Ian Mackersey is a New Zeal
maker. A private pilot, he is t
work, a widely acclaimed biog
reclusive New Zealand pilot
lonely death in Majorca. Wh
hope also to locate the ocean grave of Sir Charles King
Smith's *Lady Southern Cross*, but after six years' research, he was
reluctantly forced to conclude that the wreckage in the Andaman
Sea would probably never be found.

By the same author

CRUSADER FOX KING

RESCUE BELOW ZERO

PACIFIC ORDEAL (with Captain Kenneth Ainslie)

INTO THE SILK

LONG NIGHT'S JOURNEY

TOM ROLT AND THE CRESSY YEARS

JEAN BATTEN: THE GARBO OF THE SKIES

Smithy

The Life of
Sir Charles Kingsford Smith

Ian Mackersey

WARNER BOOKS

A *Warner* Book

First published in Great Britain in 1998
by Little, Brown and Company

This edition published in 1999 by Warner Books

Copyright © 1998 by Ian Mackersey

The moral right of the author has been asserted

A CIP catalogue record for this book is
available from the British Library

ISBN 0 7515 2656 8

Typeset in Berling by M Rules
Printed and bound in Great Britain by
Clays Ltd, St Ives plc

Warner Books
A Division of
Little, Brown and Company (UK)
Brettenham House
Lancaster Place
London WC2E 7EN

Contents

Contents

Preface

*Young airmen who had lived like hawks and poets
and paladins and died the quick death of dragon-flies*

Eric Linklater, in *Magnus Merriman*

Scattered on the rocky bed of the Andaman Sea, somewhere off
the south coast of Burma, a few weed- and mollusc-encrusted
steel components are today all that will have survived of the
wooden aeroplane in which one of the greatest of all aviators
died in the early-morning dark of Friday 8 November 1935.
Underwater cameras may one day pinpoint the spot where the
Lockheed Altair *Lady Southern Cross* plunged into the sea, extin-
guishing the life of Sir Charles Kingsford Smith. Until then the
location must remain just another of aviation's tantalising mysteries. So, too, will the cause of the accident that claimed this
remarkable and charismatic man, known to the world simply as
'Smithy'.

Charles Kingsford Smith was only thirty-eight when his life,
lived recklessly and often outrageously, came to an end. His legend
had sprung from his panache and brilliance as a long-distance pilot
who conquered the Pacific and the Tasman in both directions and
the westbound Atlantic. It had sprung, equally, from his modest
and nonchalant demeanour and the bewitching charm with which
he captivated the men and women who were drawn so magnetically into his orbit. Sixty years after his death his ghost still haunts
the Australian aviation scene. Sydney Airport and the surrounding
electorate bear his name; his portrait looks out from the country's
$1 coin. Australian children learn at school of his epic flights. The

most celebrated of his aeroplanes, the rectangular, fabric-covered Fokker trimotor *Southern Cross*, is lovingly preserved as a national treasure in an air-conditioned shrine at Brisbane Airport, visited every year by aviation pilgrims in their thousands from around the world. Standing today in this simple glass pavilion amid the aroma of jet-age kerosene, gazing upon the primitive 1920s flying machine, it is difficult for a generation accustomed to crossing the oceans at 10 miles a minute, watching movies far above the weather, to begin to imagine the fear and suffering that were the constant companions of Kingsford Smith and his crews on those great journeys.

When I began my research for this biography, I was permitted briefly aboard the sacred aeroplane that Smithy used to call his 'old bus'. Stooping through its small cabin, I crawled forward to sit for a few minutes in the tiny cockpit where a sense of his presence still seemed to permeate the cramped and claustrophobic space. Here, wrestling the great spoked bicycle-wheel control columns, he and his co-pilots had sat, unable to move about or stand up properly, for up to fifty hours at a stretch. Through the open sides of the flight deck they had been blasted by freezing air and drenched by rain. Their hearing had been bombarded to insensibility by the roar of three unsilenced engines, their conversation reduced to scribbled notes. How, trapped in this confined space without access to the cabin for a day and a half, did they empty their bladders and bowels? How, with no intercom, did they confer with their navigator and wireless-operator sitting out of sight behind the giant fuel tank they carried? How did they manage to find small islands in mid-Pacific? To survive, unstrapped in their wicker seats, in bone-shattering turbulence amid great explosions of lightning, on crude blind-flying instruments with no radar to warn them of the atomic forces that threatened to annihilate them inside every storm they so innocently tried to penetrate? The stress and fatigue must have taken them to the limits of their endurance.

Sitting there, one wondered what had compelled Charles Kingsford Smith to repeat these frightening experiences again and again. Had he become addicted to fame and the roar of the vast crowds – sometimes a staggering quarter of a million strong – who came to meet him and touch him? Beyond familiarity with the hawk-like features that stared out of pictures from the oval of his helmet, and with the daunting list of his pioneer flights, I knew little about the celebrated man behind the seemingly permanent grin. So enveloped in myth had he become, so excessively deified by the media, that it was to take me six years to separate the legend from reality.

There was already, of course, a substantial literature on Sir Charles. Its sheer volume and the determination with which it glorified and idealised him were almost intimidating. He had generated in his short years of fame more extravagant headlines, more outpourings of unrelieved adoration and sentimentality than any other Australian of his day. Almost everything he did and said had been reported. And subsequently his image had been romantically cemented into history by a succession of six reverential biographies.[1] As a reliable record of his life, however, not all, I discovered, could be safely trusted. Indeed, one author, the journalist Ward McNally, had compensated for his brief and sketchy research by casually resorting in two successive biographies to falsehood and invention. For McNally, who had a startling record of more than sixty criminal convictions for theft, safe-breaking and dishonesty, for which he had spent eight of his early years behind bars, truth wasn't a specially valued commodity.[2] He later confessed to having spiced his Smithy narratives with an extra-ordinary measure of outright fiction. This I was amazed to learn while attempting to trace a man called 'Les Branch, an old college friend' of Kingsford Smith's, to whom the aviator, McNally said, had written many revealing letters over the years – from some of which his book 'quoted' at length.

Smithy's next biographer, the Australian Pedr Davis, innocently drew in 1977 on some of McNally's narrative, briefly quoting, alas, from these 'letters'. Within weeks of publication Davis and his publisher were stunned to receive a letter from McNally in Adelaide accusing Davis of plagiarism and demanding damages for copyright-infringement. When these were refused McNally began an action for compensation in the Supreme Court of South Australia. Happily for the veracity of the record of Kingsford Smith's life, before the case finally got to trial McNally was forced to admit that Les Branch had actually never existed. He was, he wrote in a letter to Davis's publisher, Paul Hamlyn, 'fictional and from my own imagination'.[3] In the light of his confession McNally, who died in the early 1990s, abandoned his action. It was clear that, as factual sources, existing biographies of the famous Australian would have to be treated with extreme caution.

Accuracy was only part of the difficulty. The more I read of Smithy's colossal, well-documented flying feats and the wealth of colourful legend surrounding him, the more convinced I grew that something was missing: that significant truths had eluded the published record of the life of this godlike figure. No one, it seemed, had dared to explore the sensitive and complicated minefield of the personal relationships that his flying genius and compelling charm had fostered, not always happily, on every side, igniting currents of love and jealousy that surged about him through all his years as a nation's idol. Nor, it appeared, had any attempt been made to assess the toll the stress of fame and fear together had taken on his physical and mental health. There seemed to be an altogether unreal assumption of psychological stamina underpinning the superman image – a belief that he was somehow immune to trauma. It didn't take long to discover that he wasn't. Turning the pages of the old newspapers from which this small, unremarkable-looking man waved from cockpits amid enormous crowds of onlookers not seen at airports any more, one wondered what explained his capacity to arouse such singular passion and devotion. For he appears to have been a lodestone to which high drama of every description was irresistibly drawn. Two men had died for him. He was plagued by litigation, public inquiries, allegations of irresponsibility and disloyalty to Australia. One of his closest friends had sued him for a large sum of money in a sensational court action. Another had become so jealous he had resorted to legal threats for recognition in one of his books. Were they true, the persistent stories of Smithy's hard drinking, his willingness to use his fists, his inveterate promiscuity?

Who were his family and how deeply affected were they by his fame? What had gone wrong with his disastrous first marriage, so discreetly scarcely touched upon by his biographers – indeed, delicately ignored by some and doubted to have happened at all by one? What was the explanation for the constant ill health that dogged his crowded flying years, yet was rarely revealed because it didn't belong with his heroic persona? Why did Australia never reward him with a prestigious job or a major overseas air route to

operate? And when he disappeared for ever into the tropical night,
why did his country show such scant interest in locating his aeroplane and attempting to solve the mystery of the crash that killed
him?

To launch the search for answers to these questions, nearly sixty
years after his death, I first tried to establish whether Smithy's
second wife, Mary, the former Lady Kingsford Smith, was still
alive. She had left Australia in 1940 to live permanently in North
America. Many people told me they believed she was dead. In
fact, as I was presently to discover, she was still very much alive:
now in her early eighties, twice remarried, and once again wid-
owed, vigorously active and commuting between her two homes
in Toronto and Florida. I wanted to get in touch with her for two
reasons: to seek her approval for this new biography, and to draw
on her memories of her celebrated first husband. I had been
amazed to discover that not one of the authors of the six existing
biographies which had appeared between 1937 and 1977 had ever
bothered to go and meet her. Yet she had shared with Smithy five
of the most turbulent years of his short, spectacular life.

When I wrote she replied helpfully, agreeing to meet me.
However, her letter went on, disappointingly, to warn that she
now believed it was too late to find alive enough people who had
known 'Chill', as she called him, to make a new biography possible. Most of those who could have talked about him had long
gone, she said. 'I hope you won't be hurt, but personally I feel
strongly that it is a truly hopeless idea.' Happily, she was to be
proved wrong. A surprising number of Smithy's contemporaries
were still alive and well in their eighties and nineties – and all
anxious to contribute to the story of his life.

I met Mary twice, first in 1990 at her winter home on Anna
Maria Island on the Gulf of Mexico in Florida, where she and her
third husband, Frank Noldin, went every year to escape the
Canadian winter. She was a lively and sympathetic woman, who
had long ago acquired a North American accent. Her once dark
hair had silvered, yet she looked much younger than her years, still
retaining traces of the classic beauty that had captivated
Australians as she rode through the streets of Sydney all those
years ago, sitting beside Smithy, acknowledging with him the
intoxicating roar of the huge, cheering crowds. In 1991 I met her

again, this time at her large and elegant summer apartment in Toronto's northern suburbs, from which she conducted her brisk and busy life – still driving herself around the city, playing golf, entertaining, travelling the world. She had just crossed the Atlantic on Concorde. We sat in her study with its view of maple woodland, the recorder picking up the shrill calls of blue jays. On the wall above her desk hung a portrait of Smithy in flying helmet and goggles.

For Mary the interviews were obviously at times an ordeal. No one had fully interviewed her about Smithy since the 1930s, and more than half a century of life in North America lay between her and her brief existence as the twenty-one-year-old Lady Kingsford Smith in Australia. The inevitably probing process was to stir the buried memories and emotions of six decades earlier, occasionally disinterring unhappiness that would bring brief, sudden tears. It was soon clear that not every compartment of his life had Chill shared with Mary, and that for two thirds of their five years together he had actually been away from home, engaged in his restless flying adventures. But Mary had nonetheless been closer to him than any other person still alive in the 1990s, and generously recorded for me more than fourteen hours of frank reminiscences. Back in New Zealand, as the narrative began to build in the computer, I had numerous small queries to put to her from long distance. Although her memory began to fade, she continued patiently to attempt to answer my questions. She was still doing so to within a few weeks of her death from cancer in May 1997.

Mary's son, Charles Arthur Kingsford-Smith, not yet three when his father was killed at the end of 1935, has few direct memories of him. But from his home on Puget Sound near Seattle he continued, during the seven years of the biography's gestation, to facilitate my research and to relay to Mary by phone a stream of e-mailed queries as I struggled to untangle the host of mysteries and contradictions with which his father's life abounded.

Smithy's nephew John Kingsford-Smith, the son of his brother Wilfrid, was only fourteen years younger than his uncle. He had spent much time in the aviator's company in Sydney in the early 1930s and had become actively involved in many of the ups and downs of his precarious flying career. As a close observer of Smithy's private life, John was, in his mid-eighties, one of the biography's most faithful springs of information, answering persistent questions in an almost weekly flow of generously helpful letters from his home in Sydney. John's brother Rollo was another tireless source of both information and inspiration. A distinguished aviator in his own right, and a prominent figure within the Australian aviation establishment, he even set out from his farmhouse in the New South Wales southern highlands on some determined expeditions to archives and libraries throughout the country, delving on his own initiative into long-buried government aviation files in an effort to help me distil fact from myth in some of the more confusing legends that had clung to Smithy's life.

Catherine Robinson, a daughter of Smithy's brother Leofric, kindly gave me access to a treasured box packed with the diaries of Smithy's mother, Catherine. Conscientiously maintained for forty-two years, the faint pencil-written chronicles covered the entire span of Smithy's life and supplied a chronology nowhere else on record, which helped significantly to validate the factuality of the narrative. Catherine Robinson not only copied for me hundreds of the diaries' pages but, from her own impressive knowledge of many of the colourful members of the Kingsford Smith dynasty over three generations, she was greatly to aid my understanding of the dynamics of this restless and rather special family.

Soon after beginning my research I was surprised to learn that Kingsford Smith's first wife, Thelma Corboy, whom he married in 1923, was still alive in Western Australia. There was little on record about the stormy marriage that lasted only two years. The relationship had apparently become so desperately unhappy that, when I wrote to her, Thelma (now Mrs Ives) swiftly sent word back to me that the subject was totally undiscussable. However, thanks to the enterprise of Milton Baxter, one of her younger cousins in Perth, I have been able to piece together the sad and moving story of the marriage, the details of which, with admirable diplomacy, he managed to draw from Thelma in the weeks before her death in 1990. Not only did Milton unlock many long-guarded secrets, he went on voluntarily, for several years, to unravel for me in archives and libraries in Perth many other mysteries which had surrounded Smithy's flying and matrimonial affairs in Western Australia seventy years earlier.

I am grateful to many other people for recollections of their associations with Kingsford Smith. Some of the richest came from another formidable aviation figure, the late Scotty Allan, then in his mid-nineties. Flying across the world as Smithy's co-pilot, he had silently and critically observed the latter's abilities in the cockpit as well as his sometimes shocking conduct on the ground. The late Ernest Aldis, former engineering director of Qantas, who, as a young apprentice with the first Australian National Airways, was witness to Smithy's magic thrall, kindly served, with scores of clear and helpful letters, as my technical consultant. Bruce Cowan, another of Smithy's engineers, who worked on almost all his famous aeroplanes, continued to answer my questions, as his sight receded, with long and patiently taped messages.

John Ulm, the son of Smithy's celebrated partner Charles Ulm, the jealous architect of my subject's fame, gave me hospitality and many helpful interviews which aided my understanding of his father's relationship with Kingsford Smith, and made available to me Charles Ulm's frank and intensely character-revealing unpublished memoirs. At the outset of my research it became clear not only that people who had known the two aviators were often polarised into opposite camps in their regard and affection for the two men, but that the spirit of rivalry had not entirely been quenched by time.

I wrote to more than 150 newspapers throughout Australia, inviting anyone who had known, worked for or flown with Sir Charles to get in touch. Hundreds of people responded. For nearly nine months the mail poured in at the rate of over fifty letters a week, spilling sometimes from the mailbox and scattering around the garden. Fax messages up to thirty pages long curled out of my machine, piling up in heaps on the floor. And night and day the phone rang. Across Australia it was clear that, for large numbers of people, a joyride sixty years ago in the *Southern Cross*, with Smithy at the controls, had been one of the highlights of their life. They spoke of the flight as if it had been yesterday; of the honour of meeting Kingsford Smith as if he had been the King.

My appeals led me into a community of veteran aviators – pilots and ground engineers who had once been his professional colleagues – and began to open unexpected windows on his life. In an old buff envelope in Canberra I found more than fifty original letters he had written to his parents, William and Catherine, from 1915, when, as a young and frightened soldier, he was under fire in Gallipoli, to 1925, when his first marriage was falling apart in Western Australia. There had survived, too, many of the original notes scribbled in pencil that he and his flight crews had passed to one another. The terse exchanges, on hundreds of yellowing scraps of paper, reflected with enduring poignancy their minute-by-minute hopes and anxieties on those long, frightening hops they had not always expected to survive.[4]

Some of my discoveries were tinged with sadness, none more so than the vast documentation that had arisen from his fateful friendships with a fellow pilot, Keith Anderson, and a mechanic, Bob Hitchcock. Their deaths in a central Australian desert in 1929, while searching for Smithy and his crew, had made public martyrs of both men. Yet so little information about these turbid, unhappy associations was apparently recorded. Only after two years of fruitless searching within Australia's vast archive system did some of the truths begin to surface in brittle court transcripts which brought alive the nuances of the tensions between them, eerily, like television period drama.

Not all of Kingsford Smith's story was buried in Australia. In the archives of Imperial Airways at Heathrow Airport in London, there reposed once private and confidential correspondence which bristled with his name and revealed the extent of a conspiracy between Imperial and Qantas to deny his companies any role in the bitter battles of the 1930s for an operating share of the England–Australia air routes. In America, where Smithy's achievements are still remembered in aviation circles, many people emerged to help me. For the fresh information, some of it somewhat startling, that they produced about the 1928 Pacific flight, I am indebted to the kindness of two relatives of the American crewmen who joined the daunting expedition in the *Southern Cross*: William Hunt, a cousin of the navigator, Harry Lyon, and Tom Warner, son of the wireless operator, Jim Warner. I must also thank the latter for permission to quote from his father's written account of that flight.

As the search began to reach into some of the hidden crevices of Smithy's life, it became obvious that too many revelations which portrayed his character as a particle less than perfect would not be welcomed in all quarters. Among the tiny, elite fraternity of Australians who had been involved in aviation before the Second World War, his mystique had lived on; he was still idolised, his image jealously guarded. 'I hope you're not going to dig too deeply,' one elderly member pleaded. 'Just remember – he was our god.'

What few of those who worshipped him ever knew, however, was that the man who had been the first to fly some of the world's great oceanic air routes had actually suffered on many of his flights from such debilitating stress and acute fear he had sometimes become too ill to fly the aeroplane. It seemed at first like a contradiction of everything this unique figure had stood for, but it was indeed true, and the revelation was inevitably to alter the whole perception of his character. Nor were these psychological problems, which added immeasurably to the quality of his courage, of late arrival in his flying career. They almost certainly had their roots in his formative years. In his childhood, which had begun in a very modest wooden house in a suburb of Brisbane on a hot, sticky day in February 1897.

Acknowledgements

I wish to express my gratitude first of all to Smithy's family: his widow, Mary Noldin, his son, Charles Arthur Kingsford-Smith, nephews John and Rollo Kingsford-Smith, and niece Catherine Robinson.

Special thanks must also go to Mike and Jane McGovern in California for the details they so generously shared with me of both the public and complex private lives of Jane's great-grandfather, Captain Allan Hancock, who funded Smithy's 1928 Pacific flight; to Wing Commander Ken Craig, the RAF's chief psychiatrist, who offered cogent explanations for the crippling condition that threatened Kingsford Smith's life on so many of his ocean flights; to Dr Graham Clark and John Kepert of the Australian Aeronautical Research Laboratory in Melbourne for their enthusiasm, expertise and the thoroughness of the examination they did for me of the undercarriage leg of the *Lady Southern Cross*; to Garry Tee, an Auckland University mathematician, who expertly calculated many permutations which helped to plot the possible events of Smithy's last flight; to Bernard Lifka, technical consultant of the ALCOA Technical Centre in Pittsburgh, who did a spectastropic analysis for me of a sixty-year-old scrap of metal which provided clues to the location of Smithy's watery grave; to the staff of the Australian Embassy in Yangon for their perseverance in persuading the Myanmar military government to allow me to visit the country's southern coast, normally banned to foreigners, and to *Australian Geographic* for assisting the venture.

As I researched this biography I amassed such a wealth of material on Kingsford Smith that the first draft grew to three large

volumes. For the inevitably painful process of compression I have
two Carolines to thank. Caroline North, my editor, for the great
skill and objectivity she brought to the task. And my wife,
Caroline, herself a professional researcher, who shared with me the
daily agonies – and the surprises as Smithy's ultimately tragic life
was slowly reconstructed under our roof.

Many hundreds of people were good enough to respond to my
published appeals for information about Smithy. To all of them I
extend my heartfelt thanks. Others whom I approached for help
continued patiently to answer my questions throughout the seven
years of my research. I gratefully acknowledge the assistance of the
following individuals and organisations:

Australia

Doreen Affleck, Ernest Aldis, Scotty Allan, Barbara Allan, Jim
Anderson, Glen Anderson, Leith Angelo, Mabel Ashby, Wilfrid
Atkin, Milton Baxter, John Benke, Gwen Bliss, Kath Blizard, Bill
Booth, Win Boulton, Professor Maurie Brearley, Jane Brooks, Tim
Bryant (Australian Archives, Melbourne), Kathy Buckley (librar-
ian, Queensland Museum), Bill Bunbury (producer, Social History
Unit, ABC Radio, Perth), Sister Angela Burke, Bob Burnett-Read,
Jean Byers, John Chapman, Eric Chaseling, Bryan Clark, Oliver
and Dulcie Cook, Marjorie Cornish, Bruce Cowan, Pedr Davis, Ian
Debenham (curator transport, Power House Museum), Greg
Dickens (manager ANZ Bank, Cairns), Ross Dimsey, Bill Dunn,
June Dupre, Charles Eaton, Dr Leigh Edmonds, Ashley Ekins
(senior historian, military history section, Australian War
Memorial), Rod Ellison, Hon. Beryl Evans (member NSW
Legislative Council), Hon. Gareth Evans (minister for foreign
affairs and trade), Hon. Wendy Fatin (minister for the arts and ter-
ritories), John Ford, George Foster, Rt Hon. Malcolm Fraser, Bob
Fripp (past president, Aviation Historical Society of Australia),
Julia Fryar, Geoffrey Gallagher, Miles George, Peter Gibbes, John
Gunn, Eric Gunton, Terry Gwynn-Jones, Fred Haig, Margaret
Harricks, Bill and Dulcie Haskell, Colonel Keith Hatfield, Valerie
Helson (National Library of Australia, Canberra), David Hilliard,
Lionel Hitchcock, Harley Hitchcock, Richard Hitchins
(Queensland Air Museum), Noelene Hitchon (archivist, National
Australia Bank), Wing Commander John Hodder, John Hopton,

Graham Horne (curator, Aviation Museum of Western Australia), Molly Hudson, Mr T. E. F. Hughes, QC, Josephine Johnson, Owen Jones (manager, Gascoyne Trading Pty Ltd, Perth), Laurie Jones (head architect, Heritage Unit, Brisbane City Council), Peg Kelman, Lou Kent, Bette Kingsford-Smith, Ralph Knox, John Laurence, Judith Lester, Michael Lynton, Sylvia Marks, Esther Mather, Theo Mathews, John McKenzie, Jack McPhee, Keith Meggs (president, Aviation Historical Society of Australia), Roger Meyer (secretary, Civil Aviation Historical Society), Shirley Miller, Cecily Miller, Graeme Minns, Bryan Monkton, Perry Morey, John Morton (president, Early Birds Association of Australia), Anne Nathan, Canon Melville Newth, David Nicholas (Law Society of NSW), Scott Noreika (WNI Science and Engineering), Arthur Beau Palmer, Stephen Panebiango, Horrie Pethybridge, Suzanne Philcox, Graeme Powell (manuscript librarian, Australian Collections, National Library of Australia), Kay Purvis, Roland Rich (Australian Department of Foreign Affairs and Trade), Philip Rudder, Jan Ryder, Hon. Con Sciacca (minister for veterans' affairs), Stella Scott, Jean Scott, Harry Sergent, Russell Sibbison (Bureau of Air Safety Investigation), John Skipworth, Dick Smith, Moira Smythe, Jim Soorley (lord mayor, Brisbane), Arch Steinbeck, Alf Taubman, Lady Taylor, George Taylor, Yvonne Thomas, William Thompson, Patricia Todhunter, John Ulm, Valda Ulm, Pamela van der Sprenkel, Don Vandenberg (Civil Aviation Authority, Canberra), Alan R. Walden, Nancy-Bird Walton, Dr Lesley Waters, Eric Watson (president, Australian Society of World War I Aero Historians), Helen Watson-Williams, Colin Watt (Chairman, Southern Cross Museum Trust), John Westcott (Parkes Aviation Pty Ltd), David Whiteford (Battye Library), Betty Wigg, Darcy Williams, Graham Wilson, Blair Wilson, Ted Wixted.

Organisations in Australia
Aeronautical Research Laboratory, Defence Science and Technology Organisation, Melbourne, Archives Authority of NSW, Australian Archives (Canberra and Melbourne), Australian Army Aviation Centre, Oakey, QLD, Australian Army Soldier Career Management Agency, Australian Bureau of Statistics, Australian Department of Foreign Affairs and Trade, Australian Institute of Petroleum, Australian Medical Association (NSW branch),

Australian Science Archives Project (Department of History & Philosophy of Science, University of Melbourne), Australian Society of World War I Aero Historians, Australian War Memorial, Aviation Historical Society of Australia, Battye Library of West Australian History, Broome Historical Society, Bureau of Air Safety Investigation, Carnarvon District Public Library, Central Australian Aviation Museum, Civil Aviation Historical Society, Consolidated Press Holdings Ltd, CSR Ltd Archives (Australian National University), Department of Defence (Air Force) Discharged Personnel Records Department, Western Australia Department of Land Administration, Department of the Arts, Sport, the Environment and Territories, Derby Tourist Bureau, Early Birds Association of Australia, East Pilbara Shire Council, Eastern Goldfields Historical Society, Gascoyne Historical Society (Carnarvon), John Oxley Library, Lane Cove Municipal Council, Law Society of NSW, Mitchell Library, National Library of Australia, Office of Minister of Defence, Pictorial & Graphics Department, Brisbane *Courier-Mail*, Power House Museum, Queensland Museum, Queensland Air Museum, RAAF Association Aviation Museum of Western Australia, Rare Map Collection of National Library of Australia, Scone & Upper Hunter Historical Society, Shire of Broome Council, Shire of Coonamble Council, South Australian Genealogy & Heraldry Society, Southern Cross Museum Trust, Sport Aircraft Association of Australia, St Andrews Cathedral School (Sydney), St Peter's College (Adelaide), St Vincent's Hospital (Sydney), State Archives of Western Australia, State Library of NSW, Supreme Court of Western Australia, Sydney Institute of Technology, Sydney Technical High School, University of Melbourne, WNI Science and Engineering (Perth).

New Zealand

Dr Simon Barclay, Tony Harvie, David Hoskins (tidal officer, Hydrographic Office, Royal NZ Navy), Vic Hunter, Carol Kennedy, Alf Mabbett, Ross Macpherson (editor, *NZ Wings*), Errol W. Martyn, Winifred McWilliams, Tony Nicholls, Terence O'Brien, Ian Paine (technical manager, Glucina Smelters, Auckland), David Phillips (NZ Aviation Historical Society), Sally Reid (manager public affairs, ANZ Bank), John Stannage Jr, David Stringer (Research Centre for Surface and Materials Science, University of

Auckland), Glenn Taitoko (Alexander Turnbull Library), Dr Michael Taylor, Charles Wardrop, David Wilson (aviation reporter, *The Press*), Diane Woods, John Wright.

Organisations in New Zealand
Research Centre for Surface and Materials Science (University of Auckland), Hydrographic Office, Royal NZ Navy, Alexander Turnbull Library, NZ National Archives, ANZ Bank, Auckland Central Library, New Zealand Aviation Historical Society.

Great Britain
Dr Jacqueline Bower (Centre for Kentish Studies), Dr Harry Bryden (Southampton Oceanography Centre), Peggy Buchanan, Barbara Cannell, David Collyer, James Croall, James Cross, Rachel Cunningham, Fred Huntley, Freddie Kent, Wing Commander Andrew Lambert (officer commanding, 23 Squadron RAF), Paul Leaman (editor *Cross & Cockade International Journal*), Mary Lovell, Paula Mackersey, Group Captain Ian Madelin (Air Historical Branch, RAF), Sir Peter Masefield, Jonathan Peel (general manager, Shuttleworth Collection), Lois Pratt (Sheerness Library), Michael Prevost, Mrs S. C. Raftree (RAF Personnel Management Centre), Wally Rouse (archivist historian, British Aerospace Defence Ltd, Warton), Ray Sturtivant, Michael Vaisey.

Organisations in Britain
British Airways Archives and Museum Collection, Public Record Office, Centre for Kentish Studies, RAF Air Historical Branch, No. 23 Squadron, RAF Leeming (Yorkshire), Imperial War Museum, Sheppey Local Historical Society, RAF Personnel Management Centre, National Meteorological Library & Archive, British Newspaper Library, Royal Botanic Gardens (Kew), Sheerness Library, Yorkshire Air Museum, RAF Central Medical Establishment, Southampton Oceanography Centre, Shuttleworth Collection.

USA
Richard S. Allen, Kenneth Bird, Dr Herbert P. Boen, Harvey Christen, Iris Critchell, Mary Gage, Lloyd Gates, Milton J. Getker (Aero Club of Arizona), Loretta Gragg (executive director, Ninety

Nines Inc.), James R. Greenwood, Marian Hancock, Albert Hansen (editor *American Aviation Historical Society Journal*), William Hunt, William T. Larkins, Harvey Lippencott, Julian P. McCreary Jr (dean, Oceanographic Centre, Nova University), Schuyler L. Mott (librarian, Paris Hill), Bill Norin, Ron Reuther (Western Aerospace Museum, Oakland Airport), Hank Roller, Elinor Smith Sullivan, Richard E. Treat, Alfred Vlautin, Tom Warner.

Organisations in the USA
American Aviation Historical Society, the Ninety Nines Inc., Veterans Administration (Togus, Maine), ALCOA (Aluminum Company of America, Pittsburgh), National Air and Space Museum (Smithsonian Institution), Oceanographic Centre (Nova University, Florida).

Other
Canada: Keith Hawkins, Mary Pynn (Harbour Grace), Mr H. G. Rossiter (general manager, Gander International Airport); *Netherlands*: Fokker Aircraft BV, Commodore G. van Messel, Leo J. de Roo (corporate historian, Fokker Aircraft), Captain Leon Senf; *India*: *The Statesman* (Calcutta), National Institute of Oceanography (Goa), Professor P. S. Ramakrishnan (professor of ecology, Jawaharlal Nehru University), Dr Arun Parulekar and Dr Satish Shetye (National Institute of Oceanography); *Ireland*: Liam Byrne, Margaret MacNeill, Patricia Saul; *Myanmar*: Australian Embassy, Yangon (Peter Edwards, first secretary, Consular & Administration; second secretaries Peter Budd and Richard MacNeil), Herve Madeo (general manager, Total Myanmar Exploration & Production), Dr Tin Hlaing, Daw Yin Yin Oo (Myanmar Ministry of Foreign Affairs), U Ohn Kyaw (Myanmar Travels and Tours); *Singapore*: Port of Singapore Authority, Captain Don Johnston (Singapore Airlines), Dermot Taylor (managing director, Ben Line Agencies [Singapore] Pty Ltd), Richard Willdridge; *South Africa*: John Anderson; *Switzerland*: Henry Wydler (curator, Swiss Transport Museum, Lucerne).

EXTRACT ACKNOWLEDGEMENTS
I am grateful to the Manuscript Collection of the National Library of Australia, and to Charles Arthur Kingsford-Smith, for permission to quote from Sir Charles Kingsford Smith's private letters,

written to his parents between 1915 and 1925, and from his various in-flight notes written to his crews.

To the Queensland Museum for supplying copies of Sir Charles's flying logbooks, the property of his son, Charles Arthur.

To the Rare Map Collection of the National Library of Australia for copies of Harry Lyon's 1928 trans-Pacific navigation charts.

To the Mitchell Library for access to the Charles Thomas Phillippe Ulm (ML MSS 3359) Collection and to John Ulm for locating the board minutes of ANA and for permission to quote from his father's correspondence and memoirs, *My Yesterdays, Todays and Tomorrows*.

To the Australian Government Publishing Service for permission to quote from government files in the Australian National Archives and for access to the voluminous reports and correspondence created by the Coffee Royal and *Kookaburra* incidents and subsequent official inquiry, preserved in the archives in Canberra in the CP662/5, 6 and 7 series.

To the New South Wales attorney-general for permission to quote from the crown copyright transcripts of the evidence in the 1929 action brought by Keith Anderson against Charles Kingsford Smith and Charles Ulm.

To the Archives Authority of NSW for permission to quote from the evidence in the case brought against Kingsford Smith and Ulm by Henry Smith Hitchcock. Also for access to the deceased estate files of Kingsford Smith, Ulm, Anderson and Mrs Lyal Tate (née Bon Hilliard).

To the La Trobe Collection, State Library of Victoria, for access to the correspondence of Constance Anderson.

To the Museum of Transport and Technology, Auckland, for access to its Charles Kingsford Smith Collection.

ILLUSTRATIONS

In the golden years of Kingsford Smith's life news pictures of him – many taken by freelance photographers – were so widely circulated and prints so repeatedly duplicated by newspapers and picture agencies around the world that identical photographs are held by dozens of libraries. In many cases there remains no evidence of the original source and copyright-owner. Those which appear in this book are credited to the source from which they were obtained.

Author's Note

Although others sometimes did so, Kingsford Smith never hyphenated his name, a style that I have therefore followed. However, as the text reflects, most other members of his family eventually embraced the hyphen.

Unless otherwise indicated, distances are expressed in statute miles, fuel volumes and weights in imperial measure.

Except where otherwise credited Kingsford Smith's quotations come principally from his autobiography, *The Old Bus* (1932), later updated as *My Flying Life* (1937), and from the book coauthored with Charles Ulm, *Story of Southern Cross Trans-Pacific Flight 1928*. The three books were ghosted by journalists, the first two by Geoffrey Rawson, the last by Hugh Buggy, and some of the quoted material contained factual errors, which I have corrected.

Similarly, unless otherwise stated, the sources of quotations attributed to Charles Ulm are from his 1934 memoirs *My Yesterdays, Todays and Tomorrows* (which were serialised in a newspaper but never published in book form); Sir Gordon Taylor's from his books *Pacific Flight, Call to the Winds* and *The Sky Beyond*; John Stannage's from his books *High Adventure* and *Smithy*; Norman Ellison's from his biography of Kingsford Smith, 'Air Master Supreme' (which formed part of his book *Flying Matilda*); Beau Sheil's from his Smithy biography *Caesar of the Skies* and Harry Purvis's from his autobiography *Outback Airman*.

I have drawn extensively on transcripts of public inquiry and court proceedings to portray some of the human dramas that regularly attended Smithy's flying career. The verbatim records were rendered at times in such stilted and tortuous fashion that I have taken the liberty, here and there, of shortening some of the statements.

The search for original documents, newspaper stories, memorabilia and photographs recording Kingsford Smith's famous years was complicated by their bewildering diffusion in small hoards across Australia. Nowhere does there exist a central repository of it all. Even more frustrating was the discovery that of the thousands of news pictures that had been taken of Smithy in his many moments of triumph, few had survived in newspaper picture libraries anywhere. Unbelievably, it seemed, the prints and negatives of most of them had years ago been arbitrarily junked to make space for new material.

1

The Bank Manager's Son
1897–1907

The Brisbane into which Charles Kingsford Smith was born three years before the turn of the century was already a sizeable town of around 100,000 people. A collection of wooden houses and low brick and stone buildings it sprawled, among palms and banana trees, along the banks of the Brisbane River, which bustled with square-rigged sailing vessels and long-funnelled steamships. Life was leisurely. Photographs show the dusty main street, Queen Street, deserted but for a few gigs and horse-drawn double-decker trams. People travel mainly by bicycle or on horseback. Bushy bearded men with side whiskers wear bowler hats, pith helmets and straw boaters, and the women, in long white flared dresses, flutter about under parasols.

The Smith family, who had yet to add Kingsford to their name, lived in Riverview Terrace in what is today the suburb of Hamilton. The street lay on the edge of town in dense eucalypt woodland above a bend in the river about 3 miles from the centre. The unnumbered cottage, named 'Corbea', no longer exists – it was demolished sometime before 1936 – but is believed to have stood on the corner of Riverview Terrace and Whyenbah Road, on a site now occupied by a block of large, old, wooden flats (number 12 Riverview Terrace). It is a mixed sort of street, shabby weatherboard houses scattered among elegant mansions. There is nothing to commemorate the birth there of one of Australia's most famous men.[1]

His arrival, on Tuesday 9 February 1897, had been awaited by his mother, Catherine, and her husband with some dread. With good reason they believed that, because of her age – she was in her fortieth year – she might not survive the birth of this, her seventh child. It had been ten years since she had delivered her sixth, a son, and she had earlier had a number of miscarriages. It is probable that, long before, she and William had ceased trying for more. But she survived to produce the most remarkable of all her children. Catherine's diary, in which, unfailingly, she made brief, factual entries – mostly devoid of emotion or opinion – every evening for over four decades, recorded the event. 'Feeling very poorly,' she wrote the day before. 'Kept Leof [Leofric, her twelve-year-old son] at home in case of emergency. Taken ill at night. Mrs Macdiamid came to sit with me while Will went for doctor and nurse.' Around dawn next day Charles was delivered, according to the birth certificate, by Dr W. F. Marks, apparently without complication. 'Baby born at about ½ past 5 or ¼ to 6 am,' she wrote matter-of-factly.

During that following hot February week, which Catherine spent confined to her bed, the diary records a constant procession of visitors who arrived on foot, bicycle and buggy, come, in the absence of a telephone, to congratulate her and to bring the baby gifts in the shape of a large collection of frocks. In one of his earliest photographs Charles is dressed in one and, with his golden curly hair, resembles a good-looking baby girl. 'He was pretty, really pretty, with blue eyes, rose-leaf skin and the reddest lips imaginable,' wrote Winifred, his eldest sister, in a private tribute after his death.[2] However, Charles quickly developed into a tough, very masculine and unusually adventurous child, well endowed with the genes of some vigorous and distinguished forebears whose roots on both sides of the family were in rural Kent in England. William's were seafarers and tradesmen, Catherine's well-to-do middle-class farmers and businessmen. The parents of both had arrived as first-generation immigrants in search of new lives in this vast and raw land of promise.

William's ancestors are traceable back to the late eighteenth century and Catherine's to around 100 years earlier. The genealogical records are immediately dominated by the volume of material that surrounds one formidable figure: Charles' maternal grandfather, a devout Baptist, Richard Ash Kingsford. A cultivated man, tall and hugely black-bearded, who exuded, a little pompously, much dignity and charm, he was born in Canterbury,

Kent in 1821, the son of a labourer, John Kingsford, who worked at a local brewery, and his wife, Mary Walker. From this humble background in Beer Cart Lane, Canterbury, Richard went into the drapery business and prospered. By the time he arrived in Sydney, in his early thirties, in 1852, with his wife, Sarah Southerden, a governess daughter of a Baptist Kentish hop farmer, he had become sufficiently well off to redefine his occupation as 'gentleman'. Sarah, whom he had married in England the previous year, was to bear him four children. The last, delivered in her forty-sixth year, was Catherine Mary, born in Brisbane in 1857.

There is no record of what the Kingsfords did in their two years in Sydney. In 1854, they moved north to Brisbane, where Richard opened a large two-storey clothing and draper's shop in Queen Street in partnership with his brother John, a Baptist pastor. Richard went into politics and got himself elected in 1875 to the South Brisbane seat in the Queensland Legislative Assembly. The following year he became mayor of Brisbane. On losing his parliamentary seat eight years later, he started a poultry farm at Tingalpa on the city outskirts. When the venture failed in the early 1880s, he moved to the far tropical north, to the tiny settlement of Cairns, to involve himself in some new enterprises. By then Catherine had married a bank manager, William Charles Smith. Born in Sydney in 1852, William was the second son of an immigrant English sailing-ship captain, Richard Sheppard Smith, also from Kent, and his wife, Elizabeth Eldridge, whose family were Baptist Kentish farmers. Richard Smith's brother, another William, and their father – another Richard – were also master mariners. To complicate matters, Richard Sheppard Smith died in his late thirties in 1856, when William junior was only four, and his widow, left with three children, the following year married his brother, sea captain William, by whom she had five more children.

About William Smith's early life, growing up with his mother and stepfather–uncle, virtually no information exists. Early in 1874, at the age of twenty-two, he joined the Bank of New South Wales as a trainee in the central Brisbane branch, where his quick grasp of banking had him rapidly promoted. By early 1877, he had been sent to open a branch in Cairns – then a tiny, primitive settlement, little more than a camp, where his customers were gold-miners, Chinese traders, sugar-planters and fishermen. Cairns was a dangerous place. During the New Year holiday of January 1878 William joined a fishing party which was attacked by Aborigines on a nearby river. During the skirmish he was accidentally shot in the leg by one of his friends. The wound was so serious that he had to be sent by ship back to Brisbane for treatment, keeping his leg under a dripping tap throughout the five-day voyage. The surgeons only just managed to save it. When he recovered, William resumed his bank duties in the Brisbane branch as a teller, the job he held when, on 17 April 1878, still limping from the bullet wound, he married Catherine Kingsford at the Baptist Church, South Brisbane. He was twenty-six and she was twenty. Although she had grown up in Australia, Catherine had a brisk English accent, the legacy of several years at boarding school in Folkestone, to which she had been sent to become fluent in French and to acquire some of the accomplishments fitting to her family's middle-class status. It is not known how or where she met William, but because she was under age, her father had to give his written approval of the marriage, which was quickly to produce a brood of children.

William was a restless man. In 1882 he took a job with another bank, becoming acting manager of the Queensland National Bank back in Cairns. There were by now three children – Harold, Winifred and Wilfrid – soon to be joined by a second daughter, Elsie, and a third son, Leofric. The coastal voyage north from Brisbane to Cairns nearly ended in tragedy for them all. Their ship, the *Ranelagh*, in the charge of a drunken captain, was wrecked in the middle of the night near Townsville. The passengers and crew were rescued and taken to Cairns. The Smiths, who were far from well off, lost almost everything they owned.

In the four years since William had lived there the settlement had scarcely grown. It remained a primitive, unhealthy wild-west trading post. There were outbreaks of bubonic plague and everybody, sooner or later, went down with dengue fever, an endemic mosquito-borne viral disease which laid its victims low with agonising joint pains, vomiting and bouts of acute depression. But William flourished in Cairns. A prominent and popular figure, he immersed himself in the town's business and social life. He was soon a justice of the peace and a shire councillor, president of the boating club, secretary of the drama club, an executive on the local branch of the Australian National Party, a shareholder in local sugar and rice mills, treasurer of a gold-crushing company and the first captain of the volunteer Cairns Rifle Corps. There didn't seem to be any activity in which he wasn't involved.

Around 1884 the elegant Richard Kingsford and Sarah also came to live in Cairns. With his ample wealth Richard invested in property, established a fruit farm at Kuranda on the nearby table-land, became the town's first mayor and bought a large sugar plantation at Hambledon. Meanwhile, new ambitions led William to leave the Queensland National Bank. He and his elder brother, Edward, went into business together as merchants. Trading as Smith Brothers, they opened general stores in Cairns and Brisbane, to where William and his family returned and where, in 1887, their sixth child, Eric, was born. But the venture was hit by the depression of the early 1890s, and the Smiths now, for some unex-plained reason, went to Tasmania. Here, at Launceston, they rented a villa next door to a mansion which the ubiquitous Richard Kingsford had acquired. It was here, in 1890, that Sarah had died. In Tasmania he remarried, to the much younger Emma Jane Dexter who was to present him, at the age of seventy-three, with another daughter.

William and Catherine didn't stay long in Tasmania. Whatever they had been doing there, by 1893 William was forced to return to his former profession, this time as manager of the Cairns branch of the Bank of North Queensland. Two years later he was rejoined in Cairns by his father-in-law and his new wife, who built on a hill an enormous pyramid-domed house, 'Fairview'.[3] Kingsford lived there until his death in 1902 at the age of eighty. People later said that some of his generous, even-tempered, charismatic qualities flowed down to his grandson Charles – with whom, by May 1896, Catherine was pregnant.

That year William was transferred to the bank's Brisbane office. He had spent nearly twenty years in Cairns and was regarded as one of the town's founding fathers. When he and Catherine left a big banquet was thrown in their honour. Catherine's diary, only just begun, now provides the day-to-day evidence of what was soon to develop into a chronically nomadic existence for the family; a life in which they never owned a house of their own, were constantly on the move from one rented home to another and endured growing financial hardship.

The following February, Charles was born in Brisbane. From the very first day he was regarded as a special being, spoiled and fussed over by his parents and, as an unexpected late addition to the family, by his much older brothers and sisters. At the time of his arrival the youngest, Eric, was already ten, Leofric was twelve, Elsie fourteen, Wilfrid fifteen, Winifred sixteen, and Harold, nearly eighteen – in fact he had already taken a job and left home. In his first year Catherine's diary refers to Charles merely as 'baby'. He was christened in August 1897 at St Andrew's Church in the nearby suburb of Lutwyche, by which time the wandering Smiths had moved again, to 'Kingsdown', in O'Connell Terrace in Bowen Hills, nearer the town centre.

At Charles' birth William was nearly forty-five. The few pictures of him that have survived from this time show him as a small man, dapper in large bow tie with a black pointed beard and waxed moustache. People described him as quiet, gentle and unfailingly courteous. But his chronic ill health appears to have necessitated constant time off work. Scarcely a month passed when the diary did not record: 'Will in bed poorly,' or 'Will brought home from work poorly.' If it wasn't dengue fever it was rheumatism, or flu. One suspects from the various unsuccessful attempts the rootless William made to set up his own businesses that, although he was good at his job, he was not altogether happy in the banking profession. He was eventually to quit it in dramatic circumstances.

One of his granddaughters, Catherine Robinson, now in her seventies and living at Springbrook, in the southern Queensland highlands, remembers the couple from her childhood in the 1920s – particularly Catherine, whom photographs in early married life reveal as an attractive woman, her hair swept up in a roll, radiating a wistful serenity. Yet the diaries record with monotonous insistence, year after year, that, like William, she suffered from an inordinate frequency of ill health: 'Feeling very sick. Bad head . . . sore throat and headaches. Did not dress all day . . . Had bad day with pain in side . . . Still feeling poorly'. However, despite the incessant ailments that plagued her, she was, from all reliable accounts, endowed with a cast-iron stamina – and a strong will. There was never any doubt who wore the trousers in the Smith household. 'She was the driving force, the dominant partner,' Catherine Robinson said.

She was also gregarious and extrovert – both Kingsford characteristics. Always involved with other people. Always busy. Always going somewhere. She had this great sense of humour and with her brisk, educated English speech she didn't sound at all Australian. I think she was actually a lot tougher and more resilient than the diaries suggest. But Will's health really was a worry. He was never well for long. And, as a personality, he never asserted himself. He would follow Catherine's lead in everything. For him the sun, moon and the stars shone out of her. Sadly, the reverse was not the case. Although there's no doubt she was very fond of him, her feelings never went deeper than that. There had, apparently, been someone else who, for some reason, she couldn't marry.

Soon after Charles' first birthday, in February 1898, William was posted to Sydney, to become manager of the Bank of North Queensland's office there. The family went into temporary lodgings in Randwick while Catherine set out on what was to be the first of endless house-hunting expeditions as they moved with restless zeal from suburb to suburb over the years, selling and rebuying furniture as they went. Here they resumed the routine of their life and the rituals the diary typically records for the next thirty years:

Busy day unpacking and getting straight . . . went to sale and bought 30 pounds 14 shillings worth of furniture . . . Mrs Buden came to wash. Mrs Lyden and Miss Walsh called. Had to go to bed soon after with very bad headache . . . Engaged Ruby Irwin, 10 shillings a month and clothes . . . I called on Mesdames Nash and Phillips . . . Pickled onions and made quince jam . . . Wilfrid went to dentist and had three teeth stopped . . . Very busy cooking all day – six extra for tea and guests for evening . . . Wrote to Mrs Milford, Miss Paddle, Mrs McIntosh and Mrs Solomons . . Busy sewing, washing, ironing and folding clothes.

The narrative reflects an efficient, practical woman, left too exhausted by domestic rigours to have much time to commit any

philosophical thoughts to her diary. Yet, wrote Winifred, after her
mother's death, although she often began the mammoth daily
cycle of household chores at 5 am, she was 'always so poised and
unruffled after a very strenuous day and would entertain friends at
dinner – which she had cooked herself!'[4] Within four months of
their arrival in Sydney they moved again, this time to Ashfield.

Every Sunday the whole family trooped dutifully to church,
after which they would go for a picnic or fishing. The day would
end with hymns round the piano led by Catherine, 'always', wrote
Winifred, 'looking so dainty in her dark frock, with its starched
white collar and cuffs'. Everyone would choose a hymn in turn.
The family favourite was 'Eternal Father, Strong to Save' and
Charles' 'Onward Christian Soldiers'. 'He was a lovely baby,'
Winifred wrote.

> Sunny-faced, sunny-hearted, sunny-tempered. He had a
> musical voice and a very musical ear. His babyhood co-
> incided with the Boer War and he picked up many of the
> popular airs then sung. I can see him, a diminutive figure, not
> quite two years old, standing on the big polished table, sur-
> rounded by an admiring family group, lustily singing in quite
> good time and tune, Kipling's 'Duke's son, cook's son, son of
> a belty-dell [belted earl], Twenty fousand horse and foot
> doin' to Table Bay.' Many another tune, which he heard sung
> round the piano at night, were soon mastered by the little
> man.[5]

But as the humid Sydney summer began to warm up, a disaster
was brewing. The events of Thursday 5 January 1899 were to
remain a dark secret within the family. Very few people would
ever know of the personal calamity that led Catherine that
evening to make in her diary, in large, bold letters, the dramatic yet
mysteriously brief entry: 'Black Thursday.'

It had all begun on Tuesday 3 January, the day William went
back to work after the New Year holiday. Catherine had taken
Charles on his first visit to the zoo, and when they got back she
was surprised to discover that William had been brought home ill
by one of the staff. The truth which Catherine couldn't bring herself to reveal was that William's banking career, in which, until

now, he had enjoyed a high reputation for diligence and integrity, was at an end. He had resigned as a matter of honour in a human tragedy involving one of his customers. The only member of the extended Kingsford Smith family still alive in the 1990s who knew what happened was Judith Lester, living in Nambucca Heads in northern New South Wales. She had been told by her father, Smithy's brother Eric. 'Poor Will lent money without security on a fixed term to a trusted friend,' Judith explained. 'I don't know what the amount was, but it wasn't small. When the term was up the man couldn't repay it. Instead of doing the sensible thing and going back to Will to negotiate an extension, he shot himself. Will, who unfortunately was the guarantor, immediately resigned, telling the bank he would personally repay the full amount plus interest.'

However, William hadn't the least idea where he was going to find the money. But for Catherine's intervention it is likely that he would never have done so. In her positive, unruffled way, she took immediate charge. While William sat at home, demolished, writing job-seeking letters, she put on her smartest dress and went by train to the Bank of North Queensland's Sydney office, where she had several meetings with the group general manager, who had hurried down from head office in Brisbane to clear up the tragic mess. Her diary hints that she told him she would try to raise the money from her father, Richard Kingsford, in Cairns. There was no telephone link with that remote settlement, so she sent Kingsford a telegram to say that she was coming up.

At twenty-three months, baby Charles was considered too young to be left at home, so she had to take him with her. On Saturday 14 January, they sailed north on what was to prove a long and taxing expedition. 'Baby and I left Sydney for Cairns. Ill all night,' was all Catherine disclosed. She and Charles were away from Sydney for nearly a month, seventeen days of which were spent on ships in almost permanent seasickness. During her twelve-day stay she made a number of visits to another bank, the Bank of Australasia, at which, she noted, she had 'fixed business up re guarantee'.

Ninety-five years later it was not easy to throw much light on these financial arrangements. Amazingly, however, at the ANZ Bank's Cairns branch, in 1994, the late nineteenth-century customer records for its distant ancestor, the Bank of Australasia, still existed. Not only was there confirmation in neat copperplate handwriting that Kingsford had held an account with the bank from the late 1880s, but the records showed that, on 6 February 1899, an account had been opened in the name of Catherine Smith, 'wife of William C. Smith'. Since Catherine and William no longer lived in the town, clearly the account was set up during her visit to serve as a conduit for funds from her ever-generous father. 'He obviously saved the family from ruin,' Catherine Robinson said. 'Papa was very good to Catherine. He was a very indulgent father. He once gave her a cheque for £300 – something approaching £13,000 today. And on another occasion he paid their rent for a year. If they were in a financial jam there's no doubt he would have rallied round.'

Her husband's career had been destroyed, but Catherine had, at least temporarily, lifted the family out of crisis. Back home she now effectively became head of the house, assuming, with the help of a small riding whip, the role of disciplinarian. One suspects that she didn't entirely welcome undertaking what was then traditionally a husband's duties. She believed that it was the man who should prove himself strong. 'There's no fun in going through life spoon-fed, in finding the soft seat,' ran an anonymous quotation she felt moved to copy into her diary. 'That makes a man soft, and a soft man is an abomination before God and Man. Find your place and hold it – find your work and do it.'

The gentle William was to have difficulty fulfilling this ideal. Despite a stainless record in bank management, no doors in the industry were ever to open for him again. For the next four years, from early 1899 to the end of 1902, there is no evidence that he enjoyed any permanent work. He is either going fishing or making lengthy visits, job-hunting, to other parts of Australia. On the first of these, a month-long trip to Brisbane in the autumn of 1899, Catherine was house-hunting again. The search went on all through the winter until October, when the Smiths again sold all their furniture and rented a house in Manly on the coast north of Sydney Harbour. By the middle of 1900 they were running out of money. The diaries begin to record successive sums of £20 borrowed from relatives and banks, and futile journeys by William in desperate search of work.

Meanwhile, Charles was growing up. By the age of three he was filling notebooks with drawings of trains, bridges and paddle steamers – in 1901 the aeroplane hadn't been invented. 'Looking back on that period, he appears as rather a lonely little figure, for his brothers and sisters were so much older,' wrote Winifred.

Little Charlie was often the odd man out at our picnics and camps, and being *all* boy he was not always popular with the elder members of the family. However, he was always extraordinarily so with his schoolmates and, even as a small child, a born host. This sociable instinct often landed him in trouble. How annoyed we used to get when we discovered he'd invited two or three of his own ilk to spend the weekend with him, for beds were at a premium in a big family like ours. He would solve the problem by giving his guests his own room and camping on the hearth rug.[6]

The family's financial plight intensified their nomadic existence, driving them to even more frenzied house-hunting in search of ever cheaper accommodation. How they actually kept body and soul together during these desperate years no one now knows. Early in 1902 they moved from Manly to the north-harbour suburb of Longueville on Lane Cove. By now Charles was five and enrolled at Miss Clifford's kindergarten at Hunter's Hill on Sydney's north shore. He also began Sunday school – the start of an enforced religious education that was heavily to occupy his Sundays for the next ten years.

There is a story that round this time, in his Sydney backyard, he first demonstrated his interest in flying. Years later he told a New York portrait-painter about it. 'I was about six. A Professor Penland[7] was giving exhibitions in a balloon. It was white and up in the sky it looked to me like a large umbrella. So one day I sneaked into the house and got one [an umbrella], opened it, and proceeded to jump off our chicken house. If my brother hadn't seen me and rushed over to catch me I don't think I'd be posing for you now.'[8]

Late in December 1902, after four years of casual work out of banking and now approaching fifty-one, William decided in desperation to try his luck in Canada. He sailed alone to Vancouver, promising the family he would send for them as soon as he found something. He arrived without home or job in the bitter cold of January 1903. It was a harsh climatic and cultural shock for a man in his fifties so frail and unassertive. Trudging through the snow of the Vancouver streets that winter he was depressed to find there was precious little work for a middle-aged Australian itinerant with only banking skills to offer. It took him six worrying months to establish himself, and then it was only by taking a poorly paid job with the Canadian Pacific Railway company. One of the myths that has surrounded his chequered career is that he was appointed in a senior role as a superintendent. The less impressive truth is that he joined CPR as a clerk. Nonetheless, his tenuous new economic base was enough to lure his kith and kin across the Pacific. First, in April 1903, came Leofric, now eighteen, then sixteen-year-old Eric, who worked his passage as a cabin boy in a sailing ship.

Catherine didn't join William until August 1903. Since he had left she had already moved twice into cheaper houses and was now in a boarding house in Greenwich. Six-year-old Charles was missing his father and, excited at the imminence of reunion, wrote to him:

> Dear Daddy
> We are coming over to you in three weeks. I will be glad to see you. I will be playing snowballs when I am with you . . . We have sold a lot of our furnecher. We have sold the penow . . . I don't like liveing this country, and I want to see you . . . I sepose you have that toy ready for me. I do like toys. I do like train toys.
> Dear daddy with love from Charlie.

Catherine had to borrow the £85 fare to Vancouver for herself, Winifred, now twenty-two, Elsie (twenty) and Charles. Sailing with them on the *Aorangi* was Catherine's younger brother, Arthur Kingsford, now in his forties. His wife Ida, and their young children stayed in Australia. What Arthur hoped to do in Canada is anyone's guess.

In Vancouver the Smiths put down no permanent roots. Predictably, they stayed only a few months in the first house. By

November, as the first snow began to fall, and they all went down with terrible flu and colds, they moved to 7th Avenue, Fairview. Here they were presently joined from Australia by Harold, now in his mid-twenties and just married, and his wife, Elsie. Harold, who was to spend the rest of his life in North America, took the only job he could find: as a real-estate salesman. With the exception of Wilfrid, the whole family, in dribs and drabs, had now crossed the Pacific. Trying to trace their movements there through the minimal clues in Catherine's diaries is difficult. 'How the children ever got their schooling, I can't imagine,' said Catherine Robinson. 'They moved about like gipsies.' The sons and daughters, most of them now grown up, constantly came and went. There was, as there had been in Australia, an unceasing procession of visitors. Their lives were a whirlwind of activity. The house rang with the sound of voices, for they were all extremely quick-witted and, with the exception of the gentle, less volatile William and Leofric, highly extrovert, stubborn and forceful. They played pranks on one another, bandied good-humoured insults. They revelled in repartee and amusing one-line rejoinders. They enjoyed family musical evenings, when they would play the gramophone and sing together round the piano. And not only would they go to church every Sunday, they kept up the ritual hymn-singing at home, with Catherine at the piano and William reading a bedtime chapter from the Bible.

They emerge as a close-knit, immensely sociable group, loyal and fiercely supportive of one another, in constant day-to-day touch almost obsessively by phone, cable and letter when separated, however briefly. Transplanted to Canada, they had instantly recreated the tight extended family unit. The nucleus, quietly controlling, guiding and holding it together, was the tireless Catherine. It was almost certainly she who, at one of their many Vancouver addresses, was responsible for adding Kingsford to Smith. It was done to solve a mail-delivery problem when they found themselves in a street in which two other Smith families already lived. It was intended only as a temporary solution, but as it was a rather more distinguished name than plain Smith, they got to like it and it became permanent.

As the family migrated from suburb to suburb Charles moved from school to school. The only one of his Canadian school reports to have survived shows that his unsettled life had not impaired his academic success. His average mark of 78 per cent put him top of the class of seven boys. 'Will do well,' the headmaster wrote, but he also noted that Charles' conduct was 'silly at times'.[9] William's job with CPR gave Charles privileged access to the Canadian railway system, encouraging a new passion for riding steam footplates in the shunting yards. It is clear from Catherine's diaries that the family spent much of their spare time camping, salmon-fishing and sailing on the sounds that ran back through dramatic landscapes into the mountains behind the city. They had developed a liking for these very private expeditions in which only they, and those accepted into the family circle, took part. A photograph of Charles on one of them shows him dressed for the occasion in a sailor suit under a wide sombrero.

Some time during 1906 William decided to give up his clerical job with CPR and start a business of his own. It appears that Harold persuaded him there was money to be made in property sales. With his new real-estate experience, Harold joined William and Arthur in an enterprise they called Kingsford, Smith and Company. It did not do well. As they were struggling to get the business off the ground that November, for some reason never explained, Catherine packed up and went back to Australia, where she stayed for eight months. With her sailed Elsie and Leofric – both apparently still living at home – and Charles, now nearly ten, along with Harold's wife, Elsie, and their two babies, Beris and Basil. For this major evacuation the Smiths gave up their house, got rid of the furniture and William went to live with Harold. Nowhere did Catherine say why she had come home, or how she was subsisting. They spent Christmas 1906 at a house she had taken at McMahon's Point. It was a sad occasion with the family now divided by the Pacific. 'Girls, Charlie and I alone, so did not cook Christmas dinner,' she wrote wistfully.

During that hot Sydney summer Charles began to develop the close friendships he was permanently to enjoy with his cousins, Rupert and Robin Swallow (sons of Catherine's sister Caroline) and Ray, Philip and Godfrey Kingsford, the sons of Catherine's itinerant brother Arthur. On 2 January 1907 Charles, the Swallows and Godfrey Kingsford went to Bondi, Sydney's famous surf beach, east of the city. Charles and Rupert very nearly didn't come back. Godfrey and Robin, at fourteen, were four years older than the other two and much stronger swimmers. It was the height of summer and Bondi Beach was crowded with New Year holiday-makers. It was a perilous place to swim. People were sometimes taken by sharks and the fierce undertow could drag even powerful swimmers out to sea. A life-saving service had only just been introduced. It relied on swift dashes into the surf by men of enormous build attached to lines run out on reels.

People on the beach that afternoon suddenly noticed that two of the boys had been sucked out in a rip and were trapped between lines of surf, unable to get back. Panicking, Charles and Rupert had begun to swallow water and to go under. They would have drowned very quickly had not lifeguards plunged into the surf and swum out.[10] By the time they reached the boys Charles was in a bad way. People rushed to grasp the ropes and haul them in. When they were finally laid out on the beach Rupert was still conscious, but Charles, who had swallowed a lot of water, had passed out and appeared to have stopped breathing. Had it not been for a nurse who happened to be there he would certainly have died. Pushing her way through the crowd, Sadie Sweeney took over. She knelt beside Charles and began trying to resuscitate him. For a long time he did not respond. When, after half an hour, he was still unconscious, onlookers began to assume the worst. But the nurse was a persistent woman. After an hour's pumping, to everyone's amazement, he began to come round. He and Rupert were taken by a policeman to the Swallows' house in Darlinghurst.

Catherine's diary dealt briskly with the drama, describing it as a 'bad accident'. But for Nurse Sweeney, she wrote, 'he would have died, being given up by the bystanders'. She spent the night at his bedside at her sister's house. 'Both boys ill and feverish all night,' she noted. The next day she took Charles home, observing, 'Boys both better. Charlie none the worse for his terrible experience.' Physically, he was not. But the psychological trauma of those horrifying moments in the surf was never to leave him.

2

Traumas of War

1907–17

It was not until the end of August 1907 that Catherine and Charles returned at last to Vancouver. Here they had to find yet another house, Charles was enrolled at his fifth school in nine months, and the familiar ritual of settling in began. But the Kingsford Smiths were now less enchanted with Canada and remained there for only another sixteen months. They had neither prospered nor taken root in Vancouver, and their lives had been made increasingly insecure by endless financial crises. The real-estate business had foundered: they had switched from selling property to investing in it, losing most of their money in the process. So William, Arthur and Harold had split up, and William had once again been reduced to a succession of temporary jobs below his capabilities. They had all begun to miss Australia and the gentle Sydney winters. One by one they started to drift home. By March 1908, when William was fifty-six, only he, Catherine and Charles, and Harold and his family, remained. In January 1909 they, too, packed up and sailed back to Sydney. Years later, in an interview with the Brisbane *Courier-Mail*, William described how he had returned 'weary and disillusioned'. From now on he was to work always in casual, unskilled jobs.

The first, several months after their return, was with the Post Office, probably as a postman or mail-sorter. The family was living in Neutral Bay and Charles was now twelve. For the first time in his life there arrived some stability in his schooling: in April 1909 he was placed at one of Sydney's most famous central-city colleges, St Andrew's Cathedral School. Catherine took him for an interview with the headmaster, the Reverend (later Bishop) Edward Wilton, at the grey stone building with a tall, slender bell-tower in Pitt Street. The school prided itself on 'high standards of conduct, deportment, dress, courteous and Christian character'. It also set out to combat lazy diction with compulsory elocution classes. Wilton, who was said regularly to pray that some of his boys would enter Holy Orders, was also precentor of the Sydney Anglican Cathedral, responsible for its choir. Boys with singing ability got scholarships giving them free tuition, saving their families the 3 guineas-a-term fees. At his audition Charles' singing voice passed the test, he was enrolled immediately and Catherine took him off to be fitted out in the Edwardian uniform of Eton collar, long jacket, shorts, black stockings and straw boater.

Choral activities dominated life at St Andrew's. Four days a week the choristers went from the school to the cathedral for evensong and on Sundays they sometimes sang at three services. For a hyperactive twelve-year-old it was a high price to pay for a free education. A 1909 photograph of the choir, robed in white surplices for evensong, shows them moving solemnly into the cathedral in a sedate column, hymnbooks held high in front of them. Charles, captured in full voice, is clearly visible as one of the more cherubic figures. Only two of his reports have survived. That for his first term in the winter of 1909 declared him an above-average student who had deeply impressed his masters. He was placed second in the lower school of twenty-two boys and had excelled in many of his exams with a triumphant 99 per cent in English. Conduct and progress were both rated 'excellent'. 'A clever lad who has done extremely well,' his form master commented, adding: 'He has a good future before him if he accepts his advantages and keeps them. I am very pleased with him.' In the second report, for the first half of 1910, the headmaster said of Charles: 'He is holding his own splendidly and certainly approaches his tasks in the proper spirit.' The comments concluded, somewhat mysteriously, 'Charles will improve a great deal in the next half.'

In the early 1990s a few of his old schoolmates at St Andrew's were still around. One of them, Alf Taubman, in his nineties, living at Mullaway in northern New South Wales, remembered Charles well.

When I arrived he was ahead of me in the senior school, but we sang in the choir together. He was very very popular – liked by everyone, boys and masters. He was also bright. Each class had three ability streams. He was always in the top. It was a terribly strict school. You would never dare risk being a minute late for anything. We even had a fagging system. First-year boys had to run around fetching and carrying for seniors. We sat on long, hard forms at desks whose every square inch had been carved with boys' names. You weren't allowed to speak without permission. It was known as the rule of silence. If you broke it you risked getting 100 lines or six cuts on the behind with a 4ft cane. We all got our share of both.

'He was known there as Pontiac,' said a much later headmaster, Canon Melville Newth, who, in 1994, was living at Hornsby on Sydney's northern outskirts. Through the old-boy network Canon Newth had met many of Charles' contemporaries. 'The name derived from the curious haircut he arrived with. Sort of shaved on one side and swept up on the other. Not as spectacular as today's punks, but it made him look like a North American Indian. The name stuck during all his years there.' It also belonged with the Canadian accent which it took him many years to lose. 'He had a reputation,' Canon Newth said, 'for obsession with anything mechanical – especially the trams on which he came up to school from the ferry at Circular Quay. He would always insist on standing next to the driver, bombarding him with questions. He had this determined sense of inquiry.'

Catherine recalled for one of his biographers, Norman Ellison, how Charles delighted in living dangerously. Riding his bicycle at frantic speed on the suburban footpaths, careering down steep hills, hands off the handlebars. Shopping for her on stilts, once tripping in the doorway of the Neutral Bay grocer's and bringing shelfloads of goods down on top of himself, to the owner's fury. He was cautioned by the police after a courting couple reported that he had terrified them by creeping up on them and exploding a giant firecracker in a tin. Other members of the family recalled how he 'greatly enjoyed fighting – fighting, not boxing – and was never known to turn down a bout'.

'I'm afraid Charles had a reputation for being a naughty little boy,' said his niece in Sydney, Margaret Harricks, the daughter of Smithy's brother Wilfrid, now in her eighties. 'My parents were actually embarrassed to be seen with him in the street. I can remember Mother telling me that soon after they were married they were walking down George Street and they spied in the distance this small surpliced figure tearing towards them. They immediately ducked into an alleyway to try to hide. Everyone avoided Charles at that age. He was considered far too boisterous.'

When the choristers' voices broke and they could no longer deliver the treble range they would usually leave St Andrew's. There is no record of Charles' departure date, but it is believed to have been at the end of 1911, shortly before his fifteenth birthday. According to Catherine's diary, his Church of England confirmation took place early in December, a few days before his last prize-giving, at which he was one of the recipients.[1] The following year he enrolled at Sydney Technical High School, then in the Ultimo district near the central railway station, where he began to train for an engineering apprenticeship on the factory floor. What his studies comprised and what career he hoped they would provide is unclear. It appears that he was best known there as a practical joker. 'He will be remembered by his contemporaries perhaps more in the role of a prankster than as an avowed student,' a 1961 article in the school's journal observed. 'To the frantic irritation of his language master, his stunt of imitating the capture of a blowfly, complete with sound effects, was a popular entr'acte between study periods in the Ultimo technical buildings.' He was now known to his mates variously as the 'Mad Yank', 'Mouldy Tooth' (presumably for the state of his dental health), 'Stinks' (for his fondness for chemistry), 'Chilla', and 'C. E. K.'. Chilla, the result of his own first attempts to pronounce 'Charles', was his family pet name and the one by which those close to him were always to know him.

Charles spent just over a year at the high school (during which he joined the part-time Military Cadet Force, an arm of the militia), coming twelfth in the class of thirty-one with his conduct rated as 'very good'.[2] In May 1913, at the age of sixteen, he was accepted as a probationer apprentice at the engineering workshops of the Colonial Sugar Refining Company at Pyrmont in

Sydney's docklands, where he was put to work in the fitting shop. In his personnel file, still intact in the company's records, there is an internal memo commenting on his initial interview: 'We think he is a very desirable lad to take into the engineering shop.'[3] After three months' probation he applied for a transfer to the electrical fitting trade and the boring job of winding armatures. The workshops were dark, grimy and noisy places, intensely hot in summer. Photographs suggest the satanic mills of Dickensian England. It is hard to believe that Charles would have felt that his true calling lay in this repetitively mechanical environment in which some of his apprentice colleagues were barely literate or numerate. But he was to stick it out for two years.

By all accounts Charles' early teenage years on Sydney's north shore were among his happiest. He was now more or less running his own life. Lacking siblings of his own age, he found companionship in large numbers outside the family. He continued to arrive home with unannounced guests, who would be fed by the tolerant Catherine and often camp down for the night. When his parents were out, the house would jump with the noise of illicit parties at which he and his friends had begun secretly to smoke. Coming home unexpectedly one night, Winifred found one in full swing.

> To my astonishment the place was a blaze of lights, with sounds of revelry issuing from the front room through a veritable murk of smoke. Chilla had taken advantage of the family's absence to invite all his pals to a convivial evening. I peeped through the door. All the boys were smoking hard, and with their host at the piano, regaling them with comic songs, followed by choruses in which they all joined lustily. I could not have been a spoilsport, they were all so happy together.[4]

To satisfy his passion for noise and power, Charles had acquired a second-hand motorbike on which his recklessness soon earned him the nickname the 'Terror of Mosman', and numerous police warnings for speeding. Neighbours predicted that he would break his neck. But it was the bike he wrecked, smashing it one day through the wall of a dairy and ending up in a heap of bottles and confectionery.

On the small family boat, *Sao*, he learned to sail. Camping expeditions would act magnetically to rally retinues of friends and cousins to their favourite destination, in the Hawkesbury River estuary, about 20 miles north of Sydney. They visited Flint and Steel Bay, on the southern rocky, forested shore, year after year. It was accessible only by sea and their privacy was rarely intruded upon. A photograph taken there, probably in the summer of 1913, shows a happy family group beside a tent in the bush. Winifred, Wilfrid, Eric, Leofric and his fiancée, Elfreda, and Charles are all there. So are cousins Rupert Swallow and Godfrey and Philip Kingsford. Posing in these Edwardian pictures they appear as a distinctly superior-looking clan whose features and body language suggest confident extrovert personalities, and a sense of the happiness and family solidarity in which Charles flourished.

But these carefree, pampered days in the family bosom were drawing to an end. When war came in August 1914, Charles immediately announced that he wanted to enlist. The prospect of action on distant battlefronts presented an exciting escape from the boredom of a grimy workshop. At seventeen, however, he was under age, and his parents refused to give him permission to join up. Catherine told Norman Ellison he was so disappointed and angry that he threatened never to speak to her again. In the end they compromised. It was agreed that, if he waited six months, his parents would sign the papers on his eighteenth birthday. On that very day, 9 February 1915, Charles went to the Australian Army recruiting depot in Sydney and enlisted.

Within eight days, 1017 Private Charles Edward Kingsford Smith was in uniform at Liverpool Camp on the southern outskirts of Sydney. He was posted first to an artillery unit, the 19th Battery, but, 'somehow or other guns did not appeal to me, so I got a transfer to the Signal Corps'. His new unit was the 4th Signal Troop of the 4th Divisional Signal Company, based at Broadmeadow near Newcastle. Here he began training in motorcycle dispatch riding and field telephone operations.

On his first leave, in March 1915, he drove down to Sydney in uniform on a large army motorbike, proudly displaying the brassard of a dispatch rider and creating a stir in the street when he insisted on taking Catherine for a spin at an alarming speed. The family were shocked by his appearance. He had been subjected to some drastic army initiation rites and arrived home, sheepishly, with hair and eyebrows completely shaved off. On that leave he fulfilled one of his greatest wishes, acquiring a signed photograph of the famous Australian actress, Nellie Stewart, on whom, through many visits to the theatre, he had developed a schoolboy crush.[5] His sister Elsie, who had become an actress herself and was working for the same company, arranged a meeting at which, she told Catherine, she nearly died with embarrassment at the 'ghostly' sight of him. But the actress was delighted. The photograph she gave him he was to treat as a sacred possession for the rest of his life.

From the training camp he wrote to Catherine and William regularly. The letters, now and for the next ten years, reveal his zest for life, his opportunist instincts, his pragmatism, his loyalty to causes, his warmth and sense of fun. Often deeply sentimental, they abound with childlike expressions of affection for his parents and a single-minded preoccupation with his own needs and interests.[6] One of the first reported his promotion to corporal.

> Dearest Mater
>   I am badly in need of a little spare cash to last me until pay day, so if you can see your way clear to send a money order for 2s 6d [12½p] or so I would be very pleased, as the living of a corporal has to be of a better class than a private, and this, needless to say, necessitates tips for cooks etc., and there are several little things I want cash for. Come up soon and see if you can bring a bit of condensed milk or a bottle of Worcester sauce.
>   From your loving son, Chilla.

The letter concluded pathetically: 'I do miss your weekly hamper, Mummy dear.'

The 4th Signal Troop, attached to the Australian 4th Light Horse Brigade, sailed from Sydney for Egypt on the troopship *Ajana*, on 31 May 1915. It was a miserably uncomfortable and crowded voyage, during which Charles became ill with flu and many of the brigade's horses died. But it is clear from his letters that he saw the war purely as a huge and glamorous adventure. He had no idea of the carnage and horror that awaited him in

Gallipoli, where he was delivered into the thick of the battle in September. 'I've been here about ten days and under fire practically the whole time,' he wrote from his dugout on 6 October. 'Snipers are pretty bad at the foot of our gully and get our chaps fairly often. One has to do a sprint or else have a bullet after him.' As a dispatch rider, he was one of these chaps. On wings of fear he dashed to and fro between dugouts like a frightened rabbit, praying that the Turkish bullets would miss him.

> Once when coming back I got into the wrong sap and found myself in an open sandpatch near the beach and within range of the Turkish machine guns on Hill 971. I heard ping ping horribly close. I hurriedly sought shelter in a sap, but not before a bullet frayed the edge of my cap. Quite close enough for me. I have also got a piece of shell that struck the ground too close to be pleasant. The shellfire is the most troublesome of all. When a shell bursts, splinters fly in all directions with horrible noises.

The bullet-damaged cap he later proudly sent home to Catherine.

Yet as the freezing winter of 1915 crept down the peninsula, bringing sleet and snow, and the Allied armies, pinned down on the beaches, began to face military disaster, it was not a bullet, but his health that struck him down. He was overwhelmed by rheumatism so painfully crippling he could no longer run dispatches and had to be transferred to duties as a cook's mate. It almost certainly saved his life. Charles' censored letters at this time speak mainly of the agony of his rheumatism and spare his parents the true awfulness of the campaign. They never mention the severed limbs, the rotting human remains, the stench of decay, the lice, the dysentery, the faces prematurely aged or the men whose minds collapsed under the strain and were threatened with the bayonet to keep them in action. Nor does he ever hint at the fact that it was a campaign that had absolutely nothing to do with Australia. 'My rheumatism is giving me fits just now. I'm afraid if it gets much worse I'll have to go back to Egypt . . . for I can't walk without twinges of actual pain,' he wrote from a freezing dugout in mid-October. His commander, Captain Fraser, was trying to persuade him to accept repatriation to Australia. Doggedly, he refused. 'I'm determined to see the war out before I do; unless they send me back wounded or something.' By November, his letters had begun to reflect positive disenchantment with war – and terrible home-sickness. 'I don't think it's going to last much longer. When it does stop I'll be about the happiest person in existence. I didn't realise what home was until I left it. I'll close now, as I'm getting into a morbid strain.'

By the end of 1915 the disastrously failed battle for Gallipoli was virtually over. By January 1916 he was back in Egypt, his rheumatism had temporarily cleared up and he was rapt to be given the rank of corporal again. 'Dearest Mummy, you will now get 5 shillings a day from my pay.' This was half of it. Catherine put the money towards a block of land in his name at Dee Why on the Pacific coast north of Sydney. After six months' rest in Egypt his unit was sent to France. Embarking from Alexandria for Marseilles early in June, he exhibited unusual anxiety at the thought of being sunk on the way – a concern almost certainly stemming unconsciously from his near-drowning at Bondi. 'I hope we stop no torpedo on the way. I don't mind being in action on the land, but the thought of being stuck up miles from nowhere at sea with mighty little chance of rescue gives one a nasty taste.'

In France he was promoted sergeant in charge of the motorcycle dispatch section of his unit, now the 4th Divisional Signal Company, which was quickly pitched into battle with the British Expeditionary Force. The scale and ferocity of the Western Front made Gallipoli seem like a training exercise. It was an obscene place, a cratered, smoking landscape of mud, tangled barbed wire, death and destruction, where the earth was continuously rent by bursting steel. Men were blown to pieces, disembowelled by bayonets, drowned in mud. He found himself under continuous shellfire in inadequate newly dug trenches, or on his dispatch bike running the gauntlet of the bombardments that thundered round the clock. A shell landed beside him while he huddled in a shallow trench one night and he was nearly buried under an avalanche of earth and stones. Soon afterwards, another exploded in front of his bike, blow-ing him and the machine into a ditch. He tried to make light of it in his letters home. 'We've got Fritz properly bluffed down this way,' he wrote optimistically from a YMCA hut in a rest camp out of the line. But he added: 'Some of the sights out there are really sickening.'

Charles' time in the trenches was mercifully brief – less than four months. Early in September 1916, attracted by its seemingly less arduous battle conditions, he applied to join the Royal Flying Corps as a pilot. The RFC, with 100 fighting squadrons, was devouring more than 500 new pilots a month. The Australian Army was approached for volunteers and he was one of the first to be accepted. 'My intentions for the future are to take up the game permanently after the war in Australia,' he wrote. 'There'll be big possibilities for our services. It is an honourable and interesting career for a young man, as well as a splendidly paid one.' His chances of surviving the war as a dispatch rider were not high, but life expectancy in the RFC was measured in weeks. When, on 28 October 1916, he sailed for England, he had no idea that he was going from the frying pan into the fire.

At Denham, a Buckinghamshire village in rolling wooded country on London's north-western outskirts, he reported on 16 November to the RFC's Officer Cadet Battalion. It was a ground school at which they were 'prepared as officers and gentlemen'. He was often in trouble at Denham, where he was envied for his singular attractiveness to women. With one local girl he enjoyed a brief but hectic affair in which their evenings together became so protracted that he was several times booked for returning late to camp. It led to a succession of punishments in which he became a familiar sight, doubling round the parade ground with a heavy pack on his back, gasping and kept moving by a hectoring drill sergeant. He was, however, universally liked. He led poaching expeditions into the woods and his hut became celebrated for its pheasant suppers cooked over the open fire. Cadets gathered there that bitterly cold winter when the ponds froze for weeks on end and heavy snow fell. As they gambled and sang, Charles, who had acquired the nickname 'Kingy', played the guitar and piano. With his extensive repertoire of unprintable ballads, he was firmly at the centre of it all.

Chronically short of money, he had begun to appeal to his family for funds. 'By the way,' he told Catherine around Christmas 1916, 'I do hope my cabling for that £10 has not inconvenienced you people very much. I hated doing it, but one has to start with some good clothes besides the actual uniform and I couldn't get any money otherwise.' The money had been duly cabled on the

understanding that he would soon return it from some deferred
AIF pay due to him. But, reading his letters, it is clear that the
loans were rarely repaid. Inevitably, it seemed, some urgent
unforeseen financial complication would usually prevent it.

From Denham, early in January 1917, he had his first flight. An
RFC pilot flew him to Hendon as a passenger on a short hop
across the edge of north-west London. In the space of those few
minutes he was hooked on flying. 'We went up to 8,000ft and
everything looks just like a map . . . The noise is deafening and the
cold intense. I'm impatiently waiting for my own plane now to
have some more.' But before that could happen he became ill
again and, according to his military records, was whisked into
Exeter Hospital in Oxford. He didn't tell the family what had
taken him there, but he was soon discharged and, in the middle of
March, he was commissioned as an RFC second lieutenant. He was
cock-a-hoop, and so impatient to share the news with his parents
that he sent them a triumphant cable: 'COMMISSIONED.' A few days
later he was posted to Number 8 Reserve Squadron at Netheravon
in Wiltshire to begin flying instruction.

The training aerodrome was on a cold and windswept site on
the edge of Salisbury Plain. Powered flight was still in its crude
infancy and some of the Flying Corps aeroplanes were primitive
and downright dangerous to fly. The art of flying training hardly
existed. Many of the instructors were psychologically ill, their
nerves frazzled by excessive front-line combat. There were no
speaking tubes; directions were shouted above the roar of the
engine and the cockpits were open to the elements. Pupils, many
of whom were themselves traumatised by devastating experiences
as foot soldiers in France, learned to fly in machines that were
often aerodynamically unstable. Small misjudgements could flick
them into a spin from which recovery was not always possible.
Even instructors were often in the blackest ignorance of the basic
principles of flight. Crashes were a daily occurrence and, long
before they got to a squadron, one pupil in three was either failed,
seriously injured or killed.

According to his logbook[7], Smithy's dual instruction on the
Maurice Farman Shorthorn, before being sent off solo at 7.15 am
on 15 April 1917, was four hours fifty minutes. Jubilantly he
described the biggest event in a pilot's life in a letter later that

week. 'I did my first solo flight a few days ago. By jove it was grand having the "old bus" up in the air by myself. I am "some pilot" now, and can land and stunt and zoom and do anything in the aerobatics line except loop. I'd try that if these machines would do it. But they tell me that a wing is liable to go off with the strain.' But he had become overconfident. Four days after his first solo, he misjudged a landing and his engine cut out as he tried to overshoot. 'Broke undercarriage,' he wrote in his logbook. In his next letter he said: 'The machine was wrecked, but I, being marvellously lucky, only got shaken and a bit bruised . . . I ought to get my wings in about a month, and then glorious (??) France once more.'

With less than ten hours' flying and only sixteen landings in his logbook, he went in mid-May to an advanced flying course at the RFC's Central Flying School at Upavon in Wiltshire. Here he began to fly the French-designed SPAD 7, the single-seater biplane fighter he would use in combat. By the end of May 1917, with barely thirty flying hours, he had been awarded his wings. When he arrived in France early in June his total dual and solo experience was forty-six hours fifteen minutes.

His squadron, Number 23, was based at La Lovie on the flat farmland of the Pas de Calais. Its SPADs, armed only with a single Vickers .303 machine-gun, weren't regarded as very effective in air-to-air fighting and the RFC employed them largely in strike roles to attack German troops and artillery-spotting observation balloons. In the lull before his first operation, Charles wrote enthusiastically about the agreeable world of the squadron base. He was now living in the close company of young English officers, many fresh from their public schools. Their accents and use of language were infectious and soon contributing to English infusions in his letters home. 'The squadron people are a tip-top crowd and I get on very well with them. There are quite a lot of Canadians here, and very decent chaps, too . . . Work is jolly strenuous at present as the weather is A1 and Hun machines are fairly plentiful.'

For family consumption he managed to make it all sound rather jolly. The truth was too disturbing to communicate. The RFC's casualties were running at over 25 per cent a week – the equivalent of an entire squadron every month. The life expectancy of a subaltern arriving at a front-line squadron now ranged from ten days to three weeks. When Smithy joined the 23 Squadron mess he immediately sensed the strained atmosphere he never mentioned in his letters home, but which, years later, he was to describe to one of his radio-operators, John Stannage. 'There were many vacant places at the dining table and in the sleeping quarters. And the survivors, all youngsters like me – I'll never forget their faces. They were the faces of much older men. And how did they occupy their time when they weren't flying? They sat at the bar and drank. I started to do the same. We drank a lot because there was nothing else to do.' More accurately, they drank to blot out the horror and fear of mutilation or incineration that haunted them day and night. Sometimes, when huge amounts of alcohol had removed all their inhibitions, they would indulge in destructive schoolboy games in the mess, often breaking up the furniture. Some of the pilots sought less aggressive forms of release in the brothels in the towns out of firing range, but stress rendered many of them impotent. The longer they survived, the more corrosive the psychological damage. What, fifty years later, came to be known as post-traumatic stress disorder was understood by neither the commanders nor the medical officers in the front line.

Smithy flew his first combat mission on 13 July and was quickly engaged in his first dogfight. 'My gun jammed early in the fight and I put my nose towards home to get it fixed, when three spare Huns sat on my tail and kept there all the way down to the Hun lines . . . The Huns were firing all the way down. I landed with holes all over the machine and one burst of a dozen alongside my ear. I was rather badly scared.' The next day, 14 July, 'I got my first Hun this morning. Eight of us attacked about 20 Huns and had the dickens of a fight. One of the Huns dived across in front of me. So I got my sight on and let him have about 50 rounds before he could get out of the way. I had the satisfaction of seeing him chuck up his arms and fall back. The machine glided on for a little while and then nose-dived straight for the ground . . . Am OK and looking for more.' On landing he found a bullet hole in the collar of his tunic.

From now on he was constantly in battle, flying sortie after sortie for up to six hours a day over the devastated terrain whose landmarks had been obliterated by a permanent haze of drifting shell smoke and poison gas. The squadron's targets were enemy troop concentrations and the tethered balloons whose observers were the eyes of the German guns. Death or injury was a statistical inevitability, hastened by the fact that both sides flew without parachutes – the self-operated canopy had yet to be invented, and efforts to introduce the static-line 'chutes used by the balloon crews were fiercely opposed by the RFC's high command, who believed that 'possession of a parachute might impair a pilot's nerve when in difficulties so that he would make improper use of it'.[8] The pilots' worst fear was the daily prospect of being burned alive. Some, when their aircraft caught fire, chose to end things quickly by jumping or using their revolvers.

As the number of his victims rose and his reputation for forcing down German balloons grew by the day, Smithy acquired an apparent detachment from the horror of his own acts of slaughter.

> Got another Hun this morning. We were out at 4.30 am looking for something to strafe. I saw this chap flying very low just beyond the Hun trenches. So I dived and fired at him, driving him back into Hunland and lower down all the time, until he hit the ground and turned right over. So I came at him again and had the satisfaction of seeing him catch fire. Later on I killed a lot of Hun troops and set fire to some wooden huts in Hunland. So you see I had a good morning. I've been mentioned in the Army commander's report as having done bold and valuable service.

On the surface he was filled with euphoria and an appetite for more destruction; his SPAD had become his killing machine. To Stannage, however, he confided the shock of his first experience of killing; shock at the lust and satisfaction he experienced and, afterwards, the disgust. Over the lines in German-held territory one day he had become separated from his formation. Disregarding the standing instruction to head home, he began instead to look around for a target worth attacking. One soon presented itself: a long column of hundreds of German troops, resting 'in one mass of humanity' on a march up to the front in a wasteland of mud and gaunt, shattered trees. 'I didn't think about what I was about to do, but immediately decided that my business was to kill,' he later told his radio-operator.

My mind was completely occupied with one unearthly desire. Over my sights I could see men moving down the road, but there were too many of them to move quickly. I pressed the trigger. Tracer bullets zipped along the road and I saw men falling, and hundreds of them scrambling to get out of the way. I was filled with an unearthly joy. I kept my finger pressed hard on the trigger. Then I turned and roared back with my machine-gun spitting death. I saw dozens of men bowled over and I remember screaming at the top of my voice . . . I roared up to the other end of the road, turned quickly and back again . . . until my gun was empty, then streaked for home. All the way back I had nothing but these thoughts of quite unholy joy. I had killed – undoubtedly killed – lots of men.

When he climbed out of the cockpit back at base, he was overcome by a delayed reaction. 'After the noise of the engine and the gun everything, all of a sudden, was quiet. I could hear birds whistling and men talking and laughing. Contact with these realities suddenly made me realise the horror of the thing I'd done. I leaned against the fuselage and vomited. I was twenty years old, I had just killed many men and I hadn't the faintest idea why. For those few minutes I had gone completely insane. Now I felt utterly miserable and hated my weakness for doing what I did.'

Just how deeply Smithy was affected by his wartime experiences there is no one around any longer to say. With the help of his family I tried to obtain a copy of his RFC medical records from the Royal Air Force. Its Air Historical Branch said that most of the files had been destroyed in the Blitz of 1940 – and that in any case they could not have been revealed to anyone, not even his next of kin.[9] By August his letters home had become distinctly less jaunty. The strain of three weeks of frightening patrols had begun to take its toll, and for the first time he stopped disguising the fact with brave words. 'It will soon be winter now, and we RFC people will get a spell – thank goodness! We are doing frightful quantities of work now and couldn't keep it up indefinitely, or our nerves would go to pieces.' In his autobiography he was later to comment. 'You hardly ever heard of an airman having a nervous breakdown in those days, though how we managed to avoid them . . . I do not know.'

That the cumulative permanent damage to his nervous health caused by the cascading nightmares of Gallipoli, the Western Front and the air war was not more visible, and that he was spared to become one of aviation's most remarkable figures, is due to a painful event which, in the middle of August, abruptly terminated his brief career as a scout pilot.

3

A Medal from the King
1917–20

Smithy had survived with 23 Squadron for six weeks – with four enemy aircraft to his credit and a reputation for skill in aerial duelling and balloon attacks. He had forced at least nine balloons out of the sky, stopping all artillery observation during a critical period, and was regarded by the squadron commander, Major Wilkinson, as one of his most able pilots – someone with the potential to become an ace. But Smithy was already suffering from combat neurosis. A lot of his natural cheerfulness and excitement had faded, and he was no longer in the joyful state in which he had arrived at La Lovie only the previous month. There had been sixteen pilots then; now he was one of only three left.

On a dawn patrol on 14 August 1917, eight SPADs flew east to the lines, arriving there at around 6,000ft. The weather was not good. There was a lot of cloud, and visibility through the shell-smoke haze was bad. After half an hour's unsuccessful search for German aircraft, the patrol leader fired a flare to order the return to base. The formation split up and the pilots began to head home. Suddenly Smithy saw one of his colleagues turn again toward the German lines. Believing him to have spotted an enemy aircraft he decided to follow, but soon lost the other pilot in cloud. What happened next he described in a letter from England several weeks later.

I flew on about 10 miles over the lines and didn't see any Huns or anything to worry me, so I turned back. As soon as I did so, I spotted two Hun 2-seaters away below me. So I thought I'd have a hurry-up scrap and tear off home as it's not too healthy at low altitudes 10 miles over and by oneself. I proceeded to turn the old bus bang on her nose and dived at the nearest Hun at a speed of 220 mph. That was one of my last coherent recollections.

I sort of recollect a fearful clatter just in my ear and a horrid bash on my foot which made me think the whole leg had gone. Then I fainted. It turned out the bullet had busted numbers of nerves and the shock sent me off. When I came to, about 30 or 40 seconds after . . . I was spinning, nose first, down to Hunland. Little holes and chips of wood etc. were suddenly appearing all round me where Hun bullets were chewing up things. I tried to turn round to scrap. But my whole left leg was paralysed, and I could only fly straight ahead as fast and steadily as I could for our lines, and pray that the Hun wasn't a very good shot.

He had been jumped from above and behind by a lone enemy aircraft. The German pilot, seeing that he'd been hit, now came at him again.

He knew that I didn't have much more fight left in me, so he proceeded to try to finish me off which, thank goodness, he failed to do. He left me just before I got over the lines. I was feeling fairly groggy by then. Blood was gradually filling my flying boot up past the knee. I wondered if I would make it back to the aerodrome. I chanced it, and more by instinct than anything else, made a moderately good landing and then crawled out of the bus and fairly collapsed . . . It was a marvellous escape considering there were about 180 bullet holes in the machine and dozens round my head within inches. Fortunately, any that hit the engine didn't do any damage for it never conked out.

The bullets had pulped the second and third toes and destroyed a mass of tendons and ligaments immediately behind them. A large V-shaped chunk of his foot had been torn out. The surgeons tidied it up and temporarily stitched up the gaping fissure.

Back in Sydney, Catherine and William, who had been dreading the knock on the door, were relieved that it wasn't worse. The cable they received from the War Office was followed by a heart-warming letter from the squadron commander, Major Wilkinson.

> As you have probably heard by now, your son was wounded in an aerial combat yesterday. It was rather a nasty wound in the foot and necessitated the removal of two of his toes. But it should not permanently affect him in any way. I went to the hospital to see him and found him very cheerful. He goes to England tomorrow. We are most awfully sorry to lose him. I am especially sorry as he was one of the very best fighters I have had, full of grit and a splendid war pilot. He hadn't been here with us very long, but had done a lot in that short time and was universally popular. He hopes to be flying again in a few months' time. There is no one I should welcome back more warmly to the squadron. Believe me, there was only one opinion of him out here, and that was 'one of the best'.

Some of the accounts of Smithy's final combat mission have named the German pilot who wounded him as the legendary Prussian nobleman Baron Manfred von Richthofen, who, before he himself was shot down in 1918, claimed around eighty Allied aircraft in his red-painted aeroplane. The 'Red Baron' was a cold-blooded killer, aloof and unsmiling, who used to decorate the walls of his quarters with fabric serial numbers cut from the wreckage of his victims. But he probably didn't shoot down Smithy, who was himself to blame for this story. In a ghosted article published in America just before his death, he said: 'I was the seventy-eighth victim of Von Richthofen, the Red Knight of Germany, shortly before his flaming career was ended.'[1] Yet in his autobiography he made no attempt to repeat the claim – something which, if it were true, he would certainly have found irresistible. To check it out I wrote to 23 Squadron, still in existence in 1993 and based at Leeming in north Yorkshire, equipped with Tornado F3 supersonic strike aircraft. The squadron seemed unaware that one of their First World War pilots had become one of history's most famous aviators. The commanding officer, Wing Commander Andrew Lambert, managed to locate a copy of the unit's diary for the day in question, which contained an astonishing piece of information. 'Typical . . . of the spirit of the squadron is the story of 2nd Lieutenant C. K. Smith,' it said. 'On 14 August this officer was badly wounded in combat, but he pressed on to shoot down his opponent before he fainted. When he recovered he was at 4,000ft, upside down, and being shot at by machine-guns from the ground, but he managed to land safely.' Clearly this version of the incident had become badly garbled. If it is true, the German pilot allegedly shot down could not have been Von Richthofen, for he survived for another eight months.

Although the doctors feared it might be necessary, Smithy didn't lose his foot. Unlike most of his fellow pilots in 23 Squadron he'd survived intact and with his sanity. He was admitted to Ellerman's Hospital in London's Regents Park to recuperate. 'As my foot will heal, it will give me a certain Satanic aspect – cloven hoof, as it were. But that doesn't matter so long as I can walk all right,' he wrote to his family. To illustrate his point he enclosed a photograph he had proudly taken of the grossly deformed foot with his box camera. If nothing else, it settles the argument as to the number of toes he did lose: one persistent version of his metamorphic legend said that he'd lost three, another, all of them. The picture reveals, behind the two missing toes, a deep open wound stretching back almost halfway to his ankle. It seems amazing that he was able to use it again. As it was, it caused him to walk with a slightly mincing gait for the rest of his life, but only those close to him knew what a source of pain it remained.

For 'conspicuous gallantry and devotion to duty' he was awarded the Military Cross. The citation said: 'His efforts and fine offensive spirit and disregard of danger have set a very fine example.' At the Buckingham Palace investiture in November 1917 George V said to him: 'Your mother will be proud of you today.' To his acute embarrassment, as he tried to follow the instruction to move backwards away from the King, his crutches got tangled in his legs and he fell in a heap on to the floor. Aides rushed to help him to his feet and the King hurried forward to offer his arm and console him. At His Majesty's invitation Smithy waived protocol and resumed his withdrawal facing forwards, stumping away on his crutches. In his letter describing the incident he added a postscript: 'Don't forget to put Lieut C. Kingsford Smith, MC, on letters!!!' The medal meant much more to him than he would ever admit, even to close friends, to whom he liked to say, 'I got it for various acts of foolishness.'

The wound was slow to heal, and he began to develop major misgivings about his ability to fly again, fearful that he might have lost his confidence. 'I'd like to go up for a flip to see how my nerves are,' he told Catherine. 'We can't tell properly until we get in the air what state a wound has left them in. I think mine are pretty good.' But within a few weeks, later in November that year, his letters were reflecting a frankness that he was rarely prepared to display to his parents. 'My nerves have gone to the pack. I'm afraid I'm in for a breakdown if they get worse.' He was helped back from the brink of the dark canyon by six months' convalescent leave in Australia early in 1918, by which time he was able to hobble about with a stick.

Back in London in the middle of August 1918, Smithy learned that the Royal Flying Corps had been merged with the Royal Naval Air Service to become the Royal Air Force. His deepest preoccupation was still the state of his 'nerves' in the air after twelve months out of the cockpit. It was put to the test when an RAF medical board decided that, although no longer fit for combat, he could fly as an instructor. He was posted to Number 204 Training Depot Station, a busy training base at Eastchurch on the Isle of Sheppey on the Thames coast of north Kent, where pilot recruits were trained on Avro 504Ks for operational service in France. Back in the air at last he was relieved to discover that, although his handling skills were a bit rusty, his nerve had held. For instructor training he was sent, in late September, to an airfield at Shoreham on the Sussex coast between Brighton and Worthing. He found instructing boring, repetitive and restrictive. He was too impatient, many people said, ever to be a good teacher. But for the moment, temporarily in command of two training flights at Eastchurch, he had no option but to try to make a good job of it.

After the daily threat of being fried alive on squadron service, life at 204 TDS, Eastchurch was relatively relaxed. A laid-back atmosphere pervaded the officers' mess, where Smithy's thrusting personality, passion for pranks, delight in playing his banjo and rapid Australian accent once more made him a prominent figure. Again he acquired a reputation as a ladies' man and earned himself the nickname 'King Dick' for the regularity with which he was said to have attracted to his bed some of the women on the station's staff. One of his fellow instructors there in 1918 was a Lancastrian from Fleetwood, Lieutenant James Cross who, in 1993, was a sprightly ninety-five-year-old living in Wanstead in north-east London.[2] One of the last survivors of the Royal Flying Corps – he served in France with 209 Squadron – he shared, in a long and helpfully clear tape recording, some of his vivid memories of 'King Dick'. 'He enjoyed life to the full and he enjoyed specially fully the company of young ladies,' James Cross recalled.

> There were a lot of them at Eastchurch at that time in admin and clerical jobs. Some were happy to make themselves available to the officers who couldn't easily get up to London. I'm afraid it encouraged quite a bit of promiscuity in the mess. King Dick was without doubt the fastest worker. On the course at Shoreham we were billetted at an hotel where two girls were resident – one the proprietor's daughter. He amazed us all by sampling the bedworthiness of both within a couple of days. At the same time he was having an affair with an Italian violinist playing in an orchestra up in London. He just seemed to hypnotise women.

Another fellow instructor at Eastchurch was Laurie Coombes, who had fought with the Royal Naval Air Service in France.[3] He and Kingsford Smith were members of a small group of pilots quartered away from the main officers' mess in a house on the edge of the aerodrome known as 'the cottage'. Coombes was startled to learn one morning that Smithy and another instructor had taken off in an Avro 504, without voice tubes between the two open cockpits, to attempt a dangerous stunt. The idea, conceived by Smithy, was that one would work the joystick and the other the rudder. Coombes hurried across to watch the landing attempt. 'They had no means of communication except by signs till the rotary engine was switched off in the descent. I can well remember their hazardous approach over the hangars when their lurid, shouted instructions to each other could be clearly heard on the ground. But somehow they managed to pull it off and jointly land the thing.'[4]

For further excitement Smithy devised another illicit pastime:

aerial poaching. The idea was to shoot game on the estates surrounding the Sheppey airfield from an Avro trainer. The illegal
enterprise began successfully but soon went badly wrong. 'I've got
a pricelessly funny experience to tell you,' he wrote to Catherine
early in February 1919:

> I am a criminal charged, or about to be charged, in the Civil
> Court with poaching. Two of us went out in a machine to
> shoot some game for a dinner. I flew the machine and
> Dawson, the other chap, had a shotgun in the back seat. We
> couldn't see any partridges on the aerodrome, so we went to
> a nearby field and there managed to bag a few, shooting
> them from the air and then landing to pick them up.
>
> We'd just collected the bag when we saw the farmer bloke
> running over to us. So, thinking discretion the better part of
> valour, I opened up the engine and we leapt up into the
> atmosphere and came home. However the old swine took
> our number etc. and wrote to the Colonel who was intensely
> amused but told us to go over and see the farmer. We did so.
> He was furious . . . He claimed he saw us shoot a hare in his
> field. The funny part of it is that we didn't shoot, or attempt
> to shoot a *hare* at all, and we have dozens of witnesses to
> swear the same, so of course the charge will fall through the
> air. The whole squadron is going to turn out in force at the
> trial and cheer us in Court. I'm tickled to death and looking
> forward to it with eagerness.

Did the case ever get to court? It would have come up in one of
the two towns nearest the Eastchurch air base – in Sheerness or
Sittingbourne. A 1992 search of the police court registers in both
towns for the entire period of Smithy's posting revealed no record
of a prosecution; nor had the local newspapers reported it. The
farmer, perhaps deciding that the balance of public sympathy
would weigh in favour of the war veterans, had apparently withdrawn his complaint. However, the poaching had been real
enough: 'We used to enjoy the spoils quite openly at a ritual
weekly dinner every Saturday night at the Royal Fountain Hotel in
Sheerness,' admitted James Cross. He said that Smithy wrote a
jingle to celebrate the incident with the farmer and the instructors

sang it to Smithy's banjo accompaniment in the music room on their regular party nights. Cross sang the opening lines on his tape. 'If I remember, it went like this: "We went to shoot some hares, shoot some hares, oh, we went to shoot some hares, shoot some hares, but we were taken unawares and buggered off upstairs." The bit that followed, I'm afraid, was unprintable,' he apologised.

In November 1918 peace brought the halcyon Eastchurch days to an end. Armistice Day saw Smithy in the Royal Naval Hospital at nearby Chatham, a victim of the influenza epidemic sweeping Britain. The flu had developed into pneumonia, one of his lungs had filled with fluid and he was scarcely able to breathe, wracked by chest pains and spasms of crackling coughing. The navy doctors put him straight on to the danger list, instructing that his family be informed. Although he lay at death's door for several days, he pulled round, but was declared unfit to fly for three months. By then the whole training operation was being wound down and he was impatient to get out and into civil flying. While he kicked his heels waiting for his discharge, he and another Australian RAF pilot, Cyril Maddocks, began to plan a flying school back in Sydney. The idea was to buy some surplus BE2e two-seat reconnaissance biplanes from an RAF aircraft depot at Henlow in Bedfordshire, where Maddocks was working in the disposals section. 'Cyril superintends the breaking up of machines (perfectly good ones too) and he can pull many strings,' Smithy wrote home excitedly. 'Result is we are getting three or four machines for about £50 each and, after paying freight to Australia, they will have cost us somewhere about £100 each.'

The funds were to come from the £300 gratuity due to each on demobilisation. But as the money was slow to arrive they decided to go into business in England. Smithy, Maddocks and another ex-RAF pilot, Harry Hudson, formed a charter company, which they registered as Kingsford Smith–Maddocks Aeros Ltd, and ordered three brand-new biplanes. Smithy's business card, which described him as 'Director of Flying', proclaimed: 'Passenger flights undertaken anywhere in the British Isles'. Soon after they were demobbed in April 1919 – Smithy left with around 460 flying hours, sixty-five of them in front-line squadron service[5] – they were joined by two more pilots, a close friend of Smithy's, Derek Shepperson, and Laurie Coombes. But the flying circus didn't take to the air for several months. While they waited for their RAF gratuities and the issue of commercial pilots' licences, a huge distraction suddenly broke into their lives. The Australian government had, in March 1919, announced a prize of £10,000 for the first all-Australian crew to fly from England to Australia within thirty days. The route had never been flown, and this sort of money – worth £250,000 today – was a small fortune. Early in May the Royal Aero Club published the race rules. The entrance fee was £100 per aircraft and the flights had to be completed by 31 December 1920. 'Should we pull the job through it will mean that we're made for life,' Smithy wrote to Catherine. All they needed was a sponsor and an aeroplane.

Both were quick to arrive. The Yorkshire-based Blackburn company had produced during the war a successful long-range bomber and anti-submarine aircraft coincidentally called the Kangaroo. It was a large, ungainly-looking twin-engined biplane with a long, forward-protruding fuselage containing space for four open cockpits in tandem. With its dependable Rolls–Royce engines it was an obvious candidate. The company's founder, the designer Robert Blackburn, was already converting some machines for civil-airline operations in Europe and he was anxious to promote them in Australia. He invited Smithy and Maddocks to Yorkshire. However, at the company's aerodrome at Brough on Humberside, they were disappointed to discover that another Australian war pilot who had just left the RAF, Valdemar Rendle, the son of a Brisbane doctor, had already got his foot in the door. He had been promised the Blackburn entry and was going to pilot the Kangaroo, with a colleague called Booker from South Australia, as crew. Yet the Yorkshire aircraft-designer appears to have been equally impressed with the new contenders. He agreed to sponsor Kingsford Smith and Maddocks on condition that they joined forces with Rendle. They agreed. The flying-circus operation was hastily shelved and, using their entire gratuities, they arranged for two of their BE2e aircraft to be shipped to Sydney to enable them to set up their flying school when they arrived. 'Dearest Mother and Father,' he wrote on 13 May. 'We're hurrying like mad to get away before the first of next month in order to beat the monsoons round East India which would hold us up for weeks . . . When we arrive (if we succeed), we'll go straight ahead and open an aerodrome. We have

Blackburn's agency for a year to go on with.' Optimistically, he concluded, 'Possibly we will get out before this letter does.'

Almost immediately Smithy, Maddocks, Rendle and Booker
began to make news. A flight to Australia in 1919 had about it the
air of improbability and risk of failure that surrounded space mis-
sions half a century later. The London correspondent of one
Sydney newspaper wrote of Smithy: 'I judge him to be venture-
some, but not rash, efficient but not ultra methodical . . . He is a
slim and wiry Sydney type of youth with undoubtedly a brilliant
mastery over the science of flight.'

The race organisers, the Australian government and the British
Royal Aero Club, were slow to get their act together. By the
middle of June none of the entrants had been allowed to start and
it was then too late because the monsoon had broken in south-east
Asia. The race rules were changed several times, and since no aircraft had ever flown such a great distance before, questions of
safety and navigation competence had begun to crop up. With
most of their funds committed to their joyriding aeroplanes, immi-
nently due to be shipped to Australia, Smithy and Maddocks soon
ran out of money. They were forced to uncrate the BE2es and
revert to their original plan to go barnstorming in England. The
decision was to spell disaster for their Australia flight hopes.

The flying circus worked its way north from southern England
through the Midlands to the seaside crowds on Blackpool beach.
'As we could only take a minimum of luggage Kingsford Smith
flew in a check woollen dressing gown which did duty both as a
flying coat and for hotel use,' wrote Coombes. 'Some of the playing fields used for take-off and landing were hair-raising, often
being rather small and rough farmers' fields.'[6] But that summer, it
was not the state of the landing grounds that was responsible for a
succession of crashes which began to write off the three-plane
fleet. First, 'Smithy and Maddocks were flying home after a hard
day's work giving rides at a village fair,' Stannage wrote. 'An argument arose whether they should fly straight home or land in the
estate of a gentleman with whose daughter Smithy was, at that
moment, quite ardently in love. Smithy hauled one way on the
controls, Maddocks the other. Presently something snapped. It was
a control wire.' In the forced landing the aircraft crashed through
a hedge into a ditch and was wrecked. A few weeks later, trying to

land in fog, Smithy crashed a second aircraft, wrapping it round an oak tree.

Both aeroplanes were replaced in a deal with the Aircraft Disposals Board which, according to Stannage, was 'shrouded in mystery'. 'We bought these machines very cheaply from Air Ministry war stocks, and as we crashed them we would dash back and replace them,' Smithy said. 'We were young and full of beans and ready for anything.' The planes were being replaced by the insurers, who became alarmed when a third aircraft went up in smoke following an engine fire in mid-air. The fourth aircraft to go was one of the replacements. Smithy had developed a practice of offering flights to casual female acquaintances on the pretext of giving them flying lessons. The trips would often end in secluded trysting spots. On this occasion, said Stannage, 'he was taking a very lovely little nurse for a short instruction flight.' Preparing to land, the frightened pupil gripped the controls so hard that Smithy couldn't move them. The aircraft hit the ground, badly damaging the undercarriage and wing. 'There was by this time insufficient money to pay for repairs,' said Stannage. 'And most certainly they could not ask for more machines.'

They were not only crashing their aeroplanes at a frequency reflecting little credit on someone with Smithy's above-average piloting skills, but they had also, with the unwitting help of the insurers, who were covering their machines extremely well, become profitable aircraft-traders. 'Maddocks and I made about £40 in two afternoons with that one remaining machine . . . We then sold it to three chaps, who thought it looked easy to make money that way, for twice as much as we paid for it,' wrote Smithy. 'We had enough cash to buy three new and better type machines . . . I bet that before we start our flight to Australia we'll make more than the value of our buses.' But the extraordinary toll of accidents, and rumours about questionable insurance claims and the hedonistic activities of the directors of Kingsford Smith–Maddocks Aeros Ltd came to the attention of the highly principled Robert Blackburn, who was not amused. He called for a report into the company. What he learned was quickly to bring bad news for Smithy.

4

Larrikin in the Cockpit
1921

The truth about Smithy's failed attempt to enter the 1919 England–Australia air race never entered his legend. In his letters home he chose not to tell the family, and no newspaper or biographer ever revealed it. It was part of an unspoken agreement to forgive what were seen as venial lapses in a hero who was to bring great honour to his country.

According to the most persistent version of events, the Australian prime minister, the dynamic and fiery Welshman Billy Hughes had, while in Europe attending the Peace Conference, personally intervened and refused the Kangaroo's crew permission to enter the race because of their lack of navigation experience. Smithy said: 'There was a nigger in the woodpile in the form of Mr W. M. Hughes, our wartime prime minister, who was all powerful in those days. When he heard of our plan, he put his foot down. We were too young; we were too inexperienced; particularly we had no navigation knowledge for such a tremendous journey. He absolutely forbade it and that was the end of our plan.' He added: 'We sold the machine after an official veto had been placed on our venture by the Air Ministry.'

Yet the aeroplane had never been theirs to sell. It belonged to Blackburn. Nor did the British Air Ministry ever forbid the flight. An Australian government race was really none of its business. Moreover, it is unlikely that Prime Minister Hughes would have personally intervened in such sweeping fashion. He was an enthusiastic supporter of the event and in London he had attended at least one planning meeting at which he had met Cyril Maddocks, though not Smithy. Responsibility for race conditions and safety lay entirely with the Royal Aero Club, an exclusive and influential body bristling with great names from the services and the nobility. The club had undertaken to vet all entrants and refuse the unsuitable, and there is no evidence that it rejected the applications of Kingsford Smith, Maddocks and Rendle. Smithy had proved himself a pilot of above average competence with experience on nearly two dozen aircraft types at a time when long-distance navigation didn't exist as an aviation science. Most of those entering the race had been wartime fighter pilots whose operational flights had rarely exceeded 50 miles. Had lack of navigation skill been a genuine concern, it would have disqualified most of the other entrants. In any case, the navigation issue had been taken care of by the Royal Aero Club. In the middle of June, it had declared that all competing aircraft would be required to carry 'a competent navigator' who could be one of the pilots. At the same time the Australian government had arranged for the RAF to provide navigation training for any pilot who wanted it. Had this been the only impediment Smithy could easily have taken the short course.

The truth was not easy to establish seventy-five years later. The Blackburn company had long ago been swallowed up by the big British Aerospace conglomerate, and although some of its 1919 files still remained at Brough, none concerned with the air race could be found. From other sources, however, it was possible to piece together the chain of events. It is apparent that through the summer of 1919 Smithy and Maddocks were dividing their time between joyriding around England and working with Blackburn on Humberside preparing the Kangaroo for the race. 'I'm quite confident we'll pull it through,' he told Catherine on 13 June. 'The Shell company are cabling to all their representatives in the Dutch East Indies to assist us in every way and Rolls–Royce are fitting special 270hp engines . . . We had to borrow a hundred quid for the entrance fee for the race as well as spend lots rushing around.' But two months later he was much less optimistic. His relationship with Blackburn had become strained. 'I've written to two or three other concerns asking for particulars of equally capable machines and the cost of equipping one for the flight. I've also written to Harold to see if he knows anyone in America who would finance the journey. It would be

much better to be on our own, independent of Blackburns altogether . . .' In fact he had, preposterously, asked his brother
Harold if he would personally put up £2,000 for whom this
would have represented several years' income. Not surprisingly,
Harold had declined.

It is not clear when the final blow fell. The race files, preserved
in the Australian Archives, show that the problems had begun to
involve the senior Australian air officer in London, who had been
appointed Australia's official race representative in England. A
commandingly forthright figure sporting a fierce handlebar moustache, Lieutenant Colonel Richard Williams had served as a pilot
with the Australian Flying Corps and the RAF. He was to become
the first head of the RAAF, and later Australia's director-general of
civil aviation. In his autobiography, Air Marshal Sir Richard
Williams, as he was to become, disclosed publicly for the first time
what really happened.

The manager of the Blackburn Aircraft Company in London,
whose office was near Australia House, asked me to call and
see him. When I did so he asked whether I would have any
objection to replacing Kingsford Smith as pilot for the
Kangaroo . . . I said that, provided he was an Australian, it
was no business of mine to say who should or should not be
the pilot of a competing aircraft. In this case it was obviously
a matter entirely for the people supplying it. I had not even
met Kingsford Smith, who was of course to become one of
the world's great pilots.

However I was interested to know why the company
desired a change and was informed that the pilot concerned
had, with his friends, purchased an aircraft from
Government Disposals and was barnstorming in the country
and, contrary to civil air regulations, was landing in fields
not approved for that purpose. I was also told that he had
found that he could insure his aircraft for an amount in
excess of that for which he could replace it – and there had
been some crashes. The Blackburn view was that this was
undermining not only civil aviation control (they knew that
the British government would be reluctant to prosecute a
Dominion serviceman awaiting repatriation) but it was also

damaging aviation insurance, which was just getting established.

It has been stated by more than one author that Mr
Hughes prevented Kingsford Smith taking part in the race. I
know of no foundation for this assertion.[1]

Nor, said the Air Marshal, was he aware of any pilot's application
to compete having been refused on the irrelevant grounds of lack
of navigation skill. 'Aerial navigation was unknown at the time,' he
said.

When the Blackburn aeroplane finally left London's Hounslow
Aerodrome on 21 November 1919, the fourth of the six aircraft to
leave, not only was Kingsford Smith absent from the crew, but so
was Cyril Maddocks, probably as a consequence of his own
involvement in the insurance hanky-panky. The pilot was the com-
pany's original choice, Lieutenant Valdemar Rendle, the navigator
Captain Hubert Wilkins and the mechanic Lieutenant Garnsey
Potts. Flying as second pilot was another ex-Australian Flying
Corps man, Lieutenant Reginald Williams. Before his death in the
mid-1970s, Williams confided in a few people his version of
Smithy's rejection. One of them was his daughter, the Honourable
Mrs Beryl Evans, a member of the New South Wales Legislative
Council, whom I went to see at Parliament House in Sydney. 'All
his life Daddy was extremely tactful and discreet about it,' she
said. 'He was anxious not to say anything publicly that might harm
the Kingsford Smith image. However, in private, he would confirm
almost exactly Dickie Williams' version of events.' Before her
father died, Mrs Evans said, she had persuaded him to write for
the family an account of his life, including the part he played in
the 1919 race. 'When he came to deal with Kingsford Smith and
Maddocks he decided not to relate the full facts, just in case his
memoirs ever got published. You see, he only wanted nice things
said about them.'

To the end Smithy maintained to his family the pretence that
he was still involved, perhaps to spare their feelings, for they were
immensely proud of him. He wrote in October, several weeks
after he had been formally removed, that the race had been 'held
up indefinitely by the government'. This, of course, was not so.
Indeed, the first aircraft was on the point of setting off. As the six

aeroplanes began to fly out of Hounslow he must have read of the departures with great bitterness. He was probably the Australian pilot most personally obsessed with the desire to make a spectacular long-distance flight on a route that no one had ever flown. It is clear that, from this point onward, his soul was to be permanently consumed by the need to satisfy, and resatisfy, this compulsive yearning. 'My mind was filled with aviation to the exclusion of everything else.'

It was another Smith who took the fabulous £10,000 prize. Captain Ross Smith, along with his brother, Lieutenant Keith Smith, as co-pilot/navigator, and two mechanics, Sergeants James Bennett and Walter Shiers. They flew a twin-engined Vickers Vimy, arriving early in December 1919, in twenty-seven days and twenty hours, both brothers earning knighthoods. The only other aeroplane to complete the journey took nearly seven months. Two crews were killed. As for the Kangaroo that Smithy was to have piloted, one of its engines failed when an oil pipe broke over the Mediterranean and the crew were lucky not to have drowned. Rendle only just managed to limp back on the remaining motor to Crete, where they abandoned the flight.

While the Kangaroo had been making its slow way eastward across Europe, Smithy, dejected, broke and jobless, had decided to leave England. According to Reg Williams, as Beryl Evans recalled, 'Things had got a little too hot there for his and Maddocks' liking. They decided to bale out, and took off for America.' Attempts to sell the joyriding business failed. Smithy went to the USA at the end of November so short of money that he had to sell his only suit and travel in uniform. He had decided to try his luck in California, where he knew he could stay indefinitely with Harold. When he arrived in San Francisco the week before Christmas, demoralised and still weak from scarlet fever, which had seen him compulsorily quarantined at Ellis Island in New York, Harold and his wife, Elsie, and their teenage daughter Beris were shocked by his appearance. But he soon rallied with their hospitality and the joy of reunion. Harold, now forty and known simply as Harold K. Smith, had become the most successful brother. He was a manager with the American–Hawaiian Steamship Company and even owned his own home, a large, stylish-looking house set attractively among trees and lawns in Menlo Park on the city's southern outskirts. His affluence, however, was a mixed blessing. It had made him a honey pot and prop to his less fortunate siblings – Wilfrid and Elsie were also staying with him at the time – as well as a periodic source of income for his parents.

Aviation in California in 1920 offered a precarious existence. There were precious few jobs elsewhere. Desperately in need of money, Smithy pleaded with Harold to find him one with the shipping company. The only vacancies were for radio-operators. 'Poor old Charles is taking up wireless as there seems to be nothing doing in the flying game,' Elsie reported to Catherine in the middle of February 1920. 'The trouble is that Chilla is so very stony he can't wait, so Harold is going to send him away in one of his ships to South America in a few weeks. Now he is studying hard to get through but hoping madly that something more congenial will turn up. His whole heart is in flying and nothing else seems to interest him – except a pretty girl and the banjo.'

Day after day Smithy wandered restlessly about the house, dreaming of a dramatic new pioneer flight: back to Australia across the Pacific. 'Luck seems to be persistently against poor old me, doesn't it?' he wrote home pathetically, still smarting with resentment about the race.

> However, I am once more full of optimism after the last few black weeks I've had with this darned Australia flight falling through. I won't worry you with the whole details now, but when I can give you the story in person you'll see how badly I've been let down. However, dears, there's lots of fight left in me and I have every intention of coming home to you still by air – but from this country! You know there is a prize offered for the trans-Pacific job amounting to $50,000. I think I can get people over here sufficiently interested to back me. Hal's influence has already helped and I'm getting close to several big cinema concerns . . . Everybody here wants to see me do this flight, but of course I'm keeping it right out of the newspapers. No second fiasco for me thanks.

He concluded conspiratorially: 'Don't let a soul know about it, dears, until I'm actually doing it.' In fact he hadn't kept it out of the newspapers. At his behest a San Francisco daily ran his grinning portrait over the caption: 'Captain Charles Kingsford Smith, war ace, who will try to fly the Pacific.'

The US$50,000 prize for a Pacific flight was to have come from a wealthy American film-producer and director, Thomas Harper Ince. One of the major creative talents of the silent screen, he had been a former business partner of the eminent director D. W. Griffiths and of Mack Sennett, creator of the Keystone Kops. A hard-driving, ruthless man, Ince poured out westerns from his large Los Angeles studio. But for precisely which flight he was offering a prize is not at all clear. The ocean, it seems, merely had to be crossed. 'If only I could manage to do that job,' Smithy wrote, 'I would be able to justify myself in the eyes of the Australian people with a vengeance.' The disgrace of the Blackburn affair was to haunt him for a long time. Through the early months of 1920 he wrote to every organisation he vainly hoped might be interested in sponsoring him for Ince's glittering prize: aircraft-manufacturers, newspapers, film studios. He even wrote to Charlie Chaplin, one of the co-founders of United Artists. But it was a technically hopeless venture at that time, given the limitations of aircraft development and the huge over-water distances. No one had even yet flown from California to Hawaii. And presently Ince withdrew his offer. 'Poor boy,' Elsie wrote. 'I don't think he has a chance of raising the money. I wish we had some wealthy relations. However I daresay it will be all for the best in the long run and he will get over his disappointments in time.'

Smithy's stopgap career as a marine wireless-operator had got nowhere. He had discovered that as an alien he wasn't permitted to work on an American ship. In desperation he briefly took a suicidal job at Willows in the Sacramento Valley driving wild ducks off the rice fields. He piloted a small Curtiss Jenny through the marauding flocks just a couple of feet above the crop. Photographs of the aircraft after these sorties show the wings, fuselage and pilot draped in startling fashion with feathers, blood and viscera. Then he joined a flying circus which travelled about California giving joyrides and spectacular flying displays. 'AIR THRILLS', their poster announced, 'Moffett–Starkey Aero Circus featuring Chas Kingsford Smith, RAF Ace.' Almost immediately he was involved in a bad crash. As he was flying a joyrider out of a small paddock in a Jenny, his engine cut out as he tried to clear a belt of trees. He and the passenger escaped without injury, but the plane was wrecked. Next he flew for the movies, first at Universal Studios. Stunt men walked on his wings in flight, hopped from one aircraft to another and from aircraft to trains, dangled from the wing tips and clung to the struts during loops and rolls.

Tempted by the bigger money, he accepted an offer to become a stunt man himself. But the duties he was called upon to perform immediately terrified him. On his first assignment, hanging parachuteless by his legs from the undercarriage of an Avro 504K, he got stuck in the slipstream and, for an agonising fifteen minutes, couldn't swing back. A photograph famously shows the plane with his inverted, suspended torso splayed as a silhouette against the sky above the Californian desert. Close to exhaustion, his mind flooded with panic, he only just managed to grab the undercarriage cross member and swivel himself upwards. He never flew as a stunt man again. Soon a horrifying experience made him decide to abandon movie flying altogether. He watched a pilot colleague on a Fox Films night shoot, blinded by the searchlights, spin into the ground in a ball of fire. He went back to barnstorming with Moffett, who now promised to fund a Pacific flight.

But aerobatic flying in planes of uncertain reliability had begun to get to him, and he was forced to take a rest in San Francisco. His sister Elsie was alarmed. 'Poor Charles looked very thin. He has had a bad time with rheumatism and sciatica. He is also very nervy,' she wrote home. What he didn't know was that Moffett was in deep financial trouble. His plane was seized and Smithy, who was never to see a cent of the earnings upon which his latest Pacific dream rested, began to drink heavily, forced by Prohibition to frequent illicit bars serving poisonous wood alcohol that rendered him dizzy and half blind. 'It will be a good thing when he gets a good job back home and settles down away from this wild life,' Elsie reported. 'You see, Mum, after nearly a year here Chilla is no better off than when he arrived . . . He has practically only got the clothes he arrived in. I really do think his experiences are beginning to somewhat daze even his doughty heart.' Pleading with Leofric to cable him the fare, he sailed home in January 1921 to an emotional family reunion.

Catherine and William had finally come to roost in the middle-class north-shore suburb of Longueville, where they had rented a three-bedroomed, slate-roofed weatherboard house at 73 Arabella Street, just across a side-road from Leofric and Elfreda at number 75. 'Kuranda' was to remain their home until the end of their days. Now approaching twenty-four, the young pilot whom the newspapers had glamorised as a formidable contender in the air race the previous year had slipped unobtrusively back into his native land, a forgotten war hero in shabby clothes, without money or job and clinically depressed. Catherine, who had not seen her son since the war, told Norman Ellison how Charles had come off the ship looking sad and worn beyond his years. In the weeks that followed, he often retreated to his room to sit alone, plucking his banjo for hours on end. For five years he had been hyped up by excitement and mortal danger. The come-down of suburban Sydney served only to add to his blues. He was, said Catherine, 'brooding and morose'. Only slowly did the family persuade him to talk about the things he had buried: the devastating experiences under fire that had stolen his youth and wounded his mind; the terrors of stunt flying and the catalogue of his failed ventures. 'It soon became apparent to us all,' Catherine told Ellison, 'that Chilla was suffering from the effects of a great deal of hard, mental punishment.'

Within weeks of his return, he was given a tonic to lift him out of depression and self-pity: a full-time job as a pilot. It was to herald one of the wildest interludes of his life. It began – as it was to continue – in a hotel bar. Smithy went to Sydney's Carlton Hotel in Castlereagh Street, one day early in 1921 to catch up over more than a few beers with an old RFC mate, Lionel Lee. By the time they parted Lee had offered him a job with a group of thirty ex-servicemen who were forming an air taxi and joyriding venture, the Diggers Co-operative Aviation Company Ltd. They planned to operate out of the small New South Wales town of Wellington, around 160 miles north-west of Sydney, using war-surplus Avro 504K trainers.

Lee was to regret the haste with which he'd recruited his old mate for, within days of joining Diggers at the end of February at £12 a week, Smithy was astonishing his new colleagues with the recklessness of his flying and his uninhibited carousing. It was as if he had been seized by a need to live as self-indulgently and dangerously as he could. No aviation authority then existed to control the conduct of pilots. 'The public regarded them,' said Norman Ellison, 'as a special type of privileged people, expected to do the wildest things aloft and on the ground.' Smithy did not disappoint them. In the spirit of his war flying, he treated the job as an adventure driven by the fatalism that the brevity of life in the RFC had encouraged.

On his first day he was allocated one of the Avros and instructed to fly it with a mechanic from Sydney to Wellington via Oberon to pick up some joyriding business at the local agricultural show. At Oberon he landed on what turned out to be a soft and boggy paddock. The Avro's wheels sank into the mud and the aircraft tipped on its nose, damaging one of the lower wings and the undercarriage. Fearful of losing his job almost before he'd started, he decided not to tell the company. He and the mechanic called in the local blacksmith to repair the broken undercarriage, and the undertaker to fix the wing. When the repairs had been completed, he took the aircraft to Dubbo for the annual railway staff 'picnic races', the town's biggest social occasion of the year.

At the racecourse the Diggers' Avro was kept busy all day giving flights at £1 a head. The passengers went up two at a time, sitting side by side in the enlarged rear cockpit. Smithy shared the work with another company pilot. While his colleague was flying, he steadily slaked his thirst in the beer tent. Until late afternoon he flew cautiously, giving his passengers gentle circuits of the town. Around four o'clock, bored by the monotony and emboldened by beer, he decided to offer two of his customers something more lively.

His victims were a young railway clerk, Oliver Cook, and his fiancée, Dulcie Offner, a local farmer's daughter. As they were being strapped in Smithy asked, 'Would you like some loops?' They said yes, that would be very exciting. They wanted their money's-worth. The £2 Oliver had paid for their trip was a huge extravagance for a 30 shillings-a-week clerk. It took the Avro a long time to climb to a safe aerobatic height. The first loop was uneventful, but on the second something went alarmingly wrong. As they began to sweep vertically upward again, there was a loud crack like gunshot. Something had broken; exactly what is not clear. The most frequently quoted account claims that an undetected front spar fracture had cracked, allowing the lower starboard wing, damaged at Oberon, to collapse. 'The excitement was intense amongst the thousands who feared an appalling tragedy,' the Dubbo *Dispatch* reported. 'Lieut. Smith, however, was equal to the demand on his skill and nerve and he landed on a slight hill . . . without injury to his passengers or himself but with disastrous results to the plane.'

In 1992 Dulcie and Oliver Cook had been married for seventy years and their flight with pilot Kingsford Smith remained one of the most momentous events in their lives. Ninety-four-year-old Oliver said that, sitting in the cockpit, holding hands, they had been too wrapped up in each other to be aware that anything was wrong. They thought it was all part of the aerobatic performance. 'We hit the ground like a thousand bricks,' he remembered. 'The plane tipped on its nose and Smithy turned round and called out: "Are you all right?" and I replied, "Yes, but Jeez, what a rough landing." When we were clear I looked at him properly for the first time. He was shaking and in a hell of a nervous state. He'd obviously been drinking.' Dulcie produced a cracked and faded photograph of the crash, which showed the Avro with its engine partly buried in the ground, its propeller snapped, its undercarriage demolished and its tail in the air. The bottom wing, which, according to Smithy legend, had failed in the Oberon landing accident, was intact. The photograph showed that it was the visibly distorted upper port wing that had broken. An expert who examined the picture seventy-five years after the incident was in no doubt that the failure had been caused by a severe load placed on it during an exceptionally violent, tight loop – one in which Smithy's judgement of the 'feel' of the loads would have been much impaired by his drinking. Added to which the glue binding the structure's wooden components had probably dried out with age.[2]

Within days of the Dubbo disaster Smithy, unrepentant, was back in the air in the repaired Avro. After a long drinking session he set off with Lionel Lee one afternoon to mount a vigorous aerobatic display for the benefit of a nurse he was dating. To the consternation of staff and patients at the hospital he made repeated howling dives and zooms over the building, touching his wheels on the entrance drive to send up showers of gravel. His appetite thus whetted, he set off in search of riskier thrills, playing dragonfly on a nearby river, skimming the surface with his wheels as he headed, dangerously low, for a railway bridge beneath which he decided to fly. But as he dived toward the perilously small gap Lee spotted a large cluster of telephone wires in their direct path. He jerked a hand forward and grabbed Smithy's collar, forcing him to climb. They missed the wires by only a few feet.

Almost every night the pilots were at the centre of wild hotel parties. After one in Dubbo, Smithy and Lee, flying a second Avro, set off to give an air display in Coonamble. Smithy wanted to take six bottles of beer for the journey, which Lee insisted went in his aircraft. The two Avros set off in loose formation on the 90-mile flight. Within twenty minutes Smithy had landed in a large empty paddock, refusing to go any further until Lee came down and cracked open a bottle. They shared the bottle and when it was finished they knocked off another. Back in the air Smithy signalled several more landings until they had polished off the last of the beer. When eventually they arrived in Coonamble they were in carefree mood. Smithy insisted on taking the mayor, who had come to greet them, on such a stomach-churning aerobatic flight he made him violently sick.

In Coonamble the hospitality kept them in a semi-permanent state of intoxication. At one of the hotel parties mounting tensions between Smithy and his mechanic over the former's rough handling of the aircraft erupted when the mechanic attacked him with a large spanner, breaking his nose and reducing him to his knees. Ordered out of the hotel, the two resumed their fight in the main street, where the noise awoke the Coonamble police sergeant who, throwing his tunic over his pyjamas, hurried outside and arrested them both. Smithy spent the night in the cells. The next morning, battered and bloodied, he appeared before the magistrate and he and the mechanic were each fined 10 shillings. The fight left its permanent mark on Smithy: a scar and a slight bend in his large Roman nose.

The people of Coonamble were not amused. They decided to show their disapproval by boycotting the joyriding aeroplanes. The protest proved financially disastrous for Diggers, yet the co-operative was endlessly patient with Smithy, for he was their

biggest draw. They even allowed themselves to become involved in
the Pacific venture he still dreamed of. At his behest the company's manager, Gordon Wilkins, sent a cable to Prime Minister
Billy Hughes, urging him to use his influence to get from the
British Air Ministry a war-surplus Vickers Vimy to undertake the
flight. The prime minister enthusiastically passed the request to
the British Controller General of Civil Aviation, who replied that
a plane with Pacific capability 'would have to be specially
designed'.[3] Thus failed Smithy's third attempt to make a sensational flight across the world. The hard fact was that, in 1921, less
than twenty years after the beginnings of powered flight, an aeroplane with the safe range to fly the critical 2,450 miles from
America to Hawaii on a trans-Pacific flight to Australia still didn't
exist. But the Pacific trip had become a fixation. From now on
everything Smithy did was to be a means to that end.

His days with Diggers were, however, numbered. Two more
incidents, in swift succession, were, to the company's dismay,
reported by the newspapers. First, after another daytime drinking
session, he flew under the Cowra Bridge causing a team of horses
hauling a wheat wagon to career in panic into a sulky carrying a
heavily pregnant farmer's wife. She was spilled out and gave birth
then and there. By the time news of the outrage reached the
Diggers management in Wellington, Smithy had set off on another
disastrously boozy mission – a charter flight to Riverslea Station 20
miles up the Lachlan River, carrying two passengers bound for a
christening party at the homestead. On arrival he ignored the large
landing paddock, delivering his guests instead with a flourish
straight on to the front drive. As he bounced in, narrowly missing
a clump of trees, he blew one of his tyres. He laughed off the incident and joined the champagne party, a glamorous and gregarious
figure circulating among the guests, chatting up the women in his
rapid, confident way and holding people spellbound with his flying
stories.

Many hours later, he and his passengers climbed aboard the
Avro for the return flight to Cowra. All the guests came out in the
sunset to see them off. The burst tyre was forgotten. As the tail
came up the wheels began to bounce and wobble as he tried desperately to keep the aeroplane straight. But with one tyre flat, he
couldn't reach flying speed. The Avro sank a wheel into a rabbit

hole and nose-dived into the ground with its tail quivering in the air. The shocked guests ran over to find both passengers with badly cut faces and Smithy with two broken ribs. His pain dulled by champagne and shock, he was lifted out of the crushed cockpit. The insurers checked with the bar where he had spent most of the day and refused to pay out. It was a crippling blow for the company, hastening its descent into liquidation early the following year.

Smithy's first job back in Australia had lasted less than five months. All he wrote of Diggers Aviation in his autobiography was, 'I worked with them for a time.' Once again he chose to spare the family the hurtful truth. 'Dearest Mum,' he wrote cheerfully from Wellington on 20 July. 'We had a spill at Cowra and I was a bit bruised in consequence. Rather bad luck tho with the new machine, but she was fully insured and except for the delay the company won't lose.' The letter reveals that he had been sending Catherine some of his Diggers' earnings, and now the crash had created yet another cashflow crisis. In his letters he claimed he had ceased flying with the company because there wasn't another aircraft for him to pilot. He even fabricated a story that Diggers were still looking for a suitable Pacific plane for him. 'I doubt that she would have been wholly deceived,' said Catherine Robinson. 'She wasn't blind to his foibles. She knew full well she'd bred someone unique whom she actually delighted in describing as a larrikin.'

Yet Smithy left Diggers with no hard feelings. They even wrote him a glowing reference. Around the middle of August 1921, still in pain from his broken ribs, but with his spirit unbowed, he took the train back to Sydney. He arrived home at 73 Arabella Street without a penny to his name. Happily, he wasn't out of work for very long. In September he saw, to his excitement, an advertisement recruiting pilots for a small new airline in Western Australia. He applied and was accepted.

5

Nice Girl at Meentheena

1922–3

Smithy's new employer was another ex-Royal Flying Corps pilot, Norman Brearley, soon to become prominent in Australian aviation. He had come home from the war to Perth as a major with a DSO and MC for gallantry as a fighter pilot in France. In a dog-fight both his lungs had been perforated by a bullet, but he had miraculously recovered to become an instructor, emerging from the war as an aviator of rare skill. In late 1921 he had been awarded a year's contract to launch Australia's first scheduled air service, a 1,200-mile route to serve the isolated North-West. The plan was to operate a subsidised, once-weekly schedule from Geraldton to Derby using six converted Bristol fighters. He had advertised countrywide for five pilots to join his newly formed Western Australian Airways. He didn't intend to recruit them casually. Nor, he declared in a newspaper interview, would there be any place for pilots of intemperate habits. 'Flying calls for a cool head and a steady hand,' he said firmly.

Smithy's application, quoting more than twenty different types of aircraft flown and detailing his experience as an RFC instructor, was accompanied by the testimonial from Diggers Aviation which, given his spectacular trail of destruction in their employ, was mis-leadingly warm. News of his excesses had yet to reach Brearley. A highly self-disciplined man, he would have been decidedly less enthusiastic about Smithy had he known the truth. However, of his ability as a pilot, Brearley was soon to be in little doubt. He had decided that he would personally air-test all twelve of the appli-cants he had shortlisted. When the aspirants were summoned to the newly formed Royal Australian Air Force's Point Cook air base near Melbourne early in October 1921, it was quickly obvious, he wrote, that 'one young man named Smith was quite outstanding, and as soon as we were in the air I knew he was well above average'.[1] Brearley liked Smithy immediately and the respect was mutual. 'Major Brearley is an awfully nice chap and very capable as well as an excellent pilot,' he reported to Catherine from Point Cook. But the major's gentle voice masked a ruthless perfectionist for whom near enough was never good enough. His own brilliance as a pilot commanded a degree of awe. He could sideslip a biplane into a corner of a tree-lined field in breathtaking helicopter-type descents. In Smithy he recognised another pilot of similar rare ability and affinity with the aeroplane. Sadly, and perhaps inevitably, the two were destined to clash.

Borrowing the boat fare, Smithy joined Brearley in Perth on £10 a week along with pilots Len Taplin, Bob Fawcett, Arthur Blake and Val Abbott. Australia's first airline captains were soon to become folk figures in the lonely communities of the barren redlands of the tropical North-West. The country's first airliners were cheap war-surplus planes with low-powered Puma engines which, out in the bush, could happily run on motor spirit. Small and inelegant machines with big, square radiators, the rear of the two military cockpits had been converted into a cramped enclosed cabin with side-by-side space for two passengers under a bulbous hinged canopy. Despite their clumsy, home-made appearance, they were safe and reasonably reliable.

The vast state of Western Australia, four-fifths the size of India, was a profoundly empty land, much of it desert, sprinkled with tiny pockets of population. The townships of the North-West were mere clusters of brick and corrugated-iron buildings, sleepy tidal ports that existed to supply the pearl-fishing industry, gold mines and the enormous sheep and cattle stations that lay up to a week's journey away by horse and dray in the parched hinterland. For much of the year it was a shimmering, waterless landscape of oppressive heat, red dust and flies. From its starting point at Geraldton, Brearley's tiny airline was to connect Carnarvon, Onslow, Roebourne, Port Hedland, Broome and Derby.[2] The full trip was scheduled to take three days with night stops in Carnarvon and Port Hedland.

It was a perilous operation. On an augural flight up the 1,200-mile route, Bob Fawcett stalled and crashed at Murchison House Station north of Geraldton, killing himself and his mechanic. Shortly afterwards, on an airfield-proving trip, Smithy and Brearley, in another *Tourer*, were lucky to survive an engine failure over the sea. Force-landing on the beach in Roebuck Bay, they were stuck in soggy sand for several days, so badly sunburned that they subsequently had to spend a week in bed, their feet swollen into grotesque red clubs.

When regular operations began in February 1922, Smithy, now twenty-five, resumed the itinerant life, suitcase, banjo and ukulele in tow, that seemed so essential to his existence. Based nowhere in particular, moving about the North-West from town to town as services dictated, he was never sure for certain where he would spend the night as he operated on all the sectors between Geraldton and Derby. In the bars and dining rooms along the route he became a celebrity, an innately cheerful personality whose magnetic friendliness drew people everywhere into his warm ambit. Under Brearley's stern regime his flying had become for the most part safe and subdued. But, with the major hundreds of miles away in Perth, he was occasionally tempted to relieve the boredom by seeking out the monthly coastal steamer, *Bambra*, and swooping beneath the wireless aerial hung between her masts. He also introduced an ingenious solution to overbooking problems. When a pilot needed to be carried to the next town and the plane was full, he would hop up on to the lower wing and cling on for the two- or three-hour journey. A remarkable picture taken by a passenger shows Taplin 'wing-riding', propped against the strut, grinning at the camera, his jacket ballooning out in the 80mph slipstream. Below are the barren claypans of the empty desert landscape. Had Brearley known about the practice, which Smithy himself adopted from time to time, he might not have appointed him senior pilot, nor written to him so warmly in Broome in late 1922: 'I have had excellent reports about you from all and sundry. I am very pleased indeed with the way you are carrying on. I know now that you are all you appear to be, and that is saying a lot.'

Among the few who remembered Charles Kingsford Smith seven decades later in Western Australia was June Dupre, who, as a shy seventeen-year-old in Carnarvon in 1922, had gone to dances at the parish hall at which he played his banjo. 'I regarded him with utter awe, of course. He was a war hero and most people's favourite among Brearley's pilots. He was a really delightful character.' Mrs Dupre's house was close to the landing ground and Smithy, she recalled, would deliberately fly low over it on his approaches and take-offs. 'He would swoop so close to the roof that the crockery would rattle on the shelves. One washing day as he went roaring over, Mother said, "That boy's going to be embarrassed one morning when he lands with my bloomers on his wheels." I couldn't resist repeating this later to Smithy. Quick as a flash he said: "Tell your mum I'd be delighted to use them as a windsock."'

Brearley's pilots were not overworked. Normally flying on only two days a week, they enjoyed plenty of rest and recreation. In Carnarvon they stayed at the Gascoyne, a large 'bush' hotel popular with up-country station families, who would dress for dinner, which the waitresses, dressed in black skirts and white blouses, served at tables spread with damask cloths and laid with silver cutlery and starched linen napkins. In a less elegant part of the hotel known as the 'bull pen', reserved for single men, things were less formal. Here Smithy would pitch up from the bar to play the piano. 'He'd arrive in an old pair of half-mast khaki trousers with his shirt hanging out, wearing a pair of grubby white sandshoes,' remembered Kath Blizard, who was sixteen at the time and lived at Yarrie Station. 'The sandshoes were because of his foot wound. His favourite tune was "Every Little Breeze", and he'd sing it lustily as he played. He was one of the most happy-go-lucky people I've ever known.' The pain from the severed nerves in his foot was again keeping him awake at night. Catherine urged him to seek medical advice. But in a letter from Carnarvon he explained: 'The hoof isn't quite as bad now. I've avoided walking where possible. The trouble about seeing a surgeon, as you suggest, is that there ain't any surgeons up here . . . It has been mostly weakness and aching of small bones, with consequent neuritis at nights. However, it is still a foot, which is more than some poor devils have got.'

In Carnarvon he bought himself a £75 motorbike. To fund it he borrowed £50 from Brearley and cabled Catherine demanding £25 from a family-support account he had opened in Sydney, ostensibly to help them save to buy 'Kuranda'. He had no compunction about draining the account for his own needs within weeks of its creation. Although by now Leofric had been appointed as the family watchdog to control Charles' affairs, virtually taking them out of his hands, it seemed that for Catherine and William, no sacrifice was ever too great to indulge their feckless son. 'I'm still plunged in impecuniosity through the motor cycle, but am getting lots of fun with it,' he wrote happily to them. Their hearts must have sunk as they read on: 'By the way my income tax for the last two years will soon come to hand and as it will be at least £30 I'll have to get assistance from over there. So tell Leofric to make ready in a few weeks.' Preposterously, he concluded, 'Mummy dear, I want you to take a few pounds of my dough and buy yourself and Dad a little treat of some kind, and will write the "Old Dragon" re same.' It was said that, on receipt of such letters, the dragon, Leofric, would cup his head in his hands and groan with anger and exasperation. Yet, Catherine Robinson explained, 'Chilla would never have appealed in vain for assistance. Money was a commodity that went round the family according to need. Any member would be helped financially by those who had it at the time. They shared their houses and possessions, too – the family was family, one entity.'

In the North-West the pearling centre of Broome was to become Smithy's favourite town. A pearlmaster there offered to take him to the bottom of the oyster beds in a heavy suit and helmet. The area was frequented by sharks of alarming size, but Smithy, ever ready for a new experience, overcame his fear of the sea to try it. Lowered slowly into this dark green world, he was immediately stricken with the familiar panic. He couldn't get back to the surface fast enough. Sending Catherine a photograph of himself in diving gear, he wrote: 'The sickly smile is an endeavour to look as though I wasn't scared.' Ashore there were more agreeable pastimes. He began an affair with a daughter of a Spanish pearlmaster, Filomeno Rodriguez. Verona was a beautiful, capricious, intelligent and volatile widow of twenty-seven who had been left a substantial fortune by her late husband, Frederick Grave, a wealthy Perth engineer and car-distributor who had been a close friend of Henry Ford. 'Ronnie' met Smithy on a visit to her father in the North-West. 'She and her daughters were driving south out of Broome when the car broke down near Eighty Mile Beach,' said Michael Prevost, her son by her subsequent second marriage.

A search party, led by Smithy, went out and found them. The affair – and there certainly was an affair – started soon after. It was conducted, as far as I can ascertain, in Broome and Perth, far from discreetly. There was a considerable correspondence between them which, unfortunately, was all destroyed in the 1950s. I'm not sure how long the affair lasted. I believe it eventually just fizzled out. The reasons for this, I understand, were Ron's unwillingness to settle down after her very unhappy marriage to Fred Grave, and by Smithy, in turn, not wishing to be tied down to a ready-made family. Another major problem was that Ron was extremely rich, whereas Smithy was far from so. It wasn't an ideal prospect for the latter.[3]

How deeply they felt about each other is nowhere recorded. In his own long line of conquests up to this point Smithy's emotions appear rarely to have been seriously involved, and when they were he invariably confided in Catherine. None of his letters home ever mentioned the glamorous Verona. The couple appear to have lived for the moment, snatching opportunities to be alone. One local legend has it that Smithy used to land in Broome with a motorbike lashed to his undercarriage. Within minutes of parking he would be off to see Ronnie. Her liaisons around this time had made her quite notorious – she embarked on one affair after another, said one of her relatives.[4]

Into Smithy's restless world there arrived in Carnarvon around the middle of 1922 a new Western Australian Airways pilot. Keith Vincent Anderson, a tall, solid man of serious and rather sad disposition, had been hired by Brearley to replace Bob Fawcett, killed in the inaugural crash. Beyond the horrors of aerial combat and a shared vision of oceanic flight, Keith Anderson and Charles Kingsford Smith appear to have had little in common. Anderson, whom many were to describe as a 'born loser', was a gentle, measured, reticent, slow-thinking person. There seemed little about him to attract the extrovert Smithy, a natural achiever who sizzled with hyperactive enthusiasm. Yet as the two shook hands at the aerodrome and hurtled in a column of red dust on Smithy's motorbike, towards the Gascoyne Hotel, one of the staunchest and most tragic mateships of Kingsford Smith's life began.

Because he had once lived in South Africa, a myth grew that Anderson had black blood in his ancestry. But he was of white Australian descent, born in Perth in 1898, the only child of a road-building contractor, Sidney Jerrold Anderson, and his wife, Constance Willdridge. When he was ten, his father went off to Ceylon, now Sri Lanka, to manage a rubber plantation. When Constance went to join him in 1911, they decided that Keith should go to boarding school in South Africa where an older cousin lived. Sidney died suddenly in Ceylon in 1914, and Constance went to live in Cape Town to be with Keith. They were not reunited for long: early in 1917 Keith joined the Royal Flying Corps and went to England to train. According to his RFC records he served on the Western Front as a fighter pilot on Camels with Number 73 Squadron. Although he saw action for only two months early in 1918, it was to prove a shattering experience. He acquitted himself with great distinction, being officially credited with five enemy aircraft while actively contributing to the destruction of four more. Yet although he emerged from the war physically intact, he paid a heavy psychological price for those eight weeks. Repatriated to South Africa in the middle of 1919, Keith was too traumatised to work. Family photographs of him taken around this time show him looking unutterably sad. Constance was so concerned that she arranged for him to go and live on a farm in Portuguese West Africa (now Angola) to recover. Early in 1922 he decided to go home to Australia, where Brearley, assessing him as safe and reliable, offered him a job with the airline.

When Anderson and Smithy met for the first time, they talked only about their aviation ambitions: Smithy's to fly the Pacific and Anderson's, it emerged, to tackle the Indian Ocean. Apocryphal dialogue has the two deciding to join forces and fly both oceans together – on Smithy's condition that they attempt the Pacific first. It was for him as deep an obsession as ever, and he had begun to look around for a wealthy patron to sponsor him. One man who could certainly afford to bankroll a Pacific flight was Keith Mackay, who had just inherited the Mundabullangana Station on the coast at the mouth of the Yule River to the west of Port Hedland, where he lived with his mother. In his early twenties, he was the youngest of a dynasty of enterprising Scots who had come to the North-West from Skye and acquired more than a million acres of land. On his father's death Mackay had inherited immense wealth which had allowed him to embark on an extravagant lifestyle. He had a large residence in Perth, where he had become a drinking mate of Smithy's.

Smithy, Anderson and Mackay began, that winter of 1922, to develop serious plans for a Pacific crossing. On condition that he would be a member of the crew, Mackay had agreed to buy an aeroplane. They were in the market for a three-seater aircraft with a huge fuel capacity, preferably, on Smithy's insistence, a flying boat. He wrote to Leofric asking him to try to find such a plane and was amazed when his brother located someone who owned a number of flying boats. Lebbeus Hordern, another wealthy young playboy, was the black sheep of a rich Sydney department-store family. At the end of the war, in which he had served in the RFC, he had co-founded a joyriding and charter flying firm, the Aerial Company, for which he had invested in four seaplanes and flying boats. The most luxurious of these, which immediately interested Smithy, was a large twin-engined biplane described by its owner as an 'air yacht' – a Short Felixstowe F3, originally designed for anti-submarine operations. Powered by two Rolls–Royce engines, it had a 102ft wingspan, a partly enclosed cockpit and cruised at 85mph carrying ten passengers in a cabin divided into three comfortably appointed lounges. Its only drawback was its pitifully limited range of barely 500 miles, but Smithy was confident he could increase this with long-range fuel tanks. It was agreed that, early the following year, he would take leave and go to Sydney to look at this grand machine.

Meanwhile he continued his nomadic existence, living out of an old suitcase now so disintegrated that he had to carry it about, shirts and pyjamas protruding, lashed up with rope.

The 1922 winter brought the annual rash of race meetings and balls, and the chaperoned daughters of the back-country squattocracy began to arrive in Port Hedland. One of the young women who had booked for the season into Mrs Mousher's boarding

house, where Smithy stayed, specially took his fancy. She had
come down from a remote cattle station called Meentheena, 200
miles inland. At half a million acres it was larger than the English
county of Buckinghamshire, and lay in parched country on the
normally dried Nullagine River east of Marble Bar, near the edge
of the Great Sandy Desert. Within no time Smithy had persuaded
Brearley to give him two weeks off to go inland on the pretext of
finding emergency landing grounds for the medical evacuation of
isolated settlers. In the first week of October he reported to
Catherine: 'I'm going as far as Meentheena Station where I'll stay
a few days and then come back (nice girl at Meentheena).'

At the end of October he revealed more.

Returned from my holiday to Meentheena a couple of days
ago. Had a bonzer time, but had to come back as far as
Marble Bar per horseback (65 miles) and needless to say was
pretty sore and stiff for a while. It was a hot and dry trip,
about 107° (42° C) in the shade (of which there ain't any)
and absolutely waterless and uninhabited. I can easily understand men doing a perish in such country. The station, apart
from being so hard to get to, is a bonzer place. Mrs McKenna
and Thelma gave me a splendid time and I enjoyed the break
immensely . . . Thelma Corboy (Mrs McKenna's daughter)
heap nice girl. Am very interested!

The stages of Smithy's rapidly developing relationship with
Thelma Corboy are difficult to reconstruct for, uncharacteristically, he chose to keep his parents largely in the dark. Nonetheless,
from the limited information he did provide, they can hardly have
been left in much doubt as to his intentions. 'Next weekend I go
out again to Meentheena for a few days spell,' he wrote at the end
of December. 'Guess I'll end up a family man all right. Can't find
anyone I fancy better and I'm tired of pub life. What say you?' The
letter concluded: 'Still hoping to get a trip to Sydney soon (will
come on my honeymoon!)' A month later came: 'Dearest Mum
and Dad, I think I'll jolly well *have* to get spliced. Not that I relish
losing my erstwhile freedom, but I must have a home at this job,
otherwise I'll have to chuck it. It's a ghastly coast after one has
been up and down it a few dozen times; and to finish one's run

with the only prospect of going "home" to a bush pub – Gawd! Wish I could aviate across the Pacific or do some damn thing. But even that is fading into "things impossible tho longed for."'

Whatever the family in Sydney understood about the imminence of a wedding, the event, when it came, left Catherine and William stunned. A bombshell of a telegram dispatched by Smithy from Marble Bar on 6 June 1923, simply read: 'MARRIED FIVE MINUTES AGO THELMA AND SELF SEND FOND LOVE – CHILLA.' That day's entry in Catherine's diary, in which, as usual, the momentous and the trivial enjoyed equal prominence – 'Letter from Carrie Smith. Wire from Chilla saying he is married to Thelma Corboy. Quite a shock. Making pie melon jam. Phil (Kingsford) here for dinner' – disguised a sense of bewilderment and hurt that Chilla, the apple of their eye, had not given them the chance to attend the wedding, for which they would surely have mortgaged their souls, or even to meet the woman they would automatically embrace as another daughter-in-law.

After a flurry of phone calls and telegrams to flash the news round the family, Catherine sat down and drafted a congratulatory telegram in which she apparently found words to express some of the disappointment she could not commit to her diary. The wire, along with all her correspondence to Smithy, he did not keep. But his reply from Hedland three days after the wedding, has survived. As always, finding himself on the wrong foot and seeking parental indulgence, he laid on the affection.

Port Hedland
9 June 1923

My darling Mum and Dad,

Of course you got the shock of your lives to learn of Thelma's and my marriage. As a matter of fact we are rather surprised ourselves, but very happy and absolutely content and satisfied that we have done the right thing.

I had it in mind all the time – as you could probably see from my letters – to fix it up sooner or later, but was coming to Sydney to look around generally and see you all . . . However, some days ago, I went out to Meentheena to bring Thelma in to the Marble Bar ball. While we were in the Bar we sort of came to the conclusion that, after all, why wait –

anything might happen in the interim and we would be losing the best time of our lives. When I told Thel that it might prove unfair to her to take on a partner whose future might prove somewhat uncertain, she said that, if she couldn't face the downs of life as cheerily as the ups with me, we shouldn't get married at all. Anyway we definitely made up our minds at about lunchtime and were married by special licence at 3 pm . . . We hope to come to Sydney in about a month's time and, of course, will stay at 'Kuranda' . . .

You will both love the kid and admire my taste when you see her. We haven't rushed into this in any rash way at all, but we do understand each other and can be and are very happy and content . . . Thel will add a few lines to this. Goodbye for a little while dear folks. Fondest love to your-selves and all at home – from your loving son (and daughter)

Chilla and Thel

Thelma had added: 'My dear new Mum and Dad, Chilla is too much in a hurry to write at length this time, but I will write by the next south-going boat. I am looking forward immensely to meet-ing you all soon . . . Fondest love from Thelma.'

The burning question for the Kingsford Smiths was: who exactly *is* Thelma Corboy? She was to remain one of the most successfully kept secrets in Smithy's normally exceedingly open life. In his own autobiography he made no mention of her, refer-ring only to his second, happier and durable marriage. Similarly, the first two biographies of him, written with love and admiration by longstanding friends, completely ignored his first wife. Another referred to rumours of a marriage to a red-headed 'Irish migrant girl . . . with a blistering temper and a tongue to match'. The author, Ward McNally, claimed that 'this hectic marriage lasted only a couple of weeks and then blew up after a wild fight between Smithy and the Irish girl in the bar of one of the hotels'. He added, 'If this marriage did take place I have not been able to verify it and I know other writers have tried to get to the bottom of the story with as little luck.'[5] However, ten years later, in a revised edition of his biography, McNally confirmed that there was a marriage, to a Miss Thelma McKenna, with whom Smithy had public rows in bars 'over whose turn it was to buy the drinks'.[6]

From these descriptions and a later portrayal in an Australian television mini-series,[7] Thelma came to be represented as a formidable, hard-drinking, permanently trousered cowgirl, readily given to strong language, who could hold her own in the toughest male company in any outback bar. The truth was surprisingly different. The real Thelma was not red-headed, rarely wore trousers and was seldom seen in bars. Moreover, for a girl from an earthy North-West background, she was distinguished by both the quality of her education and the range of her cultured interests. Given the liberties taken with her character, it was with surprise that I learned early in 1990 that she was alive and well in her eighty-ninth year, and was living in Perth. It seemed curious that no writer had apparently ever gone to hear at first hand her recollections of her time as the wife of one of the most famous figures in Australian history.

Thelma, by then Mrs Ives, was traced by a Perth social welfare executive, Graham Wilson, who was writing a biography[8] of a well-known part-Aboriginal pastoralist, Bill Dunn. Dunn, in his eighties, still lived at a lonely bush camp on the Yule River near Port Hedland. As a boy, Wilson told me, Dunn had worked at Meentheena. Not only had he known Smithy and Thelma there, he had actually gone to their wedding in Marble Bar. Wilson had hoped to persuade Thelma to talk to him about her days at Meentheena and Kingsford Smith. He did not get very far. 'Mrs Ives is very *un*willing to talk about her short-lived relationship with "the great aviator", as she refers to him, somewhat cynically. I had to give an undertaking not to mention her in my book by name.' Hoping for greater success, I wrote to Thelma Ives to ask if she would agree to meet me. I was taken aback by her response, which came swiftly late one night in a phone call from a first cousin once removed, Milton Baxter, an electrical-appliance salesman in a Perth store.

'Thelma has asked me to ring you,' he began, somewhat hesitantly. 'She got your letter about Kingsford Smith. I'm afraid she was extremely upset you'd discovered her address. The problem is she refuses absolutely ever to talk to anyone about him. He's a totally taboo subject.' I inquired why. 'I don't actually know,' he

said. 'She won't discuss him, even with her closest friends and relatives. But you can take it as a definite no-go area. I'm sorry to
have to say this, but she's asked me to tell you not to write to her
again, or phone, or attempt to visit her.' I was stunned. 'It's all
rather complicated,' he apologised. 'She doesn't want anyone to
know she was ever married to him – especially her neighbours and
friends. If you're coming to Perth I can explain it better.'

Embarrassed to have blundered into territory of such sensitivity,
I wrote the next day to Milton Baxter to say that I was sorry my
letter had created such distress and expressed the hope that
Thelma might be persuaded to reconsider her ban. He replied
helpfully, suggesting that I make my plea in a taped message which
he would play to her, though he wasn't optimistic. In the recording I promised that the text of any interview would not be
published without her consent. Baxter duly took it round and
reported that she listened to it intently, but remained unmoved.
'All he wants is to make a bit of money out of me,' she told her
cousin. And that was the nearest I got to meeting Smithy's first
wife. It was some weeks before the reasons for her reticence
became clear and many months before I was able to penetrate the
cloak of mystery she had imposed on the little-known marriage.

Ironically, the revelations came in the end from Baxter himself.
He had tenaciously researched his own genealogy, and when we
met in Perth in April 1990 he showed me the data that had
enabled him to connect his side of the family with Thelma's own
roots. He told me that my letter had forced her to break her
silence on Smithy. 'If she was going to ask me to keep you at bay,
she had no option but to admit the truth.' Baxter had taken her a
newly published book about the pioneers of the North-West,
which featured the wing-riding photograph of Len Taplin. 'She
studied it for a long time in silence. Then she looked up at me and
said: "I want to tell you something about this picture. The pilot of
that plane was Kingsford Smith. He was my first husband." Of
course, I had to feign surprise, because not only did I know, but the
neighbours, all her friends and every one of dozens of relatives
knew.'

Baxter introduced me to some common relatives and, generously, in the circumstances, offered to try himself to extract from his
suspicious cousin some memories of her years with Smithy as he

sought her assistance with information for his family tree. We agreed that anything he might learn from Thelma would not be published in her lifetime without her consent. When I spoke to other relatives, some of whom had known her since the 1920s, it become clear that Thelma had indeed not discussed the marriage with any of them. However, thanks to the warm relationship that sprang up between her and Baxter, he gently persuaded her to relent.

'She is a very striking old lady. Rather fierce-looking, with beautiful snow-white hair and prominent, black bushy eyebrows. Arthritic legs force her to walk with a stick and mostly she spends her days reading and listening to classical music surrounded by mountains of books.' Baxter found Thelma a very emphatic, decisive person, still clear-minded, with strong, articulate views on almost every subject. He grew to like her. Although she had at last admitted to being Kingsford Smith's first wife, he had been warned by relatives to be extremely cautious in asking her about the marriage. 'At one stage I suggested, for my genealogical purposes, using a tape-recorder. Bloody hell, you should have seen her reaction. She bridled and snapped out just one fierce word: "No." I never mentioned it again.' Nor did he dare risk producing a notebook. 'I had to memorise everything and hurry home to type it up before it went out of my head,' he told me later. 'I must have been the first person for decades she'd confided in.'

Through the winter of 1990, with gentle encouragement from Baxter, Thelma gradually began to talk for the first time about the marriage she wanted to forget. Their meetings went on at intervals for nearly six months and her memories began to grow in his typed narrative. One day, in September, he arrived at her suburban bungalow to discover that she had been taken ill and was in hospital. Before he had a chance to visit her she had died, taking with her many of the secrets she had so obstinately guarded into her final winter. Among her possessions, in a small case, he was touched to find newspaper cuttings of quite recent stories commemorating some of Smithy's great flights. With Thelma's passing a number of people close to her no longer felt constrained to keep silent about what they knew and it became possible to reconstruct something of her life with the mercurial aviator. That relationship, it turned out, was not the only unhappy episode in the past she wished to bury.

Born in Perth in 1901, Thelma was the first of five children of a New Zealand Irishman, William Corboy, and his wife, Gertrude Jeffries. Corboy, who spent his life moving between gold-mining and running cattle in the Marble Bar area, had deserted Gertrude for the Kalgoorlie goldfields when Thelma was nine. The abandoned family was rescued by another Irishman, Maurice McKenna, who, with a partner, Mick Doherty, had taken up the lease to create the vast Meentheena Station which, in 1923, he managed. A tough working man of little education, who, back in Ireland, had known only poverty, potatoes and the Church, McKenna appears in photographs as small, round-faced, pugnacious-looking. As was then the custom among the white pastoralists, he had helped himself freely to the wives and sisters of his black workers. A half-Aboriginal son, Clancy McKenna, was to become a well-known figure in the Pilbara community. But Maurice was a rough diamond, people said, with a heart of gold. He gave Gertrude and her five children a home through the years of the First World War and, in 1918, when she had divorced Corboy, they married. In the meantime Maurice had paid for Thelma and her sister Irene to go to boarding school in Perth and was later to send them to an expensive finishing school in Sydney.

Thelma was twenty-one when she first saw Smithy in Port Hedland. 'Mother and I were in Mrs Moseley's drapery shop buying material for new dresses for the race-week grand ball,' she told Milton Baxter. 'The shop had an open front and sauntering past came this group of five or six young men amid a lot of laughter and banter. They were so conspicuous that mother asked Mrs Moseley who they were. "It's the Kingsford Smith crowd," she said, indicating the shortest of them, a slight-looking chap with a big nose. "And that's Kingsford Smith himself, the airways pilot – you must've read about him."' To Thelma he looked quite unremarkable but, she added, 'He was obviously someone with a special reputation because Mrs Moseley drew mother aside out of my hearing and began talking about him in a low voice. It naturally made me rather curious and, as we left the shop, I asked her what she'd been told. She refused to say and became very prim and embarrassed. "You don't need to know," she said, quickly changing the subject.'

Back at Mrs Mousher's boarding house Thelma discovered that

Smithy was a fellow guest. But it wasn't until the night of the race ball that she was introduced to him and they danced together. Early next morning she and her mother caught the train back to Marble Bar and she put Smithy out of her mind. She was amazed when, a few weeks later, he emerged in a shimmering mirage over the horizon at Meentheena, materialising out of the scrub, a lone figure on horseback. The temperature was in the brain-numbing forties. 'He had come the 60 miles from the railhead at Marble Bar through that appalling heat. He was dripping with sweat, sheathed in dust and exhausted. He explained that he'd come on behalf of the airline on a tour of back-country stations looking for emergency landing grounds. It wasn't true, of course. He didn't visit any other station and he stayed rather longer than he needed for the purpose. Later he admitted that he'd come solely to see me.'

At Meentheena's timber-slab and corrugated-iron homestead at Baroona Hill the McKenna family welcomed him hospitably. He instantly hit it off with the easygoing Maurice, and with his fund of stories from around the world brought welcome stimulation to this lonely place. He was immediately popular, too, with the Aboriginal station hands, who called him 'Kingy'. Bill Dunn, the subject of Graham Wilson's biography over sixty years later, was a close friend of Maurice's half-black son, Clancy. In 1994, Dunn warmly recalled for me Smithy's Meentheena visits. 'He became one of us. He was so popular and easy to be with, always joking and pulling our legs. He'd come out mustering cattle with us and in the evenings would come across from the house with his banjo and sit by the fire with we black fellas, singing songs and talking about flying.' On his first visit Smithy and Thelma rode over the vast property's sun-scorched ranges of bare granite, sparsely sprinkled with scrub and spiky blue spinifex grass. 'The station seemed to cast a spell on him,' Thelma said, 'and during those early months of 1923 he became a regular visitor. He was just so relaxing to be with. Though such a little man, he had this distinct aura – an air of someone of consequence. I think it had a lot to do with the very brisk, authoritative way in which he always spoke.'

There was no hint, according to Thelma, of a marriage proposal until early in June. Setting out for Meentheena to ask her to marry him at last, Smithy was surprised to bump into Thelma and her mother in Marble Bar. In the parlour at the Ironclad Hotel that evening he took Gertrude to one side, and with her permission, proposed to Thelma. 'My answer was an immediate yes,' she recalled. 'Had I known him better I don't think I would've been in quite such a hurry. But he was an exciting, interesting person to a girl in her early twenties largely innocent of the world. He appeared to promise a much more stimulating life than the outback.'

They married after an engagement lasting barely three days. Bill Dunn, then twelve, remembered the wedding as a major event of his early life. 'I can still picture it all. They drove into the Bar in Maurice McKenna's old red Model-T Ford, "Red Wind". He'd given it them as a wedding present. There was Thelma, Smithy, Maurice and Gertrude, with old Maurice driving. Me and my mate, George Munga Munga, escorted them on the big bronco horse to pull them through all the sandy dried-up creeks.' The mid-afternoon ceremony was conducted by the Marble Bar postmaster in the register office in the Government Building, a large stone structure resembling a Victorian prison, perched on a hill on the edge of town. The marriage certificate, which gave Smithy's occupation as 'aviator', shows that he was twenty-six and Thelma twenty-two. Outside the register office a small crowd had gathered. 'As they came out people cheered and clapped,' said Bill Dunn. 'They got into "Red Wind", under which some big empty kerosene cans had been tied, and drove off to a great rattling noise.'

There was no formal reception. Instead an impromptu party quickly got underway in the bar at the Ironclad. It was race week and a lot of squatters and miners who had come into town soon joined the celebration. It developed into one of the longest parties anyone could remember. Bill Dunn listened to the revelry from the dusty street outside, where he and George Munga Munga waited patiently under a tree with the horse. 'I'll never forget Smithy coming out in the middle of it all with a bag of oranges and apples for us. We'd never seen those fruits before. He was a thoughtful fella,' he recalled. 'The wedding created a sensation right through the Pilbara,' Kath Blizard said. 'The news spread around the stations by bush telegraph. I remember we were driving in from Yarrie to the races when we met a neighbour on the road. "Have you heard?" he said, "Kingsford Smith was married in the Bar today."

'"Who to?" we all chorused.'

Smithy and Thelma spent their wedding night back at Meentheena. When they returned to Marble Bar the next day, the party at the Ironclad was still in full swing. All the revellers left the bar to accompany the couple to the railway station, where Smithy strapped their suitcases on to a small, open trolley, started the engine and, amid loud cheering, set off for Port Hedland, where he and Thelma resumed their honeymoon at the Mousher boarding house beside the Indian Ocean.

In the first week of July they took the train from Perth to Sydney, where they were met at the station by a welcoming committee of Kingsford Smiths curious to inspect Thelma. They all made a great fuss of her, yet were not quite sure how to take her unexpected refinement and exquisite manners. They noticed that Smithy always called her 'Bebe', which he pronounced 'Beeb', after the American film star Bebe Daniels. It was a nickname that close friends used for the rest of Thelma's life. The only Kingsford Smith still alive in the 1990s who had any memory of Thelma was Smithy's nephew, John,[9] a son of Wilfrid, who was twelve at the time. 'I remember her as a very pretty, well-built woman, extremely well spoken, obviously from a good school. She and Smithy seemed very fond of each other and he made a great show of affection for her.'

Thelma was not to see a lot of Smithy during their stay in Sydney: his mind was on other things. Within twenty-four hours he had gone to meet Lebbeus Hordern, the playboy with the flying boats. An urbane, baby-faced man in his early thirties who wore rimless spectacles and expensive suits, Hordern drove Smithy out to look at the big Felixstowe in a hangar on the shore of Botany Bay. The £14,000 aircraft had never been assembled and flown, and Smithy's heart sank when he saw that the hull had begun to deteriorate and the wings were still in crates – Hordern was now bored with flying boats and moving on to luxury ocean-going yachts. It would take a lot of money to restore the Felixstowe to flying condition. Hordern said he could have it for a bargain £2,000, but Smithy said he would need to talk it over with his sponsor.

For Thelma the Sydney visit was not a great success. 'He spent most of the time drinking with old mates in bars,' she told Milton

Baxter. 'Most days and many evenings it was like that. I was just left with these elderly parents, old enough to be my grandparents. We kept running out of things to talk about. After about two weeks of this I complained to Charles and demanded to be taken back to the west. But he wouldn't hear of it. He was so absorbed by his own needs that I began to wonder if things there mightn't be just the same.'

Her fears were all too well-founded. Back in Port Hedland, married life became a nightmare of separation and insecurity as Smithy, chronically restless and constantly broke, began to search for more fulfilment and financial reward than could be gained from route-flying. Despite his above-average salary they were permanently in debt. 'He may have been a brilliant aviator,' Thelma said, 'but he couldn't begin to handle money. From the very first week of our marriage we were being pressed by creditors. Yet he always seemed to have enough to buy himself and his army of friends a drink.' Only rarely, she said, did she join his drinking sessions. 'I observed the deep need he had to be the focus of attraction with his stories, jokes or making music. He always had to have an audience. His favourite party trick was to drink beer standing on his head. It used to bring the roof down. But after I'd watched it several times I began to find it embarrassing.'

Sometimes Smithy would take a few days off and he and Thelma would hire the Marble Bar trolley and go out to Meentheena. On one of these trips Maurice McKenna suggested they took over a pastoral block, a crown lease of 63,000 acres immediately east of the station, which had become vacant. Although mostly dry, rocky scrubland, it could, in theory, support several thousand cattle. To allow Smithy to keep his flying job, McKenna offered to manage the block for them. Excited by this fresh potential source of income, Smithy seized the offer. The 92 square miles of rough grazing country between the Oakover River and Yilgalong Creek, where the Pilbara bush country began to fade into the Sahara landscape to the east, was registered as lease 3421 in the name of C. E. K. Smith. Connected to Meentheena by the dried-up bed of Elsie Creek, it was not far from a smaller 40,000-acre block, called Ripon Hill, on which Gertrude McKenna had acquired the lease.

In the late winter of 1923 Smithy was bursting with ambitious plans for these barren acres, and was even contemplating giving up his airline job to devote his whole energy to the project. 'It is possible that I may leave Airways . . . as really this station proposition looks so remarkably good that it seems worth while for me to spend some months helping to get it started. It doesn't mean I'd like to give up flying altogether, but I'm a bit sick of this job,' he told Catherine, adding hastily, 'Of course, should anything turn up re Lebbeus Hordern I will jump at it and let the others look after my station interests for a while.' In the end he decided to stay with the airline, instead persuading his sister Elsie and her husband, Bert Pike, and his cousin Phil Kingsford to come out west and work on the property. They arrived in the spring and went to live with Maurice and Gertrude at Meentheena. Smithy had conceived an enterprising scheme for an ex-servicemen's commune. 'The idea is to get one or two more returned soldiers into it and start on a bigger scale as a sort of pastoral syndicate,' he wrote in November. 'Everything points to a good thing coming for us.' The letter concluded: 'Thelma sends fond love – I'll make the little baggage write next week's letter as punishment for not writing before. Tons of love to yourselves and all at home – your loving boy, Chilla.' The commune never got off the ground. He was too busy flying to organise it and soon lost interest.

Between a £10 share he had acquired in a brand-new gold mine, flying the route, trying to deal with his remote, undeveloped property, the endless meetings with Anderson and Mackay and flurries of telegrams to Leofric in Sydney about the flying boat, he was unaware that Thelma, languishing in Mrs Mousher's boarding house, was already wondering how long the marriage could last. Keith Mackay had now, subject to the value of his seasonal wool-clip, agreed to offer Hordern a maximum of £2,000 for the Felixstowe in assembled certificated condition. To avoid the cost of equipping it with long-range tanks and now desperate for any sort of flying adventure, Smithy had decided to circumnavigate Australia in it. Before he could begin to plan the expedition, however, a series of disasters killed the venture stone dead and changed the immediate course of his life. The first blow fell in February 1924, when Brearley fired him from Western Australian Airways.

The Cattle-Ranching Aviator
1924–5

His dismissal came as a shock to Smithy. It was the unhappy outcome of threats by the pilots to strike for more money. He was one of the signatories to a letter the majority had decided to send to Brearley requesting a substantial rise. 'With a nice literary flourish,' said Brearley, 'the letter explained what failure to meet their demands would mean: "Like Arabs, we will fold our tents and silently steal away."'[1] Whether these words were Smithy's is not certain, but people who knew him well thought the spirit of defiance was suspiciously in keeping with his style. In any event, he was indubitably one of the ringleaders. If the six pilots had assumed they were indispensable they had not reckoned with the tough and uncompromising stand of the managing director. His airline was flourishing, but he needed bigger aeroplanes to extend his routes and the directors decided that the company couldn't afford a wage increase. The pilots' £600 a year was already three times the country's basic wage and equal to the pay then enjoyed by British airline pilots. Summoning them to a meeting in his Perth office, Brearley presented them with a simple ultimatum: accept their current salary or go. Two of them decided to climb down, but the other four, including Smithy and Keith Anderson, refused to withdraw their demands. Brearley immediately asked for their resignations.[2]

It was the second time he had been fired in two and a half years. Smithy was again reluctant to admit the truth to his parents, who had come partly to depend on his uncertain remittances. When he wrote from Port Hedland on 15 February 1924 to break the bad news, he disguised it as resignation on a matter of principle. 'I've been putting up a stiff fight with Airways (they are immensely well off now and can afford it) for more pay for the pilots. Anyway,' he wrote, in a curious reversal of the truth,

> I've got the increase all right but they want me to climb down in various ways which I refused to do. The alternative remains – resign and Airways are so far standing firm and I am ditto and have resigned. Tomorrow I fly to Perth and finish there. The other pilots are all for me and would come out, too, should I ask, but my principles never included Bolshevik methods of strikes so I won't hear of it. It leaves my good name intact which is a fine asset. Of course if I had nothing up my sleeve in the way of jobs I'd have hung out a good deal longer but this truck proposition is too good to miss . . .
>
> Thelma is very philosophical about it all. She is a great little kid, God bless her, and stands by me in everything.

Privately Thelma was far from unperturbed. 'Philosophical was not exactly how I would have put it,' she told Milton Baxter.

Smithy left the airline with around 2,600 hours, 1,000 of which he had accumulated flying for Brearley. He had also gained a ground engineer's licence. The only comment on departure offered by his autobiography was: 'For two years I flew backwards and forwards on this service, covering thousands of miles, acquiring experience and gradually becoming bored with the monotony of it all.'

The 'truck proposition' was a haulage business he and Anderson had been considering to finance their Pacific dream. It is clear that, now he had burned his boats at WAA, his life was at another of its perennial crossroads and that he was ready to leap in any direction that promised some quick money. In March 1924, within a few weeks of leaving the airline, he and Anderson decided to take the plunge. They bought into a garage and petrol station in Carnarvon owned by a man called Tom Carlin, registered it as the Kingsford Smith Carlin Transport Company and ordered an American-built 3-ton Republic truck. The idea was to carry wool into the port from the scores of huge stations in the

Gascoyne district, which stretched inland for hundreds of miles behind Carnarvon, and take back supplies, a service traditionally performed laboriously by camel train. Funding his stake in the company had presented Smithy with an all too familiar problem. The lion's share of the capital he personally needed eventually came from a surprising quarter. 'I got over the difficulty through the goodness of Mrs Anderson, the mother of Keith Anderson, our third partner. She offered to lend me, free of interest, for six months, £150 to see me out of the very real difficulty I was in – which offer, needless to say, I accepted with great gratitude.' It is fairly certain that she also stumped up Keith's equity.

Smithy travelled the 770 miles down to Perth to collect the new truck they had bought on hire purchase. When he arrived back in Carnarvon he found Thelma deeply distressed. She had just heard from her mother that Meentheena was so hopelessly in debt that the bank had foreclosed on McKenna and Doherty, putting them out of business. The station had been placed under new management and the McKenna family had been forced to leave. In despair, Maurice had turned again to gold-prospecting. Elsie and Bert Pike had gone back to Sydney. With the collapse of Meentheena all Smithy's hopes for his pastoral syndicate died. He and Anderson now threw themselves into their haulage business seven days a week. One big contract followed another, and within four months they had bought Carlin out and renamed the company Gascoyne Transport. Soon they needed more trucks and drivers. Since neither partner had a shred of administrative ability, Smithy brought back Bert and Elsie to manage the business.

From an iron garage behind the Settlers' Hotel in Carnarvon, Smithy and Anderson hauled their loads inland across the roadless mulga and spinifex plains, following the wheel tracks of the camel wagons. In summer it was oppressively hot and the radiators boiled dry in temperatures that could touch 52°C. In the wet season the wide, dry, sandy riverbeds became unfordable torrents that could delay them on the bank for a week. It was hard, physical work, struggling with bales of wool, lifting sheep singlehanded and wrestling with the heavy steering wheels. Almost every hour a tyre would be punctured by rocks or spiky scrub. When they ran out of patches for the tubes they stuffed the tyres with spinifex.

Smithy, who weighed at this time only 9½ stone (60 kg), began to develop bulbous arm and shoulder muscles.

A former truck-driver, Lou Kent, who sometimes drove in convoy with Smithy and Anderson, recalled, in Perth, the striking difference in the temperaments of the two partners.

> Smithy was a happy-go-lucky, well-organised, jovial sort of bloke – the complete opposite to his mate. Anderson was a real dreamer: slow, careless, almost helpless. We'd come across him stranded out there with a puncture in forty-five degrees heat and no means of repair. He'd have no toolbox, no pump, no jack. He'd have forgotten to put them on board. Or he'd have set off without his tucker box. Or just fallen asleep on the road. He never mixed with people. Always sat apart from us all, alone in his cab with a distant look on his face.

'I'm sure the only thing that held them together was this great flight dream,' said June Dupre. 'Andy was quite the most irritatingly slow person I've ever known – slow-moving and slow-thinking. He lived in the clouds. Yet Smithy was always so patient with him.' Few others knew what the war had done to Keith Anderson.

The trucking life took further toll on Smithy's marriage. He was often out in the bush for a month at a time. 'I'd be left on my own in the Gascoyne Hotel for weeks, with no money and creditors knocking on the door,' Thelma said. 'On the rare occasions he was in Carnarvon he'd spend his evenings in the bar with mates in noisy drinking sessions. I would lie there listening to the sound of the boozing, waiting for him to come staggering up in the small hours. Trying to discuss this miserable way of life would always lead to a row – to which his standard response was to go out and get even more drunk. So the cycle would begin all over again.'

On 16 July 1924 came a major blow. Keith Mackay, Smithy's Pacific flight patron, had chartered a Bristol Tourer from Western Australian Airways in Port Hedland to fly the 40 miles down the coast to his home at Mundabullangana. Within minutes of taking off the aircraft suddenly plunged into the sea in sight of the town. The pilot, Len Taplin, and his mechanic had swum ashore unharmed, but Mackay, who was said to have been drinking before the flight, had suffered a blow to the head and was drowned inside the plane.[3] Smithy was shocked and more disappointed than he could express. 'Keith Mackay's death was a tragic thing wasn't it? It upsets the whole apple cart re my probable flight . . . I'm afraid that's my last hope gone west.'

The Pacific dream receded even further with another disturbing event that winter. One day Smithy found a plain-clothes policeman from Perth waiting for him at the garage. Detective Sergeant Harry Manning was conducting an investigation, he said, into allegations of cattle stealing in the Nullagine River area. Thelma and Smithy listened aghast as he outlined some of the evidence. During a muster late the previous year, a white stockman at Warrawagine Station, immediately north of Meentheena, had found a steer with a strange ear mark and a brand on its rump which had obviously been tampered with. The Warrawagine brand, O1O, had been crudely amended with a small stroke in the first 'O' to read Q1O, the brand registered to Gertrude McKenna. In a subsequent round-up, Smithy was dumbfounded to hear, brands had been found altered to his own OKQ, and both he and his mother-in-law were prime suspects. Smithy convinced the detective that as an absentee leaseholder he had had no opportunity to commit such an offence. Gertrude, too, was able to demonstrate her innocence, but the evidence against her husband was damning. Maurice McKenna, it eventually emerged, had, with the assistance of his black stockmen, been helping himself to Warrawagine's cattle for years. In the vast, unfenced tracts of the Nullagine it was all too easy. He had created, his stockmen had told the police, a secret camp to which he'd been driving the stolen steers for rebranding before mixing them with Meentheena's cattle.[4]

Better news was that, by early 1925, Smithy and Anderson were, for the first time in their lives, accumulating money. The fortunes of Gascoyne Transport, which was eventually to own six trucks and trailers, went from strength to strength. 'The business is looking most promising,' Smithy told William in February in a letter reporting that he had become a freemason and was about to be initiated into the Gascoyne Lodge in Carnarvon. 'The end of our third year ought to see us clear of everything and with a thousand or perhaps more in the bank.' But in the same letter he mentioned yet another setback to his Pacific flight hopes. 'Anderson went south a few weeks back to see his uncle re backing . . . He was quite confident of his support but, alas, like many other bright hopes, it did not eventuate. Uncle wouldn't come to light with the necessary.' The uncle was Harry Vincent, the wealthy husband of Connie Anderson's sister Beatrice. He had made his money as a builder in Melbourne, where he and his family lived in a large mansion in fashionable Toorak. Vincent took the view that a Pacific attempt could only end in disaster.

But for Smithy, the flight remained an obsession. The office at Gascoyne Transport had become a flight-planning centre, and trucking was getting less and less of his attention. So was Thelma. 'He should never have married,' she told Milton Baxter. 'He had far too many other priorities. He didn't want the responsibility of a wife. He most certainly didn't want children. I began to see him only infrequently and he never discussed the company or its finances with me. He just assumed that a woman wouldn't understand, or had no right to know. All he could think and talk about was the damned Pacific. It had taken hold of his very being. I became irrelevant.'

The marriage finally ground to a halt in June 1925, just two years after its whirlwind beginning. At the divorce hearing three years later Smithy was to allege that another man, whom he didn't name, was involved in the break-up.[5] Finding his wife 'growing very cool' towards him, Smithy told the divorce-court judge, he had asked Thelma 'whether there was anybody else'. She had replied 'Yes,' and had mentioned the name of a mutual friend. Smithy had immediately gone to see the man. 'I accused him of having alienated my wife's affections. The man admitted that he loved my wife but he assured me that there was nothing improper between them. I am satisfied that there was not.' According to Smithy's testimony, Thelma had then gone to Perth for a holiday. He drove down to try to persuade her to return to Carnarvon with him by car. She had refused and travelled back by ship. On her return he had tried to patch up the marriage, offering to do anything that would help to keep them together, but Thelma had said it was too late and that she was now determined to leave him. When he next returned to Carnarvon from a trip up-country, she had gone.

The other man was probably the Carnarvon resident magistrate, Henry Moseley. His developing relationship with Thelma in Smithy's absences had not gone unnoticed in the small settlement. 'She was very friendly with him,' said June Dupre. 'He was a widower whose wife had died the year before. He was a very cultivated man and I think they had a lot in common. But it was never more than just a friendship.'

Close witnesses to the disintegration of the marriage were the Pikes. Elsie, now in her early forties, had never entirely approved of Thelma and lost no time in involving the family in what she saw as her brother's latest hour of need. From the middle of June, Catherine's diary begins to bristle with brief entries logging a surge of letters and telegrams between 'Kuranda' and Elsie in Carnarvon. 'Long letter from Elsie re Chilla's troubles,' Catherine wrote on 1 July. 'Ethel Laing helped draft lettergram, recommending Elsie send Chill over at once.'

'He was always Nan's baby,' said Catherine Robinson. 'Her baby had been hurt and her immediate response was to get him quickly back into the family bosom. There was, one suspects, an element of unstated relief that the marriage had failed. It seems that not all of them had exactly taken to Thelma in Sydney. They used to mutter about her snobbishly as "that woman", and would whisper a word they weren't allowed to utter – "common" – for which they had created family code: "K".'

Yet it would seem that Smithy quickly recovered from the shock of Thelma's departure. His letter to Catherine in the last week of July, acknowledging her sympathy, is the last that has survived of his correspondence with his parents. It suggests that he already had much more on his mind than the collapse of his marriage.

Dearest Mum,

Thanks muchly for your letter and understanding of my troubles. They are pretty heavy on me and will take some getting over, but all will be OK some day . . .

I hope that there really is a good chance for this Pacific flight as I want to come over next month, but cannot risk being away unless it is justified. I need the change tremendously and if there is something doing [with Hordern's flying boat] I will be able to throw myself into it with some energy . . .

The business is going strong and I really think we are well on the road to future prosperity . . . so shortly I will be able to send something along. I am sending Thel £2 weekly and think that will be enough to make things easy. Unfortunately my income tax has just hit me with a bang (£30). Lord knows how they can possibly reckon I owe that much, but anyway I'm used to being in debt and will be amazed if I am ever out of it. Fondest love to your dear self and Dad and all at home.

Your loving son,
Chilla.

Indeed, there is no evidence that Smithy suffered any remorse or serious regret that the marriage hadn't worked out. Thelma never acknowledged any of the £2-a-week maintenance payments. They quickly became spasmodic and, before long, he stopped them altogether. Thelma told Milton Baxter that when she walked out she had determined to write Smithy out of her life. 'They were two years I really wanted to forget. I got rid of all his photos and every letter he'd written me. I needed to divorce myself from all memory of him. Later, of course, when he became so famous and his picture was everywhere, even on the stamps and bank-notes, it was difficult to escape from a sense of his presence. He really deserved all the acclaim he got. But by then I had not a shred of feeling for him.'

Although Thelma never discussed the marriage with any of her many relatives or close friends, a view of it did exist among them. 'It didn't stand a chance,' said Thelma's cousin Edith Anthony. 'He was an impatient, frustrated, very gifted man who wanted to show the world what aviation could do. His mind was permanently in the sky. On the ground he was a restless roamer, never creating a stable home and spending as fast as he earned. The sad thing was they were both such nice people.' A less sympathetic slant came from Charles Fowler, who married Gertrude Corboy's sister Lillian. Before he died he expressed to his daughter, Ivy Thorpe, some old-fashioned sentiments about Smithy. 'My father was a man of high principles and strict morals,' Mrs Thorpe said. 'He was appalled at the way Smithy behaved towards Thelma. He told me he gave her a very rough time – was a bad drinker, never paid his debts, and was a womaniser. "Not a very honourable man," I can remember my father saying very disapprovingly.' Those who knew Thelma in later life unfailingly spoke of her with great affection. They talked of her lively intelligence, her wit and humour and her great love and knowledge of the arts and travel, some of which she had shared in her final days with Milton Baxter.

Within the Kingsford Smith family Thelma was rarely discussed, either. John Kingsford-Smith said: 'There was this persistent belief that she was happy to be married to a pilot but not to a truck-driver. Of course, the truth was that none of us ever really knew much about her at all.' Catherine Robinson explained: 'The break-up of a marriage in those days was seen as such a disgrace it was discussed only in whispers. So it became a bit of a family skeleton that people carefully avoided talking about.'

When Thelma left Carnarvon in June 1925 she travelled north, intending to join the displaced Gertrude and Maurice and her brothers and sister at a gold mine Maurice was now developing in the Nullagine. But when she arrived she was greeted with the shocking news that her stepfather had just been sent to prison. A few weeks earlier, Detective Sergeant Manning, after eighteen months' investigation, had ridden out from Marble Bar to the McKenna camp and formally charged Maurice with cattle-stealing. Maurice appeared first in the court in Marble Bar, where the conclusive evidence of one of his Aboriginal stockmen was heard. Bill Dunn, who was in court, told me: 'There were no two ways about it – old Maurice was guilty, all right. I was there at the yard watching him. He was branding big stuff, big bullocks in broad daylight to make quick money. I think he may have been doing it to surprise Smithy and Thelma, to send a big fat cheque as a wedding present.' Among exhibits of bullock hides and branding-irons, the jury had listened for six days to the evidence. Smithy wasn't called but, inevitably, his name was publicly revealed as the owner of the OKQ brand which the accused had tried to replicate. It was also revealed that Maurice had once been fined for altering the brand on a horse. The jury found him guilty and he was sentenced to two years' imprisonment with hard labour.

After serving his time in Fremantle Gaol, McKenna returned to the Nullagine to resume mining. Up there, it was said, he told a number of people that Smithy had rustled the cattle. 'Years later,' wrote Kathleen Mallett of Limestone Station, 'he had the effrontery to say that he took the rap but was the innocent party. He said Charles Kingsford Smith was the man who did it.'[6]

'Of course he didn't,' said Bill Dunn, the only person still alive who had quietly observed Smithy's comings and goings at Meentheena and witnessed the branding operations day after day. 'Him and Thelma never knew anything about it.'

McKenna never went back to pastoral pursuits. Smithy's lease, which had so briefly held the promise of prosperity, and Gertrude's both lapsed. 'The two properties just withered away,' said Bill Dunn. 'Smithy never put down a single post on his. Never fenced it, built a homestead or named it as a station.' To this day the huge Kingsford Smith property remains a number on a pastoral lease map. The original Meentheena homestead which McKenna built at Baroona Hill was destroyed in 1941, washed away in a big flood that surged down the Nullagine River, removing almost without trace the house that had known the charm of Kingsford Smith and witnessed the wooing of Thelma Corboy. 'It was all very sad,' said Bill Dunn, 'all those nice people coming together and everything ending in tragedy.'

7

Enter a Tall, Dark Stranger
1925–7

At the family's persistent urging, early in September 1925 Smithy went home to Sydney on what was to become a very long, lotus-eating holiday.

Catherine, Eric and Leofric were at the station to meet him. Expecting to find him bowed from his matrimonial traumas, they were surprised when he bounced off the train 'looking very well and fit', as Catherine wrote with relief. His robust and bronzed appearance contrasted with that of his brothers. Eric was now suffering from tuberculosis contracted in the navy, and Leofric from chronic bronchial problems and ankylosing spondylitis, which had stiffened his spine and reduced him to walking with a stoop.

Back at 'Kuranda', as they listened to Chilla's account of the collapse of the marriage they had believed to be so happy, the Kingsford Smiths were unaware that Thelma, now calling herself 'Miss Smith', had already begun an affair with another man. Her friendship with magistrate Moseley had ended when she left Carnarvon, but almost immediately she had fallen in love with someone else. Len Ives was a war-wounded Perth clerk who had turned unsuccessfully to gold-mining. What was remarkable about him was his startling resemblance to Smithy. In build, and with his handsomely hawkish features, he could have been the former's double. Ives, however, was already married and the father of three children. His wife, Ethel, was the attractive and spoiled daughter of a powerful and wealthy Perth businessman, Nat Harper, who so disapproved of the constantly unemployed Ives that he had refused to speak to the couple for two years. The marriage had

descended into violence and Len and Ethel had split up. Ives had
gone north to try his luck gold-mining in the Nullagine, where he
had befriended the McKenna family. Finding no gold in the North-
West, he returned to Perth, bringing the McKennas with him.
Soon afterwards his affair with Thelma began. For the moment it
was being conducted furtively in Perth hotels, but before long, it
was to lead to a sensational and highly publicised divorce case.

While all this was brewing, Smithy was enjoying life in Sydney.
Within days of his arrival he had drawn another woman into his
turbulent orbit. Lyal Hilliard, whom everyone called Bon, was the
daughter of a prosperous Sydney solicitor, Arthur Hilliard, and his
domineering wife Maude. Smithy had been instantly captivated by
Bon – bewitched, people said, by her vibrant, outgoing personality
and her sensuality. She was soon a constant visitor at 'Kuranda'
where the family, falling under her spell, made a special fuss of her.
Bon, said her cousin, Jane Brooks, was a 'specially charming
person – fair and very pretty. You wouldn't believe the number of
men who fell in love with her. There was something about her, a
caring affectionate quality she just radiated.'

During the last months of 1925 Smithy and Bon were rarely
apart. They swam, played tennis, went on picnics and to the
theatre. He began to spend nights at the Hilliards' home and
sometimes stayed for days at a time. He was so smitten that he
tried to persuade Bon to marry him when he was free. To expedite
matters, just before Christmas he went to see a solicitor, who
urged him to write to Thelma to clear the air. As she had technically deserted him he was advised to go through the hypocritical
formality of asking her to return:

Kuranda
26 December 1925

My dear Thelma,

    I would like to take this opportunity of wishing you and
your mother the compliments of the season, and to hope
that all your Xmases may be happy ones. Now, I am writing
again to ask you to come back to me, but if you are determined not to do so, you might at least write and tell me, as
one doesn't like one's letters ignored.

    If you are willing to return, I can offer you at least a home, although you didn't seem over-anxious to share one with me prior to your leaving me when I was in the west. Unfortunately, dear, I cannot truthfully tell you that I have anything financially attractive to offer you, as the longed for Pacific flight seems as far off as ever, and I have almost decided to give up the whole flying game for something steady, if uninteresting, in the way of ground jobs over here or back in Carnarvon. However, Thel, this place is really my home, and if your affection for me is what it should be, you will, I know, return to me. But, if not, please tell me and don't keep silent. You know you haven't even written to acknowledge the allowance I have, from time to time, been sending you since you left me.

So there it is in a nutshell, Thelma, and I am asking you to come back to me, and if you won't do that, do at least let me know.

Your affectionate husband,
Charles

It was to be months before he got a reply. Meanwhile, he had resuscitated his negotiations with Lebbeus Hordern, whose big flying boat still lay unassembled in its shed on Botany Bay. Hordern was now prepared to let it go, as it lay, for £1,000. Smithy got the RAAF's chief technical officer, Squadron Leader Lawrence Wackett, a young pilot and aircraft-designer, to estimate the cost of getting it into flying condition. Wackett reckoned it would take at least £1,000, but that it would be a waste of money: the aircraft wasn't capable of lifting off with sufficient fuel to fly for even 1,000 miles. And so Smithy finally abandoned the project. The Felixstowe slowly deteriorated in its shed, the wings rotted away and Hordern eventually gave it to a local man to use as a fishing hut. Wackett tried to interest Smithy in another aircraft: a single-engined biplane amphibian, the Widgeon, that he had designed and built for the air force. But after early take-off problems were solved, it transpired that this aircraft couldn't lift enough fuel even to cross the Tasman. It seemed no plane in existence had the range to tackle the vast Pacific.

Smithy's every waking thought was now focused on the ocean flight. When he wasn't with Bon Hilliard, fishing with cousins

Rupert Swallow and Ray Kingsford or out drinking with Terry Trousdale, his closest friend outside the family, he was pursuing every conceivable person he thought might provide him with a long-range aeroplane. He wrote to the prime minister, Stanley Bruce, appealing for funds; he went to Melbourne to pressurise the defence minister, Sir Neville Howse; he approached the Vacuum Oil Company, who promised free fuel. But the only promise of money was an offer from the managing editor of Sun Newspapers, Herbert Campbell-Jones – if the flight ever took place – of £500 for the exclusive news rights.

It was not until early April 1926, that, promising Bon Hilliard he would be back before the end of the year, he reluctantly returned to Carnarvon. Awaiting him was a hostile letter from Thelma.

> Perth,
> April 8, 1926
>
> This is an answer to your letter of 26th December, just received, in which you ask me to return to you.
>
> I have no intention whatsoever of returning and absolutely refuse to live with you again.
>
> I am contented at home and am capable of supporting myself, as I have done for the last four or five months, since you went to Sydney.
>
> Do not trouble to write again, as this is definite.
>
> Thelma.

Although he was hurt by this aggressive response, he was at the same time hugely relieved.

The haulage business had begun to bore him, and, back behind the wheel of his truck out in the hot, monotonous bush, he yearned for the cockpit. He applied for jobs as an instructor, first with the New South Wales Aero Club in Sydney, then with the Aero Club of Victoria in Melbourne. Failing to get either, he began to wonder whether his wild past was beginning to catch up with him. Fearing for his chances of government funding for the Pacific project, he wrote in August to Colonel Horace Brinsmead, the controller of civil aviation, anxiously seeking reassurance that he wasn't on some unofficial blacklist. 'I know you will tell me, Sir, if my once-good name has, for any reason, become tarnished.'[1] The essence of tact, Brinsmead, who knew full well of Smithy's spectacular reputation, wrote him a bland letter of reassurance.

Smithy now persuaded Keith Anderson that they should sell Gascoyne Transport,[2] buy a couple of second-hand aeroplanes and start up an air-charter company in New Guinea to serve the gold mines in the inaccessible interior. The idea was to make some quick money to acquire a Pacific aeroplane. The sale of the business was completed in November 1926, and while Elsie and Bert Pike went back to Sydney, Smithy and Anderson travelled triumphantly to Perth to buy from Norman Brearley two of his elderly Bristol Tourers. The £500 for each plane, plus several more hundred for spares, made a large hole in the hard-earned proceeds of two and a half years of trucking. The aircraft – G-AUDJ and G-AUDK – could not be spared until late January so, early in December, the partners went to Sydney to try to raise further capital for the New Guinea project.

In Sydney, just before Christmas 1926, Anderson went with Smithy to visit the Hilliards and to meet Bon, whom Smithy now regarded as his unofficial fiancée. He was unaware, as he presented his close mate to her, that she was instantly attracted to this tall, gentle giant. While Anderson went back to Perth to spend Christmas with his mother, Smithy, blissfully ignorant of her feelings for Anderson, began to plan his holiday weeks around Bon. He went to stay with the Hilliards at their cottage in the Blue Mountains in January. It was not until the middle of the month that he reluctantly tore himself away from Bon and went back to Western Australia to collect the planes for New Guinea.

In Perth, where Anderson was waiting, they were to be joined by a third man, Henry Smith Hitchcock, known as Bob. Hitchcock was an aircraft-mechanic colleague from Western Australian Airways with a lot of experience on the Bristols, and Anderson had suggested they invite him into their venture.

Hitchcock was a deeply religious, churchgoing man whose life had been one long battle for survival. It showed in his heavily jowelled, prematurely lined face. The son of a nomadic bricklayer, he had left school in Kalgoorlie at twelve to begin an odd-jobbing existence. He'd become a mechanic, married at twenty, and had been wounded at Gallipoli. Now thirty-five, he had three children, was chronically short of money and his marriage had been lurching from one crisis to another. He had eventually left home but his strict upbringing in the Church of Christ ruled out divorce. People who knew him described Bob as unimaginative, but enormously dogged, hard-working and reliable. His niece, Gwen Bliss, saw him as 'a quiet, cheerful, dependable plodder'. He and Anderson were natural kindred spirits.

Hitchcock was led to believe that the New Guinea venture was merely a precursor to a trans-Pacific flight which he would join as a full team member. The precise terms of his involvement, casually agreed between the three men, but sealed in a Perth bar with handshakes and a celebratory drink in late January 1927, were never put in writing and probably did not, at that time, seem of critical importance to any of them, so accustomed were they to the binding nature of verbal commitments. But the events of the next eighteen months would sadly test the loose arrangement and lead to outpourings of great bitterness in a Sydney court in which both Anderson and Hitchcock would separately bring massive claims against Kingsford Smith.

When Smithy and Anderson took delivery of the two Tourers from Brearley, to defray the costs of shipping them from Sydney to New Guinea, they decided to take some fare-paying passengers across Australia and try to break the Perth–Sydney record of three days, created in 1920. To publicise the event they invited a journalist, John Marshall, Perth representative of the Sydney *Guardian*, and his wife to join the flight. The two aircraft made the trip in formation. Although they failed to break the record, the flight gave Smithy his first small taste of fame. Waiting at Mascot to greet the first woman to cross Australia by air were reporters and newsreel cameras. It was his first chance to present himself publicly as the aviator who would fly the Pacific. He would soon be doing it, he told Australia, with Keith Anderson and Bob Hitchcock. Smithy's craggy face beamed briefly from the news pages; then, just as quickly, his name was forgotten. 'There we were,' he wrote, 'in the Big Smoke of Sydney, stony broke but with a couple of old planes . . . Meanwhile the years were passing.' Now thirty, he lamented: 'This was 1927 and it was nearly ten years since the war had ended . . . I had nothing to show for those ten years which the locusts had eaten.'

The locusts went on eating. Seduced by the fleshpots of Sydney and spoiled by Catherine at home, he was in no hurry to commit himself to a risky venture in the malarial jungle. However, while he and Anderson marked time and socialised the money ran out. The New Guinea plan was abandoned. The partners decided instead to look for charter work in Sydney. They formed a company, Interstate Flying Services, and rented a small office in Eldon Chambers at 92 Pitt Street in the middle of the city. Here Bert Pike was installed as business manager, while Hitchcock, still on the payroll, maintained the Tourers out at Mascot. There were to be depressingly few calls for their services.

The partners were rarely seen in the office. Happily driving about in their Chevrolet, they spent much of their time visiting friends around Sydney and enjoying weekends in the country. Their favourite destination was the Blue Mountains where, at the Hilliards' cottage, they were frequent guests. It was here, in the early months of 1927, that the relationship between Keith Anderson and Bon flowered. Bon and Keith, who had known each other barely three months, created a mild sensation – and a major shock for Smithy – by formally announcing their engagement on 21 March.

Why did Bon so suddenly switch her affections? 'I think perhaps she realised that Keith was really the man she'd been looking for,' said Jane Brooks, 'It wasn't just that he was incredibly tall, dark and handsome. He was also a very sweet, quiet and gentle person with so many admirable qualities.' A cousin of Anderson's, Richard Willdridge, explained: 'It was really quite simple. She chose the better man – the more decent bloke.' According to another cousin of Bon's, John Laurence, a QC and former New South Wales crown prosecutor, 'Maude would certainly have had a say in it. I think she may have seen Keith as a more dependable investment than Smithy.' What Smithy's private feelings were we shall never know. Outwardly, he appears to have emerged from the triangle undis-mayed. The Kingsford Smiths and the Hilliards remained friends, apparently without embarrassment. Bon Hilliard's decision could have had disastrous consequences for Smithy's relationship with Anderson, yet remarkably, it appears that it did not. Instead their bond was about to be threatened from a quite unexpected quarter.

Interstate Flying Services did not prosper. There continued to be few passengers, and neither Smithy nor Anderson had the slightest flair for marketing. 'Aeroplane flights arranged to any part of the world,' their leaflet fantasised, but they were never even asked to fly to another Australian city. Every week they slid deeper into debt. The company would not have survived beyond the middle of 1927 but for a twist of fate that was to change the course of the lives of everyone involved. It began with a letter which Bert Pike found in the mailbox on the office door early in April. It was from a solicitor, a Mr Cherry Willis, who said he had a client interested in aviation who would like to meet the partners to discuss a 'proposition'. Pike immediately phoned the solicitor and made an appointment for the client, a Mr Charles Ulm, to meet Smithy and Anderson a few days later.

The meeting between Charles Kingsford Smith, Keith Anderson, Bert Pike, Leofric (Smithy's financial guardian) and Charles Ulm in the small central-city office was to launch one of the most successful partnerships in aviation history. The tall, dark, curly-haired, saturnine man, dressed in a well-cut suit and waistcoat, who arrived that afternoon clutching a hat and briefcase, was someone who commanded immediate respect. There was about him an intensity, an aura of self-confident authority and slight pompousness, that suggested someone of importance. As he introduced himself he reminded Smithy that they had met very briefly about six years earlier out at Mascot Aerodrome during the latter's time with Diggers Aviation. He came quickly to the point. He'd read, he said, about their Perth–Sydney flight, and had heard that they were now short of work. Although he was not a pilot – war wounds prevented him from passing the medical, he explained – he had a passionate belief in the future of civil air transport in Australia. He saw money in it. But more immediately he was looking for some established pilots to join him in a bid for the government contract to operate an Adelaide–Perth air service.

Smithy knew that Brearley, whose company had now been renamed West Australian Airways, had, along with many other hopefuls, tendered for the route, planning to fly it with big three-engined de Havilland Hercules fourteen-seater biplanes. Beating Brearley to this subsidised operation was a challenge that appealed to him. He had taken immediately to this slick, fast-talking man who had obviously done his homework and by whose enthusiasm and incisiveness he was impressed. Ulm, who couldn't have known of the parlous financial state of Interstate Flying Services, seemed to need them more than they needed him. He later told the Supreme Court: 'I said to them that I felt that my tender would be stronger if their firm joined with me and we made it a mutual tender.'[3] The more Smithy listened to this articulate stranger, the more it seemed to him that they were 'twin souls'.

Keith Anderson, however, did not so easily fall under Ulm's spell. As they sat there, all chain-smoking, in a heavy blue haze, he felt a strong unease that Ulm could be a formidable threat to his own easy relationship with Smithy. He would have been even more disturbed had he known how the visitor had already summed him up. 'Keith Anderson,' Ulm was to write in his memoirs, 'was a simple soul with a broad grin and an intensely parochial outlook.' Ulm, Anderson noticed, rarely smiled. The expression on his broad, rugged face remained grimly serious. If he wasn't a pilot, what role did Ulm see for himself? they asked. His strengths, he explained, were in management, in organising things, in fund-raising and publicity. He had already done his sums for the Adelaide–Perth service. He had made detailed cost–revenue estimates and drawn up a full submission. He handed them the document. It was much more professionally presented than they could ever have managed.

It was now Bert Pike's turn to feel disquiet. The management of Interstate Flying Services was his job, and he, too, felt threatened. But Ulm was a single-minded and determined operator, and he saw in Smithy and Anderson and their two aeroplanes a going concern ripe for entrepreneurial exploitation. He had summed up Kingsford Smith as well. 'Smithy, wizard pilot though he was, had little more idea of organising big-scale finance than he had of conducting a Sunday school.'

None of them was to know that this deceptively prosperous-looking visitor was actually on his beam's end as well. His commanding presence was a bold bluff. He had no money, no permanent job, no office. He was making ends meet at that moment doing casual work in billiard saloons, being paid by the hour to partner customers. Behind him, since his return, badly wounded and mentally traumatised, from the war, lay a rather chequered career in which he had acquired a reputation as a 'hard doer', quick to indulge in litigation. Indeed, one of his flying enterprises had, only a few weeks earlier, terminated in an aircraft crash that

had left him heavily in debt. It is doubtful that any of them had
heard about the unflattering description of Ulm recently given to
the Australian Aero Club in Melbourne by Edward Hart, the
editor of Australia's leading aviation magazine, *Aircraft*. 'Ulm,' he
had said unkindly in an address reviewing the history of civil flying
in the country, 'holds the Australian record of having been actively
concerned with the formation of no fewer than five extinct aviation companies in Sydney, and is thus entitled to special mention.'

At the end of the meeting Ulm concluded: 'I'm offering you the
figures on which you can base an excellent tender. It'll stand a better
chance coming from Interstate Flying Services than from an independent person. You fellows chew over the figures and I'll come back
tomorrow.' Contrary to many of the stories and screen dramas that
have since attempted to recreate this celebrated meeting, a Pacific
flight was never mentioned. After Ulm had gone they sat there talking about him. Smithy was so excited by the proposition that he
soon persuaded the others to accept it. They studied Ulm's master-
ful Adelaide–Perth submission. Their teetering company had little to
lose: they had debts of £700 and just £49 in the bank. Perhaps the
thrusting Ulm really could turn around their fortunes. Bert Pike said
little. There wasn't room for two organisers and he knew he couldn't
compete in skill and intellect with this slick opportunist.

When Charles Ulm duly joined Interstate Flying Services in
April 1927 they drew up a partnership agreement, a document
prepared by Arthur Hilliard, initially only to cover the trans-
Australia tender. With his curt manner and forceful personality,
Ulm in no time came to dominate the business. He was brimming
with good suggestions for rejuvenating the flagging charter operation, and Pike's fears were all too quickly realised. 'Pike,' Ulm said
later, 'had very little aviation experience. I often used to give him
advice as to people with whom he might make payable contracts.'
Demoralised by Ulm's superior business flair, Bert offered to leave.
Ulm was acutely conscious that, as an 'interloper', as he put it, he
might be seen as having taken a badly needed job from Smithy's
own brother-in-law. But, in the interests of keeping the company
afloat, the plodding, good-natured Pike was sacrificed.

Ulm was signed up as business manager on a retainer of 30
shillings a week, but the commission on the charter business he
immediately drummed up quickly bolstered his weekly income.

When the Australian federal capital moved from Melbourne to Canberra in May, Ulm organised a successful joyriding operation there at the opening of the new Parliament buildings. The partners all went down and lived in tents on the airfield. In the intimacy of this flying camp the others stopped addressing him as Mr Ulm. 'In a day or two,' Ulm said, 'we were calling each other Smithy, Andy and Charles.'

Meanwhile Ulm had created for them a syndicate to support the route tender. They had no funds to set it up so they borrowed from a moneylender at a steep rate of interest. Ulm persuaded a popular public figure, Major General Sir Charles Rosenthal, a distinguished, much-wounded Australian soldier, to chair the syndicate. But the general's reputation was not enough to win the day and the Adelaide–Perth contract went to Brearley, who had easily convinced the government that he knew how to run a successful airline. Interstate Flying Services were seen as cowboys on the fringes of the industry. Although Ulm had been brought in expressly to win the trans-continental licence, he managed to persuade Smithy and Anderson that they still needed his business skills to survive. It was agreed that he would stay on. Soon he had dropped the word 'business' from his title and was signing his letters 'manager'. To Anderson this looked like the writing on the wall, but he kept his resentment to himself as he observed the growing friendship between Smithy and Ulm, who began to spend more and more time together socially.

Ulm, who had a failed marriage behind him, was now engaged to a schoolteacher, Mary Josephine Callaghan. She was a plain, bespectacled, academic-looking woman, regarded with universal affection by those who remembered her as a gracious, cheerful and generous person. Ulm boarded with Jo, as she was known, and her younger sister, Amy, a nurse, who tended his still painful war wounds. Smithy drove him home in the evenings and began stopping off for a drink. Their Lavender Bay flat soon became a centre for discussion of their grandiose plans for Australian aviation. It was here, as Smithy and Ulm got to know each other better, that Ulm slowly revealed more about himself.

Eighteen months younger than Smithy, Charles Thomas Phillippe Ulm was born in Melbourne in 1898. His father was a Parisian artist – the German family name came from their roots in

Alsace-Lorraine – and his mother an Australian. 'I was, I believe, a very ordinary child,' he wrote in his autobiography, 'quick of temper, inclined to obstinacy.' He was also, it appears, something of a loner. He would spend hours at the top of a tall pine tree near his home, 'staring intently out over the sea'. Aged only fifteen when war broke out, he had enlisted in an AIF infantry battalion, lying about his age and using a false name. By the time he was sixteen he had been sent to Gallipoli, wounded in the foot and – along with hundreds of other young Australian soldiers – had been returned to Australia to be discharged from the army, according to his military records in the Australian Archives in Canberra, 'for medical unfitness due to VD'.[4] Another reason for his premature discharge was the army's discovery that he was under age. However, as soon as he was eighteen, he was urged by his father, a man with a singular hatred of the Germans, to get back into the war. 'You've still got all your limbs,' Ulm recalled him saying harshly. So, in 1917, he had re-enlisted and had been dispatched as a private to the Western Front, where he had been wounded again, this time in the knee.

He claimed in his memoirs to have been sent on an officer training course in England. But his detailed AIF service records, listing all his wartime postings and promotions to temporary NCO ranks, contain no evidence of this. According to the memoirs, he had had his first taste of flying at a training school on Salisbury Plain. At a nearby airfield he made friends with some RFC pilots and made an illicit solo flight. It was to change the direction of his life. 'Illegally I had discovered something that appealed to my entire heart and brain. I suddenly perceived the possibility of money and public prominence through this new and exciting medium of travel.' He saw aviation, he wrote, 'as a way of escape from my own repressions and inhibitions.'

Back in Australia Ulm was involved in a series of failed aviation ventures, which included unsuccessful attempts to raise money to fly round the world, round Australia, across the Tasman and over the Pacific. When all these dreams evaporated, he and a pilot called Billy Wilson had turned to what he called 'the airman's last resort – barnstorming'. This had ended, early in 1927, in a crash on a New South Wales mountain range, the Barrington Tops. Almost everything Ulm had turned his hand to had ended in disappointment, with unhappy consequences for his domestic life. In 1919, on his return from the war, he had married a shop assistant, Iris Winter. Their son, John, who was to become a Second World War Spitfire pilot and later public relations director of Qantas, recalled the circumstances in which his parents had separated. Having grown up with his mother and a stepfather, he had met his natural father on fewer than a dozen occasions and referred to him distantly, always in the third person. 'My mother told me that because none of his businesses were succeeding, Charles Ulm suggested one day: "It's probably best for the boy if we separate. When I make my name I'll come back and pick it all up again." He was to become famous, but he never came back.' Charles and Iris Ulm divorced.

An event which took place in the late autumn of 1927 electrified Smithy and Ulm into revealing to each other for the first time their identical vision of a trans-Pacific flight. An unknown American airmail pilot, Charles Lindbergh, arrived in Paris on 21 May at the end of a spectacular non-stop thirty-three-hour solo flight from New York. The Atlantic hop had stirred the world, making Lindbergh instantly famous – and very rich. Both Smithy and Ulm now feared that someone, possibly Lindbergh himself, using the same successful long-range aeroplane, a Ryan cabin monoplane, might quickly capitalise on the Atlantic success and cross the unflown ocean of their dreams. The prospect was so unthinkable they agreed to meet in Jo Callaghan's flat to discuss joining forces. Smithy knew that this would inevitably precipitate a showdown with his original Pacific partners, but the sheer force of Ulm's personality had quite mesmerised him. 'He was ambitious. He wanted to do something that would make the world sit up. He had a good business head. He was a born organiser,' Smithy wrote. 'Why should we two not capitalise on our combined assets? We began to talk of some Big Feat which would bring us what we wanted – fame, money, status. We wanted also to do something which would not only advance aviation and confound the sceptics, but bring fame to our country.'

The terms by which they decided that day to seek fame together were, initially, casually agreed. The gist of the conversation – as Ulm tried to recall it later before a jury – is rendered unambiguously, if ponderously, in the court transcript. 'If I get the finance will you come along with me?' Ulm thought he remembered saying.

'You bet your life, I'm all for it,' he claimed Smithy had replied.

'I said to him, "Well, as it stands now, if I get it, it's Kingsford Smith and Ulm going on this flight. We'll be quite sure about that?"' Ulm, who knew he had no skills to qualify for any vital crew role on a trans-Pacific flight, waited uneasily for the reassurance be sought:

'He said, "Yes."

'I said: "You will have to bear in mind, if it does come off, you'll have a problem with your partner Anderson. He'll naturally think you are dropping him if you join with me."

'Kingsford Smith said, "We'll take care of that difficulty when it arises."'

It was to arise within days.

To solve the funding problem Ulm proposed an attempt with one of the Tourers on the 7,500-mile round-Australia record – set in 1924 at twenty-three days – to get themselves known and 'induce somebody, preferably the Government', wrote Smithy, 'to aid us financially in executing the Big Idea to the glory of Australia'. When Smithy told Anderson, the co-owner of both planes, of the plan, the latter assumed that he would share the flying. But this was not what Ulm had in mind. Having made a sponsorship deal with Sun Newspapers in return for daily progress reports, he declared that he, not Anderson, would accompany Smithy.

Anderson felt insulted. The Bristol Tourer had only one cockpit and there were no dual controls. Only a qualified pilot could fly it. Ulm couldn't relieve Smithy; he would merely be a passenger, Anderson protested. His outrage led to the first headlong clash in Ulm's brief membership of the team. Anderson was not readily given to anger, but now his resentment exploded in violent indignation at Ulm's increasing dominance and high-handedness. The row brought to a head the triangular conflict that had lain uncomfortably near the surface since the day Ulm had breezed into their office. It was to be the first of many in which Smithy would side with Ulm at the expense of his friendship with his slower-thinking mate. Theoretically, they could all have gone – the Tourers had two seats in their cabins and could take three people. But to break the record, it would be necessary to make some long hops for which the aircraft's normal range would have to be greatly extended. An extra tank would have to be fitted under the pilot's seat and petrol cans for refuelling in flight stacked in the tiny cabin. There just wasn't room for a third man.

The impasse did not augur well for harmony on the 'big feat.' It laid bare the qualities that distinguished the disparate personalities of the team. Anderson's languid gentlemanliness openly irritated Ulm, while the latter's aggressive self-confidence unnerved Anderson. Between them stood Smithy, the brilliant pilot they both admired – unflappable, disorganised, radiating the magnetism the other two lacked. Ulm now recognised, to his private alarm, that the bad blood spilling between them threatened to wreck the partnership and imperil his Pacific ambition. He suggested a compromise: to attack the round-Australia record with both aeroplanes. Smithy could fly one with him on board to telegraph back the press bulletins, and Anderson, accompanied by Hitchcock, could take the other. Ulm offered to try to find a sponsor for the second flight. Assuming that the two Bristols would cruise round Australia in formation, supporting each other in a team effort, Anderson reluctantly agreed. He went out to Mascot to tell Hitchcock, who was naturally delighted.

Within days Ulm had found another sponsor, George Bond & Co., a well-known hosiery manufacturer. Unfortunately, what he didn't immediately tell Anderson were the conditions of the deal. The company agreed to charter the aircraft as a publicity stunt, promoting the trip as the first commercial flight round the country. Their advertising manager was to go along as an observer. Anderson's aircraft would therefore require twice as many refuelling stops. By the time he learned of this tortoise-and-hare affair it was too late to cancel the charter. Furious, he accused Ulm of deliberate deception. As if this were not enough, Anderson now discovered that Ulm had agreed another condition with the two sponsors: the Bond flight would not start until he and Smithy had returned or abandoned their own trip.

The currents of discord had come at an unfortunate time for the families now so emotionally involved in the fortunes of Interstate Flying Services. A warm friendship existed between Maude Hilliard and Catherine Kingsford Smith. And Constance Anderson, still highly protective of Keith, had arrived in Sydney to be near him and, for a time, even went to stay at 'Kuranda'. It is likely that Smithy chose not to alarm Catherine by revealing the rising tensions at the company. And whatever the Hilliards knew, it didn't inhibit them from throwing a big send-off party for both teams.

Smithy and Ulm made astonishing progress as, amid daily headlines, they headed for Perth via Brisbane and Darwin. The
disgruntled Anderson soon decided to ignore Ulm's diktat to await
the return of the first plane. He and Hitchcock decided to set off,
along with the hosiery company's man, in the hope that the first aircraft would fail in some way and allow him to overtake it. The
second flight also made good progress round the continent, but
because of its need for twice as many refuelling stops, it never stood
a chance. It did not help when Anderson made a serious navigation
blunder over the middle of Queensland, flying 120 miles off his
course. Smithy and Ulm proved impossible to beat. They completed
the circumnavigation in ten days and five hours, less than half the
previous time.[5] When they landed back in Sydney on 29 June, they
were welcomed as celebrities and greeted in person by the NSW
state premier, Jack Lang. Kingsford Smith and Ulm, for the first
time linked publicly as partners, were acclaimed as national heroes.
'They have,' Lang said, somewhat extravagantly, 'accomplished
something as hazardous as Lindbergh's epic flight across the Atlantic
Ocean.' Smithy wrote: 'Australia began to talk about us. At a bound
we had jumped into prominence. We had done something.' Ulm,
having promised to marry Jo if the record attempt was successful,
celebrated by fulfilling his promise the same day.

On his own plodding journey round the country, Anderson had
begun to talk openly about the Pacific dream. In Melbourne he
told reporters that he and 'Captain Kingsford Smith were ambitious to be the first airmen to do it', adding, 'We hope to
undertake the flight at an early date.' It was therefore with hurt
and bewilderment that, the next morning, he opened his newspaper to read that Smithy and Ulm were planning to fly the
Pacific, in a single-engine Ryan, without him or Hitchcock. They
were, he read, on the point of sailing for San Francisco to enter, as
a preliminary and potentially money-making adventure, an air
race from California to Hawaii, sponsored by a wealthy Hawaiian
pineapple magnate, James Dole. Smithy and Ulm intended to
borrow an aeroplane in an attempt to win the huge prize money
which would buy their Pacific aircraft. Not a word of this had they
communicated to Anderson, and only slowly did the full extent of
their treachery dawn on him.

Had Anderson ever seen the proposal drafted by Ulm to

support their bid for sponsorship he would have been astounded that Smithy was prepared to put his life in the hands of a man who was neither pilot nor navigator. The desperate plan was for both men hurriedly to try to acquire the necessary navigational skills. Given the critical importance of locating small islands in the pre-radio-navigation era, the scheme was a recipe for disaster. Yet it had already gained support in helpful quarters. Vacuum Oil had agreed to buy them a Ryan and supply the fuel, provided the cost of the aeroplane was guaranteed by one of the governments. Jack Lang's Cabinet had duly guaranteed the operation up to the sum of £3,500, on condition that the Pacific flight was made within six months. In one stroke the way had been opened to the fulfilment of Smithy's golden dream.

By the time Anderson and Hitchcock took off from Melbourne on the last leg of their marathon journey, Smithy and Ulm had begun a marine navigation course, tied up a £500 news-rights deal with Sun Newspapers and booked two passages on the *Tahiti*, due to sail to San Francisco on Thursday 14 July. Concerned that their sponsorship might not cover all their costs, they were still determined to enter the Dole race. But not a breath of this was conveyed to either Anderson or Hitchcock. Anderson was now desperate to get back to Sydney to confront the man he had believed was his Pacific partner. But severe winter conditions had struck the Australian Alps, and as he found himself flying over a landscape as bleak as his own thoughts he and Hitchcock were caught in a blizzard and forced to return to Melbourne.

An apocryphal story has it that Anderson that night sent a telegram to Smithy and Ulm demanding that they book his passage to America as well. This is not so: Anderson, who couldn't bring himself to recognise any role for the man who had usurped his position, was determined to have it out face to face with Smithy, and Smithy alone. The next day, Friday 8 July, he and Hitchcock managed to get back to Mascot, where an elaborate ceremony awaited them. Smithy, Ulm, Catherine and Leofric were there as the band struck up to salute them for a flight that, remarkably in the circumstances, had taken only four days more than the first. But for Anderson there was little joy in the occasion. The speeches of praise and flattery rang emptily in the sour atmosphere that enveloped him. All he wanted now was an immediate showdown with Smithy.

8

Seeds of Conflict
1927

Anderson and Smithy met that evening at the Hilliards' house, where Anderson, since the announcement of his engagement to Bon, had been living. Smithy received a cool greeting from Bon, who was all too aware of the crisis that had brought him. He emerges from the tense meeting, as it was later reconstructed in court, as guiltily defensive. Ulm, who privately thought Anderson ineffective and a liability, had told Smithy, the court heard, that he was 'in no way willing that his arrangements should be shared in by Anderson'.[1] Now Smithy had to listen to Anderson's entreaties and the expression of his deep hurt.

Smithy did not excel in moments like this. He lamely tried to justify casting Anderson aside, saying that, because Ulm was now doing so much work on the Pacific venture, 'it is only fair that, it being an arrangement for two, he and I should go'. The 'arrangement for two' was the single-engined Ryan. The weight of any more men on board would create a severe fuel penalty which would threaten their long hops. Anderson had replied that one pilot couldn't handle all that flying – up to thirty hours at a stretch. It would be suicidal, he said, pleading with Smithy to drop Ulm and take him.

Reading the brittle, yellowing transcripts of these emotional exchanges nearly seventy years later, one is struck by the total dominance that Ulm, within the space of three months, had come to exercise within the group. The force of his absent personality somehow seemed to reach into that room. Amazingly, despite his non-pilot status, he had virtually taken over the Pacific operation. And Smithy had yielded so far to his forcefulness that, he was, it is clear, ready to abandon five years of precious friendship with Anderson. Was he prepared to ditch Keith, some people wondered, because he had swept Bon away? Those who knew Smithy best think that he was too generous of spirit and lacked the capacity for such resentment. Rather he knew that Ulm, not Anderson, had the ability to make the Pacific flight happen, and that the price he might have to pay was to fly this ambitious man with no practical aviation skill as a supernumary.

And so, as he sat there that night, Smithy floundered in search of compromise. He tried to buy Anderson off with the suggestion of an oceanic flight of his own. Why not a first-ever to New Zealand? he suggested. 'I didn't see why he shouldn't have the credit of doing that flight as I considered he was perfectly capable of undertaking it,' Smithy told the court. 'Ulm and I would do what we could to organise it.' But Anderson wasn't in the least interested in being fobbed off with a smaller ocean.

Smithy had been afraid at first to reveal the exciting, still confidential news of the state government guarantee for fear of Anderson's reaction, but now he plucked up the courage to tell him. Anderson listened incredulously. They were not talking any longer of a theoretical flight, but one that was in all probability going to happen at last. His emotional outburst took Smithy by surprise. Anderson accused him of double-dealing, of casually sacrificing five years of their trusting relationship. Angrily he demanded that Smithy make up his mind once and for all whom he wanted as his Pacific co-pilot. As he left Smithy suggested they meet Ulm over the weekend to discuss the impasse. Bon, Maude and Arthur came out with Anderson to see Smithy off. It was a strained farewell: they had all heard the raised voices.

Events moved fast in the next few days. The three met in a private lounge at the Carlton Hotel in Castlereagh Street the following day. Earlier Anderson had gone along to Sun Newspapers to see Herbert Campbell-Jones, the managing editor, to find out precisely what offers had been made in his absence. Although Smithy had told him the night before that Campbell-Jones was only prepared to put money behind a two-person team, he no longer trusted either Smithy or Ulm. He was not surprised to hear that while Campbell-Jones had struck a deal with Ulm and Smithy alone, he had made no stipulation limiting the size of the flight crew. Anderson left the editor in no doubt that the composition of the team was by no means resolved.

At the Carlton Anderson, incensed by what he'd just heard from Campbell-Jones, struggled to keep his cool. He reminded Ulm that he and Smithy had been involved in planning and seeking sponsorship for the venture for two years before Ulm had come on to the scene. Indeed, his own family's money had gone into both the trucking business and the aviation company with the sole purpose of buying a Pacific aeroplane. Looking hard at Ulm, he accused him of having contributed nothing. Ulm couldn't even fly or navigate, he said. If there was only going to be room for two, then it had to be Smithy and him. Ulm would just have to drop out.

Ulm responded aggressively. Once and for all, he said tersely, they had better get it into their heads that if they thought he was going to solve the problem by standing down, they were wrong. Smithy appears to have played an uncomfortably passive role in the debate. He was not yet a celebrity, and although he really had no more right to a place on the flight than the others, his entitlement to it was never for a moment questioned. He tried to justify the importance of Ulm's participation. It was Ulm's enterprise that had been responsible for the round-Australia flights that raised their profiles and brought the money. He'd sold the news rights and arranged free fuel from Vacuum. 'It wasn't fair to expect Mr Ulm to stand down,' Smithy was to tell the judge.

Anderson was unimpressed. Smithy had got the promise of a rights deal two years earlier and they had both obtained precisely the same oil-company offer back in 1925. Ulm had merely capitalised on the goodwill they had already established. 'If you'll drop out,' he told Ulm, 'I'd be happy for you to take a third of the proceeds.' Ulm wasn't interested. 'I had designs on the big prizes of life,' he later wrote in his memoirs. 'I am an ambitious man determined to push aside all obstacles in my path.' John Kingsford-Smith said: 'There was no question about it: Ulm tried to push Anderson right out of Smithy's life.'

The stalemate continued acrimoniously for hours. Desperately they tried to find a compromise in which no one would lose face. Despite his apparent self-confidence, Ulm was an insecure man, and it was he who conceded first. He knew his was the weakest position. What was more, he was so utterly bereft of money that he didn't even possess his boat fare to America. Embarrassingly, it would have to come from one of the others. With extreme reluctance, he suggested a solution: 'If Smith is agreeable, I don't mind including Anderson and making the party three. We'll sink or swim together.'[2] None of them was exactly overjoyed with the compromise. It would reduce quite critically the range of the single-engined Ryan upon which they had set their hearts. But by now they were so emotionally drained that they shrank from rekindling the squabble. Instead they shook hands and went into the bar to celebrate. They had solved one problem, but they had overlooked another: the role of Bob Hitchcock.

On Monday 11 July they paid for their passages on the *Tahiti*, Smithy and Anderson lending Ulm his £60 fare. Then they went to the state Parliament to meet Premier Lang and sign the government's six-month £3,500 guarantee. As the Ryan company was selling its suddenly famous monoplane for around £2,400, the venture seemed secure. It was agreed that, on their arrival in America, the money would be made available as needed by the Vacuum Oil Company, acting as the government's agent.

Back at Eldon Chambers their elation was soon dampened. Bob Hitchcock, isolated out at the aerodrome from the current of events, had finally got wind of what was going on. Although there could be no in-flight role – or space – for a mechanic, he appears to have been quite sincerely convinced that he was still a member of the team. He had persuaded Anderson to raise the matter with the others that afternoon. Ulm reacted fiercely. According to Smithy, 'He became rather explosive and shouted, "Damn Hitchcock – haven't we had enough worry trying to agree to three going on the flight?"' Smithy said: 'I'm sorry for Bobby, but things have changed. There's no room, and he's had no experience on American aeroplanes.' Ulm told Anderson that it was not open to discussion. He'd better tell Hitchcock to forget the idea once and for all. But Anderson thought this unfair. 'I'd rather you and Smithy told him,' he said unhappily.

Hitchcock was invited to the office the next day. The stunned mechanic could not believe what his colleagues had to say. 'Kingsford Smith said: "Bob, we're going on the Pacific flight and we've got to leave you behind."' Hitchcock reminded them that he had resigned from his job at their invitation specifically to join the flight. 'And now you're turning me down. Is that right?' Smithy replied, 'No, Bob, but there isn't money for the four of us to go. Andy and I must go, Ulm insists on going, therefore we'll have to leave you behind. But we've agreed that on our return to Sydney we'll pay you a thousand pounds for dropping you out.' Ulm added, according to Hitchcock, 'That'll do me, because on my going I'm pushing you out.'

The devastated Hitchcock went back to Mascot determined to plead with his partners again before they sailed. But getting to meet them proved difficult. They were caught up in a crowded round of farewell parties, culminating on the eve of their departure in a lavish dinner hosted by Catherine at 'Kuranda'. The party went on, with singing round the piano, until 2.30 am, and within a few hours, there were more celebrations in the city. When Hitchcock went to the office around midday the place was deserted. The other three were in the Carlton bar. Hitchcock sat down nervously to wait. Presently, he heard their happy, raised voices approaching up the stairs.

Smithy was the first to walk in, flushed and a little unsteady and grinning widely. He was in expansive mood. 'Well, Bob, we sail today,' he said, as Hitchcock remembered it. 'We're very very sorry to leave you behind. But it can't be helped, old man. On our arrival back here, Bob, there'll be a thousand hard for you.' And Ulm, he recalled, added: 'Yes, you'll hear a knock on the door and I'll say, "Sir Charles, Robert awaits outside about his thousand."' Smithy went on: 'And I'll say, "Show the boy in."' This conversation, repeated word for word, by Hitchcock later, was to constitute a vital element of his case against them. Ulm, who denied that any such offer had been made, explained it away by declaring: 'We were all half-sozzled at the time.'

Smithy, Ulm and Anderson travelled in style on the three-week voyage to San Francisco. They went first class, cultivating some of the ship's officers, from whom they received some elementary instruction in navigation and radio direction-finding techniques.

When they docked on 5 August they were met by Smithy's brother Harold, still working as a shipping executive and now a naturalised American. Also on the wharf was a Vacuum Oil Company man, Herbert Dickie, bearing news of the preparations for the Dole air race to Hawaii. He'd taken the liberty, he said, of obtaining an option on an aircraft which could be made available to them. The next day they went out to Oakland Airport to look at it. Their hearts sank as soon as they saw it. It was a totally unsuitable open-cockpit biplane named *Miss Hollydale*. They were not surprised to learn a few days later that it had failed an under-carriage-strength inspection by the race officials.

They abandoned all thought of participating in the race – prudently, as it turned out. For the event, when it got underway on 16 August, was the most disastrous air race in aviation history. Of the eight aircraft – all single-engined – which started, only two ever reached Honolulu. Three competitors were killed testing their aeroplanes before it even began. Two more planes, grossly overloaded, crashed on take-off on the day of the race. A further three had mechanical problems and returned within minutes of leaving Oakland. Three plunged into the Pacific and were never found. In nine horrifying days no fewer than twelve people – contestants and searchers – had been killed. The Dole debâcle was to change quite fundamentally the assumptions with which Smithy's team had so gaily left Australia. 'It was now clear to us,' he wrote, 'that any attempt to fly to Honolulu on one engine appeared fore-doomed to failure.' Clearly, using a single-engined Ryan to fly to Australia was out of the question. They began to look for a multi-engined machine which could safely carry big fuel reserves as well as a professional navigator and wireless-operator. It didn't take them long to select a three-engined Fokker monoplane – or to discover that it was well beyond their means.

With one of these cabin planes, fitted with Wright Whirlwind engines, the US Army Air Service had recently made the first-ever flight from California to Hawaii in twenty-six hours. In another, the American polar explorer Richard Byrd and his pilot, Floyd Bennett, had, from Spitzbergen the previous year, completed the first successful flight to the North Pole and back and had subsequently flown the Atlantic from New York to France. The Fokker trimotor FVIIB-3m, with a big wooden wing supporting a square-looking fuselage, was the creation of the Dutch designer Anthony Fokker, whose deadly First World War fighters, spurned by Britain, had been used to ruthless effect against the RFC by the German air force. After the war Fokker had opened a factory at Hasbrouck Heights outside New York, where he assembled wings and tubular steel-framed fuselages shipped out from Amsterdam. Although the trimotor was to become one of the most widely used airliners of the years between the two world wars, in the middle of 1927 there were very few in existence. It was therefore with some amazement that, in late August, within days of identifying their trans-Pacific plane, Smithy's team received a telegram from Seattle offering them one.

It came from a fellow Australian, Captain (later Sir) Hubert Wilkins, who had been a member of the crew of the ill-fated Blackburn Kangaroo from which Smithy had been excluded in 1919. Wilkins, now a famous polar explorer, had read in the newspapers of Smithy's need for a long-range aeroplane. He had just returned from an aerial expedition in the Arctic on which he had used two Fokkers, one single-engined, the *Alaskan*, and one trimotor, the *Detroiter*. He now urgently needed to sell them both to finance a single replacement, a Lockheed Vega, in which he planned the following spring to make a trans-Arctic flight from Alaska to Spitzbergen. His trimotor, built in late 1925, was clearly ideal for Smithy. Wilkins was offering it, without engines or instruments, for US$15,000 – around £3,000 – which he claimed was a mere third of its value. The New South Wales government's £3,500 would not stretch to Wilkins' aeroplane and the engines, instruments and extra tanks it needed, but nevertheless they invited the explorer down to San Francisco and cabled Premier Lang in Sydney to plead for further funds.

Smithy, Anderson and Ulm immediately took to Wilkins, a portly man, who, with his bald head and sharply pointed black beard, bore a strong resemblance to Lenin. His recent operations with his two Fokkers in the ferocious cold of the Arctic had, they learned, been plagued by disaster. Both aircraft had been badly damaged in a series of take-off and landing crashes in the Alaska snow. To get one flyable aeroplane, Wilkins had temporarily created a composite machine by switching the big wooden wing of the trimotor, minus its engine mounts, to the fuselage of the single-engined *Alaskan*, naming the hybrid the 'Big Fokker'. After his expedition he had had the two planes shipped back to Seattle, where each had been refitted with its original wing.[3] Wilkins, desperate to make the sale, offered to accept the £3,000 payment in stages. But to turn a bare fuselage and wing into a fully equipped aeroplane would take at least three times this sum. Just when the whole venture was beginning to look hopelessly beyond their means, they were presented, to their joy, with a gift of £1,500 from Sidney Myer, owner of one of

Melbourne's biggest stores, who had been spending the northern summer in San Francisco. To their further delight, the New South Wales government agreed to add another £1,000 to their guarantee. Smithy rashly sent a telegram to Wilkins sealing the deal.

In the autumn of 1927, at the Boeing Aircraft Company's factory in Seattle, the engines were at last fitted and the aircraft was ready for a test flight. At Wilkins' insistence the maiden forty-five-minute flight was made by a former US Navy test pilot with trimotor experience. Commander George Pond was a rotund, boyish-faced man, so short that he had to look up to speak to the diminutive Smithy, who flew as co-pilot. By today's standards the Fokker was an extremely crude machine. The pilots sat side by side on hard metal seats on a tiny, draughty open-sided flight deck into which the icy slipstream and rain poured. It cruised at barely 90mph, was heavy on the controls and uncomfortable to fly. The pilots, wrestling with its large, circular control wheels, couldn't talk to each other because of the mind-numbing, deafening noise. There were only the most basic flight instruments, no trim controls to relieve the strain on the pilots, no flaps, no brakes, and no automatic pilot. It had to be flown for every second of flight exhaustingly by hand. But, thanks to its huge, load-bearing wooden wing, it was an inherently safe aeroplane, and the Whirlwind engines were supremely reliable. Smithy and Pond flew the plane, bearing on its fuselage only the word 'Fokker', no registration letters, down to Mills Field, on the site of today's San Francisco airport. It was here, at Anderson's suggestion, that they named her *Southern Cross*, after the southern-hemisphere constellation.

They now needed to fit the aeroplane with long-range tanks, flight instruments and wireless, but their money was fast running out. The venture was once again threatened. To drown their sorrows, when the *Tahiti* was in port on her passages from Australia, they would go aboard for a free meal and to drink with the ship's officers who had befriended them on their voyage over. They had persuaded Second Officer William Todd to join them as flight navigator and wireless-operator. Todd had taken unpaid leave and was now impatiently killing time in San Francisco, comfortably accommodated, at his colleagues' expense, alongside them at the Roosevelt Hotel, where his bill was adding an alarming £100 a month to their costs. Todd was a huge man, then weighing 19 stone (121 kg), but Smithy, convinced of his navigational skill, had insisted, 'He's worth his weight.' However, as the weeks passed and they still hadn't financed the expedition, Todd grew restless and began to complain that he had been induced to give up his livelihood with unrealistic assurances. He and Ulm developed a mutual antagonism. Todd, a highly emotional man, began to drink heavily, and when he rolled the team's car down a bank, Ulm angrily told him to get out of their lives. Embittered and privately bent on revenge, Todd went back to sea.

Meanwhile, out of the blue, there came shattering news. A change of government in New South Wales in the third week of October saw Labour premier Jack Lang replaced by a new coalition administration led by Thomas Bavin. Bavin regarded his predecessor's investment in the Pacific flight as irresponsible. He promptly cancelled the £4,500 worth of guarantees. Pressure on the team to abandon the flight now mounted in Australia, where the newspapers began exhorting them not to risk their lives and go the way of so many Dole race pilots. But, so close now to the realisation of their dream, they were determined not to retreat. To pay Wilkins they borrowed $7,500 from Locke Harper, the Vacuum Oil Company's west-coast manager. It was a generous and risky gesture by Harper, for the money came out of his own pocket. But nothing, it seemed, could stem the flood of their uncontrolled outgoings. Nor was the ocean of debt limited to the huge sums they owed in America. Their creditors in Australia were growing restless. One of them, embarrassingly, was Anderson's mother, who had put in £400 which she now needed back. They cabled Leofric instructing him to sell one of the Bristol Tourers and liquidate all the local debts.

Tramping the streets of San Francisco, Ulm went from 'interview to interview', he wrote, 'from oil company to aircraft builder, from Jew to Gentile, seeking backing for a project which nobody in the world apparently thought was possible'. Neither Smithy nor Anderson, it seems, took any part in these desperate excursions. Smithy, frustrated by the setbacks, had decided to spend the time more pleasurably. He had been introduced to a network of speakeasies – America was still in the grip of Prohibition – and was amusing himself with the local women.

Ulm's singlehanded struggle to find a sponsor failed. Their debts mounted and they were forced to mortgage the still incompletely equipped *Southern Cross* to the San Francisco *Chronicle*. And Ulm did a deal with the Associated Oil Company of California which would clear everything they owed if the trimotor, circling over San Francisco, could break the world flight endurance record, then standing at fifty-two hours twenty-two minutes. As the aircraft needed to be strengthened for the attempt, Anderson plucked up the courage to cable his uncle, Harry Vincent, pleading again for a loan. This time the Melbourne builder relented. He sent the requested £600 as a personal loan to help his nephew, on the clear understanding that Anderson would share the flying to gain vital handling experience under heavy fuel loads. Ulm issued Anderson with a receipt, and later in December had a further agreement drawn up in which the three declared themselves equal partners in the ownership of the *Southern Cross*. The document stated that if one of the three withdrew from the flight he would cease to be a partner and the other two would acquire all the assets and liabilities. A further clause stipulated that they would divide equally any profits from any flight made 'by any of them' in the aircraft.

Meanwhile, with the help of Vincent's cash, the trimotor was flown 350 miles south to Santa Monica in Los Angeles where, at the Douglas Aircraft factory, extensive work was commissioned to strengthen and tank it to stay in the air for over two days and nights. The fuselage was repainted and, for the first time, the plane's name was displayed on the side. Then a fresh complication arose: the San Francisco *Chronicle* was not, understandably, prepared to see the aircraft make such a risky flight while it was still a mortgagee of the plane. Just when the end of the road seemed in sight, the supportive Harper once again stepped in and personally took over the $10,000 mortgage from the newspaper. Yet the three Australians continued to pour into the project with quite reckless abandon money they now didn't have. One gets a sense that they regarded the historic significance of the flight as justification for sprees of purchasing, on credit, everything they needed, from aircraft and engine accessories to meals, hired cars and hotels. They took the view that if the flight was successful the proceeds would quickly pay off the bills, and if it wasn't, then it wouldn't be their concern.

The first attempt on the endurance record, made by Smithy and Pond, ended prematurely. Early in the flight they were forced to dump their petrol and auxiliary oil and return to Mills Field with what felt alarmingly like tail flutter. The fuel had been frantically jettisoned over a San Francisco suburb, splattering the Monday-morning wash on scores of clotheslines. The next day they tried again. But now there were problems of rudder control flying at slow airspeeds close to the stall. A larger rudder was fitted. Then they ran out of fuel. After the third attempt, once they had mastered the control and fuel economy techniques, Anderson suggested that he should fly the fourth trip, but Smithy adamantly refused to let him. The aircraft stayed aloft for forty-nine and a half hours – only three hours short of the record – so they decided to mount a fifth and final attempt. Again Anderson pleaded to be allowed to go with Pond, but Smithy 'wouldn't hear of it'. Why Smithy so firmly barred him from the San Francisco flights was never revealed in the subsequent court case. Such was Pond's experience on Fokker trimotors that he could have backed up either of the Australian pilots. Whatever the explanation, Anderson regarded Smithy's refusal as a deep slight which relegated him once more to junior status in the partnership. It was also soon to have wider repercussions. On hearing that his £600 had not been used to help his nephew to fly, Harry Vincent felt he had been deceived, and when, later, his beneficence might have solved some of their remaining problems, he turned them down.

The final record attempt was delayed until 17 January 1928. Their need to succeed this time was given an edge of desperation by the arrival the same day of a devastating cable from Bavin, the new state premier in New South Wales. Having withdrawn the Lang administration's funds, he now instructed Vacuum Oil to arrange for the immediate sale of the aeroplane. The cable also contained a brisk edict that the three were to abandon any further attempt to fly the Pacific, and demanded that they confirm immediately that they had done so.

After watching the take-off from Mills Field that morning, Ulm drove to the Vacuum Oil Company's office and drafted a cable of capitulation. Anderson, having made another futile plea to go in Smithy's place, went back to the Roosevelt to pour out his resentment in a long letter to Bon Hilliard. His days with the expedition were numbered. Smithy, crawling in a wide circle over San Francisco Bay, knew it could well be his last flight in the thundering machine he already regarded with so much affection.

A Millionaire to the Rescue
1928

The final endurance attempt failed. When, after circling San Francisco for fifty hours, they were forced to land three hours short of the record, Smithy and Pond, deaf, frozen and ill with exhaustion, had to be helped out of the cockpit. For the first time Smithy accepted that they were beaten: 'The sun of our fortunes seemed to be setting. We had been six months in America and were no nearer achieving our ambition. Our creditors were pressing us; we were so poor we had not even loose cash in our pockets to buy a meal.'

In February they left the comfortable Roosevelt Hotel, owing the management hundreds of dollars, and moved into the first of a series of downmarket hotels, all crowding into one small room. They stopped eating properly and began to lose weight. Only the generous Locke Harper, constantly fending off their creditors, kept them from starvation, slipping them dollar bills for food. Living on top of one another in seedy rooms, permanently hungry and stressed, put new strains on their relationships. Almost daily, Ulm wrote, 'bitter arguments and petty squabbles' broke out among them. Anderson, who, from his mother and Bon, received the biggest stream of personal mail, was being urged by both women to return to Australia. Smithy, too, was ready to retreat. But Ulm refused to give up.

Gaunt and desperate, his few clothes visibly worn out, he continued to knock on corporate doors and pour out a stream of letters seeking sponsorship. However much it belonged in their fantasies, there remained in them the belief that the world in some way owed them the means to fly the Pacific; that they were destined to perform this self-appointed task. Scrounging some petrol at Mills Field, Smithy and Ulm flew down to Los Angeles to try to persuade Union Oil to pay off their accumulated debts and buy the *Southern Cross*. In return they offered to fly her across the Pacific to promote Union's products, or to give the company the Fokker in return for jobs of any description. Union didn't immediately reject their proposal. Hopes raised, the Australians thumbed a lift back to Rogers Airport. Conspicuous by their Antipodean accents and down-at-heel appearance, they had become figures of pity among the pilots and mechanics at the airports. Sometimes, lacking the price of a bed, they would doss down in hangar offices, where people would buy them a coffee and a hamburger. 'It had become a nightmare existence,' Ulm wrote. 'Smithy thought we should return to Australia, but I kept pressing for a few days longer.'

It was now the third week of February 1928. While Ulm stayed on in Los Angeles, living on his wits and charity to await the Union Oil verdict, Smithy flew back to San Francisco. Within days of his return, Anderson, still simmering over his dumping from the endurance flights, announced that he was going back to Australia. His fare had been cabled to him and he was leaving in two days' time. When Ulm heard about this he was furious. 'For God's sake, wait until I get up there and let's hear what it's all about, because I don't hold with this at all,' he told Smithy angrily on the telephone. 'We three came over together and we three should go back together. Put Andy on the line.' Ulm recalled later: 'I thought it was absolutely rotten that they should talk about either of them going home, while I was away on the affairs of the three of us, without consulting me or giving me a voice in it.'[1] Having failed to talk Anderson round, he rushed back to San Francisco on the night train. Locke Harper had to wire him the fare.

At a depressing meeting in Harper's office at Vacuum Oil the next morning, Anderson remained adamant that it was futile staying on in America. Their debts had risen to $16,000; they had been ordered by the New South Wales government to sell the plane and abandon the flight, and had agreed to do both. They were destitute, an embarrassment to the government in Sydney and the butt of growing public criticism. Smithy agreed: for him all the fun had

long gone from the venture. He was bored by the ceaseless in-
activity and low living. His real interest had only ever been in
physically flying the Pacific – the business side he didn't want to
know about. In desperation, Ulm suggested they sell the trimotor
and buy a cheaper single-engined aircraft. Anderson refused to
have any part of it. It was absurdly risky, he said. But Smithy
agreed to give it a go. It was never to happen.

Ulm borrowed a typewriter and that night in their shared hotel
room, he and Anderson spent several hours drafting a document
for the latter to sign agreeing to the sale of the *Southern Cross* –
the aeroplane he had named but which he had never been allowed
to fly. When, around midnight, they finally arrived at a suitable
form of wording, the document, legally phrased by Ulm, contained what was to prove one crucially important clause: 'It being
understood that should any such sale or disposal of the said monoplane result in our partnership being employed or engaged to fly
said monoplane to Australia or New Zealand, I (Anderson) shall be
one of the pilots'. It was resolved that if, by some eleventh-hour
miracle, Ulm was able to pull off a deal with Union Oil, he and
Smithy would cable Anderson to return immediately. The two of
them sat in their room talking until around 3 am. During these
final hours of their turbulent relationship, Ulm tried to persuade
him to change his mind. Why, in view of his highly critical opinion
of Anderson, is not clear, but it is likely that he recognised that the
Pacific flight needed two experienced pilots and he didn't want to
see an American hired as co-pilot. He wanted the triumph, if there
was to be one, to be an Australian triumph. The obvious man to
replace Anderson at this time, as Harper had suggested the previous day, was George Pond. But Ulm didn't like Pond. He found
him difficult to deal with and was later to describe him as a 'dis-
senting spirit'. Anderson, however, was now beyond persuasion.

On 24 February, two days after Keith Anderson sailed away,
Smithy and Ulm flew the *Southern Cross* to Los Angeles, where, if
Union Oil turned them down, they intended to sell the aeroplane
and go back to Australia. On 16 March Union Oil at last formally
declined their proposal. Now, with exactly 18 cents between
them, they decided to take one final chance and make use of a
letter of introduction from a friend in San Francisco. It was to save
them from descent on to skid row. The Samaritan, who lived in

Glendale on the northern fringes of Los Angeles, was a surgeon, Dr
F. T. Read. He and his wife, Ann, virtually adopted Ulm and
Smithy, and, together with their friends Robert and Cora Wian,
who owned a Glendale furniture company, they set out energetically to try to find a Pacific backer. 'Doc' Read went with Wian on
a round of meetings with bankers, but no one was prepared to
finance a repetition of the Dole calamity.

At this, their blackest moment, their luck, amazingly, changed.
To help unscramble their financial mess and dispose of the aeroplane, Ulm sought the advice of Andrew Chaffey, president of the
California Bank. A serious, rather worried-looking man in his fifties
with rimless spectacles, Chaffey greeted him with affable charm.
Ulm was surprised to learn that, as a young man, the banker had
lived for many years in Australia, where his father had worked as
an irrigation engineer at Mildura. The meeting couldn't have got
off to a better start. The next day Chaffey drove out to Rogers
Field to view the *Southern Cross*. He sat on the flight deck and listened to Smithy explaining how the aircraft could safely cross the
Pacific. Chaffey had set out merely to try to help the partners to
sell the aeroplane and clear their debts, but now had another idea.
He knew an experienced marine navigator, who, he believed,
would be fascinated to hear of their plans. A few days later, in the
third week of March, they had an urgent call from Chaffey to say
that his friend would like to meet them that afternoon and see the
aeroplane at Rogers Field. The man turned out to be another
director of the California Bank, which his wealth had helped to
found. He was said to be one of the richest men in the state. His
name was Allan Hancock.

Hancock didn't look in the least like Smithy's conception of a
millionaire. He was a short, stocky, serious and softly spoken man in
his early fifties, with receding black hair and glasses. Smithy and
Ulm were struck by his old-fashioned politeness and his obvious
genuine interest as he listened to their story, and surprised by his
extensive knowledge of oceanic navigation. But it wasn't entirely
clear to them what had prompted this unpretentious oil magnate in
his tweed cap and leather jacket to find time to meet them. They
presumed he was thinking of acquiring the Fokker for one of his
companies, and hoped he would offer them the $16,000 they
needed to clear their debts. They took him for a flight over Los

Angeles, and afterwards Hancock thanked them courteously and drove off in his Cadillac. As was the case with so many of the casual acquaintances they made, it was the last they expected to see of him.

They were flabbergasted, therefore, when, two days later, Chaffey phoned them at the aerodrome to say that Hancock was about to set off on a twelve-day voyage to Mexico and back on one of his ships and had invited the Australians to go along as his guests. Had this man merely taken pity on them, or was he the fairy godfather who had been sent to realise their dreams? They sent a presumptuously exuberant cable to Anderson: 'SPENDING FORTNIGHT WITH MILLIONAIRE FRIEND . . . WHO LIKELY TAKE OVER WHOLE PROPOSITION.'

Self-conscious in hurriedly hired ill-fitting clothes, Smithy and Ulm boarded the *Oaxaca* at the Los Angeles docks in the third week of March. The vessel was a 1,400-ton freighter, built as a Q-ship for the British admiralty during the First World War to be used in U-boat attack operations masquerading as a cargo vessel. Hancock had bought her to carry tomatoes from his farms at Mazatlan on the Mexican Pacific coast to Los Angeles and had fitted her out luxuriously for cruising. On the 1,000-mile voyage to Mazatlan the Australians discovered that their host, whom everyone called 'the captain', was a fully certificated master mariner who commanded the ship in uniform on the mahogany-timbered bridge. Beyond that, as they basked in sybaritic comfort, being plied with fine food and wine, they learned virtually nothing about the genial benefactor who was about to launch them on the road to fame. Indeed, the captain was to remain a romantic but shadowy figure in the literature of Kingsford Smith's life. Little about Hancock, whom the newspapers always referred to as a 'Los Angeles capitalist', was revealed at the time, and seventy years later it proved difficult to lift the veil that he had drawn over his private life. The only two biographies,[2] both commissioned by the subject, are so steeped in obsequious praise – 'the career of Captain Hancock is something joyous to contemplate' – that his true character is obscured.

However, in the 1990s, some of his descendants living in California were able to shed more light on his somewhat reclusive life, which ended in 1965. He was born in California in 1875 to an American lawyer and surveyor and the aristocratic daughter of an émigré Hungarian count. At the foot of the Santa Monica mountains outside Los Angeles, the family had acquired a former

Mexican Spanish property, the Rancho La Brea. Its 4,500 acres covered rich deposits of bubbling tar, gas and oil and, as a young man George Allan Hancock borrowed $10,000 from his mother to start drilling them. He struck oil in rich quantities, then added to his wealth by selling off the entire 7-square-mile property. Lying between Wilshire and Sunset Boulevards, and embracing a large piece of Hollywood, it was to become one of the most expensive tracts of real estate in the world. Hancock later moved north, investing in more land and expanding his wealth. In the Santa Maria Valley he acquired another oilfield, three more ranches and a railroad. He founded a shipping company, entertaining Albert Einstein and Lord Mountbatten on voyages, and a bank which, through mergers, became the California Bank, run by his school-friend, Andrew Chaffey. At some stage he had gone to sea, serving as a deck officer and navigator in the Pacific and Atlantic. Later, he took his own ships on scientific expeditions to the Galapagos and Alaska. As well as commanding his own ships, he drove the loco-motives on his Santa Maria Valley railway and qualified as a pilot at his own flying college.

By 1928 Hancock had become fascinated by the challenge of the Pacific. Shocked by the Dole race tragedies, he wanted to see confidence restored with safer, better-equipped flights. In the *Southern Cross* he believed he had seen for the first time an aero-plane that could make it to Australia. But were its crew worth investing in? The cost of it all he would hardly notice, but he didn't like his projects to fail. Aboard the *Oaxaca* he quizzed his guests about their Pacific plans. 'When I boarded the ship I knew that if I were to make any headway with the financier I would have to be brutally frank and reveal the whole miserable state of affairs,' Ulm wrote in his memoirs. 'I lacked the nerve to ask Hancock if he would buy the aeroplane to satisfy our creditors. But I did have a vague notion that if he would take it over he might give us the job of running it for him. Kingsford Smith, more or less resigned to fail-ure, and grateful for the unexpected comfort which a kindly providence had showered upon us, prepared to settle down com-fortably and leave the business to me.' They spent a week at Mazatlan, visiting Hancock's tomato farm, swimming in the small tropical harbour and racing about in the *Oaxaca*'s speedboat.

It was on the return journey that the captain made the decision

to help them. There are many versions of the dialogue that is supposed to have taken place at this turning point in their lives. Ulm,
in his memoirs, took the entire credit for selling the venture to
their host.

A few days before the ship was due back in Los Angeles,
Hancock turned to me and put the question: 'How much
money is required to put you boys on the right side?' I
gulped, my tongue stuck to the roof of my mouth. The query
came as a shock. But I told the frank truth: 'Sixteen thousand
dollars.'
   'I'll buy your machine for that sum,' said Hancock. I
fought down my mad desire to dance around the chartroom.
I tried not to look excited. But in thirty seconds the whole
world had changed. Our battles, struggles and anxieties were
not to be in vain. The Pacific would be flown for the first
time.

But was this exquisite moment enjoyed exclusively by Ulm? In
his own autobiography – and in the witness box in the Supreme
Court back in Sydney – Smithy claimed that he was also in the
chartroom at the time and that the captain, calling them both in,
had actually said: 'I'll buy the machine from you boys,' adding, 'I'll
see my attorneys and decide the best way to do it so you can use
it to fly to Australia.' A third version of events comes from
Hancock himself, who recalled that he left the news of his decision
until the moment of disembarkation. As he shook their hands he
said: 'You're going to fly to Australia in the *Southern Cross*. I don't
know how just yet, but we'll take the matter up later. But, rest
assured, you're going.'[3]
However the news was communicated to them, and whoever
swayed the millionaire, Smithy and Ulm, replete from good living,
walked ashore in Los Angeles on 2 April 1928 in ecstasy. But back
at Rogers Field a shock awaited them: the *Southern Cross* had disappeared. The aircraft had been seized by bailiffs and flown to
another airport. At the behest of one of their creditors, it was due
to be sold at auction in a few days' time. Hancock instructed his
lawyer to forestall the sale by paying off all the debts, and as a
result he became the effective owner of the aeroplane. He loaned

it to the Australians under an arrangement whereby they would
pay for it out of the money they would make if they succeeded in
crossing the Pacific. The Fokker was flown back to Rogers Field
and they set about preparing it for the great flight.

Smithy and Ulm moved into the Hotel Clark at the corner of
Los Angeles 4th and Hill Streets, which was run by a well-known
local pilot, P. G. 'Bud' Morriss, a jolly and sociable character.[4] They
even had some dollars in their pockets again: Hancock had
advanced them money for living expenses. At last they were able
to replace their worn-out trousers and shoes. One of the first
things they did when they got the aeroplane back was invite Keith
Anderson to rejoin them. His right to a place on the flight was
now reinforced by the agreements they had all signed. Indeed,
ironically, he had been the only one of the three to contribute his
own money to the project. So, in a cable to Arthur Hilliard on 6
April, they said: 'UTMOST SECRECY IMPERATIVE. FINANCES COMPLETELY
ARRANGED EVERYONE'S SATISFACTION HENCE ESSENTIAL KEITH RETURNS
FIRST STEAMER ADVISE LEAVING DATE – CHILLACHAS.'

This less than informative summons did not meet with the
enthusiastic response they had expected. Anderson had arrived in
Sydney penniless. He had gone to live with the Hilliards, borrowing £10 from Arthur to buy a new suit to go Pacific fund-raising.
It proved a hopeless mission. Just as the Dole race disasters had
dampened the enthusiasm of potential sponsors for oceanic adventures in America, a tragedy on the Tasman early in the year had
done the same in Australia.[5] It was at this point that Anderson,
unsure where next to turn, had received the terse cable recalling
him to America. He discussed it with Hilliard, who agreed that it
was exceedingly lacking in the specifics of the new flight plans. On
the solicitor's advice Anderson replied on 12 April: 'NO FINANCIAL
HELP HERE . . . REQUIRE DETAILS WHAT MACHINE WHO OWNERS DATE
DEPARTURE ROUTE CREW MY STATUS. YOU FURNISH MY FARE TAHITI SAILING
19TH – ANDERSON.'

To his annoyance, his questions were not answered in the reply
that came two days later to Arthur Hilliard, demanding to know
whether Keith was coming. Again Anderson cabled asking what his
role on the flight would be. To that request came, on 18 April, a
heavy-handed personal response from Ulm: 'STATUS CO-PILOT PER-
SONALLY URGE YOU COME TAHITI FAILURE SO TO DO NATURALLY LOSES

YOUR INTEREST WHICH I WILL CONSIDER TREMENDOUSLY DISLOYAL –
CHARLES.' However, Anderson, who bitterly resented these stric-
tures from Ulm, didn't have his boat fare, and told them so. Ulm
then sent him an impatient ultimatum: 'ARE YOU COMING OR NOT?
NO REPLY BY NINETEENTH APRIL CONSIDERED AS YOUR TOTAL WITH-
DRAWAL.' This last cable pointing a pistol at his head did not reach
Anderson until the day of the deadline. But he refused to be bul-
lied. He had still not been told about the miracle of Hancock's
patronage, what the aeroplane was – he didn't know that the
Southern Cross had been refinanced – when they were planning to
leave, what their intended route was, what total crew. He was now
being torn in many directions. From Arthur Hilliard he was getting
advice on his legal rights under the partnership agreement, but it
wasn't at all clear whether the agreement still related to the
Southern Cross since the cables from San Francisco made no mention of the trimotor. Hilliard urged him not to return until Smithy
and Ulm were more forthcoming; he believed that their cryptic
messages reflected a suspicious covertness.

Constance Anderson, who had seen what the traumas of war had
done to her son, didn't want him exposed to the stress of an ocean
flight. Maude Hilliard, who dominated her own family and usually
got her way, was openly opposed to Keith's further involvement.
'She thought it far too risky,' said John Laurence. 'She saw Keith as
a glamorous war hero and a gentleman, and she badly wanted him
preserved for the marriage.' Bon, on the other hand, was a young
woman with a mind of her own. Although she had come to have
reservations about Smithy, and had not forgiven Ulm for coming
between him and Anderson, she believed that, if there was to be
glory from a Pacific flight, then her fiancé deserved to share it.

Stung by Ulm's aggressive cable, Anderson was convinced that
his mates didn't actually want him back. Openly accusing them of
this in his reply, he announced that he was claiming compensation.
He formally demanded a third of the proceeds if the flight was
successful, saying he would accept $13,000 'in full satisfaction'.
The shock tactic worked. The cable bothered Smithy and Ulm,
who had now brought the Fokker back to San Francisco, where
they were staying at the Hotel Bellevue. They knew they were on
weak ground in persisting in withholding so much vital information from their legal partner, and why they did so has never been

explained. Sensing the threat of a lawsuit, they decided to adopt a more helpful tone.

They began at last to drip-feed him an outline of some of the facts, though in such vague terms as to obfuscate the full truth. All they told him, mysteriously, was that they had sold the aircraft for $16,000 and 'repurchased' it with money from a private backer. They were unable to raise his fare, they said, and urged him to work his passage, concluding: 'HONOUR DEMANDS REPLY IMMEDIATELY STATING COMING OR NOT THIS OUR LAST WORD.' Instead of the friendly 'CHILLACHAS' they signed off with a stiff 'SMITHULM'. They still had not explained the dramatic turnaround in their financial fortunes, or declared a departure date, or said who else would be on board. However, on receipt of this cable, on 23 April, Anderson decided at last to try to get back to America. All that appeared to stand in his way now was the lack of his fare.

At this point, for some unaccountable reason, Anderson created a problem for himself. Not only did he refuse to try to work his passage, but he insisted on travelling first class, which, at £60, was more than double the cheapest fare available. He attempted to borrow the money from Arthur Hilliard, but Hilliard was still uneasy about the resuscitated venture and said no. Then he asked Leofric, who couldn't help him, then Herbert Campbell-Jones. The newspaper editor, who strongly disapproved of the way they had all allowed themselves to get into such appalling debt, very firmly refused. So did Vacuum Oil. Anderson had now exhausted all avenues.

One cannot escape the feeling that it was all terribly sad and unnecessary – a problem that, sixty years later, would have been solved in a couple of days by phone, fax, or e-mail. On the one hand a generous millionaire had arrived to finance the flight to any level of cost in crew and equipment that would guarantee a successful mission. He did not quibble over the dollars: had anyone asked him to pay a co-pilot's boat fare to America he would not have questioned it. But neither Smithy or Ulm was prepared to do so. Was Ulm still resentful that Anderson had deserted their sinking ship? Was requiring him to find his own fare intended as a penance? And why did Anderson take such an inflexible line? Why did he choose this moment, when the flight for which he had suffered so much was about to happen, to stand on his dignity on an unimportant principle over a first-class cabin? Was he really incapable of borrowing the £25 that would have got him to California third class, or of signing on to work his way across? Did he really *want* to go? Or was it that his partners' reluctance to be open with him rankled too strongly? Because it seems that he made no further effort either to get to America or to communicate with Smithy and Ulm.

The crisis also stirred up the families involved. Constance Anderson was apparently in Perth but Catherine Kingsford Smith learned from Maude of the Hilliards' distress at Keith's predicament and about what was viewed as the uncompromising attitude of his partners. In her diary Catherine recorded that she met Maude at their favourite rendezvous, Griffiths' tea shop in the city, where they had a long, womanly talk about it all. The same day she met Bert and Elsie Pike, also 'to talk re Andy'. Afterwards she went home and drafted a letter to Maude, the contents of which were, it seems, so delicate that she decided to show it to Bert and Elsie for their approval before posting it. The letter has not survived, but we can assume that the diplomatic Catherine was trying to pour oil on turbulent waters.

Meanwhile, in San Francisco, Smithy and Ulm were perplexed that no reply had come from Anderson. When the *Niagara*, the last ship that could have brought him there in time, sailed from Sydney on 3 May, they discovered that he was not on board. They waited another week and then, on 11 May, in exasperation, cabled that their offer of a third interest in the new flight was now formally withdrawn. Anderson ignored this communication too. To reinforce their position Ulm wrote him a long letter accusing him of deserting them and informing him that he had no further rights in what they regarded as a completely new expedition. This letter, signed by both Smithy and Ulm, spelled out the lengths to which they had gone to keep a crew position open for him. Still refusing to name their benefactor, they concluded: 'This letter closes all our dealings with you in connection with the proposed flight to Australia with which you were connected and which failed ultimately with the forced sale of the plane.'[6]

What they didn't tell Anderson was that they had been forced to abandon their plan for an 'all-Australian' flight. They had already recruited two Americans to join them: a navigator called Harry Lyon and a wireless-operator, Jim Warner.

10

'Guess we are Lost'

1928

One of Hancock's conditions for backing the Pacific flight was that Smithy and Ulm carried both a professional navigator and a wireless-operator. Air navigators didn't then exist, so they had to find a marine one. Their first choice was the *Tahiti*'s third officer, Harold Litchfield, but he was away at sea. So anxious were they to give the job to an Antipodean that they were even prepared to take back the troublesome William Todd. They radioed him at sea, but this time he declined.

Harry Lyon was suggested by the chief of the Hydrographic Office in San Francisco, Captain J. T. McMillan. Lyon, he warned, 'was a bit of a wild man', with a bizarre sense of humour at times, but a superb ocean navigator. He held a master's certificate and had commanded his own ships in the merchant marine and in the US Navy during the war. The captain was between commands and would like to meet them.

In his own little-known account of the Pacific flight, Lyon described his first encounter with Smithy and Ulm. 'My first impression of these two chaps was of their extreme earnestness and confidence, not only in the feasibility, but of the absolute success of the flight. I was impressed by the uncanny thoroughness with which they had been preparing for it. We talked for several hours. I had never navigated in the air, but had flown several times as a passenger. I asked if I could think it over. Needless to say I hardly slept that night. But when daylight came I'd made up my mind. I would take the job.'

It is unlikely that Smithy and Ulm learned very much at that first meeting about the colourful background of this short, chubby-faced sea captain with thick, prominent lips and black swept-back hair, upon whose skill their lives would soon depend. They were happy to accept McMillan's assurance that he knew how to get them to Australia. Very little was ever written about Harry Lyon, yet, although he was treated as a temporary hired hand, this tough, witty and slightly cynical upper-class American, whose trademark was a neat bow tie, was to become a full hero of the Pacific flight.

Harry Lyon died in 1963 and his second wife in the 1970s. They had no children, and as Harry had been an only child, it seemed that his branch of the family might have died out. However, early in 1992, after two years' search, I discovered a third cousin of Lyon's at Vero Beach in Florida. William Hunt, a retired aeronautical design engineer, had known him well. And Schuyler Mott, the local librarian in the tiny Maine village of Paris Hill, where Lyon lived for much of his life, told me that the village museum had a small permanent display featuring both the navigator and his distinguished father, Henry Lyon, an admiral in the US Navy. The family home, 'Lyonsden', still stood on the village green. 'There are many stories here about Harry,' Mr Mott confided intriguingly. 'I hesitate to pass them on, even though I heard some from Harry himself.' Lloyd Gates, an aviation historian in the nearby township of Norway, had acquired some unpublished memoirs, handwritten in pencil by Lyon around 1929. The narrative concluded with a description of the first part of the Pacific flight. From all these sources it was possible to piece together a career remarkable for its constant involvement with danger and adventure.

Born in 1885, Lyon tried to follow in his father's footsteps but, lacking academic discipline, he had been kicked out of the prestigious Annapolis Naval Academy where, in his first year, the class of 1907, he failed his exams – ironically, most dismally of all in navigation. His indulgent father then sent him to a famous Ivy League university, Dartmouth College, but he walked out after one term to sign as a deckhand on a full-rigged sailing ship, rejecting the lifestyle of an educated gentleman his father had planned for him to become a permanent wanderer, knocking about the world in an endless succession of small, seedy tramp steamers. His

hard-drinking career in sail and steam took him round the Horn
before the mast, into fist fights, armed mutinies and fires at sea; a
plunge overboard from the yardarm of a windjammer; wartime
U-boat attacks, illegal rum-running on the California coast and, in
1924, into the midst of a revolution in Mexico in which he was
sentenced to death but reprieved.

'Harry was a delightful person,' said William Hunt who, twenty-
four years younger, was a boy when he first met Lyon. 'He was a
man full of outgoing charm, amusing, with a lively, active mind.
His background showed in his educated New England speech. His
early academic failures were really no reflection of his brightness –
he was just rather lazy. But he did become a brilliant navigator. He
was actually quite a lonely man – after one brief unhappy marriage
he didn't marry again until very late. In the rough life he led, he
had become, by the time he met Smithy and Ulm, a deeply
unhappy person who drank to forget.'

Lyon introduced Smithy to wireless-operator Jim Warner, with
whom he had served during the war on Atlantic convoys. After
sixteen years' service Warner had left the navy and was now
working as a door-to-door salesman selling trousers – 'peddling
pants', as he put it – in San Francisco. Even less existed in the vast
literature of the Pacific flight about him. Whereas Lyon had
begun life self-confidently in the comfortable ambience of an
admiral's home, wanting for little, Warner had suffered a horrifying childhood which had left permanent emotional scars. He
was a slim, slightly built, rather withdrawn and nervous man
with a small moustache, his retiring and unassuming demeanour
in marked contrast to Lyon's thrusting ebullience. I traced
Warner's son, Tom, to Pompano Beach in Florida, where he is a
boat-builder. In a large wooden chest he had kept his father's
extensive Pacific flight archive. Jim had shared with his son over
the years his memories of the historic journey. Not all of them
were happy.

Warner's life had been haunted by insecurity which had created
a deep need to be loved and wanted, something he sought in turn
from no fewer than six wives. He was born in 1891 in Lawrence,
Kansas. His parents split up when he was four, and he was dumped
in an orphanage from which he was fostered for several years by a
family who ultimately decided to send him back. He was returned

to the institution with a cracked skull, having been kicked by a horse. At seven he was adopted by a German maize-farmer and his wife and put rigorously to work under the most brutal discipline. He was constantly beaten at home and at school. 'He got no affection from any quarter,' said Tom. 'He often used to go out into the cornfields to hide and just cry his heart out.'

At fourteen Warner ran away from the farm, and for the next six years he wandered about the west, picking up casual work on farms and construction sites until, in 1911, he found security in the navy. He became a wireless-operator, serving on gunboats in China and, in the First World War – during which he was twice sunk – on destroyers and on the cruiser *St Louis*, where his radio skills impressed the navigating officer, Lieutenant Harry Lyon.

The Americans were engaged on weekly pay to go only as far as Suva, through which it had been decided to route the flight despite the absence of an aerodrome there. Beyond Fiji, Smithy believed, they would not need either navigator or radio man as they could hardly fail to miss the huge land mass of Australia. Warner was offered US$40 a week and Lyon – presumably because his role was considered more vital – a higher rate of which there is no longer a record. If they made it to Fiji both were to receive a bonus of US$500, supplemented by a further $500 if the *Southern Cross* reached Australia safely. The Americans agreed informally to these terms in the belief that they had entered into a gentlemen's agreement.

A role still had to be found for Ulm, whose energy and persistence had been largely responsible for the remarkable turnaround in the fortunes of the expedition. Although he could not take off or land an aeroplane, and therefore couldn't operate technically as a full co-pilot qualified on the trimotor, it was decided that he would occupy the right-hand seat as 'relief pilot', handling the controls in the air in the less demanding moments out of cloud. To this job description Ulm at first added 'organising manager', but neither term caught on with the media so, with Smithy's agreement, he redesignated himself 'co-commander'. Although it was a curious title, it took root. However, aeroplanes cannot be flown by committee, and there was no question that Smithy was the captain and pilot in charge. But he was by now sensitive to his colleague's concerns about his status and far too laid back to make an issue of it. Besides, had it not been for Ulm, they would have been back in Australia, in disgrace and huge debt.

The last two weeks of May saw the team in frantic activity preparing the *Southern Cross*. Success depended principally on two things: engines that would not fail, and accurate navigation. The rest would be endurance and pilot skill in handling a grossly overloaded aeroplane in the destructive tropical storms they would meet. With Hancock's money they were now in the happy position of being able to afford to make the flight a model of safety and efficiency for its time. They hired one of the world's finest aircraft engineers, an Englishman and ex-Royal Flying Corps flight-sergeant mechanic who had come to work for the Wright Corporation. Cecil Maidment, known as 'Doc', had been Lindbergh's engineer.

Not only did they have three motors – although at all-up weight the loss of even one would have put them into a long and fatal descent to the sea – but they had three radio transmitters, one for emergencies installed in the wing, and four compasses. The latter were Lyon's concern. As he had never before navigated an aeroplane, he was slightly nervous as he began to adapt his marine skills to the much less forgiving medium of the air, where a course error of only a few degrees could be disastrous. Oceanic flights were then made with simple magnetic compasses, navigating by the ancient nautical art of dead reckoning, which relies on a running plot showing, by no means always reliably, where the aircraft should, in theory, be in mid-ocean, based on its estimated ground-speed and compass course. The huge imponderable was the wind and the extent to which it was invisibly slowing or speeding progress – or pushing the aircraft off course. The vital calculations of this drift were based on crude visual estimates of the aeroplane's often imperceptible sideways movement over the lines of the waves.

To establish position more precisely, periodic fixes were obtained by sextant and an approximate latitude and longitude arrived at from the angle of the sun or stars – provided that they could be seen at all. The marine sextant required the navigator to read at sea-level the angle between the horizon and the celestial body. But, in an aeroplane, the ocean's horizon could not always be seen. So an aviation sextant had been developed in which it was represented artificially with a bubble, a sort of spirit level. Harry Lyon had never seen one of these things, and he didn't at first have much confidence in it. Nonetheless he set out to simulate on the ground the unsteady platform of an aeroplane bouncing through turbulence. Night after night he was driven in a car at high speed along a rough beach road outside San Francisco as he practised taking sights on the stars. Then, with Smithy at the controls of a borrowed biplane, he began to master the bubble sextant in the air.

Lyon supervised the installation of the four compasses. They included a then revolutionary new device called an earth-inductor compass. It worked electromagnetically and its generator, a wind-mill on top of the fuselage, was driven by the slipstream. It fed its directional information to a simple needle in the cockpit. By steer-ing a heading that kept the needle central, the aircraft could be made to follow a course preset by a handle at the navigator's table. A navigation table had been put behind the big, oval-shaped 800-gallon tank which blocked access from the cabin to the cockpit, and a sliding hatch had been fitted in the roof through which, by standing on a box, the navigator could poke out the sextant. In addition to two conventional steering compasses in the cockpit, the navigator had a heavily dampened master magnetic compass, a large, nautical-looking instrument called an 'aperiodic' which sat on a tripod on the cabin floor. A crude sighting contraption, with three parallel wires for judging drift over the white crests of the waves, was mounted on a bracket on the side of the fuselage outside the entrance door. The door had to be propped open against the slipstream to allow Lyon to lie on the floor and stick his head out to squint through it.

Immediately behind the navigation table on the port side of the fuselage, Warner's radios, installed on metal shelves, were quaintly insulated from vibration – as was Lyon's chronometer – by sus-pension on rubber cords. Today the two main transmitters, with their brass tapping keys, are museum pieces. One was for short wave, for long-distance position-reporting and news bulletins, the other a medium-frequency unit for shorter-range communication with ships. The short-wave system operated with a single valve; to switch frequencies Warner had to resort to the clumsy expedient of completely removing one coil and screwing in another. Power for the two transmitters and the aircraft's lighting batteries came from two small wind-driven generators mounted on each side of the fuselage. His two aerials – the short-range one was 400ft long – trailed behind the aircraft, reeled out from drums on the cabin floor. Sometimes the wires would wind round each other and it could take up to an hour to disentangle them.

Lyon and Warner sat close together in wicker chairs supplied by Robert Wian's furniture shop. Incredible as it may seem, they were neither anchored nor provided with seatbelts. The cabin around them was a bare shell with no interior lining or insulation of any kind. They sat inside the framework of the tubular fuselage among criss-crossing bracing wires, protected from the elements only by thin fabric. In the air the hideous noise of the engines made it impossible to communicate even by close-up shouting and, regardless of the cotton wool they stuffed into their ears, rendered them all deaf soon after they were airborne. They communicated with the cockpit by means of scribbled notes clamped with a large paper clip to a long broomstick. When the Americans needed to send forward a message they clipped on a note and pushed the broomstick round the fuel tank into the cockpit, poking Smithy in the back of the neck to attract his attention. Smithy or Ulm would agitate the stick to signal that they wished to send a message.

In the third week of May they began to fly out of San Francisco on shakedown flights as a four-man crew for the first time. Smithy, aware that their lives would depend on his ability to fly safely for long periods, day and night, blind in bad weather, had hired George Pond to give him several hours of instrument-flying training on the Fokker. He took every opportunity to head deep into cloud to build his confidence in the techniques. He had provisionally scheduled their departure for the full moon of Thursday 31 May. In their last week he and Ulm conscientiously maintained a fitness programme designed to keep them going around the clock without sleep. 'We tested ourselves,' Smithy wrote, 'by driving an automobile for 12 or 15 hours, then flying three or four hours, then running for an hour or two, then flying some more, then more driving and so on for a total of 35 or 40 hours on end – until we knew that the "human element" would not let us down.' Meanwhile Ulm was cabling Sun Newspapers with stories which created huge public excitement across Australia. In terms of perceived peril, a trans-Pacific flight was viewed in the late 1920s with the sort of awe that had surrounded Columbus's voyage to the New World, and Smithy was already being described as a new-age Magellan. They had taken the *Southern Cross* from Mills Field across the bay to Oakland Airport, which had a less obstructed climb-out path. The Oakland Chamber of Commerce put them up at a first-class hotel near the aerodrome and a car-distributor lent them each a brand-new Buick sedan. Besieged by reporters and photographers, they were now celebrities throughout California.

At the eleventh hour, Lyon and Warner were stunned when Ulm suddenly produced formidable-looking legal agreements for each of them to sign. They had not expected this degree of formality, not having reckoned with Ulm's thoroughness or his determination to limit their ability to profit from the flight. 'They put it under my nose the night before take-off and after reading it I didn't know whether to laugh or get peeved,' Warner wrote. 'It was quite a work of art.'[1] The agreement confirmed his weekly pay at $40 and the $1,000 in two bonuses if the aeroplane got to Australia, and offered a first-class boat fare back to America from Fiji. It was 'specifically understood' that the $500 bonuses would, in addition to their weekly pay, be the limit of their reward from the flight. The document also indemnified the Australians against any death or accident claim. But what was to prove its most contentious provision was a clause under which the Americans agreed not to give interviews or write articles 'without the express permission of the owners in writing' until they returned to America, a condition both men would come to resent.

'Isn't that a daisy? Or would you prefer to call it a peach?' observed Warner cynically. 'It struck me that some folks held my life pretty cheap, but I wasn't to get the full-blown beauty of the thing until later.' In his own memoirs Lyon refrained from commenting on these contracts. 'Harry was much more philosophical about it than Warner,' said his cousin, William Hunt, 'but then, he was a much more laid-back guy. He did tell me, however, that he thought it was a very stiff contract. He put it down to Ulm's heredity. He always believed – wrongly, as it happened – that Ulm was German which, in his mind, explained his autocratic approach to life. Talking to me, he often referred to him as the "Kraut". Of

the two he preferred Smithy. They hit it off right from the beginning. As did Jim Warner and Smithy. Neither of the Americans
found the same warmth in Ulm. They thought him a bit taciturn
and ruthless.'

'I signed it,' Warner said. 'I had to. Everyone knew I was going,
and if I didn't sign it I couldn't go. If I didn't go it would have
looked as though I had suddenly developed cold feet.' But sadly, it
seems that is exactly what Jim Warner did develop, although
whether it had anything to do with the contract is not clear.
Warner had certainly been deeply affected by the Dole race
tragedies. He had been the radio-operator aboard one of the US
Navy ships along the race route which tried fruitlessly to pick up
the desperate transmissions from the doomed aircraft. 'It touched
our hearts,' he had said in an interview, 'to know that they had
dropped out of sight without any word – not even a goodbye to
their friends.'[2] His change of heart was later described by Locke
Harper, who said that Warner 'had to be locked in as well as talked
to most of the night because, at the last moment, he was afraid to
go and wanted to back out. Which was understandable, since he
had not in excess of twenty hours altogether in the air in the
Southern Cross.'[3]

During the night a bitter-sweet cable for Smithy and Ulm
arrived from Keith Anderson in Sydney. Although he wished them
Godspeed, the real purpose of his message was to warn of legal
action to follow: 'YOU HAVE BEST POSSIBLE MACHINE. IF YOUR COMPAN-
IONS' SKILL EQUALS YOUR DETERMINATION YOU WILL SUCCEED. GOOD
LUCK. REGRET FAILURE FURNISH MY FARE ENSURING MY PARTICIPATION
WAS NOT FIRST CONSIDERATION. EXPECT A LITTLE JUSTICE AND COMPEN-
SATION UPON YOUR ARRIVAL HERE – ANDERSON.'

Several hundred people turned out at Oakland Airport to see
them off on that fine, misty morning on the last day of May.
Among them was Allan Hancock, who had come up to San
Francisco in the *Oaxaca*, which he was about to sail down to his
estate in Mexico where he intended to go to ground while the
flight was in progress. At the airport he insisted on remaining
incognito, mingling with the crowd in his cloth cap and making no
attempt to approach the blue and silver aeroplane, which was
groaning with nearly 4 tons of fuel for the twenty-seven-hour first
leg to Hawaii – a flight that today takes only five and a half hours.

Smithy's brother Harold was there, and 'Doc' and Ann Read and Robert and Cora Wian had come up from Los Angeles. Ann gave them a bouquet of flowers, which they placed in the cockpit, and presented Smithy with a full-sized horseshoe to add to his collection of good-luck charms. He already had a crinkled portrait of Nellie Stewart to sit on and a Felix cat badge pinned to the front of his leather flying helmet. Just as they were about to board, a Mrs Evangeline Eichwaldt handed Smithy a silver ring which had belonged to her navigator son, Alvin, whose aircraft had spun into the sea at night while searching for missing Dole race pilots the previous year.

Reporters crowded round the aircraft, shouting up questions. 'Do you think you'll make it?' one asked.

'You bet your life,' Smithy said. 'We're so sure, we're not taking parachutes, lifejackets or a dinghy.' If they ditched they would jettison the contents of the long-range tank so that it became a flotation chamber. Once in the sea they would saw off the two outboard engines. The wooden wing contained a saltwater still and the emergency radio with a gas balloon to hoist the aerial.

They were dressed in an assortment of highly unsuitable clothes. Pictures taken that morning show them boarding in collars and ties. Smithy and Ulm wore tall riding boots. Smithy's sports jacket, crumpled up like a concertina, looked a size too small, Ulm had chosen a loose blouson and Warner, the smartest, a suit with a patterned sweater and a large white panama hat. Lyon, by contrast, wore a sloppy sweater and bow tie. Although the Australians had stowed rabbit fur-lined flying suits in the cockpit, the Americans were to cross the Pacific dressed as if they were going to spend a day at the office. As most of the flight would be at low level through warm latitudes, they were happy to travel like this.

It was a few minutes before nine o'clock when they lifted off. As the tail slowly rose and the plane bounced gently across the field, petrol sloshed out of an overflow valve in the main tank behind Smithy's head, drenching his shoulders and back and filling the cockpit with noisome fumes. He gripped the control wheel with both hands while Ulm held the throttles wide open until they were well clear of the ground. They were followed into the air by a host of small aircraft carrying photographers and newsreel

cameramen. The full power of their three engines was barely
enough to keep the aircraft above its stalling speed, and they were
to remain in this critically dangerous state for several hours. Once
they were safely established on the climb, struggling for height
over the white disembodied spires of San Francisco's skyscrapers,
which poked up through a blanket of brown smog, Smithy and
Ulm turned to each other and shook hands. For Smithy, aged
thirty-one, with 3,300 flying hours, it was a moment of sweet
exultation. For eight years his every waking thought had revolved
around his obsession with the unconquered Pacific. 'A sensation of
relaxation and relief from worries and anxieties of the past nine
months. A tremendous elation at the prospect before me,' he
wrote in *My Flying Life*. 'All our troubles were over. What lay in
front was a glorious adventure.' If they made it to Hawaii they
would be the fifth aircraft to do so, but no one had ever made the
giant hop beyond there.

'As we headed out over the Golden Gate, where the morning
mists drifted seaward like light smoke, we felt that the gods had
smiled on us,' Smithy said. 'Someone had given us a tiny silken
Australian flag. It was only a minute thing, but it was a reminder of
home. We placed it between the petrol gauges where it fluttered
proudly in the morning sun.' The last they were to see of any land
for more than a day and a night was the small cluster of the
Farallon Islands breaking through the carpet of mist. As the humps
of land disappeared astern, a sense of great loneliness descended
upon them. 'We seemed to be leaving the world for a new one of
our own. Before us swept an immensity of silent ocean.'

Cocooned in their separate compartments, out of sight of one
another on either side of the big tank, theirs was a disorientating
world of acute sensory deprivation. The pervasive flood of noise
pounding their eardrums would be considered injurious by today's
standards; indeed, it was gradually to impair Smithy's hearing permanently. 'It seemed to get right into the bones at the sides of the
forehead,' he wrote. All heavy smokers, the crew suffered acute
nicotine withdrawal symptoms. The absence of a toilet added to
the discomfort. They emptied their bladders into lemonade bottles
and poured the contents out into the slipstream. Bowel movements were suspended for the duration in the cockpit, but in the
cabin, where there was more space, Warner resorted to squatting

over a sheet of newspaper which he jettisoned through the sliding cabin window.

Soon the message stick was passing scribbled sentences fore and aft in notes that, before the crew reached Australia, would run to hundreds and one day become collectors' items. The notes paint a vivid picture of the concerns that exercised them all hour by hour as they crawled south-west at 88mph, 1,400ft above the blue North Pacific.[4] The four communicated questions and answers, passed on radio messages, position information and courses to steer, made jokes to relieve the boredom and shared their fears and anxieties. Their handwriting was sometimes reduced to barely decipherable hieroglyphics by turbulence, cold and the vibration of the engines. As they settled down to work as a team, the notes were much preoccupied with the need to establish the aircraft in the centre of a radio beam that pointed them along the Great Circle course to Hawaii. There was no pilot-friendly cockpit indicator to follow: the signals arrived in Warner's headphones, and the heading corrections would go forward on the stick. But 400 miles from the coast they flew out of the beacon's range. Now their only link with the world, since they had no voice transmission, was the torrent of Morse code that flowed to and from the parabolas of their two dangling aerials. 'I remember wondering,' wrote Warner, 'whether anyone was getting my position reports and how long it would take someone to get to us if the motors decided to quit and we were forced to make a wet landing.'

Lyon soon emerged as the crew wit. His messages notifying Smithy of the changing courses to steer were interspersed with jokes and anecdotes. 'I bet a woman a dollar that I was older than she,' he wrote apropos of nothing in particular. 'I won by just four days so she paid the dollar and tore a corner out for luck.' He persuaded Warner to transmit personal messages to his girlfriends around the world. Ulm had strictly forbidden any transmission without his express authority, but he was out of sight in the cockpit and unaware that Lyon's greetings were being surreptitiously dispatched by short-wave: 'Miss Betty Warren, 1528 Sutter Street, San Francisco – Sorry to leave so abruptly. Are now 400 miles out and going strong. All well. Love Harry Lyon.' Lyon's laid-back approach extended to the conduct of his navigation. Instead of filling a logbook with scores of minute-by-minute calculations, he preferred to scribble the arithmetic on small scraps of paper which he would screw up and throw out of the window.

In the first hours, cruising smoothly in bright sunshine low over the sea, the crew were in high spirits. 'We're as happy as Hell, cracking wisecracks ad lib.' Ulm wrote in his flight log. 'Everything 100% perfect this end – how are you lads functioning? Cheer-up – Charles,' ran a note to the Americans. And in a perky radio report to the San Francisco *Examiner* he joked: 'Smithy must be in love. I can't make him eat. He's had only three to my ten sand-wiches to date.' Unfortunately, the message didn't reach the newspaper intact: it arrived as the non-sequitur: 'I must be in love . . . he had three to my ten sandwiches to date.'

The engines hadn't missed a beat. 'So long as they roared in har-mony no Wagnerian chorus could have given us greater pleasure,' recalled Smithy. The weather remained ideal, and from his drift and sextant readings Lyon was confident that they were nicely holding the gentle curve of the Great Circle. With the release of the pre-flight tensions, their inhibitions melted away and a warm camaraderie began to draw them together. The remarkable thing about the flight was that it was largely uneventful. Smithy, whose boredom threshold was low, wrote that their biggest enemy was monotony. Also remarkable was the flow of wireless messages, which, by the sheer volume of information they poured out and the great distances they covered, made aviation history. Across North and Central America, the Orient, South Africa and Australasia, commercial operators and amateurs picked up their talkative dots and dashes, sitting up through the night to follow their progress. One-valve radios were brought into schools throughout Australia so that children could share in the wonder of it all. On the *Oaxaca*, now cruising toward Mexico, Allan Hancock hung about the radio room for the reassuring signals confirming that his investment was intact. When he was not transmitting mes-sages, Warner would screw down his key to produce a continuous whine which told the world they were still in the air somewhere.

So successful were their signals in reaching a worldwide audi-ence that they created a problem for the newspaper and radio groups with whom Ulm had done exclusive deals. They had seri-ously underestimated the level of international interest in the flight. When Warner idly asked a ship what stories were leading the world news he was surprised to hear the reply: 'You are.' Amateur operators in America began to intercept his bulletins and sell them to rival radio stations. The *Examiner*, whose property they were, radioed an angry complaint to the aircraft, accusing the crew of breaking their agreement by supplying the big news agency Associated Press. Ulm sent a curt denial and instructed Warner to put out a warning that amateurs selling their messages would be prosecuted. Almost immediately, however, he had second thoughts about the wisdom of this threat – which could have alienated the keen private operators upon whom they might well depend in an emergency – and had a new, friendlier message sent to all stations.

The venture must rank as quite the best documented of the pioneer flights of the 1920s. In addition to the subsequent memoirs published by each of the crew, and the sheaves of in-flight notes, Lyon's charts have been preserved as artifacts.[5] As well as his reports to the San Francisco *Examiner* and the Sun group in Australia, Ulm, in a brown covered school exercise book, kept an amazingly detailed log in which he conscientiously recorded in pencil their progress and instrument readings, at times literally from minute to minute. Furthermore, an enterprising US Navy radio-operator, Charlie Hodge, a former shipmate of Warner's on the *Omaha*, now in Pearl Harbor in Hawaii, dutifully logged every transmitted word he heard. The navy's radio-operators were then a small, elite community, and they all recognised one another from the individual rhythms of their Morse transmissions. Hodge embellished his log with affectionate comments reflecting his worries for the Fokker's safety and his anxieties whenever the short-wave signals from the *Southern Cross*'s call sign ceased because Warner was talking to ships at close range on his other channel. 'No signals from Jim. Guess he is working steamer,' he would note. Then: 'He is not giving us much news. I suppose he is getting QTE [radio bearing] from sum commercial op.'

From time to time Ulm took over the controls, having acquired an elementary familiarity with them. But if anything had happened to Smithy they would have been in deep trouble. Ulm could not fly safely on instruments in turbulent cloud; couldn't recover from a stall or a spin; he couldn't have been confident of being able to land the Fokker without mishap. As night fell they went up to 4,000ft. The moon came up behind them, illuminating a silver path along the ocean. Their engines spurted vivid blue flames from their exhausts. Lyon measured the aircraft's drift, throwing out calcium carbide flares which, on hitting the sea, ignited into a brilliant white blaze which he observed through the wires of his sight. But, although they were holding their course well, they were anxious to verify their position with a ship. Eventually Warner made contact with a freighter, the *Maliko*, which carried a radio direction-finding loop. It gave them its position and a bearing which showed Lyon that they were some distance north of the Great Circle. To get back on to it they turned and headed for the ship. At 1.50 am the *Maliko*'s lights appeared on the horizon. 'Sighted ship on port bow,' Ulm recorded. 'I flew plane round while Smithy signalled them with searchlight.' Forty minutes later they overflew a second ship, the *Manoa*. Again they circled and signalled and Warner got another precise latitude and longitude. They were 1,600 miles from San Francisco and well over halfway to Hawaii.

At dawn, when they discovered they had picked up a helpful tailwind in the north-east trades and were reaching nearly 100mph, their thoughts turned to their landfall, now less than 400 miles away. Their fate from this point was in the hands of the Americans. As the plane approached the Hawaiian Islands from the north-east, fears began to grow that they might miss them. Lyon was worried that his bubble sextant hadn't been providing accurate sun angles above the true horizon he was accustomed to using at sea. Warner, who appears to have been the most frightened, was so deafened by now that he could no longer hear the signals accurately. To make matters worse, one of the wind-driven generators had broken down early in the flight and the radio batteries for the aircraft's receiver and short-range transmitter were now almost flat.

By 9 am California time they had been in the air for twenty-four hours. Looking ahead over the centre engine, Ulm spotted what looked like a cliff rising out of the sea on their port bow. Excitedly he pointed it out to Smithy. They gripped each other's hands in triumph and relief and dispatched a jubilant message to the cabin. But Lyon greeted the news with consternation. 'In over four years of inter-island trading I felt I knew the islands well,' he wrote. 'It appeared to be a few perpendicular rocks sticking up and no other land in sight. This worried me as I knew of no such rocks. I began to wonder if I had passed the island of Kauai and was off a little island called Kaula to the south and west of Nihau. The sensation of having missed my landfall was sickening.'

These islands were at the extreme western limits of the Hawaiian cluster – 150 miles off their course. Alarmed at the scale of such an error, Lyon feverishly rechecked his calculations, which he was convinced placed them correctly to the north-east of Oahu. Warner, sensing that something was wrong, eyed Lyon nervously. Smithy had turned the aircraft and now flew for twenty minutes toward the rocks they could all now see. 'As we neared them,' wrote Lyon, 'they suddenly came up out of the water and drifted away. They were clouds. The reaction of the crew was peculiar: the other three took it as a great disappointment. I was elated. We changed back to the original course.' Said Warner: 'Several times we thought we sighted land, but it always turned out to be more cloud formations. I thought yet again of the Dole flyers. I wondered if they, too, had become uneasy and started desperately changing course at random.' He thought of the sea, in which he had twice before found himself close to drowning. 'I scribbled a note to Lyon and asked if he was lost.' To Warner's dismay, Lyon seized the note and hurriedly wrote a big 'YES' across it.

Smithy and Ulm were blissfully unaware of the navigation doubts behind them. Warner, however, was so physically gripped by fear that he involuntarily emptied his bowels into his trousers. He gripped the brass key and, with his battery's fading current, sent out the message: 'GUESS WE ARE LOST.'

11

Pacific Conquest

1928

As he had already radioed that they had sighted land, Warner's message caused confusion and shock around the world. Operator Hodge, on the *Omaha*, heard him next say, 'Batteries down can't receive any—'. For twenty-five long minutes there was no further signal from the *Southern Cross*. In Honolulu, where radio stations were interrupting their programmes with newsflashes of the plane's progress, listeners had begun to fear the worst.

Then from the Fokker came a plaintive stream of 'V's. Lyon, his faith in his navigation temporarily shattered, had scribbled a note to Warner pleading for a radio bearing. Although his signals were growing steadily more feeble, Warner received one faint reply reporting that they were bearing 340 degrees from a station whose call sign was so distorted they couldn't identify it. Then, to Hodge's relief, came a reassuring message: 'Land in sight now.' But, five minutes later: 'Thought we had sighted land but guess not. Our batteries down can't receive anything . . . These clouds everywhere we turn . . . We only got one more hour gas now.'

This last dramatic news electrified Warner's listeners. If he was right, and they were more than 90 miles from land, they wouldn't make it. In fact they were still around 180 miles north-east of the islands, but, although they didn't know it, they had a good deal more than an hour's fuel left. At last Warner made out a signal from a powerful shore station at Hilo, over 200 miles south-east of Honolulu on Hawaii Island. The operator said they were bearing 4 degrees east of north from him. Lyon's chart shows the providential bearing line he now ruled northward from Hilo and its interception with his Great Circle dead reckoning course, 176 miles out from Honolulu.

Almost immediately Lyon managed to get a good sun shot which, to his huge relief, gave him a position that coincided with the Hilo bearing. It was a stroke of luck, for the radio batteries finally packed up, and from then on they could only transmit, using the wind generator. Warner did so energetically, pouring out his personal fears. '26 hours and a half in the air – now about time . . . Wonder if you're getting me now. Tell Uncle Sammy to keep them destroyers leased . . . we don't need 'em yet.' Hodge noted approvingly: 'This is sure good. Wish more of the Navy operators could have heard JW say this.' Almost immediately, Warner added pessimistically: 'I mite have swimming exercise yet. About time we were sighting some terra firma. Stay with us.'

For another nerve-wracking hour they cruised round one huge cloud heap after another, peering ahead and watching for the long-overdue landfall that refused to appear. Warner expected to hear the engines beginning to cough at any moment. He sent a note forward to Smithy: 'How about some altitude until we spot the land.' With the Fokker now relieved of most of its fuel, Smithy, at 1,200ft, immediately obliged and cruised up to 4,500ft. Up here there was revealed to the south a most wonderful sight. 'I noticed a long, thin black line over some clouds on the port bow,' Lyon wrote. 'I took a quick map bearing and laid it off on the chart. It was Mauna Kea.'

The 13,800ft volcano on Hawaii Island, mantled in snow, was sitting on the horizon over 100 miles away, exactly where his navigation put it. His course had been immaculate and the landfall they made over an hour later at Oahu was a triumph. The agony of suspense had been created by lighter tailwinds than he had calculated. The tension on board evaporated and a new wave of cheerful notes began to surge fore and aft. 'Damned good work Harry, Old Lion. Keep on doing your stuff – Smithy and Chas.'

'If we get a cigarette and cup of coffee we'll feel like flying back – ha, what, Old Top,' Lyon scribbled back.

Yet Warner's private anguish over the fuel had by no means subsided. Even as they crossed the coast of Oahu he kept the world in suspense – 'It's going to be a race whether we make it to landing or not before fuel is exhausted' – but the motors kept up their hammering beat. As the *Southern Cross* flew over Honolulu, 'bells rang wildly, whistles shrieked and thousands stood in the streets'. The flight had taken twenty-seven hours and twenty-five minutes. Furthermore, as they were to discover when they drained the tanks the next day, there was more than 130 gallons of fuel left – enough for another three and a half hours flying.

As Smithy, red-eyed and unshaven, switched off the engines the sudden silence was disorientating. 'It left us feeling blank and wondering what had happened. The roar was still going on in my head and, as I stepped down, I caught sight of a sea of faces advancing on me from every direction.' There were 15,000 people waiting at Wheeler Field to greet them. As they stepped out of the Fokker they were adorned with mountains of leis and besieged by the media. They were welcomed by the governor of Hawaii but, though they saw his lips moving, they heard not a word of his eulogy, so profoundly deaf had they become. With a siren-wailing police escort, they were whisked, like visiting heads of state, into Honolulu and installed in the Royal Hawaiian Hotel, where they were fussed over, waited upon and endlessly photographed and interviewed. In Sydney 'Kuranda' was inundated by reporters demanding the story of Smithy's life, which was unknown to Australians. William and Catherine were soon talking proudly of his childhood, his years as a choirboy, his war service with the RFC, his narrow escape at Bondi. Catherine spoke of his fear of heights. 'He has always hated standing in exposed places like cliffs and the tops of tall buildings,' she said.

The crew were keen to press on from Hawaii. For the long sector to Fiji they needed a fuel load to sustain around thirty-five hours in the air. They knew that Wheeler Field wasn't big enough for the long, heavy take-off run, and so they flew as they had planned to Kauai, the outer island to the north-west, where Keith Anderson, on a reconnaissance trip the previous year, had located a suitable beach at Barking Sands.

On Sunday 3 June, they were up at 3 am. The *Southern Cross*, bustling with army mechanics, gleamed in the moonlight. Their petrol and oil load this time represented nearly 60 per cent of their all-up weight, now at $7\frac{1}{4}$ tons, precariously close to the Fokker's lifting limits at full power. As he looked at the silent aircraft, Smithy knew that he was about to commit himself to a take-off that could end in a ball of fire – and to a flight which had a strong chance of running out of fuel. The 3,150-mile Fiji hop was around 700 miles longer than the first leg. But they could squeeze into their tanks only another 100 US gallons, just 300 miles' worth of fuel. Today the flight would be regarded as a suicide mission, but their obsessive commitment to their goal was now so total that Smithy was prepared to ignore the stark arithmetic of consumption. A number of people in Hawaii had urged him to abandon the flight, declaring that it was irresponsible, but 'these criticisms had no effect on us whatsoever. Drake and Magellan and Columbus had not been dismayed by doleful predictions.' The islands dotting the Pacific were not then equipped with big concrete runways for emergency diversion, and there was nowhere to land and refuel between Hawaii and Fiji. However, in Honolulu the crew had been shown photographs of two uninhabited atolls, Enderbury and Canton, which lay in the Phoenix group near their intended track. On both there were small beaches on which, if they could not make Fiji, they could probably get down safely, though they would not be able to take off again. Lyon and Warner were nonetheless much reassured.

It was still dark when they boarded and started the engines. Their rations for up to thirty-six hours in the air were forty-eight sandwiches and $4\frac{1}{2}$ litres each of coffee and water. Again they carried no lifejackets or emergency dinghy. A naval-officer friend of Lyon's had given him a rubber dinghy with paddles and inflation bottle. Smithy was horrified. 'He refused to take it. Far too much weight, he said,' Lyon wrote. 'I think he even begrudged the weight of my sextant.'

At 5.20, as dawn began to break, Smithy started his long take-off run. Waddling on its rubber shock-absorbers in the soft sand, the aircraft began sluggishly to gather speed. Smithy knew that the great fuel weight had raised his stalling speed to a point perilously close to his full-power maximum. In the cabin Lyon and Warner sat tensely in their unsecured wicker chairs, holding their breath. 'She ran 3,000ft before leaving the ground – but then settled back again,' Lyon wrote. Warner described three futile attempts to get airborne, in all of which the Fokker rose a few feet only to sag heavily back on to the sand. 'We reached the end of the beach,' he said, 'and it looked like a bad day for the home folks.' According to

Smithy they finally crawled into the air 100ft short of a man who had been stationed at the 3,500ft mark. For several critical moments, as the trimotor staggered out to sea, its wheels were almost in the water. 'We skimmed along the top of the waves for several miles,' said Warner. 'I think Smith "wished" her into the air and held her there by the same method.' It was 25 miles before they managed to climb more than 10ft, Lyon recalled. Then he wrote feelingly to Warner: 'We just barely did get off that ground.'

They flew almost due south at first to intercept the Wheeler Field army radio beacon which had been specially pointed toward Fiji, but they were still so low that, even after 100 miles, Warner couldn't reel out his 400ft aerial to capture the signals for fear that the cable would hit the sea. He asked Smithy to climb. They went up to 500ft where, as they turned on to their west of south heading for Suva and the sun came up, the comforting buzz of the beacon came strongly into Warner's 'phones. 'We all in good spirits,' radioman Hodge on the *Omaha* heard Warner call. The flight had got off to a promising start: they had picked up the north-east trades, which gave them a helpful 10-knot tailwind, pushing them along at well over 100mph in good weather under fluffy lumps of gentle cumulus.

Two and a half hours into the flight they had their first fright: a suspected petrol leak. The drips came steadily from one of the tanks above the cockpit. Terrified of fire, Smithy and Ulm began a frantic dialogue, short-circuiting the notes and instead spelling out words with their fingers on the windscreen. Smithy stood up and tried to trace the source of the leak. He sniffed the fluid, dabbed some on his tongue and Ulm saw him grin and give a thumbs-up. 'Glory be!' said his note. 'It's only water. Cheer up Old Tops.' But the effect of the scare stayed with them for hours afterwards. It was a sobering reminder that they must never weaken and light up a cigarette.

Next the port wind generator packed up again, leaving Warner only one source of power. He could no longer transmit on either short or medium wave and simultaneously keep charging the batteries that kept his receiver alive. Worse, his whole charging circuit had blown. For nearly three hours he knelt on the floor taking his equipment apart, trying to trace the fault. The howl of the engines was so painful it diminished his ability to think the problem through. Before long the batteries totally lost their ability to receive. From that point on, less than four hours into the flight, there is no record that they ever received another message before reaching Fiji, nearly 3,000 miles away. But what was more important was that they retained the facility, with the remaining generator, to transmit. Indeed, for the first time in history it was possible from their diligent position reports to plot reliably an aeroplane's progress, hour by hour, across the globe.

Six hundred miles out of Hawaii, at around midday, they hit the inter-tropical convergence zone, the permanent belt of ferocious rain and towering thundercloud that girdles the earth. Smithy had never before seen anything like it. A huge purple-black mountain of cloud, exploding awesomely with lightning, rose from the sea to heights – nearly 7 miles – which they could not hope to climb over. Nor was there any way round the cloud: the menacing wall hung across their path from one side of the horizon to the other, reaching down in black rain curtains to the wavetops. The phenomenon of this tropical frontal system was not much understood by pilots in the 1920s. To Smithy it was merely a frightening collection of thunderstorms capable of breaking up the fragile Fokker. But he knew that if they didn't get through them they might as well abandon the Pacific flight and return to Hawaii.

At low level they plunged straight into the boiling cloud mass. Flying now entirely on his few elementary instruments, the most sophisticated of which was a primitive turn-and-bank indicator, he struggled to keep the aircraft straight and level, no longer knowing from his own senses whether they were upside down or the right way up. It was, he wrote, 'a nightmare experience'. The aircraft was plucked up and down like a leaf, rolled and bounced about in violent, shuddering convulsions. The noise of the engines merged with the roar of the rain. It was like flying through a giant waterfall. It poured all over Smithy and Ulm through the seams of the windscreen and cascaded in through the open cockpit sides, drenching them from head to foot.

Back in the cabin the Americans were frightened out of their wits. Nothing had prepared them for this horror. Their loose wicker chairs were repeatedly hurled on to the floor as Smithy, trying to avoid the turbulence, made some hair-raising steep turns, flinging the Fokker almost on its side at full power. The manoeuvres slopped the petrol about in the cabin tank and the nauseous fumes had the Americans gagging. Lyon, who had weathered countless fearful storms at sea, but nothing as alarming as this, sent an anxious note forward: 'What the hell's going on?' He got no immediate reply. Smithy and Ulm, who likewise had no safety harness and whose light chairs began to float about the cockpit, were too busy fighting their own battle, wrestling the dual wheels together. The pathetic note, wobbling at the end of the stick, hung there, ignored.

Struggling up to 1,000ft they flew briefly into calm air, but within minutes, in the base of another cumulo-nimbus, the aircraft was flipped almost on to its back. 'It was an unusually difficult and very heavy aeroplane to fly,' said Peter Gibbes, who once piloted the famous trimotor. 'She had to be flown hands-on continuously. Aileron control was particularly sloppy at low speed. It was like doing U-turns in a car. It had this really tiny rudder which required quite mammoth movements on the pedals. In turbulence it was utterly exhausting. I don't think anyone now can conceive of the superbness of Smithy's skills in handling that thing on instruments in rough weather in cloud on that Pacific crossing. Whenever I flew it I used to think of him and marvel at the achievement.' In the blackness of the cloud the starboard engine began to falter. 'It sounded quite menacing,' Smithy said. 'Were the motors going to let us down after the wonderful comradeship they'd shown us since leaving Golden Gate? Our ears had become sensitised to the slightest irregularity . . . Was it only a passing hesitation? But no. It came again, definite and unmistakable. Another splutter and a kick.'

Thoroughly alarmed now Lyon pushed a further agitated note into the cockpit. Warner grabbed the key and rattled out a message to all stations. 'QST QST QST. One motor going bad.' Radio operators around the world waited as the rough running went on for an agonising eight minutes. Smithy searched in vain for the cause. The engine's temperature, pressure and revolutions were showing normal. He concluded that some dirt had got into the fuel line. Suddenly to everyone's relief, the motor resumed smooth running. It was a long time before any of them could breathe normally. The flight had lost all its fun.

Eventually they broke through the main belt of the inter-tropical front and out into clear weather. By 5.30 pm, when they had been in the air for twelve hours, Lyon's dead reckoning showed that they had theoretically flown 1,240 miles and were over a third of the way there. Smithy sent a confident message to Catherine: 'Will be in Suva tomorrow afternoon. All well. Love Chilla.' For several hours they cruised down through humid skies towards the equator, their thoughts on the Phoenix Islands. There the amount of fuel remaining would determine whether the flight would have to end or could continue. But long before they reached that lonely cluster of atolls they flew into another strand, hundreds of miles wide, of the convergence zone, another great black mass sizzling with lightning.

When they hit it at dusk the trimotor nearly flipped upside down. Smithy, fearing they would be destroyed if he pressed on into this latest cauldron, quickly steep-turned out of it and began a long, circling climb to try to struggle through higher up. The ascent took them to 8,000ft, devouring precious fuel and advancing them not a mile on the map. He asked Lyon to set a course to Enderbury Island, where he knew they could land, ending the whole expedition if necessary, at dawn. Lyon's chart shows the new heading which now diverted them about 15 degrees to the east of their Fiji course. The chart is smeared with a large splodge created when his ink bottle overturned in turbulence.

Smithy began the most taxing instrument-flying of the journey so far, trapped within that 'prison of clouds'. The lighting batteries were flat and Ulm had to play a torch on the instrument panel. Every few moments a brilliant white cyclorama of forked lightning would flood the cockpit, giving them brief photo-flash images of each other. They prayed they wouldn't be struck and the petrol explode. Ulm wrote in his log: 'We see a rotten night ahead.'

Around 8 o'clock, they emerged into a starlit sky in which they were cheered to pick out the stars of the Southern Cross beckoning them. At about 11.30 pm Lyon announced that they had crossed the equator. At midnight, he reported that they should be over Enderbury Island. They could not, however, despite intermittent moonlight, see any sign of it. It was decision time. They were 1,900 miles from Hawaii with another 1,200 to go. If they pressed on, their fuel might not get them to Fiji. But the thought of ending his life's dream ignominiously as a castaway on an obscure atoll was too painful for Smithy to contemplate. The discussions at that critical moment appear to have been minimal.

Strangely, Lyon's memoirs abruptly cease at this point, and the accounts of the other three ignore the conference that decided their fate. Warner appears to have sent out no report about their Enderbury crossroads. Whatever the case, the note that Lyon now pushed up on the pole must have encouraged Smithy in his decision: 'Smitty: As per instructions I steered to cut the Phoenix Group. We should be over now. They're very small. However, the course I was steering would take us to Vernon Group [American-owned Swain and other islands about 500 miles south]. Would suggest squaring away for Suva. I've given myself the worst of the argument and it may be less than 1100 [nautical] miles. I know not more. Can we do it?'

Smithy and Ulm held a scribbled fuel discussion, passing a notebook containing their messages to and fro. They agreed that probably around 500 gallons remained. It would be touch and go. There was no margin for climbing over bad weather and they might not have enough to cope with the south-east trade headwinds that lay ahead. But the prize was too great. Even if the fuel wouldn't get them all the way, they reckoned that it might take them to the coast of Vanua Levu, 180 miles north of Suva. Unknown to them, the liner *Sonoma*, en route from San Francisco to Australia, was at that moment passing the Phoenix Islands. The officer of the watch heard the Fokker pass right over the ship, and its radio-operator, intercepting a transmission from Suva to Warner, tried repeatedly to contact him. But he got no reply and soon the sound of the aeroplane had faded away to the south-west.

On board the *Southern Cross* the remaining fifteen hours of the flight became an agony of worry about fuel and their true position. In more storms they lost sight of the stars Lyon needed to get a fix. Turbulence threatened once more to tear their fragile fabric shell apart. Again and again Lyon and Warner were flung on to the floor. Lyon, his handwriting distorted almost into illegibility, and his dead-reckoning calculations upset, sent forward a perturbed note: 'Where the hell are you going? Are you turning back?'

As dawn approached there was a fresh problem: they began, as they dreaded, to be slowed down by the vigorous south-east trades. Their speed over the sea slowly dropped to a worrying 55mph against a powerful 35mph headwind. 'Fuel is alarmingly low,' Ulm logged at 6.05 am. 'Unless the main tank gauge is wrong we cannot make Suva and will have to land in the water. Not so good . . . 6.10 am. Lyon and Warner just sent further notes asking whether fuel will hold out. I wish we could honestly reassure them.' Morale hit a depressing low. Again and again, scribbling on his knee, Smithy reworked the discouraging arithmetic of groundspeed and consumption. He had now convinced himself that, if they continued toward Fiji, they would finish up as flotsam. To Lyon he wrote the first message in which his real concern is evident: 'Harry, can't you get a star position at all? Or can't Jim get a radio bearing. Getting pretty serious if we don't get one in a few hours – Smithy.' But the stars were invisible above cloud and no radio bearings could reach them with their hearing and batteries so attenuated.

Smithy studied the map, trying to find some islands nearer than Fiji to which they could possibly divert. The closest were in the Ellice group – now Tuvalu – which were presently abeam them, about 150 miles to the west. Anxiously he consulted Lyon. 'Some suggestions, Harry. Could you fix a position to guarantee us running for the Ellice group – or too risky? Maybe your noon reading (lat) will show closer to Fiji than we suppose. What about deviating a shade to try and sight one of these little islands around here? My compass reads South 45E [he meant South 45W]. Isn't that too much?' The note ended ominously: 'We have 5 hours gas and are only making about 60 knots against wind.' Shaking his head, Lyon passed the note to Warner, who was later, cynically, to comment: 'That left about 170 miles to swim.' If Smithy was right, they had fuel for only another 300 to 400 miles. The nearest land in Fiji was still over 700 miles away. '7.15 am. Smithy says if forced down will wrap this logbook in waterproof bag and address it to Sydney Sun and San Francisco Examiner,' Ulm logged bleakly.

When, around dawn, they hand-pumped up the last of their fuel from the cabin tank, they were relieved to discover they had more than they thought – certainly enough to reach the Fijian coast. 'Whoops of joy on board,' Ulm noted. To Lyon he wrote: 'If you can find the shortest way we can easily make it, Harry, my darling, lead and I shall follow. Find that Bloody Suva and Smitty will land this buzz wagon – Chas.' When the sun came up, Warner said in his memoirs, 'we just congratulated ourselves upon still being aloft'. Lyon sent up to Ulm: 'Chas, when Jim Warner and I get back to U.S. we sure are going to try and have Smitty made President.'

During the last hours of the flight their main worry was finding the Fiji Islands. The 3,000-mile journey had been made without sight of any land to confirm their dead reckoning and celestial navigation and without a single radio bearing from shore or ship. The constant detours from their course during the night had played havoc with Lyon's navigation. When he was able to get a shot of the sun that morning, he found, his chart shows, that they were around 120 miles west of their Hawaii–Fiji course. Instead of approaching the islands correctly from the north-north-east, they had finished up due north. Nonetheless, flying in low over the brilliant blue sea, there was a feeling of new confidence on board that the conquest of the Pacific was in their grasp. Warner slid open the window and poked his head into the slipstream to freshen up. He was surprised to find that it appeared to be raining. He scribbled to Lyon and pointed to the window. 'Warm rain,' the navigator read. But Lyon suspected there was another explanation. Squinting through the portside gap between the fuel tank and the side of the fuselage, at the end of which the pilot was visible, he saw immediately what he was expecting. He took Warner's note and, crossing out his words, scrawled, 'No – Smithy!' Kingsford Smith had been emptying into the slipstream from his lemonade bottle the contents of his bladder.

'Shortly afterwards there was a moment of further embarrassment for Warner, Harry told me,' related Lyon's cousin, William Hunt. 'Caught short, he had laid out some newspaper on the floor and was squatting, doing his business, when, most unfortunately, they hit some turbulence. Because of the heat Jim had earlier stripped off most of his clothes and was now wearing only his BVDs – a singlet-and-pants combination. The plane lifted and dropped very violently, hoisting him and his newspaper into mid-air, with particularly unpleasant consequences for the BVDs – and his trousers. He was forced to discard them.'

The last hours were the longest. As the south-east trades strengthened, depressing their groundspeed still further, their pessimism returned. The world was alarmed to hear, soon after 9 o'clock: 'Now about 500 miles north of the Fiji Islands. Have about five hours' gas left. We may be able to make Suva, but doubtful.' Ten minutes later Hodge, in Hawaii, heard Warner desperately pleading for a bearing. But if anyone tried to send one he didn't hear it. To Hodge's concern, there was now an unusual silence from the Fokker which lasted for all of a nail-biting hour. Fears grew that the *Southern Cross* had gone into the sea. But then, to his relief, Warner came back on the air to say that they were only 180 miles north of Cape Udu on Vanua Levu.

They sighted land at 1.10 pm Hawaiian time. It was the northern coast of Vanua Levu. 'We were on the verge of triumph,' wrote Ulm. 'It was a dramatic moment.' It was also a staggering feat of navigation by Harry Lyon. With the aid of his marine sextant, elementary drift sight, simple magnetic compasses and nautical charts, some of 1903 vintage, he had, despite hours spent in cloud out of sight of sea and sun, delivered them, for a very modest fee, to the Fiji Islands.[1]

Over myriad green islands and sparkling white beaches they swept low. In those moments of elation Ulm passed Smithy a note: 'The rest is easy. It's hard to realise it's over and that, at the moment, we are exceedingly famous.' A few minutes later he added a significant footnote: 'I've nearly changed my views re taking Jim on to Aussie with us. Remind me to talk with you re this.'

Arriving over Suva early that afternoon, Tuesday 5 June 1928, Smithy was horrified by the diminutive reality of the town's only landing area – a small sports ground, Albert Park. Not only was it too small, but it was surrounded on at least three sides by higher ground. The landing he eventually made was to become one of the most applauded feats of his legend. Much less known were the steps he took to try to find somewhere else to come down. 'Smithy was so aghast at the sight of that pocket handkerchief, Harry told me, that he decided to fly off and look at some of the nearby beaches,' said William Hunt. 'They flew over several that looked OK, but he was worried the sand might be too soft. As his fuel was almost finished, he had to make a swift decision. He decided to have a shot at the park, knowing that he might well be forced to abort, in which event he'd decided to put down in the sea.' To deal with this contingency the government ship *Pioneer* was standing by.

Two things worried him. He wanted to be sure that Harry and Jim could swim, and he wanted – for the park or the sea – to approach by dragging her in, in the slowest possible tail-down attitude. So he sent a note through telling them to undress and climb back as far along the inside of the fuselage as they could get. Harry stripped down to his one-piece underclothes – Jim, of course, was already naked. Getting back to the rear of the fuselage wasn't as easy as it might sound. There was only a few feet of solid wooden floor around the radio–navigation area. Aft of that the fuselage was just a skeleton of thin steel tubes and diagonal bracing wires encased in fabric. Scrambling through these obstacles, they could easily slip and fall, bursting right out into space through the bottom fabric. Well, they eventually squeezed their way back, both stone deaf, exhausted out of their minds, unable to see anything outside and frightened as hell. It must have seemed like a bad dream, not knowing whether they were going to finish up in a pile of wreckage on land or underneath the sea.

To mark the historic event the British colonial governor, Sir Eyre Hutson, had declared a public holiday. A large crowd of whites, Fijians and Indians who had poured into Suva from the villages and plantations were held back by soldiers in khaki shorts and pith helmets as the plane touched down and careered towards a jungle-covered bank less than 200yds away. But as people gasped and shouted, the plane suddenly performed a spectacular manoeuvre: Smithy swung hard left in a dramatic ground loop that miraculously spun round a tree, passing narrowly between this and another tree. The starboard wing barely missed the palms on the edge of the field. William Hunt said:

The wheels hit some soft ground and she began to tilt on her nose. Harry and Jim, huddled in the back, hanging on to bracing wires and trying to keep their weight off the fabric, felt the tail rise. It teetered for a moment, then fell back hard. As it dropped, poor Jim was knocked off his perch and crashed right through the fabric on to the ground. He hit his head and was knocked out cold.

I suppose he was lucky the tail skid didn't run over him, because Smithy couldn't see what had happened and taxied away, leaving him there unconscious without a stitch on. According to Harry, as he began to come to, he was rescued from his embarrassment by a uniformed British nurse. She ran out from the crowd, took off her cape and wrapped it round his nakedness while she rendered first aid.

The *Southern Cross* had flown the 3,150 miles from Hawaii in thirty-four hours thirty minutes. Of the 1,300 US gallons of fuel they had set out with, there were 85 gallons left – much more than they had believed. 'We looked on our air conquest of the Pacific as being complete,' Smithy wrote. 'As I stepped out to face the crowd I had a feeling of exaltation, a sense of accomplishment. The *Southern Cross* had made the longest non-stop ocean flight on record.'[2]

Once again they were all stubbled, dazed and deaf. Warner, now conscious and dressed, rejoined them. Smithy looked at his colleagues. 'Lyon's eyes were sunk in his head. Warner looked pale and cadaverous. His eyes were half closed. Ulm looked at the point of exhaustion, weary in body and mind.' They had no idea who the people were who had come to greet them with smiles and hand-clasps. 'A man approached me and held out his hand,' Smithy said. He learned later that the man had said, 'I congratulate you. Will you all lunch with me tomorrow?'

'"Yes, isn't it," I replied. He brought his face closer to mine and said something. "Excuse me," I said, "I didn't catch your name."' The man was Governor Hutson. Lyon kept saying apologetically to everyone in turn: 'Excuse our appearance, sir.'

News of the epic flight's success had quickly been cabled around the world. Everywhere it seized the imagination of media and public alike. In California the newspapers rushed out special editions; it was the lead story all over Australia and prominently featured in London. Overnight Kingsford Smith had become an international hero. The brilliance of his achievement had also drawn much attention to the contribution of the Americans. Under the terms of their contracts, however, they were now expected to catch the first ship back to America and simply fade gracefully away. Ulm had insisted that if they were to arrive in Australia victorious, it must be an Australian triumph, its financial rewards undiluted by American involvement. Grateful as he was for their contribution, he wanted Lyon and Warner paid off, although, from his note to Smithy as they approached Fiji, it

would seem that he had begun to have some reservations about
the wisdom of parting with Warner. He may have seen the radio-
operator as more valuable than Lyon on the final sector for his
ability to keep the flight, hour by hour, on the world's front pages.
Lyon, with his slightly bumptious charm, certainly represented a
bigger threat through his tendency to draw the media spotlight
away from the Australians.

But Ulm hadn't bargained with public opinion. Back in
Australia there was already dismay at the decision not to bring the
Americans on to Brisbane. Sydney newspapers started to point
out the unfairness of it; questions were asked in Parliament in
Canberra. At least one MP wrote to the prime minister. And,
according to Jim Warner, William Kingsford Smith, who had been
deeply upset by his son's readiness to dump Keith Anderson the
previous year, sent a private cable to Chilla in Suva. 'It said, in
effect,' Warner's son Tom recalled, '"Unless you bring the
Americans don't bother coming on to Australia."' Most unfortunately of all, rumours of a rift in the now-famous team began to
appear in American newspapers.[3]

Reporters in Suva, where the Americans, with their approachability and natural charm, had proved instantly popular, took a
lively interest in their fate. Smithy and Ulm were compelled to
accept that they had a delicate diplomatic situation on their hands.
When the four got around to discussing it in private, on their
second night in Suva, it was, Lyon told William Hunt, not an ideal
moment. It had been a taxing day. There had been a relentless
round of hard-drinking social activity in their honour: lunch with
the governor, a civic reception, two cocktail parties, a ceremonial
welcome by Fijian chiefs and a mayoral ball. Reeling away from
the ball around midnight, they arrived back at the hotel distinctly
the worse for wear.

'Ulm, despite the public pressure, was still implacably opposed
to their going any further,' said Hunt.

He hoped they would disappear, as originally intended, on
the *Aorangi*, due to sail in forty-eight hours' time. Smithy
apparently didn't feel so strongly. He believed Harry and
Jim deserved to share in the acclaim. Ulm came up with the
proposal that the Americans should follow them to Australia

by sea. This of course meant, as Ulm intended, that they would arrive when all the initial adulation had subsided. Anyway, it was at this point that Harry told me he saw red. Harry got up, put his elbow against Ulm's chest and slammed him against the wall in sheer rage. He was just about to follow this up with a hard punch when Smithy intervened. He told Harry to cool it and made it clear to Ulm that he wanted the Americans to fly on with them. Ulm had to climb down. He said he'd have a new contract drawn up. But I don't believe that, privately, he ever forgave Harry for threatening him that night.

The confrontation with Ulm was, of course, rooted in more than a sense of injustice that they were being dropped in Suva. After all, that was the original deal they signed. It was equally the fact that Harry was used to commanding his own ship and giving the orders. With Ulm he felt that he had considerably subordinated himself to someone who was quite unused to authority and the niceties of leadership. It was Ulm's autocratic style that finally got to him.

Lyon also resented what he saw as Ulm's inconsistency. In public, the Australian was now at pains to sing the praises of the hired crewmen. At the civic reception that afternoon, while Smithy was inspecting a possible take-off site at Naselai Beach, Ulm had made an emotional speech to the top strata of Fijian society. 'I am telling you on behalf of myself and Smithy that we would have been cold meat but for the aid of our two American friends,' he had declared amid loud applause. Lyon and Warner had listened to this eulogy, cabled round the world, with cynicism.

As Smithy was not in the least interested in the legal straitjacket his partner now proposed, he left it to Ulm to seek out next morning a Suva solicitor to draft a new agreement. The result was a quite intimidating document which went to inordinate lengths to ensure that Lyon and Warner should not benefit in any way from the rewards of the flight if it succeeded in reaching Australia. 'It was done,' said Hunt, 'with what Harry regarded as exquisite Teutonic thoroughness.' In a preamble the document declared that 'the owners' had 'incurred a personal liability of upwards of $50,000' to mount a Pacific flight 'in the interests of aviation and for the promotion of amity and communication between the United States of America and the Commonwealth of Australia'. It stated that Lyon had already been paid $1,767 and Warner, for some reason, $500 less – $1,267. These payments terminated all the 'owners'' current obligations. Under the new deal, 'to foster good feeling between USA and Australia', the Americans were invited to 'proceed to Brisbane, but not further . . . as an act of sportsmanship'. On arrival in Brisbane Lyon and Warner would each be paid 'as an act of grace' a further £100 (then around US$500).

For the Americans the agreement's harshest conditions were those excluding them from the tiniest morsel of the fruits of success: 'And so far as they the said Lyon and Warner may be deemed to be entitled to any interest, claim, or share in any sum or sums payable or paid by any government, corporation, or person, to the crew of the "Southern Cross", or any of them, in respect of the said flight, they hereby assign and transfer, release and surrender to the owners any such interest, claim or share . . .' As if this wasn't disheartening enough, the document concluded with what, in the circumstances, the Americans viewed as some quite extraordinarily tactless sentiments: 'The said Lyon and Warner hereby record their appreciation of the generous performance of the owners . . . and of the owners' sportsmanlike act in inviting them to proceed in the "Southern Cross" to Brisbane.'

'Yes, we signed it,' Warner wrote in his memoirs. 'You know the saying, "when in Rome" . . . well, when in the company of sportsmen, reward true munificence by a like gesture; in other words, act like a sport.'

The spiritual end to the flight was, of course, Sydney. It was Smithy's and Ulm's home; it was Australia's most significant city. It was where they were determined to mark their triumph the following Saturday evening with a private celebration dinner. It would also, without any doubt, be the place where, for the conquering aviators, the fervour of the welcome and the scale of the accolades would be greatest. Ulm did not believe that the Americans' contribution, compared with the heartbreak and hardship of organising and funding the flight, merited their participation in the inevitable welter of public hero-worship.

Warner had taken into adult life the insecurity that had plagued his early years. Although he was inwardly seething, he was glad to be allowed to go on to Australia, even if it was only to Brisbane, and he didn't challenge the conditions. 'They were just hired hands,' said Tom Warner. 'From years in the navy he'd got used to doing what he was told. I don't think at the time, though, he fully realised what he was denying himself. As things were to turn out, that agreement cost him a small fortune.'

Indeed, the rewards had already begun to arrive in Fiji. They were showered with gifts, including a fine tortoiseshell casket with £200 in gold sovereigns raised in a local collection. The community intended the money to benefit the four of them, but Smithy and Ulm shared it between themselves. 'I don't think Harry actually cared all that much,' William Hunt said. 'He wasn't really out for the money. Yes, he badly wanted to go on to Australia, but all he looked for was recognition, professionally, for the navigation achievement.' To counter their critics in Australia, Ulm issued a brisk press statement in Suva, in Kingsford Smith's name, to announce magnanimously that the Americans would be flying on to Brisbane. Still people wondered why Lyon and Warner should be dropped off there, particularly given the more frequent sailings back to the States from Sydney.

Smithy flew the *Southern Cross* from Albert Park to Naselai Beach, where they fuelled and eventually took off on Friday 8 June 1928. They hoped to complete the final 1,700-mile leg to Brisbane, the shortest of the three hops, in less than twenty hours, for which they didn't need a full fuel load. As the Fokker flew low over Suva and headed, in a brilliant blue tropical sky, out to sea, they were intoxicated with excitement. The difficult flying and navigation was, they thought, behind them, and they were on the home stretch. In this atmosphere of euphoria Ulm decided that the moment had arrived for their patron saint, despite his desire to remain anonymous, to be publicly named and thanked. 'Now we are sure of success,' he radioed, 'we wish to announce to the world that we could not have made this flight without the generosity and wonderful help of Captain G. Allan Hancock, of Los Angeles. Details cannot be given here. We take this opportunity of publicly thanking him in the most modern way, by radio, in the first aeroplane to cross the Pacific.' When the message reached the reticent millionaire, still cruising off the Mexican coast aboard the *Oaxaca*, he was upset and embarrassed. But it was too late. His patronage was quickly seized upon by the Californian newspapers and he was forced to plan a public announcement to explain his benevolence.

On board the *Southern Cross*, thundering towards Australia, the jaunty mood did not last long. Soon after night fell, they flew headlong into the biggest and fiercest electrical storm they had encountered since leaving America. If they had been badly frightened by the violence of the inter-tropical front, this one, boiling across their course between Fiji and New Caledonia, proved a much more horrifying experience. Lacking the power to climb over this towering inferno of cumulo-nimbus which reached down to the waves, Smithy plunged them straight into it at low level. But for his blind-flying training back in California the trimotor would have finished up in the sea that night. They were forced up to the bitter cold of 9,000ft. Smithy and Ulm struggled into their flying suits but they were soon drenched by the rain. The turbulence was ferocious. The Fokker, according to their altimeter, was being sucked up and down in switchbacking surges of up to 400ft at a time amid continuous explosions of alarmingly close lightning.

As the aircraft twitched and shuddered, rolled and pitched, Smithy and Ulm, clinging to their control wheels, were repeatedly flung out of their seats. The wicker chairs toppled as fast as they righted them and they found themselves 'sitting in the air grabbing wildly'. Back in the cabin, Lyon and Warner were subject to G-forces that rendered them semi-weightless. They too were pitched off their chairs and Lyon several times found himself entangled in bracing wires on the ceiling. 'Harry told me that during the turbulence he seriously expected the wing would collapse,' recalled William Hunt.

So that the world would at least know they were still airborne, Warner screwed down his key and sent out a continuous high-pitched note which had Charlie Hodge at Pearl Harbor worried. Now surrounded in the *Omaha*'s radio room by a large group of the ship's company who were following the historic flight, Hodge monitored the rapidly changing note of the signal as the generator speed see-sawed with the turbulence. 'Call shrieked with violent pitch,' he wrote. 'I think plane has evidently plunged downward through storm. They seem to be in very bumpy air. We want news bad.'

The ordeal lasted for five hours, from 7 pm until around midnight. It was impossible for Lyon to navigate. He did not see the lights of Noumea, which had been left on all night for them on the instructions of New Caledonia's governor. Weaving, circling, corkscrewing in cloud, they were now miles off course. They had not the least idea where they were within 100 miles. Lyon sent a note of encouragement forward: 'Keep up the old courage and you will get us through.' Just keeping the aeroplane in the air was their only concern as fears grew that the water-drenched magnetos would fail.

In the early hours of Saturday 9 June they emerged from the storm exhausted, bruised and shivering with cold. From Smithy came a note: 'If anybody hereafter suggests to me that I go practise blind flying, I'm going to caress them gently on the skull with a pisspot.' But his bravado masked emotions that on this occasion he chose not to record. Reluctantly, Warner now had to broadcast: 'Exact position unknown.' Lyon's charts show that they were heading for a point on the Australian coast roughly halfway between Brisbane and Sydney, a long way south of their intended track. Warner tried to get a radio bearing from Brisbane, but the port generator had failed again and his batteries were too low for reception.

When land failed to appear, Lyon decided, after taking a sun shot, that it was time to alter course from south-west to due west. At around 8 am Australian time, a long, grey shadow began to rise over the horizon. 'We felt disposed to yell . . . we nudged each other in the ribs, all smiles.' Again Smithy and Ulm reached across and shook hands. In the cabin Lyon and Warner did the same. As the brown coastal cliffs loomed up, they didn't at first recognise their landfall. Circling the town which today boasts a monument commemorating their historic mistake, Smithy identified it as Ballina in northern New South Wales. They were 110 miles south of Brisbane.

As they flew up the coast, their hearts singing, a squad of welcoming biplanes came south to meet them. Circling Eagle Farm, they were amazed to see a stream of cars converging on the aerodrome and a large crowd waiting behind barriers. They were not aware that millions of people across the country had been anxiously listening to their progress on radio all night. Many Australians had eaten breakfast that morning with crystal-set headphones clamped on their heads. Thousands had been late for work. Catherine and William had refused to go to bed, sitting glued to their radio until dawn brought reassuring news. 'Very anxious time,' Catherine wrote. 'Boys flying through storms last night. Wireless going all hours. All feeling fagged.' Through the night the phone had rung incessantly with calls from newspapers and radio stations, friends and relatives.

Fifteen thousand people poured out of Brisbane to meet them, many of whom had been waiting patiently in frost since 3 am. Shortly before 10.15 the *Southern Cross* made its historic landing. Although the flight had taken eight and a half days, they had covered the 7,200 miles from San Francisco in eighty-three hours and fifty minutes.[4] Smithy had been at the controls for over fifty of those hours and Ulm for more than thirty. As 'the giant Fokker monoplane' circled twice before making a perfect touchdown, an orchestra of car horns rent the air and the crowd, shouting and cheering, broke the barriers and began to swarm across the field. A contingent of mounted police galloped out to head them off and a uniformed inspector, afraid that someone would be decapitated by the propellers, shouted what were to become the immortal words: 'Get back. Get back. This is no ordinary aeroplane.'

Slowly, the trimotor, with Smithy's grinning, helmeted face peering out from the open cockpit side, taxied up to the barricade where the state governor and premier waited with a large body of ministers and senior government officials. Smithy and Ulm, in their soggy flying suits, squeezed stiffly out. Smithy's first words were, 'Hello Aussies – my kingdom for a smoke.' A young woman ran up, thrust a garland of red and white roses round his neck and kissed him on the cheek. He was quickly grabbed by other women calling, 'Kingy, you darling,' as they smothered him with kisses. Men fought to shake his hand, saying repeatedly, 'Good old Aussie.' For Charles Kingsford Smith it was the start of an era of pop-idol fame.

People were shouting, 'Where are the Yanks, Smithy?' Someone opened the cabin door. To their amazement there was nobody inside. Harry Lyon and Jim Warner, the co-heroes of the Pacific, had vanished into thin air.

12

Triumph and Conflict
1928

The extraordinary events surrounding the arrival of Harry Lyon and Jim Warner in Brisbane were not reported by the Australian newspapers; nor were they mentioned in their memoirs by either Smithy or Ulm. In the 1920s, the press was less inquisitive than it is today, and there was a reluctance to play up indelicate things that might tarnish the image of famous men. Amazingly, by today's reporting standards, the journalists who flocked to Eagle Farm that winter morning described the epic moment as if the Americans had in fact emerged from the cabin in front of the phalanx of dignitaries. One reporter wrote how, when the aircraft stopped, Lyon 'pushed his head out of the window, grabbed a felt hat and swung himself down the ladder'. In reality Lyon, at this moment, was nowhere near the aeroplane. It seems that he and Warner had got out at the end of the landing run in the middle of the airfield, and, by the time Smithy and Ulm had climbed out, they were walking purposefully away from the crowd, hoping they wouldn't be noticed. 'Lyon and I climbed out as soon as the plane came to a standstill,' Warner wrote, 'it being our intention to make our way unobserved to the train for Sydney.'

However, they were spotted by the eagle eye of the Sydney *Daily Guardian*'s air correspondent, Norman Ellison, known, for his prominently large nose, as 'Cocky', short for cockatoo. Before his very eyes, this major aviation story had acquired a bizarre twist. Why were the Americans who had just helped to make history hurrying away from their tumultuous welcome? Ellison broke into a run and headed them off. 'The chunky chap,' he recalled, 'fumbled with a handkerchief, took out a denture, slewed it into his mouth, and said, "I'm Harry Lyon, and this is Jim Warner." After handshakes, I asked, "Why did you leave the plane? And where are you going?" Lyon said this was an Australian welcome for the two Australians. He and Warner were keeping out of it. I managed to convince them they were wrong – that they, too, were being welcomed. They, too, were to be guests of honour at the official enclosure.' In their navy-blue suits and brightly coloured bow-ties they contrasted so curiously with Smithy and Ulm, in oil-stained overalls, that at first the crowd took the Americans for welcoming officials. But once they were recognised, people swarmed around them. They were snatched bodily from Ellison and, in a seething wave of humanity, swept towards the enclosure.

Although the newspapers diplomatically chose to gloss over the incident – Warner 'was the last to descend', said the Brisbane *Courier* with helpful tact next day – evidence of it was captured for the record by a photographer from the city's *Sunday Mail*. In his front-page picture two lonely figures, too small to be identified, can be seen walking across the airfield some distance behind the *Southern Cross*. Did the negative still exist, I wondered? In the *Sunday Mail*'s picture library the staff obligingly located it for me. Sixty-five years later it was still in good condition. Skilfully they enlarged the fuzzy shapes of the two men who occupied only a few millimetres of the shot. The portly figure, hairstyle and head of Harry Lyon are unmistakable, and the slightly taller Warner can be instantly identified by the high-crowned panama hat that was to become his trademark in Australia.

Was an arrangement made in Fiji, or on board the aircraft as it approached Australia, that the Americans would discreetly fade away in the middle of the airfield immediately after touchdown? None of the surviving notes from the final leg provides the smallest clue to such an understanding. Yet Smithy must have known, for instead of keeping the Fokker rolling once he was on the ground, he brought it briefly to an unnecessary full stop before starting to taxi.

Unwillingly drawn into the welcoming frenzy, Lyon and Warner were hoisted shoulder-high amid the cheers of the crowd as hats were hurled into the air. 'The Americans modestly tried to efface themselves while Kingsford Smith and Mr Ulm were being lionised,' one reporter wrote. 'Captain Lyon, as happy as a school-boy, cracked jokes and shook hands with the crowd, saying, "It's just like Lindbergh's reception in Paris."' In contrast Warner said little. Yet people specially wanted to see the man whose messages had led the news for days. As he was carried towards Queensland's premier, Mr McCormack, one of his bearers shouted, 'Have a look at him. He's the boy that worked the keys.'

The flimsy wooden railings marking the official enclosure eventually collapsed as the police lost control. Cameras were knocked out of the arms of press photographers. Lyon and Warner joined Smithy and Ulm in an open tourer, in which they were driven, waving, round the aerodrome. Six policemen stood on the running boards to fend off boarders. A procession of raucously honking cars, several miles long, followed them along what is now Kingsford Smith Drive, passing, in the suburb of Hamilton, Riverview Terrace, where Smithy was born. Along the route people rushed into the roadway to cheer them. As the convoy, now joined by a squad of mounted police, slowed down in the central city, traffic was brought to a halt. Hundreds leaned out of office windows, squeezed on to balconies and hurried to the tops of buildings.

At Brisbane Town Hall, Smithy and Ulm, still in their sodden, greasy flying suits, stood with Lyon and Warner listening to endless speeches and tributes. 'Four brave men have completed one of the most amazing feats in history,' said Premier McCormack. 'It has done something very material, I believe, to bring closer together the English-speaking peoples upon whom, after all, civilisation depends.' Six hundred miles away in Canberra, the federal Parliament had decided to award a government grant of £5,000 – today worth over £100,000 – to the aviators. The message from the Australian prime minister, Stanley Bruce, 'to you and your gallant comrades', was greeted by Smithy and Ulm with surprise and joy. It was clear that the money was intended to be shared among them all. 'We are grateful,' it said, 'that in this achievement you have been associated with two citizens of our great sister democracy beyond the Pacific. I ask you and your companions to accept a cheque of five thousand pounds in recognition of your epoch-making flight.'

When Smithy rose to speak he brought a wave of laughter with the joke that was to become his opening favourite: 'The only difference between a parrot and an aviator is that the parrot can talk but cannot fly, whilst we can fly but cannot talk.' In serious vein he said: 'This is a very big moment in our lives. It is the fulfilment of my life's greatest ambition.' Conscious that the adulation was again sharply focused on him, he told the audience: 'Mr Ulm is an equal co-leader in this expedition with me. We are very much overcome with emotion for the magnificent reception and the munificent donation by the government. This is a very wonderful thing indeed.' Lyon and Warner listened in silence as Smithy went on: 'We are particularly delighted and honoured to have our two Yankee friends come through with us . . . The flight was not an individual thing. It was the magnificent co-operation between four people who understood each other and worked together for the common good.'

The Americans, who had not been slow to work out that £5,000 was around $US25,000 dollars, wondered whether the prime minister's intention that they should all share the reward would be honoured. When, later, Warner diffidently raised the matter with Ulm, he was firmly reminded of the Suva agreement he had signed.

Ulm's grip on the whole venture was now almost total. Smithy, who normally found it easier to say yes than no, seems to have been prepared to allow his partner the autocratic control he was increasingly exercising. The Australian newspapers were beginning to compare their opposite personalities. 'Kingsford Smith, the most outstanding figure of the party, is the typical Australian pictured by the novelist,' wrote a *Courier* reporter after meeting them both at Lennon's Hotel.

A powerful, lean frame, thin face and jutting jaw burnt brick red. He has an easy frankness of manner and a refreshing dry humour. Mr C. T. P. Ulm is the businessman of the party with a brusque, direct manner and he speaks with the curt rapidity of the machine gun. A suggestion that Captain Kingsford Smith should issue a message of greeting to the people of Queensland, to which the pilot showed signs of compliance, was instantly vetoed by Mr Ulm who vouchsafed the information that the fliers were bound by newspaper contracts not to divulge any information concerning their flight.

During these first heady hours of the crew's veneration, the immediate fate of the Americans had not been resolved. It seems that Ulm hoped they would somehow quietly fade away. The next ship back to San Francisco was due to sail from Sydney, and the Americans intended to travel there unobtrusively by train, leaving Smithy and Ulm to fly down for what promised to be a spectacular reception. But they had reckoned without the sharp news instincts of Norman Ellison.

Late that afternoon, bumping into Lyon in the hotel lounge, Ellison was amazed to be told that he and Warner would not be flying on to Sydney. 'It didn't make sense, I said, for the really big national welcome would be in Sydney, and the two Americans just had to be there . . . But Lyon cut in. Their contract ended in Brisbane, he said. Besides, he admitted, at Suva he had been drunk. He had blotted his copybook.' Lyon told Ellison of his confrontation with Ulm, and said that, as a result, the Australian was emphatic that he and Warner must leave the flight as soon as they got to Brisbane.

Ellison, who would probably not have wished to have struck a discordant note by reporting the strange circumstances in which the Americans had left the *Southern Cross*, knew that this time he had walked into a sensational story. The *Guardian* was less squeamish than its rivals about stirring up conflict, and a rift in the ranks of the Pacific crew was a front-page lead. Furthermore, it would confound the *Guardian*'s Sun Group competitors, who enjoyed exclusive rights to Ulm's dispatches, which were going out of their way to convey the impression of a bunch of warmly united buddies. What was more, Sydney's leading hotel, the Australia, had publicly announced that it wanted the Americans to stay there as its guests. As soon as he could, Ellison excused himself and hurried off in search of the aero-club official who had been appointed Smithy's and Ulm's minder.

I said to him that I wanted to see them both on an urgent matter. Couldn't be done. They were getting ready for the official dinner. Then, I said, would he put these questions to

them: were Lyon and Warner going on in the *Southern Cross*
to Sydney? If not, why? Also, would he tell Smithy and Ulm
that if the Americans were out, the *Guardian* would charter
a plane and fly them to Sydney to arrive at the same time as
the *Southern Cross*? I would wait half an hour, I said, and
then, if I couldn't get the interview, I would phone through
to Sydney my interview with Lyon and then charter the
plane. Incidentally, I wasn't empowered to undertake this,
but I felt sure the *Guardian* would have approved.

Ten minutes later, several other reporters by now having
arrived, the secretary came back to the lounge. He
announced that Smithy and Ulm would like the press to
come to their room. There Ulm was the spokesman. He said
there seemed to be a story around that the two Americans
were being left in Brisbane. Not so, he declared. They were
coming on to Sydney in the *Southern Cross*.

For the second time in three days Ulm had been forced to
accept that Australia was not going to allow the Americans to disappear. Had the *Guardian* flown them separately into Sydney, as
Ellison would most certainly have done, the colossal fame that
was now his and Smithy's would have been for ever soured in the
history books. Moreover, the need for some demonstration that the
Americans weren't regarded as second-class members of the team
acquired even greater urgency with the news of the involvement
of another of their countrymen in the triumph. When the *Oaxaca*
finally got back to Los Angeles, on the day of the trimotor's arrival
in Brisbane, Allan Hancock called a press conference on board. Not
only did he confirm that he had funded the flight, he announced
that he wished to make a gift of the *Southern Cross* to Smithy and
Ulm, as well as writing off the large sums he had laid out in loans
and in settlement of their enormous debts. The total value of the
package was probably of the order of US$50,000, then around
£10,000. Its present-day equivalent would be close to £250,000.[1]
Hancock told reporters: 'Give me no credit for the successful
flight. I merely saw an opportunity to advance the science of navigation in the air. Aeronautics have been advanced many years by
their success.'

The fairytale of the penniless Australian aviators and the

American millionaire was cabled round the world, and the Kingsford Smith legend had well and truly begun. In London *The Times* said, 'A new and glorious mark has been cut in the record of aerial achievement.' The Paris newspapers were ecstatic; one described the flight as a tour de force of navigation by which Atlantic flights paled into insignificance. The San Francisco *Examiner* commented: 'Captain Kingsford Smith came from obscurity to become the aerial Columbus of the Pacific.' In Australia the newspapers were calling them the 'kings of the air'. Ulm's flight logs, now published in full by Sun Newspapers, were being likened to the diary of Scott of the Antarctic.

Their arrival in Sydney still ranks as one of the most memorable events in the city's history. It is difficult today to envisage the surge of humanity that poured out to the small, muddy cow paddock surrounded by Chinese market gardens at Mascot on the afternoon of Sunday 10 June 1928. Two hundred thousand people,[2] probably the greatest crowd of airport-greeters in history, arrived by tram, car, horse and cart, bicycle and on foot, dressed in their Sunday best – some men even wore morning suits and top hats. They came to see the aeroplane that had done the impossible, but there was little doubt that they came principally to see the man who was now the talk of Australia. As the trimotor flew in over Sydney, escorted by welcoming aircraft; as ferries whooped and factory sirens wailed, Smithy and Ulm could not, in their wildest moments, have imagined the extent of the pride and patriotism their flight had unleashed among ordinary people across the country. The tops of buildings were clustered with people. The roads leading south to Mascot were jammed with columns of traffic. The pilot of one of the Moths now in proud formation around the Fokker waved to Smithy. Although he didn't know it, it was Keith Anderson.

On the official dais at Mascot was gathered a contingent of the high and the mighty. Also there were the diminutive figures of William, with his white beard, and Catherine, in a fur-collared coat and cloche hat. It was all becoming a huge strain on them both. 'Not feeling well,' Catherine had written the previous day. 'Boys got doctor to come in evening and give us sedatives and stimulants ready for tomorrow.' Drawing deeply on his first cigarette, Smithy brushed off attempts to steer him towards the governor-general and headed straight for his parents. He took them both in his arms and hugged them. Catherine, observing his stubble, is alleged to have said loudly, 'Chilla, you dirty brat – go and have a shave.' Observers noted that he was uncharacteristically overcome with emotion and momentarily had difficulty speaking. Nearby, Ulm was saying, 'Well, that's that. We could do it again.' The speeches of the governor-general, Lord Stonehaven, and the prime minister, Stanley Bruce, were drowned by cheers and interrupted by young women who rushed the dais and imprinted bright red lips on the cheeks of the four heroes. Warner got swept away by the crowd and was carried back through the mud by two policemen, his face now covered in lipstick. The heroes were hoisted on to the back of a truck and driven victoriously round the airfield.

At the flying clubhouse, where Keith Anderson fought his way forward to congratulate them, the aviators gave a press conference. Curiously, apparently by agreement, Smithy, the star attraction, handed over to Ulm. 'They stated,' reported the *Sydney Morning Herald*, 'that they preferred to make a joint statement and Mr Ulm was deputed spokesman.' The reason soon became clear. Ulm immediately addressed the unhappy matter of the Americans' involvement. One suspects that, as his partner had been the architect of the hard terms imposed and the one most reluctant to bring Lyon and Warner on to Australia, Smithy had insisted that Ulm try to mend the fences himself. He did so with panache, in their presence launching into a well-prepared tribute to the Americans. But his main purpose was to stress that they were not partners, merely technicians hired at the last minute. 'Those two chaps were strangers to us two weeks ago. We got them on the advice of the highest technical authority in America, and we have paid them for their services. Naturally we felt it our duty – as neither of the men had flown before – to pay them a high daily rate for a hazardous flight.'

Warner, who did not consider his rate of around £1 a day particularly generous for the hours of bowel-loosening fear he had endured, heard Ulm explain that an 'uplift in our finances' had enabled them to fund the Americans' wages for the further day's flying from Fiji to Australia. Lyon and Warner were puzzled that their tiny daily costs on the expedition's large budget should require any significant increase in its funding, but, encouraged by the warmth of his sentiments, Warner decided to approach Ulm with a request for a small share of some of the minor rewards of the flight. Meanwhile the Americans went out of their way to avoid drawing any of the spotlight from their employers. '"This is not our show," protested Mr Warner in an interview. "We were passengers – no more."' The newspapers now began to describe them quaintly as 'salaried assistants'. The *Guardian*, without which they would not have been in Sydney at all, decided not to rock the boat. Ellison's interview with Lyon, with its deeply embarrassing revelations, was never published.

A large suite at its Pitt Street headquarters, complete with staff, was provided for Smithy and Ulm by the Atlantic Union Oil Company. Ellen Rogers, the company's managing director's secretary, was one of those seconded to this glamorous operation. An attractive young woman with an Eton crop who wore a jacket and tie, she was to become a shrewd observer of Smithy's and Ulm's dissimilar characters. She went on to work for Ulm devotedly, and with secret unrequited love, for the remainder of his short life. Ellen, whom they called 'Rodge', quickly discovered how remarkably unindustrious Smithy was out of the cockpit. While Ulm was a veritable powerhouse of energy, conscientiously conducting countless interviews and daily dictating scores of letters, Smithy showed little inclination to be drawn into the business routines of the treadmill of fame. 'He seemed to spend most of his time chatting to his cousins and friends,' she wrote.[3]

A torrent of letters poured in, many from women for whom Smithy had become a potent sex object, offering in their hundreds to marry him. Although he had been separated from Thelma for three years, he was still legally married to her, but the existence of Mrs Kingsford Smith had been discreetly ignored by every newspaper. As a result most Australians believed that he was single. 'Dearest Captain Kingsford Smith, I am dreaming wonderful dreams with you always as my hero. If only they could come true, one would feel in paradise with Prince Charming. I would just explode with wonderful feelings.'

'Dearest Airman, what would I not give to have you as a husband. From the moment you hopped off from Oakland I knew you would succeed and have loved you silently ever since.'

Some pleaded to be taken on a flight, an opportunity for casual affairs that Smithy was soon to find irresistible.

Everywhere the crew went they were followed by traffic-paralysing crowds. But there was no pomp and circumstance around these men. They were disarmingly human, casual, informal and accessible. They shouted back wisecracks and allowed people to grasp them. At ceremony after ceremony they were fêted by premiers and governors, cabinet ministers, military chiefs. Almost anything Smithy wanted was presented to him free. Hotels put him up in their best suites, and even his petrol was supplied without charge at the insistence of Atlantic Union. That first week the four airmen made a triumphant tour of the country in the *Southern Cross*, accompanied by Catherine, who everywhere was treated like the Queen Mother. What appealed to people at every level about Smithy was his uncomplicated personality, so devoid, in fame, of the least affectation, and his total approachability. Outwardly he appears not to have taken his Pacific feat very seriously. Newspaper reports of what he said in his brief speeches, laced with simple jokes, reveal little profundity and surprisingly few references to earnest hopes for the establishment of regular Pacific air services. The truth was that their flight had been an appallingly dangerous operation that had pushed the margins of safety to limits unacceptable to public air transport. Indeed, scheduled services between America and Australia would not begin for nearly two decades.

At a Sun Newspapers ceremonial lunch at the Hotel Australia in Sydney, Keith Anderson sat dejectedly in the background, far away from the VIP table. Nor did his heart respond when Ulm's speech touched on his role and people turned to look at him. 'You probably don't know what the gift by Mr Hancock of the *Southern Cross* means to Smithy and me. It means,' he said, his tongue loosened by champagne, 'four thousand pounds.' And that was £4,000 each, Anderson knew. 'I also have a feeling of regret,' Ulm went on boldly, 'that Andy was not able to accompany us. It was he who suggested the name "Southern Cross". I am very proud that he was associated with us in the early stages of the venture.' Anderson, like Warner, had done his sums, and he had already decided, at Bon's urging, to make a bid for a share of the rewards, as had the disenchanted mechanic, Bob Hitchcock.

With his new riches Smithy was generous. Within weeks of his return, as a gift to his parents, he had bought 'Kuranda' for £1,350, enabling them to live rent-free for the rest of their lives. And he created a trust into which he put £5,000 from which his parents received a helpful £4 a week.[4] 'Chilla's new relative wealth completely changed their lifestyle,' John Kingsford-Smith recalled. 'Until then they'd hardly possessed a brass farthing.'

Among the honours showered upon Smithy and Ulm were an Air Force Cross each and, to the surprise of many of its serving officers, honorary commissions in the Royal Australian Air Force. Smithy was made a squadron leader and Ulm a flight lieutenant. Almost immediately they began to appear in their officers' uniforms, Smithy sporting air force wings on his tunic. Ulm had yet to qualify for the flying badge, but nonetheless he boldly decided to have one sewn on to his own tunic – a rash move he was quickly to regret. In *Aircraft*, the editor, Edward Hart, denounced Ulm's 'effrontery in putting up a pair of wings on a RAAF tunic without the least authority'. The illicit insignia also drew a howl of outrage from the Air Force's commander-in-chief, Air Commodore Richard Williams, who, nine years earlier in London, had been asked to remove Smithy from the 1919 air race. He publicly denounced what he regarded as a colossal cheek. 'People must never wear wings unless they have earned them,' he declared.[5] Reluctantly Ulm removed the insignia. Yet the honorary ranks and medals were regarded in some quarters as inadequate recognition. Among ex-servicemen there was a feeling that Smithy and Ulm should have been knighted, as Ross and Keith Smith, winners of the 1919 race, had been. Within the family it was believed that Chilla would most certainly have been so rewarded but for his untidy marital situation. The embarrassing consequence of the elevation to Lady Kingsford Smith of his unknown and estranged wife was something that Stanley Bruce's government clearly shrank from.

While the Pacific celebrations were still at their height, the embittered Bob Hitchcock decided it was time to strike. In the middle of June he went to the Atlantic Union office and demanded to see the famous partners. When he asked for the £1,000 he understood he had been promised, Smithy responded, according to Hitchcock, by claiming that he had in their absence failed to maintain the Bristol Tourers left in his care. They were therefore under no obligation to pay him anything. And Ulm had said of the alleged promise: 'We were all half sozzled at the time.' 'I said [to Smithy], "Don't break your word to me, Charlie . . . Please don't break your word to me,"' Hitchcock recalled. 'And all he said was, "It can't be helped, Bob. You go home and chew it over."' Hitchcock did not go home. He went to see a lawyer.

No reliable record now exists of the money Smithy and Ulm made from the Pacific flight. In his autobiography Smithy wrote that the total they shared was £20,000. However, there is evidence that it was considerably more than that. They had been presented with an expensively equipped aeroplane worth around £8,000. A grateful Australian government had given them £5,000. Sun Newspapers had opened a public subscription that brought in nearly £3,000. A special performance of *Rio Rita* staged by a Sydney theatre, for which the famous singer Gladys Moncrieff auctioned the seats, raised an amazing £1,000 in a few minutes. The New South Wales government which had so hastily withdrawn its original guarantees had guiltily restored the £4,500 backing and voted them an additional cash grant of £2,500. On top of all this a wealthy Victorian grazier and benefactor, Marcus Oldham, sent Smithy and Ulm a cheque for £4,000.[6] There was also speculation at the time that the rich Lebbeus Hordern had privately contributed a further £5,000. Even from the confirmable sources the income Smithy and Ulm finished up sharing was probably nearer £30,000 – approaching £700,000 in today's terms. Most Australians, awed by the achievement, believed it was no more than their just entitlement. It is also clear that the public was under the impression that the Americans were sharing in the bonanza.

But none of it ever came their way. They were not even permitted to accept cash offers to advertise products. 'I tried to get Ulm to release Lyon and me from the terms of our Suva contract,' Warner wrote. 'The flight was over and several firms were trying to give us rewards for our share in it. But Ulm ignored my requests for more than ten days, after which it was too late.' On 23 June, he and Lyon sailed back to America. Meanwhile, Warner's unease was being shared by some members of Parliament in Canberra. Replying to their questions, the prime minister pointed out that Kingsford Smith and Ulm had spent twelve months organising the flight and had borne 'all the anxiety and responsibility of financing the venture'. But Stanley Bruce was careful not to close the door. He had left the distribution of the money, he said, to the discretion of Captain Kingsford Smith.[7] Smithy saw that discretion, within the three-way San Francisco agreement with Keith Anderson, extending only to Ulm.

As the largesse continued to stream in, Anderson decided to act. His decision was prompted by the news that Smithy and Ulm were about to make another first-ever oceanic flight, this time to New Zealand. At the urging of his wife and daughter, Arthur Hilliard had devised a legal strategy. Believing that Anderson might succeed in getting a much bigger sum than the US$13,000 he had earlier demanded, he drafted for him identical letters to Smithy and Ulm telling them he now wished to claim 'as a creditor'. In the third week of June Anderson went along to the Atlantic Union office to deliver the letters in person. He reminded Smithy and Ulm that his family had put the equivalent of more than US$3,000 into the venture, some of it at critical junctures. Smithy as usual left the hard talking to his partner. Ulm, openly exasperated, was curt and businesslike. He saw the history of their relationship in quite simple terms, he said: when Hancock had rescued them they had immediately summoned him to return to America, but he failed to do so. From that point he had removed himself from the original partnership. He had spurned their offer of a third share in the refinanced *Southern Cross* expedition, thus forfeiting his stake in the aeroplane and the rewards. Their only indebtedness was for part of the $3,000 he had contributed. To settle this he and Smithy, there and then, each wrote him a cheque for the Australian equivalent of $1,000, totalling around £400. Anderson, warned by Hilliard not to settle at any token level, refused the money. He stood up, said they would be hearing further from him, and left.

Hilliard now advised Anderson to demand a full statement of accounts showing every item of income and expenditure incurred during the purchase and preparation of the *Southern Cross* for the Pacific flight. When Anderson went back with this bold request he got a frosty response. Ulm, point-blank, refused to show him the accounts.

The move into court was hastened, early in July, by the discovery that Smithy and Ulm had recruited a new navigator and wireless-operator for their Tasman flight as well as a first-ever non-stop transcontinental hop to Perth. Hilliard urged Anderson to clip their wings with an immediate claim on their most precious asset. So, on 19 July, he petitioned the Supreme Court, seeking an order preventing the *Southern Cross* from being flown out of New South Wales. He also sought a judgement declaring that the original partnership of three still existed. Moreover, the petition demanded that the aeroplane be sold forthwith and that a receiver of the partnership assets be appointed. 'I was pained and surprised,' Smithy wrote. 'Andy's action was a real body blow,' said John Kingsford-Smith. 'Of all the disappointments in his life, having his old mate sue him was probably the bitterest.' Bon Hilliard's cousin, John Laurence, commented: 'The pressure to take that drastic step almost certainly came from Maude Hilliard. She would have called all the shots.'

But the writ didn't immediately stop Smithy and Ulm in their tracks. When the petition came before the chief judge in equity in the first week of August, he ordered only that the *Southern Cross* should be within the New South Wales jurisdiction of the court when the full case came to trial. They were therefore free to make both their flights in the meantime. Sitting in court, Smithy and Ulm were amazed when Anderson's counsel then jumped to his feet to seek an order 'that the plaintiff be allowed to take part in any active flights by the defendants'. The judge refused. He would most certainly not ask the defendants to fly with Mr Anderson, he said. 'There might well be a dispute in the cockpit.' Smithy and Ulm were greatly relieved. To have been compelled to take Anderson would, apart from relegating Ulm to the role of passenger in the cabin, have created unbearable tensions on board.

The dispute was not to be settled for many months, and not before it was joined by further expensive litigation. The new claim arrived infelicitously in front of Smithy during a Returned Soldiers League banquet in Sydney Town Hall. It was a writ claiming £1,000 compensation from Bob Hitchcock.

13

'The Extreme of Human Fear'
1928

The legal claims on Smithy's and Ulm's new-found wealth were to dog their lives for nearly nine months. They devoured weeks of their now precious time and ran up huge lawyers' fees. They also plumbed depths of bitterness whose effects were still felt among the Anderson and Hitchcock families seventy years later. First to be heard, in the Equity Division of the New South Wales Supreme Court, was Keith Anderson's claim. How he funded his King's Counsel in his parlous financial state, no one knows. The essence of the case was the status of the partnership between the three men. The defendants insisted that the flight originally proposed had been abandoned when the New South Wales government withdrew its backing. The successful flight, although it involved the same aeroplane, had been a quite separate venture. As powerful evidence they produced for the court the partnership agreement they had all signed in San Francisco in December 1927, which declared that, if one of the three withdrew, the other two would 'assume all of the assets and liabilities'. They denied that Anderson had returned to Australia with their agreement to try to raise further money. Rather, they insisted, he had abandoned them and the whole enterprise.

The preliminary hearing took several days. Anderson, and Smithy and Ulm, who had also engaged a KC, gave lengthy evidence. The transcripts provide a far more piercing insight into the dynamics of the partnership than the heroic portrayal of the protagonists by the adoring media. Smithy comes across as a helpful witness, although casual, always vague and imprecise on business detail; Ulm as a defensive, prickly person, but tersely businesslike about money. Every letter signed by them both had been written by Ulm. So had every financial document. 'Pardon me for being vague,' Smithy several times said of joint letters he and Ulm had written to Anderson, 'but it was compiled by Mr Ulm.' Anderson's evidence reflects his slow and measured personality, his careful use of language suggesting an educated man. Trying to disinter this bleak episode in their lives, one feels a raw and eerie sense of their presence in these tragic events of so long ago. As the embers of their relationships were raked over by lawyers the greatest sadness was that Smithy and Anderson's friendship should end like this.

Early in July the case was adjourned to await the collection of statements required from Hancock, Locke Harper and Harold Kingsford-Smith. In the meantime Smithy and Ulm were free to make their planned non-stop flight to Perth to demonstrate the potential of inter-state aviation. They had already engaged a navigator. This time Harold Litchfield, who had been unavailable for the Pacific flight, was able to join them, along with a New Zealand wireless operator, Tom McWilliams. McWilliams was appointed for the trans-Australia hop principally to familiarise himself with the Fokker's radio systems for the Tasman flight to follow, for which Smithy and Ulm had decided, as a gesture, to take on a New Zealander. McWilliams was superintendent of the Union Steamship Company's wireless training school in Wellington. An extremely shy man, he had suffered a severe foot wound in action as an infantryman in France, which had left him with a slight limp.

The 2,000-mile flight to Perth was a minor challenge after the high-risk Pacific flights. They set off from the RAAF aerodrome at Point Cook in Melbourne because there wasn't a long enough runway in Sydney. The *Southern Cross* had now acquired the British registration, G-AUSU,[1] the last two letters standing for Smith and Ulm. The twenty-three-and-a-half-hour journey was made through the night of 8 August in freezing rain that showered stinging ice pellets into the cockpit and formed a great sheath of ice on the wing.

In Perth Smithy discovered that he was now famous for more than his Pacific feat. In a recent widely publicised divorce hearing in the Supreme Court in Perth, the co-respondent cited by Len Ives' wife, Ethel – described discreetly at first as the 'unknown woman' – had been soon revealed as none other than the wife of the celebrated aviator. The newspapers began eagerly to report the case in unusually salacious and sensational detail with titillating evidence from private detectives. They had spied at night on Mrs Thelma Kingsford Smith and Ives at the latter's Maida Vale fruit farm, and been rewarded by the sight of her having a bath in a tub in front of him in the living room before they retired to bed. Despite this and other conclusive evidence that pointed to a permanent relationship between Ives and Thelma, the judge, to wide amazement, had dismissed the petition. Thelma had refused to appear in court. Perth headlines cried, 'WHERE IS THE FAMOUS AIRMAN'S WIFE?' She had gone into hiding in the city.

Thelma's relationship with Smithy had meanwhile been making news as well. It was three years since they had parted, then the minimum qualifying period for divorce on grounds of desertion. On his return from America, he had decided to end the long-dead marriage, and while in Perth he resolved to try to find her. He went to see one of the spying private detectives, who led him to the McKenna family. He arranged to meet Thelma at her mother's home in Gertrude's presence. It quickly became obvious that the public perception of his new wealth was going to put a price on her willingness to co-operate. The sum of £250 was mentioned, and, subject to the court's approval, he agreed to make her such a present on condition that she didn't contest his petition.[2]

Back in Sydney in the last week of August, Smithy and Ulm were impatient to make more aviation history. They announced that early in September, the *Southern Cross* would fly to New Zealand. Almost simultaneously, Keith Anderson told Sydney newspapers that he, too, was about to embark upon a major flight. With Bob Hitchcock, he was planning an imminent attack on the England–Australia record of fifteen and a half days created earlier in the year by Bert Hinkler, this time travelling in the opposite direction, from Australia. Smithy was staggered to read that they intended using the remaining Bristol Tourer jointly owned by himself and Anderson. Anderson appears to have considered he had the right to help himself to the aircraft without his old mate's agreement. Still burdened by a nagging sense of guilt toward him, Smithy decided not to question his plans. On the eve of another epic flight of his own the last thing he wanted was further unpleasantness and more embarrassing reports of squabbling among the aviators. 'It was a colossal cheek, of course,' said John

Kingsford-Smith. 'But the family were genuinely fond of Andy. They believed that he was simply being manipulated by the Hilliards.' 'He had been very ill advised,' Elsie Pike wrote to June Dupre in Carnarvon at this time. 'And also weak-minded to be so swayed by his fiancée and her folk.'

> It is a hard thing to say, but I am sure they are responsible for the way Andy has been acting. She is a very ambitious girl and it is a bitter blow Andy not being one of the famous Pacific fliers. They are trying to push him to either get some share of the results, or to do something big on his own.
>
> Everything seems all a muddle and mix-up with regard to Andy these days. I can't help feeling sorry that the friendship between those two, which lasted so long, has come to such a wretched end. We used to like Andy so much and Bert and I have many pleasant memories of the old days when we saw so much of him, that it makes me sad to see all this unpleas- antness now. Do you remember how he and Charlie used to plan and plan the Pacific flight and Bert used to get mad with them paying more attention to their dreams than to the transport company! Well, Charlie has attained his dream, and Andy is a disappointed man. But it's all his own fault. He went over with the others and had the same chance to make good. It's a funny old world isn't it?[3]

Anderson and Hitchcock, in the commandeered Tourer which they had named *Old Pioneer*, were halfway to Darwin when, at dusk on 10 September, the *Southern Cross*, with Smithy, Ulm, Litchfield and McWilliams aboard, left on the 1,250-mile flight to New Zealand from the RAAF's Richmond Aerodrome out near the foothills of the Blue Mountains. About 500 miles out from Sydney, the Fokker flew into a violent, unforecast storm. As the plane was snatched into a cauldron of turbulence and rain of un- believable ferocity, Smithy began the worst blind-flying ordeal of his life. Water poured into the cockpit and, for the first time, into the cabin. McWilliams' radio was drenched and some of its com- ponents were hurled into the back of the aircraft far out of his reach. The 400ft-long short-range trailing aerial was struck by lightning and the discharge flashed back to the cabin, burning out the coils of the transmitter and nearly killing McWilliams. From then on, although he laboured through the night to create some makeshift arrangement, only intermittent peeps of Morse were to be heard from the Fokker for the rest of the flight.

Incredibly, despite the bitter lessons of the Pacific turbulence, although they had secured the cockpit seats and fitted lap straps for the pilots, they had left the other two frail wicker chairs unanchored and unharnessed. Litchfield and McWilliams were soon being flung about the cramped cabin, hanging on only by gripping the fuselage stanchions around which they were twirled and shaken like puppets. Litchfield was unable to navigate. Around him the thin, cotton fabric of the fuselage walls flapped and rippled as if the cloth was about to peel off, leaving him and McWilliams exposed to the tempest outside. The up- and down-draughts were registering 2,500ft a minute, a rate the Fokker had never experienced before. It was a paltry, vulnerable craft faced with forces as brutal as these, and Smithy did not understand their terrifying power. He seems merely to have seen his task as a test of nerve, a battle of airmanship, of man against the elements. It is one of the many miracles of his career that he and his crew did not plunge into the Tasman that night.

At 10,000ft, the *Southern Cross* could climb no higher and began to ice up with awful speed. Soon every exterior surface was covered. Smithy felt the controls growing heavy and sluggish as they struggled to deal with this dangerous new weight. 'The plane,' he said, 'began to sink, and, to my surprise and dismay, our airspeed indicator, on which I relied while flying blind, went from 95mph to zero.' Wrongly, he assumed that they had stalled. His response nearly put them all into the sea. 'I pushed the controls forward as far as possible to build up our speed. But nothing happened except the terrific roar of the air past the machine and the steady fall of the altimeter from 8,000 to 2,500ft . . . I'd lost all this height before realising that the speed indicator had ceased to function.' The external intake, the pitot head, had frozen over, blocking off the air pressure that drove the instrument. A glance at his engine rev-counters revealed the true state of affairs. 'The needles were quivering at 2300rpm instead of 1800! We were diving down at a terrific angle at the enormous speed of 150mph or more. Below us – and not far below – was the angry Tasman Sea.'

With precious little time to spare Smithy, with only his

engine-counters to tell him whether he was climbing or descending, managed to pull out of the dive and regain straight and level flight. Outside he could see nothing; the windscreen was an opaque skin of ice. To make matters worse a hail squall now began to slice chunks out of the propellers, unbalancing them and setting up such a violent vibration that the crew feared the motors would at any moment leap from their mounts. 'Encrusted with ice. Our radio failed. Alone in the middle of the deserted Tasman Sea. We could see nothing, hear nothing. We didn't know where we were. I think that night I touched the extreme of human fear. Panic was very near and I almost lost my head. I felt a desire to pull her round, dive – climb – do anything to escape. We were like rats in a trap – terrified, dazed with fear.'

This account of his dread and desperation, published in the first version of his autobiography, *The Old Bus*, shows that Smithy was not the totally fearless figure his mythology painted him. The paralysing panic he recalled – the terror exceeded anything he had ever experienced in aerial combat, he told reporters – was in fact never far away during almost all the great flights he made. His own published descriptions of his oceanic journeys, and the frank post-flight interviews he gave, confirm that these attacks, which sometimes created an overwhelming urge to get out of the plane and out of the air, occurred most acutely, perhaps not surprisingly, out of sight of land in bad weather. That he chose again and again to expose himself to this anguish added a quality to his natural courage that was recognised by very few.

It was nearly daylight, and they were approaching the New Zealand coast, before the short-wave radio began feebly to work again. However, few operators in New Zealand heard the signals. Most thought they had gone the way of Hood and Moncrieff, who had disappeared while attempting to fly the Tasman eight months earlier. When at last they broke out into a clear moonlit night, the ice melted and the airspeed indicator flicked back into life. As the sun rose ahead, Litchfield was able to make his first celestial observation for many hours. Amazingly, it showed that they were virtually on course. Smithy, his spirits revived, decided to celebrate their arrival with a joyful orbit of the capital, Wellington, at the foot of the North Island.

No aeroplane had ever flown into the country from overseas

before: had it arrived from outer space it could not have created a bigger sensation. Men came out of their houses bare-chested and waved their pyjama tops; women in flannel nighties 'threw modesty to the wind' as they rushed from their bedrooms to cheer. Traffic ground to a halt and trams stopped to let passengers off to salute New Zealand's first international arrival by air. As radio stations spread the tidings, the entire country rippled with relief and excitement.

From Wellington they flew south to Christchurch, to the country's only large aerodrome. When news of their approach reached the city, normal life all but ceased. More than 30,000 people, a quarter of the population, swarmed out to the airfield, broke down the barriers and overwhelmed the police as the aircraft taxied in. Men leaped on to the struts and tried to pull Smithy and Ulm out before the aircraft had even stopped. The mayor and the reception committee never reached the aviators, all of whom were seized bodily and carried away shoulder-high as a military band played 'Hearts of Oak'. Smithy, disorientated by deafness, looked drawn and exhausted, and the horrors of the night had made him uncharacteristically irritable. 'Let a man down,' he exploded angrily to the human phalanx carrying him.

At their hotel they were greeted by the sad news that Anderson's and Hitchcock's record attempt had failed. The Tourer's water-cooled engine had boiled dry in the heat of the Northern Territory, and at Pine Creek, south of Darwin, Anderson had been forced to drop the aircraft into trees, wrecking it. Although he had escaped unhurt, Hitchcock had suffered leg and shoulder injuries and a deep cut to his bottom lip. It was a humiliating end to the venture. They were forced to sell the engine to a hotel-keeper at Katherine to pay their fares back to Sydney, where billboards had declared heartlessly: 'SMITHY TRIUMPHS – ANDERSON CRASHES'. The crumpled Bristol was left in the bush to be eaten by ants. Because it was uninsured, Anderson had effectively written off Smithy's investment. But Smithy didn't have the stomach for yet more litigation. Besides, he was now a hero in New Zealand. In Wellington the prime minister, Gordon Coates, presented him with a cheque for £2,000. 'I'm very grateful for this cheque, sir,' responded Smithy. 'It'll help our plans along very nicely. But we didn't fly the Tasman to collect two thousand quid. We flew here to link two countries which have hitherto been outposts of the empire.' People assumed that he would share the money equally with the others, as Coates had intended. But Ulm, using as models the contracts he had produced for Lyon and Warner, had signed up Litchfield and McWilliams as mere hired hands, not as financial participants. They got nothing. Smithy and Ulm took £1,000 each.

The crew spent a riotous month in New Zealand, living for free as government guests. Outside Christchurch there were few landing grounds big enough to take the trimotor, so the country's Permanent Air Force flew them on a tour of the main towns in three ancient Bristol fighters. Smithy was given the temporary rank of major in the Territorial Air Force. Wherever they went the normal life of towns ground to a halt and a kind of hysteria took over. Some schools were closed and children bussed from miles around for a glimpse of the megastars. At others pupils waited for hours, standing in rows in the playgrounds, fluttering flags and handkerchiefs, for the aviators to fly over. Away from the aerodromes, they travelled in a squadron of cars from reception to reception, ball to ball, banquet to banquet. The hotels in which they stayed trembled to the racket of the wild parties that erupted spontaneously wherever they went.

The tour was conducted on two separate levels: one highly visible, the other largely out of public view. The latter, characterised by carousing and Smithy's womanising, was whispered about, but the deeply respectful and cautious newspapers of the day would not have dreamed of even hinting at any scandalous behaviour of a figure so hallowed. More than one person who remembered the 1928 visit confided that Smithy had acquired a reputation for being 'a bit of a rogue'. The drinking binges sometimes resulted in smashed-up hotel furniture, and as ever there were persistent stories of his casual sexual encounters, in which it appears, he wasn't always terribly choosy – or discreet.

At the end of the grand tour the crew returned to Christchurch and, on 28 September, flew the *Southern Cross* up to a large paddock at Woodbourne near Blenheim. Planning to make the return flight to Sydney from here to avoid flying over the Southern Alps, they booked into the Criterion Hotel to await suitable weather. They were to wait for over two weeks. Tom McWilliams' girlfriend, Winifred, later his wife, travelled from her home in the North Island to say goodbye to him, chaperoned by her mother. At the Criterion they became aware, to their deep embarrassment, that both Smithy and Ulm had acquired resident companions. 'These two Australian women had come over to New Zealand by sea to be with them,' Mrs McWilliams said. 'It must all have been prearranged in Sydney. They were pretty tough-looking girls, very smartly dressed with fox furs. I never discovered their names because we were never introduced. They appeared only in the evenings when Smithy and Ulm would come down to dinner escorting them. At bedtime they would all just disappear. My mother, as you can imagine, was absolutely horrified by these goings-on.'

During the long wait in Blenheim there was an exciting development in Ulm's life. He completed some flying instruction, provided as a gesture by the New Zealand Permanent Air Force, who had given him the temporary rank of flight lieutenant. At Blenheim he graduated on to a Bristol Fighter and was awarded New Zealand Air Force wings. He could now legitimately sew the emblem on his uniform and stand proudly beside Smithy as a qualified pilot.

To avoid another night of terror on the Tasman they decided to fly back to Australia in daylight. But a fierce westerly headwind reduced their return journey to such a crawl that they nearly ran out of fuel. When, around midnight, they reached the Australian coast, it lay under heavy fog. They couldn't find Sydney. At Richmond, where 30,000 people were waiting, their quavering warbles of Morse began to reflect the panic on board as Smithy called again and again for a searchlight. The lights were already arcing about the sky, but he couldn't see them. When at last, through drifting skeins of stratus, the lights of the city suddenly appeared wonderfully beneath him, the *Southern Cross*'s tanks were almost dry.

It was 2.15 on Sunday morning, 14 October,[4] when they touched down. The first-ever flight from New Zealand to Australia had taken twenty-three hours. Smithy climbed out, looking strained and unshaven, and walked over to hug Catherine, huddled in a fur coat, only to be rudely seized from the embrace and carried away on peoples' shoulders. A bulky microphone was thrust under his nose. 'How do you do, everybody,' he said tiredly. 'We have only three gallons of petrol left – but here we are.'[5]

14

Coffee Royal

1929

For several months Kingsford Smith and Ulm basked once again in the glow of great triumph, their names linked in one of the most successful double acts in aviation history. Every great flight they had attempted they accomplished with apparent nonchalant ease. There were renewed calls in the New South Wales Parliament for the pair to be knighted. However, in Smithy's case there remained the impediment of his unresolved marriage to Thelma.

At the divorce hearing in Sydney on 26 October 1928, Thelma did not appear and the other, marathon, divorce case in Perth which had created her current notoriety was not referred to. Smithy's application to make Thelma the agreed gift of £250 was approved and, on the grounds of her desertion, he was granted a decree nisi to be made absolute in six months. The headline 'FLYING HERO'S FREEDOM' summed up his feelings. However, Ethel Ives, her own divorce refused by the first judge, was seeking another hearing. To Smithy's embarrassment the evidence promised to implicate Thelma even more deeply, and his ever-rising fame guaranteed that the case would be reported more sensationally than ever.

On 12 December 1928, Smithy and Ulm announced the formation of their own Australian inter-city airline, Australian National Airways, registered in Sydney with a nominal capital of £200,000.[1] It was to operate – bravely and, some said, foolishly – without government subsidy, daily passenger and mail services between Sydney, Melbourne, Brisbane and Tasmania. A group of prominent businessmen rallied to their support and enough money to get the airline flying was quickly found. The biggest single shareholder was Federick (later Sir Frederick) Stewart, governing director of Sydney's Metropolitan Omnibus and Transport Company, who personally invested £16,000 and became the company's first chairman. By the end of the year Australian National Airways had set up its headquarters in Challis House in central Sydney's Martin Place. Here Smithy and Ulm presided over the fledgling business as salaried joint managing directors. Ellen Rogers became their first secretary.

While Ulm threw himself into the huge task of creating an operating airline, Smithy, from the outset, was rarely seen in the office. The unglamorous administration processes bored him. His only interest was in the physical operation of the aircraft – five Fokker trimotors due to be built under licence by the Avro company in England to meet the Australian government's requirement that, within the spirit of empire, they used only British aircraft. During the long, hot Sydney summer of 1928–9 while Ulm toiled for twelve hours a day at Challis House, Smithy was engaged in the more pleasurable pursuit of roaring about Sydney Harbour in a powerful speedboat he'd just bought. His nephew John, who was only fourteen years younger than his uncle, had begun to spend a lot of time with him and looked after the boat. In his late eighties, and still looking strikingly like his famous relative, John was one of the few surviving members of the family old enough to remember Smithy at that time. 'He kept his speedboat down on the Lane Cove River and he'd often spend the day with mates aquaplaning behind on a board. Because it wasn't fast enough for him, he borrowed a Gipsy Moth floatplane to tow the board at a hair-raising 70mph. He was quite obsessed with speed.'

When he got bored with the boat Smithy would go out to Mascot and tinker with the 'old bus'. Returning in his new Studebaker, 'Lady Clara Vere de Vere', one day with John, there was an incident which demonstrated that, when his anger flared, he could react with physical violence. 'We came to a stretch where a gang had laid new tar and begun to spread fine gravel chips.' John recalled. 'Chill slowed down to a crawl. But, as he went past, one of these guys deliberately flung a whole shovelful at the side of the Studebaker. Chill let out an oath, jammed on the brakes and hopped out. He strode over to this guy and, without a word, just grabbed him by the collar and smashed his fist into his face. It was all over in a second. I can still see the man reeling, with blood on his face, and Chill swearing at him. Then he just jumped back into the car and drove on without a word. It was really quite awesome.'

When Smithy wasn't careering round the harbour he was driving up-country to stay with friends, showing off doing aerobatics in a Moth over Arabella Street, or being fêted at never-ending functions. But it wasn't always pleasure that kept him from the office: 'Tues. 12 Feb. 1929. Chilla not very well,' records his mother's diary. '13 Feb. Chilla in bed all day not very well.' His illnesses were always described as 'flu'. The true nature of these bouts of sickness with high temperatures which dogged his life was never questioned.

The extraordinary thing about his enormous fame was its lack of impact on the unassuming tenor of his life. He had no desire to buy a grand home or a luxury yacht; instead, his base was the small, very ordinary, room he had occupied since 1921 at 'Kuranda'. Nor had celebrity affected his friendships. He was the adored nucleus of an enormous tribe of mates and relatives who seemed to swarm through the house almost daily, arriving for lunch, dinner and often staying the night, sleeping on camp beds on the veranda. Catherine, although now in her seventies, still took it all in her stride, providing an effortless flow of food and makeshift bedspace. William was not much help to her any more. Seventy-six and now seriously debilitated, he was a proud, stooped figure in an old red tam-o'-shanter who shuffled about in the background in his slippers, or lay for hours on a bed on the veranda watching the new bridge creeping over the harbour.

At the end of November the Ives divorce case in Perth burst back into the headlines. Ethel Ives had won her appeal for a new trial on the grounds that she was now in possession of fresh evidence to prove that the co-respondent was undeniably Mrs Kingsford Smith. More witnesses gave evidence that Thelma was openly living with Len Ives and being routinely introduced as his wife. The judge was finally convinced of the adultery, but he accepted Ives' claim that Ethel had connived at it. He refused to grant the divorce. Ethel's father, Nat Harper, was so angry that he announced that he would fund a third hearing: an appeal to the

Full Court of Western Australia. The affair was to haunt Smithy for another seven months.

Meanwhile, he was casting about for fresh flying adventures. The latest was for the *Southern Cross* to complete a circuit of the world with a flight to New York and San Francisco via England. To take care of the first leg he persuaded Ulm that they should both fly the trimotor to London to discuss with the Avro company their order for the British-built Fokker airliners and to recruit some pilots with multi-engined experience. To add excitement to the trip and get a newspaper to pay their costs, he suggested they attempt to break Bert Hinkler's fifteen-and-a-half-day record in the opposite direction. Sun Newspapers quickly snapped up the exclusive rights to the story.

Their departure was delayed for several months by the resumption of Anderson's case in late February 1929, but the hearing, before the chief judge in equity, Mr Justice Harvey, didn't take long. For some reason – perhaps the overwhelming weight of evidence that he had made no serious effort to return to America to join the refinanced Pacific flight – Anderson was persuaded that his demand for a share of the profits was unsustainable. The records of the legal arguments that finally convinced him no longer exist in the New South Wales state archives, but what have survived are the terms of the settlement reached that day. They represent a sad and total retreat.

Anderson was forced to concede to a painful catalogue of facts: that his departure from America had dissolved the partnership agreement under which his claim had been made; that the original Pacific venture had been abandoned; that he had returned to Australia voluntarily; that he had been invited to join the Hancock-backed flight, but did not do so; that the defendants had never agreed to pay his boat fare back to America; that he had no interest in the *Southern Cross*, nor in any of the proceeds of the Pacific flight. The only concession he succeeded in wringing out of Smithy and Ulm was a moral one: 'The plaintiff's non-return to the United States . . . was not the result of any lack of personal courage.' It was a humiliating and crushing defeat for the man who was one of the nicest people Smithy had ever known. But he had lacked Ulm's thrust and tenacity. Anderson and Smithy between them would probably never have succeeded in organising the round-Australia, Pacific or Tasman flights, nor would they have managed to create an inter-city airline. But for Charles Ulm, Smithy would still be virtually unknown. Yet this uncomfortable truth did nothing to dispel his unease that a former good mate had been publicly demolished.

Under the terms of the settlement both sides agreed to pay their own costs. As Anderson had little money, doubtless Arthur Hilliard, still expecting to become his father-in-law, would have offered to stump up the £400. Surprisingly, however, it was to arrive from elsewhere. On the day the case ended the conscience-stricken Smithy, 'to show our old friend that we entertained only the warmest feelings towards him', presented him with a cheque for £1,000. Ulm contributed half the money. The present wasn't quite as generous as it sounded, for Smithy and Ulm were still in debt to Anderson for the £600 his family had contributed to the partnership in San Francisco. Smithy and Ulm had each, of course, tried to pay back their share, but the fact that Anderson had refused to accept their offer did not expunge the debt.

Nonetheless the gift enabled Anderson not only to pay his legal costs, but it was almost enough to fund the purchase of his own aeroplane, a British-built Westland Widgeon III,[2] with which he planned to begin a charter business. After paying his legal bill, he found himself nearly £300 short and, incredible as it seems, he asked Kingsford Smith if he could help him out. Smithy did so without hesitation, signing a promissory note for the shortfall.[3]

All that prevented Smithy and Ulm setting off for England now was Bob Hitchcock's claim for 'the thousand hard' he maintained they had promised the day they sailed for America. This case, which began on 19 March, was heard in the New South Wales Supreme Court. One of the subsequently published versions of the litigation claimed that, because Anderson had been involved with Smithy in luring Hitchcock away from Western Australian Airways, he had been named by the mechanic as a third defendant. However, in the records of the hearing in the state archives, Anderson's name is not mentioned. Nonetheless it is clear that Anderson did strengthen Hitchcock's case by confirming to the mechanic's Sydney solicitor that he and Smithy had both promised a role for Hitchcock in the Pacific venture. There is evidence, too, that Anderson may have suggested to the solicitor that his case might be helped by producing evidence detrimental to Ulm, whom Anderson had still not forgiven for coming between him and Smithy. It might therefore have been on Anderson's suggestion that Hitchcock went down to Melbourne to try to get from Edward Hart, editor of *Aircraft*, a statement of his concerns about Ulm's record in the aviation industry. Hart refused to confirm these formally. Although he had accumulated a small dossier on the less successful activities of Ulm, and probably had a file, too, on some of Smithy's more reprehensible conduct during his bibulous flying days with Diggers Aviation, he was certainly not willing to be summoned as a witness in the unpopular role of character-assassin of two national idols.

The case lasted three days, Smithy and Ulm having engaged one of the most eminent and ruthless barristers of the day, Richard Windeyer KC, to ensure its swift demolition. The hectoring Windeyer set out to bully and intimidate Hitchcock from the moment he entered the witness box.

Patronisingly, Windeyer demanded: 'You were merely a mechanic were you not?'

'Yes.'

'You knew nothing about navigation?'

'No.'

'You could not have done any wireless work?'

'No.'

'You were not a pilot?'

'No.'

'Do you realise you would have been only dead weight, absolutely useless while they were in the air?'

'While they were in the air.'

'I suppose you realise, or you won't deny, will you, that at every place where these people would stop it would be possible to find good mechanics?'

'No.'[4]

And so the cross-examination went on, Windeyer several times contempuously reminding Hitchcock of his inferior status.

Smithy's brother-in-law, Bert Pike, was called to give evidence about Hitchcock's work with Interstate Flying Services. So was Leofric, who had the painful task of detailing how Hitchcock had allegedly neglected the maintenance on the Bristol Tourers while

Smithy was in America. For hour after hour, Kingsford Smith stood in the witness box while Hitchcock's counsel led him minutely through the history of his relationship with his client and the offers allegedly made to him. The transcript suggests that Smithy was sometimes extremely economical with the truth. Despite Hitchcock's elaborate recollections of the conversations, confirmed by Anderson, Smithy categorically denied ever offering him a role on the Pacific flight. He lied about the planned New Guinea venture, saying that it 'was not connected in any way with the trans-Pacific flight by any proposition', when in fact the hopes of raising money for the latter had been its sole purpose. He also flatly denied any knowledge of a conversation in which Hitchcock had been promised £1,000.

The odds seem to have been hopelessly stacked against the mechanic who had the temerity to challenge the word of two heroes who had brought such lustre to their country. With the tone set by Windeyer, which implied that the claim verged on the impudent, the humble Hitchcock didn't stand a chance.

The judge decided that the Pacific flight for which Smithy and Anderson had originally, and perhaps foolishly, recruited him, planned to use a single-engined Ryan. This venture had been abandoned in favour of a larger aircraft which Hitchcock had not been invited to join. The claim was dismissed. 'Boys won their case against Bobby Hitchcock,' Catherine's diary noted, probably with a little sadness, since Hitchcock had been a popular visitor to 'Kuranda' in happier days. That evening, it would appear, Smithy and Ulm went out to celebrate, for Catherine added: 'Chilla did not come home last night.' It was a frequently repeated entry.

The two court cases took their toll on Smithy. He hadn't enjoyed watching Windeyer making Hitchcock look small and contemptible. Privately he would have preferred to have given the mechanic some money and kept an old friendship alive. The stress of it all had begun to affect him physically. 'Chilla sickening for flu,' reported his mother's diary immediately the hearing ended.

The anticipatory anxiety of his next major flight may also have contributed: he and Ulm had planned to leave for England as soon as the hearings were over. Their departure again had to be postponed because of Smithy's illness. For the rest of the week, he dragged himself out of bed to set about the preparations at Richmond for the flight. They had again signed up Harold Litchfield and Tom McWilliams, both carefully described as 'employees'. The England venture promised to be much less arduous than its oceanic predecessors, and although, in 1929, there was still a lack of proper aerodromes, most of the route was over land. They had decided to begin with two big non-stop hops: from Sydney direct to Wyndham, 300 miles south-west of Darwin in north-west Australia, and from there to Singapore, after which they would fly through Burma, India and the Middle East to Europe.

But whether Smithy was still unwell, or Ulm too preoccupied with the affairs of their embryonic airline, it is clear that neither devoted to the enterprise the care for which they had come to be so widely admired. Still intoxicated by the success of their earlier flights, and perhaps because the largely overland route had taken some of the anxiety out of it, they appear to have become uncharacteristically blasé. They set off without adequate tools and equipment, survival rations or a single flotation device for use in the event of ditching. They did not take the seawater still they had carried on the Pacific, or an emergency radio. They didn't even bother to wait for an up-to-date destination weather report from Wyndham. For some of these lapses they were to pay a heavy price.

Most difficult to comprehend was their apparent indifference to the appalling unseasonal weather at that moment lying across their route through north-west Australia. A senior official of the Atlantic Union Oil Company, Clive Chateau – an experienced commercial pilot who had flown with the Royal Flying Corps – had gone on ahead to Wyndham, which then had no road link with the rest of Australia, to locate a landing ground big enough for the trimotor to take off with enough fuel to reach Singapore. By the last week of March he had found three separate sites and, subject to the weather, was ready to receive the *Southern Cross*. Unfortunately the North-West's annual monsoon rains, which should have retreated, were still deluging the whole area. Day after day Chateau dispatched telegrams to Sydney emphatically warning that conditions were unsafe for landing.

However, Smithy and Ulm do not appear to have taken his

advice very seriously. They had set Easter Saturday, 30 March, as their departure date and seemed determined to leave that day willy-nilly. On Good Friday, they sent an impetuous telegram to Chateau: 'SOUTHERN CROSS LEAVING 10 O'CLOCK SATURDAY MORNING UNLESS YOU ADVISE GROUND DEFINITELY UNSAFE FOR LANDING.' To which Chateau replied cautiously: 'WEATHER FINE DRYING WIND. AM JUST GOING OUT TO INSPECT NO.2 LANDING GROUND WHICH IS PROBABLY UNSUITABLE AT PRESENT MOMENT STOP FURTHER ADVICE LATER.' Amazingly, and for reasons they were never satisfactorily to explain, Smithy and Ulm decided to ignore Chateau's reports of the actual Wyndham conditions. They consulted instead the forecast in the previous day's issue of the *Sydney Morning Herald*. Twenty-four hours out of date, it misleadingly showed no unfavourable weather in prospect along their intended route. So, without waiting for the vital all-clear from Chateau, whose carefully selected landing grounds were at that very moment being rendered unusable by further drenching storms, they announced that they would definitely depart as intended the next day. Catherine was concerned that her favourite son wasn't fit enough to tackle the two-week flight. 'Chilla not at all well,' she wrote anxiously that Saturday.

The four members of the crew cheerfully recorded farewell radio messages on to primitive gramophone discs. They were the last words the world was to hear from them for over two weeks. At 10.50 on a fine autumn day the *Southern Cross* took off on its 1,860-mile flight across Australia. As they cruised north, struggling with their great fuel load to gain enough height to clear the hills around the Hawkesbury River, McWilliams reeled out his two trailing aerials.[5] Twelve minutes after take-off, Litchfield, sliding open one of the cabin windows to get a drift reading, accidentally knocked the release mechanism of the receiving aerial. Before his horrified eyes it swiftly unreeled to its full 450ft length and broke away. The *Southern Cross* could no longer receive any messages.[6]

McWilliams reported the disaster to Smithy with a note on the stick. He and Ulm conferred. They were less than 20 miles from Sydney: to land safely back at Richmond would mean dumping most of their 800 gallons of fuel, something Smithy was reluctant to do. Nor did he want any further delay. It seems that, at that moment, neither he nor Ulm could conceive of any message that it would be vital for them to receive. Later they and McWilliams were to argue that reception on board, degraded by engine noise, electrical interference from fifty-four spark plugs and deafness meant that they would not have heard any messages anyway – a claim that was to be strongly challenged by radio experts. In his autobiography Smithy gave a quite different and – considering Chateau's far from reassuring messages – somewhat baffling explanation: 'In view of the fine weather report from Wyndham and the fact that reception was not imperative to us in these circumstances, Ulm and I decided to go on.' The decision was to prove one of the biggest errors of judgement Smithy was ever to make.

McWilliams now rigged up a short emergency receiving aerial inside the cabin. It proved totally inadequate: he could hear only sizzling static. Whether they would have heard it or not, within two hours of their departure, there was, unfortunately, a critically important message to be flashed to them by Sydney radio. But the operator, now advised by McWilliams (who could still transmit on the other aerial) of the disaster, decided that it was pointless sending it. The message, from a deeply anxious Chateau, who had just learned that Smithy was determined to set off on the Saturday, was a warning of deteriorating conditions at Wyndham. When his telegram reached Sydney the Fokker had been airborne for nearly two hours.

When Chateau heard later that morning that Kingsford Smith was actually on his way he was flabbergasted. 'CANNOT BELIEVE SOUTHERN CROSS WOULD LEAVE WITHOUT DEFINITE OK FROM ME,' he telegraphed in bewilderment. The weather was so bad he urged that they be recalled, but there was nothing anybody could do. The unseasonal storms had now set the entire North-West awash. The rivers had risen to rushing brown torrents and the area had grown dark under low cloud that cloaked the hills and reached almost down to the sea. Chateau knew that, in this ferment, no pilot could hope to find the inconspicuous little port – and if, by some miracle, he did, there would be nowhere safe to land.

It was around 3.30 am, over the Tanami Desert, about 400 miles from Wyndham, that the *Southern Cross* ran into cloud and rain. For the rest of the night Smithy flew on instruments in a twitching, turbulent black void with what must have been

growing misgivings and also, if his autobiography is to be
believed, with surprise at this worrying change in the weather:
'We had received favourable weather reports from Chateau . . .
Torrential rain poured down and hour after hour I flew on blind,
mentally chiding poor Chateau . . . It was a horrible night.'

When a bleak dawn arrived around 7.30, Litchfield calculated,
on his dead reckoning, that they were close to Wyndham. But
they were trapped in cloud and rain, afraid to descend for fear of
flying into high ground. Wyndham lay at the head of Cambridge
Gulf on the Timor Sea, flanked to the immediate west by the
remote Kimberley country. In 1929, virtually uninhabited except
for a few tribes of nomadic Aborigines and a handful of white missionaries, this big chunk of Australia, 300 miles across, was not
fully explored or properly charted. The only maps they carried
were a page of the whole of Australia from the *Times* atlas and
some admiralty charts of the North-West coast which were virtually devoid of information on land beyond the coastline.
Forbidding, trackless, heavily bushed country, its mountains rose to
3,000ft.

Locked in cloud, Smithy cruised blindly north-west, praying
for daylight and a break in the weather. Eventually, in the half-
light, he found a small gap through which he fleetingly glimpsed
land through sheets of rain. He banked steeply and spiralled down.
At long last perhaps they would discover where they were. But the
country bore no resemblance to anything he remembered from his
last visit to Wyndham. They were over a long canyon whose river
they followed down to the sea. 'Just met large river, either Ord or
Victoria,' Ulm logged. He was wrong: the Ord and Victoria both
ran into the sea to the east of the Cambridge Gulf in which
Wyndham lay.

Turning to the west in the belief that the coast would soon
lead them up the gulf to their destination, they were dismayed to
find 'no Wyndham but plenty of angry-looking sea'. They were
hopelessly lost. For more than an hour, through driving rain and
banks of mist, they flew about in growing despair, forced by the
cloud base to fly dangerously close to the most awful terrain any of
them had ever encountered. The entire landscape was ruckled
with knobs and outcrops of rock. They came down to within 20 or
30ft of the tops of the trees, and at times Smithy found himself so

trapped by high ground on all sides that he was forced to claw his way back into the cloud, praying that they wouldn't slam into an invisible mountain range.

Reluctantly, they began to accept that they had overflown the town, travelled in cloud the length of the Kimberley and fetched up on the northernmost coast, more than 150 miles north-west of Wyndham. They were right. They had reached the sea, Litchfield was to realise later, at Port Warrender. If that small gap in the cloud had not so providentially appeared, they would have flown out over the Timor Sea. From their nautical chart they could now see, correctly, the precipitous cliffs on the edge of what looked like Admiralty Gulf. But they didn't hint at the name of the gulf in their anxious radio messages to the outside world. Or their intention now to follow the Kimberley coast back eastwards to try to find Wyndham. Nor, even more puzzlingly, that they suddenly, to their delight, in this ghastly wilderness of crags and ravines, came upon a small habitation. It was a mission station, a collection of huts lying among rice fields and coconut palms, about a mile inland.

Smithy circled low as scores of black people began to appear from nowhere. Ulm quickly wrote a message: 'PLEASE POINT THE DIRECTION OF WYNDHAM', put it in a handkerchief which he tied to a torch, and dropped it out of the cockpit window. While Smithy banked, Ulm watched to see if the message, which had fallen into a patch of grass, would be picked up. He thought it was. After circling for fifteen minutes over a crowd of excited Aborigines, they saw a white man appear. Looking up at them, he raised his arm and, to their utter astonishment, stood rigidly like a statue, pointing to the south-west. This was shattering information. Wyndham should have been south-east.

The community they had found was the Drysdale River mission, a lonely outpost in the far north of the Kimberley run by a Spanish Benedictine order. It had no land connection with the outside world: it was accessible only by sea in a voyage taking several days from Wyndham. It had no radio and luggers from Wyndham called only infrequently. It was so remote that the Spanish fathers, it was said, didn't get the news of the First World War armistice until early in 1920. They must have looked up at this orbiting three-engined aeroplane with utter amazement.

Smithy and Ulm discussed their dilemma in abbreviated sentences in their notebook. If Wyndham was south-west of here, then they must have finished up north-east of it, somewhere near Darwin. They were not to know that their message had not been picked up – it wasn't discovered until three days later. The Spanish priest, believing they were looking for somewhere to land, had pointed toward a possible site a few hundred yards away. It was a calamitous misunderstanding. As they flew off on the south-west course they believed they'd been given, they were actually heading for Derby and Broome.

As midday (Sydney time) approached and they had been in the air for twenty-five hours, they began to get low on fuel. Ulm, normally so thorough in keeping the log, did not record that they had flown over an unidentified settlement, and it was to be many days before this highly relevant fact became known to the outside world. The principal record of the remaining hours of the flight come from the aircraft's increasingly helpless transmissions, logged by stations between Darwin and Perth.

'12 noon. We can't see where we are yet but it's somewhere on coast at mouth of a river. Steering south-west trying to avoid the clouds but they are all about us.' They all believed they were travelling south-west down the east coast of Joseph Bonaparte Gulf, heading for the smaller Cambridge Gulf within it that contained Wyndham. They were actually now more than 350 miles to the west of that area, laboriously following the Kimberley coast around all its indentations of promontories and fjords on a slow south-westerly journey that might eventually have brought them to Derby.

At 1.50 pm there came from McWilliams a more hopeful message: 'Passed over a mission or something like that and threw down a note. A chap gave us the direction and I think 150 miles.' The second mission on which they had stumbled was a Presbyterian station called Port George. It was on the western side of the Kimberley and, like the first, could only be reached by boat – in this case, over treacherous open sea from Broome, a three-day voyage away. It lay about 3 miles inland in rolling hills densely cloaked in cypress and spinifex. There was nowhere they could possibly land safely. Everywhere lush green grass, taller than a man, concealed carpets of wicked boulders. The coast nearby offered no better prospect: beneath towering vertical crags of red rock lay massive boulders. There was not a beach in sight.

Once again the arrival of an aeroplane out of grey lowering cloud created a stir among missionaries and Aborigines, who rushed out from the small collection of houses and huts as another message fluttered down. The missionaries and their wives were amazed to recognise the famous aeroplane. 'When the machine was nearly overhead we all cried out, "The *Southern Cross*!"' wrote one of them, George Beard. 'We could see the name quite plain. It came right over us, circled, dropped a note asking us to place three white sheets on the ground in a line pointing the direction of Wyndham and to mark the mileage on the centre one. We did this. I stood at the end pointing due east.'[7]

When Smithy and Ulm saw the direction in which Beard was pointing they were dumbfounded. They were equally stunned to see the distance dutifully marked for them, in numerals created by twists of sand on the sheet: 150. They began to wonder if they were losing their reason. Had they known that the well-intentioned guess at the mileage was a serious underestimate they would have been shattered: the true distance was nearer 230 miles. They had no idea what this place was and it wasn't shown on their maps. They were now more unsure than ever where, in the whole vast spread of the Kimberley, they actually were. In the cockpit Smithy and Ulm conferred frantically, scribbling fuel estimates in the notebook and on the windscreen.

'I wrote on the windowsill with my finger "1.40" [one hour forty minutes],' Ulm recalled afterwards. But Smithy, he said, disagreed. 'He said, "No, less than that." I said, "I still think there is 1.40 or more. If we have a following wind we can make it. If not we can turn back."' Ulm's dangerously optimistic estimate allowed not a minute's margin. It assumed they could fly to Wyndham unerringly, without any homing aids, through rain and cloud, across the badly mapped ranges vaguely indicated in the *Times* atlas. It assumed somehow that if they got there it would be easy to find the township, for which, moreover, they had no precise heading, merely a vague easterly direction indicated by a man on the ground. It assumed that throughout the flight they would be able constantly and accurately to measure their drift. Smithy's more cautious guess would have seen them theoretically out of fuel well short of Wyndham. But these were both calculations in which desperation had blinded them to the harsh arithmetic. It was a suicidal decision, later to be strongly criticised, that they now took: to have a go at finding their original destination.

And so they climbed away from this friendly place and set course east. Why Smithy, with four lives in his hands, should have allowed himself to be persuaded to risk their necks in this way, he was not convincingly able to explain. Asked by an experienced pilot investigating the events of that day, 'But you did not actually consider the question of whether you had sufficient petrol before you left Port George?' Smithy replied lamely: 'I do not remember considering it.' They flew east into what proved to be a head-wind. Had they not detected it, it is almost certain that they would have pressed on and discovered too late that Wyndham was much further away than 150 miles. Even so, they appear to have flown away from the coast, where there were mudflats suitable for an emergency landing, for nearly an hour.

Shortly after 2 o'clock they abandoned the ill-conceived flight and turned back. By now the cloud base was lowering again on to the ranges ahead of them and they were scarcely able to see the ground. By the time they should have reached the Port George mission there was no sign of it. It was, Smithy wrote, 'the last and cruellest blow'. They were never to locate the tiny habitation. Through steep, mist-covered ranges sprinkled with the bulbous shapes of baobab trees, they wove their way back toward the western estuaries of the Kimberley, now accepting that their hugely publicised flight to England must end ignominiously in an embarrassing forced landing. Even in this dire emergency Ulm did not forget his sponsors: the last message McWilliams tapped out was to the Sydney *Sun* and the Melbourne *Herald*: 'Have been hopelessly lost in dense rain storm for ten hours. Now going to make forced landing at place we believe to be 150 miles from Wyndham in rotten country. Will communicate again as soon as possible. Cheerio – Ulm.' What he failed to state was the direction from Wyndham, an omission that was to create days of confusion among those who set out to look for them.

Around 3.30 Sydney time – 1.30 in the Kimberley – when they could no longer see any fuel sitting in the gauges behind them and knew they were living on borrowed time, they emerged from the hills into desolate estuarine country where wide, tidal rivers snaked through low-lying bush and mangrove swamp. Although all messages from the Fokker had now ceased, McWilliams had screwed down his Morse key and in Darwin the whine of his generator could be heard, eerily telling the world they were still airborne. But there was no direction-finding equipment to say where, in the great expanse of the North-West, the spooky rising and falling tones were coming from.

In fact they had drifted well south of the mission. The swamplands below looked too boggy to receive the weight of the aeroplane, but they had no option. Smithy made a wide circuit and lined up the Fokker with a flat patch of mud, lying amid swamp and large patches of bush. 'The wheels ploughed into the mud and as we forged through it, she tilted dangerously forward. I thought she would turn over on her nose. But she sank back on a level keel – and came to rest. Again the dear old bus had saved us.'

But neither they nor anybody else had the least idea where they were.

15

Snails and Grass
1929

Smithy switched off the engines and they all climbed out. The landing had been a miracle: the starboard propeller had sliced through a sapling and arrived within 5ft of a much bigger tree. They had been in the air for twenty-eight and a half hours, and there remained barely enough fuel for another fifteen minutes' flying. Their initial reaction was euphoric relief. Unable to hear one another, they shouted with the sheer joy of being alive – they had not expected to survive a landing in this wilderness. The crew seized Smithy, slapping him affectionately on the back as they bellowed congratulations on their deliverance.

Although the Fokker appeared undamaged, the heavy landing had fractured the lower fringe of the centre of the main spar. Concealed by the wing's plywood skin, the break wasn't visible and they were to remain blissfully unaware of the dangerous condition of the aircraft. 'Where were we and how were we to get out of this dreadful spot?' Smithy wrote. 'The place was a great swamp, bordered by tidal inlets where, we later discovered, there was a rise and fall of nearly 40 feet. Fortunately we'd landed above high water mark. We believed we were within 50 miles of the mission. But whether it lay north, south, east or west, was quite unknown to us.'

The Port George mission was actually much nearer than they believed. It lay, modern topographical maps show, only 12½ miles in a direct line almost due north of the mudflat. But they couldn't see it. All they could see was a flat expanse of muddy claypans, tropical woodland and wet grass which stood 8ft high, concealing sheets of thigh-deep water. In the near distance were some low hills and one of these, a hummock around 100ft high, they climbed for a wider view of the landscape. To the south, about half a mile from the aircraft, was a large, tidal river, curving through salt flats and tall mangrove swamps. The river, which was to be made famous by their sojourn near its blue, slimy banks, was a tributary of the Glenelg known as the Gairdner. At dusk they trooped back through the squelching bog to the aircraft and began to take stock of their position.

The first thing they discovered was that their emergency food was missing: it had apparently been stolen from the locker before they left Sydney. All they had were seven stale sandwiches and around 3 kilos of tinned babyfood they had been taking to a sick child in Wyndham. That night they made their first attempt to get the radio working. Their transmitter was normally powered direct from the Fokker's wind-driven generators, which only rotated in flight and also charged the batteries used for reception. McWilliams rigged up an aerial, hanging a wire on one of the aileron posts, and soon waves of Morse were pouring in with concerned communications discussing their disappearance. Although he had the means to do so, McWilliams made no attempt to convert his receiver to a transmitter and inform the world that they were alive. To celebrate their survival they opened the bottle of emergency brandy, lacing the remains of their coffee with it and naming the spot Coffee Royal. Smithy walked back along the deep tracks of their landing run to see if the surface would permit a take-off when the mud dried out. If they could get back into the air, the radio generators would enable them to get a brief message out. Given a few days of dry weather, it looked feasible. He went into the cockpit to check the fuel gauges: there was only enough for two or three minutes' flight. Before long even those precious drops had evaporated.

With nightfall came hordes of vicious mosquitos. Soon the four men were punctured and bleeding from head to foot. To try to get some sleep they pulled on heavy clothes in which they sweated uncomfortably in the stifling tropical heat. They put on gloves and looped rubber bands round the bottoms of their trouser-legs, but were still bitten on every inch of their bodies. In desperation, around dawn, they stoked up the fire and stood, coughing, in the smoke, trying to comfort themselves with the thought that they wouldn't be there for long. They were convinced that, once they could light signal fires, searching aircraft would quickly spot the Fokker's big silver wing.

Their disappearance, making headlines around the world, was baffling those trying to decide where they were. False hopes based on one of their radio messages were at first raised that they had made a safe landing near the Drysdale River mission. But the mission couldn't be quickly contacted: it took three days for messages to travel by Aboriginal runner from Wyndham to Drysdale. Sun Newspapers decided to charter a search aircraft to go to Drysdale.

Extraordinary as it seems today, when the Fokker vanished there was no automatic response from anybody. The rescue appears to have been left entirely to individual initiatives like that of the Sun's managing editor, Herbert Campbell-Jones, intent on a journalistic coup. There was no one in the whole of Australia at that time with the responsibility or the funds to co-ordinate and direct the hunt. The new Australian National Airways as yet had no aeroplanes – it didn't even own the Southern Cross. All it could do was charter a second aircraft from West Australian Airways in Perth. In Melbourne the defence minister, Sir William Glasgow, said cautiously that the RAAF would help only 'if required'. For two days after the Southern Cross disappeared, not a single search flight was made by anyone. On the third day the Sun Group's chartered DH50 flew out from Wyndham to the Drysdale River mission to question the Spanish monks, using an ingenious system of dropped questions to which the missionaries responded with semaphore-like gestures. It was established that the aircraft had passed over the mission before flying off south-west.

Meanwhile, the Southern Cross crew, growing weak and hungry, had been reduced to a diet of mud snails collected from the nearby mangrove swamps, and tiny sago-like beans they found on some of the grass. The snails, which they boiled in hundreds, breaking the shells with stones, made them feel sick; they tried to counteract the nausea by sipping glycerine from a bottle of lubricant. They had discussed making spears to fish in the Gairdner River, but the water, which ran in swift tidal flows, was perilous. Along the banks they sank to their waists in blue, oozing mud. And lurking there were huge saltwater crocodiles, up to 20ft long, which could leap up and seize a man in seconds. They decided to stick to the snails. With the ample rainwater they were confident they could survive on this disgusting diet for weeks.

On their first full day on the mudflat, Easter Monday, 1 April, while they still had some strength, they had busied themselves lighting signal fires and fixing their position with the sextant. Litchfield calculated it as latitude 15° 35' S, longitude 124° 45' E – within a mile and a half of their true position. On their marine chart they could at last fairly accurately pinpoint where they were: south of Port George IV Inlet, about 3 miles north of what they believed to be the Glenelg River. But as they had no reference to the name or location of the Port George mission, they still didn't know in which direction it lay. They could also see what a staggering distance they were from Wyndham.

On their battery receiving set they listened in frustration to reports that the search was still concentrating on the Drysdale River area, far away to the north-east. In a desperate bid to broadcast their latitude and longitude, they tried to use one of the Fokker's big landing wheels, 4ft in diameter, to turn the generator by friction. To get the wheel running they dug a hole beneath it after building a supporting trestle for the undercarriage from a tree laid between piles of rocks. Lacking a suitable tool with which to fell the tree, they were reduced to hacking it down with a screwdriver hammered by a rock. To turn the heavy wheel, Smithy carved from a branch with his pocket knife a wooden bearing into which the aircraft's engine-starting handle would fit. Then he fashioned a wooden friction roller to attach to the generator they had taken off the side of the fuselage. It was to be a whole week before all these desperate devices were ready to test.

During that time they discussed the possibility of converting the battery short-wave receiver to a transmitter. Technical instructions on how to do it were repeatedly broadcast by Sydney radio. McWilliams denied ever hearing these messages. He may have been afraid to admit to having received the advice for fear of censure that he hadn't tried to follow the simple instructions. Smithy admitted that they had indeed heard the guidance. He added that McWilliams already knew anyway how to reverse the receiver to transmission mode. Why McWilliams didn't try even for a few minutes to send out an SOS remains one of the many enigmas of the whole unhappy episode. Had he done so it is conceivable that the crew could have been found within forty-eight hours, sparing much of the misery their disappearance would cause.

In Canberra the air force's impotence was being roundly attacked by MPs, who were pressing the prime minister, Stanley Bruce, for action. But the army-dominated Defence Department didn't believe that the *Southern Cross* would be found from the air. A briefing note to Bruce said: 'The search can most effectively be carried out to finality by a practical mobilisation of the natives under white leadership.'[1] While the government procrastinated, the people of Sydney decided to act. The city commissioner, John Garlick, a forthright figure and a personal friend of Smithy's, had in exasperation formed what he called the 'Citizens' Southern Cross Rescue Committee' to raise immediate funds and mount its own search. The public response was overwhelming. Within hours $4,000 had been collected. The committee chartered its own search aircraft – a big, single-engined biplane, the *Canberra*, a six-passenger de Havilland DH61, known as the Giant Moth – piloted by its co-owner, Captain Les Holden, an experienced ex-war pilot. There were unconscionable delays in the *Canberra*'s departure from Sydney with a wireless-operator, doctor and mechanic on board. By the time it got to the Kimberley the *Southern Cross* had been missing for nine days.

By then an attempt had been made at last to communicate with the Presbyterian missionaries at the Port George station. The pilot of the DH50 chartered by Australian National Airways went there and immediately discovered, from ground signals in response to dropped notes, that this, not Drysdale, was the last mission station to have seen the trimotor. The missionaries abruptly stopped harvesting their corn, peanuts, rice and potatoes and most of the station's inhabitants, black and white, left on foot, donkey and boat to join the search.

'My, but we are all weak!' Ulm wrote on the eighth day. 'Tobacco ran out this morning. Have tried since smoke leaves but they awful . . . More strength-sucking efforts turning generator. We each turn for 10 to 15 seconds, then all have quarter-hour's spell.' Cranking the aircraft's wheel, with its tyre driving the generator, was, finally, in brief, strenuous bursts, producing a small flow of current to the transmitter. They worked it at night while

McWilliams tapped out their position. But they lacked the strength to give it the sustained effort it demanded, and their signals were never heard.

Their disappearance had now become a national crisis, discussed daily in the federal Parliament, where Bruce was concerned at the growing public anger, emanating most stridently from ex-servicemen's organisations. Because the *Southern Cross* flight had not been a government venture, the RAAF had still not committed a single aeroplane of its own. It was to take a tragic development to spur them into action.

Keith Anderson, still vainly trying to promote his own reputation as an aviator, had fitted his Westland Widgeon, which he had named *Kookaburra*, with long-range tanks to attempt a world endurance flight record circling over Sydney. A group of Smithy's drinking mates at the Custom House Hotel, led by the publican, Jack Cantor, disgusted by the government's inertia, approached him to make a search, which they offered to fund. For £500 Anderson agreed to go. He was convinced that the *Cross* had come down near Port George, and that the search was being conducted in the wrong part of the Kimberley.

What possessed Anderson to undertake this mercy mission it is now only possible to guess. The gesture, one suspects, must have been inspired by his enduring affection for Smithy, despite all the rebuffs and humiliations. It is clear that he badly wanted to keep their fragile friendship alive, and putting Smithy in his debt would certainly have helped. It might also have led to a prestigious job as a captain with the new airline. 'He undertook the flight from a spirit of sympathy and fellowship for Kingsford Smith,' Jack Cantor later told the newspapers. It is also possible that Anderson saw this as his last chance to redeem a rather unsuccessful career in aviation.

Perhaps more surprising was the revelation that the mechanic Anderson had engaged to accompany him, for a fee of £100, would be none other than the man who can be assumed to have been nursing an even deeper grievance against the lost aviators: Bob Hitchcock. He appears cheerfully to have turned the other cheek, embarking on an expedition which, people said, he saw as his Christian duty. The need for the £100 may have had something to do with it. Bob Hitchcock's niece, Gwen Bliss, whom I traced in

Perth, said: 'In those days mates were mates, weren't they? If a mate was in strife and you could assist, then you went and looked for him.' When, at Coffee Royal, Smithy and Ulm heard on Sydney radio that Anderson and Hitchcock were about to join the search, they were astonished. Yet Smithy never revealed his true feelings. In his autobiography he merely recorded: 'The most dramatic and poignant attempt to fly to our rescue was that made by our old friend and former companion, Keith Anderson.'

The preparations for the *Kookaburra*'s departure from Sydney were as careless and casual as had been those for the plane they were going to look for. Arriving at the aerodrome, Anderson discovered that there was no compass in the aircraft. After a series of frantic phone calls he located one somewhere in central Sydney. As the auxiliary steel tanks he had installed would affect the instrument's accuracy, he arranged for an engineer to adjust it to compensate for the metal-induced error. Although he had been offered an emergency radio he decided not to carry one because its batteries were too heavy. Less comprehensibly, he took only a small amount of emergency food and water. Nor, like Smithy, did he bother to carry a light axe with which to clear scrub for a take-off in the event of a forced landing. He intended to take a tyre pump but left without it. The only maps he had were an inadequate set of small-scale pages torn from an atlas, together with a section of a South Australia railway map.

On the morning of Sunday 7 April 1929, Anderson left behind the relative luxury of his fiancée's home in upmarket Cremorne, warmly dressed for the flight in a suit with waistcoat and collar and tie under a heavy leather flying coat. In his bare and shabby room in unsalubrious Tramway Street, Hitchcock left almost everything he possessed in the world: one of his two Bibles, an aircraft propeller, some tattered underclothing, a waistcoat and two shirts. Once more on his beam's end, he arrived at Richmond inadequately dressed for flight in a worn and crumpled worsted suit with a scarf tucked into the jacket. Much more worryingly, he was far from well. His injured leg, badly gashed in the Tourer crash the year before, had become persistently infected and had recently required further surgery to drain it. He had been discharged from hospital only a few days earlier, still in much pain.

Just a few people came to see them off, among them Bon

Hilliard. Things were tense between her and Anderson. The resentment she felt toward Smithy and Ulm had not subsided and when
she had heard of Keith's search plan there had been a bitter row.
'She had threatened that if he went to look for Smithy, he could
regard their engagement as terminated,' John Laurence said.

With an enormous overload of fuel, the *Kookaburra* bounced
soggily for hundreds of yards across the airfield before slowly staggering into the air. Anderson hoped to get to Wyndham in three
days, stopping overnight at Broken Hill and Alice Springs. Less
than 100 miles from Richmond, at the small town of Blayney, low
cloud forced him to land in a paddock, in the process of which he
damaged the tailskid. Between Broken Hill and Alice Springs he
got lost, ending up, after flying 200 miles on a wrong heading, at
Port Augusta at the head of the Spencer Gulf in South Australia –
almost as far from Alice as when he had left Broken Hill. He had
not noticed that their entire tool kit, stowed on the floor of the
front cockpit, as well as the *Kookaburra*'s spare parts, had been
stolen during the night at Broken Hill. The resulting reduction in
the mass of metal so close to the compass had badly skewed its
accuracy.

On the third day, at Algebuckina, a few miles south of
Oodnadatta, the engine began to play up. Anderson landed in a
clearing in the scrub and Hitchcock quickly rectified the problem:
a loose tappet on one of the four cylinders. In Alice Springs they
learned that the Giant Moth had reached Wyndham and had been
searching the Kimberley all day. One suspects that Anderson
prayed that pilot Holden would not beat him to the Fokker. To
Anderson's delight there was also a telegram from Bon. She had
had second thoughts about her threat to call off their engagement. Her affectionate message has not survived, but it is known
that she said she still wanted to marry him.

From Alice he determined to strike across the Tanami Desert
direct to Wyndham in one 700-mile hop, something he had been
strongly advised against because of the dangers of a forced landing
in this waterless wilderness, where no animals existed and no birds
sang. Two days earlier Holden in the *Canberra* had skirted the
area in a long detour to the north. But Anderson, in his desire to
get to Smithy first, rejected this option, even though the risky
short-cut amounted to a saving of only an hour and a half.

Furthermore, he decided to sacrifice emergency drinking water for fuel, taking only 3 litres. The little aeroplane was tanked up with nearly 90 gallons of petrol – vastly more than was necessary, even allowing for a fierce headwind. The man who was fuelling the Widgeon from four-gallon cans paused before pouring in the last and tried to persuade him to take instead its weight in water. 'No thanks,' Anderson is said to have responded. 'Petrol is worth more to me than water.'[2]

Anderson and Hitchcock had replaced some of their stolen tools at Alice, but didn't bother to have the compass readjusted. They no longer had the least idea by how many degrees the instrument was deviating from true. Moreover, the stoical, uncomplaining Hitchcock was probably in no state to continue the flight. His leg was now giving him so much pain that he had to have it treated by a nurse in Alice. The wound was swollen and infected, but all she could do was disinfect and rebandage it. They took off at 7.15 am on Wednesday 10 April, having left details of their intended route at the Alice police station. They followed the telegraph line 90 miles north to Woodforde Crossing – between Aileron and Ti-Tree on the present Stuart Highway – and then set off north-west across the pink, featureless scrubscape of the Tanami.

Now in their tenth day at Coffee Royal, the crew of the *Southern Cross* had been listening nightly with disbelief to reports of the *Kookaburra*'s plodding progress toward the Kimberley. They still couldn't come to terms with the irony of being searched for by Keith Anderson and Bob Hitchcock. Gaunt and bearded, they watched in frustration while planes at last combing the Port George area passed to and fro without spotting the Fokker's white wing or their smoke-signals. 'Smithy is failing fast,' Ulm wrote that day. 'He reels as he walks. Hunger pains are nearly driving Mac and me insane. Today I collapsed five times.'

On the eleventh day the government at long last responded to the rising public concern. Prime Minister Bruce announced that the seaplane carrier *Albatross* would leave Sydney for an air search of the Kimberley. The ship's amphibious biplanes would be lowered over the side in the Timor Sea. But it would take the carrier nearly a week to get there. While the naval crew were being recalled from shore leave, some disquieting news reached Sydney. The

Kookaburra had failed to arrive at Wyndham. Two aeroplanes and six men were now missing. As the *Albatross* steamed out of Sydney on its long voyage to the other side of Australia, Bruce, fearful now of a double tragedy, decided at last to involve the air force. Obsolete and unsuitable as they were, he announced that a flight of DH9A biplanes would leave immediately from Melbourne for the North-West. Scarcely had he made the announcement that Friday, 12 April, when a dramatic message arrived in Sydney from the Giant Moth. 'Found, found found', it said as the *Canberra* circled triumphantly over the *Southern Cross*. 'Found alive all well. Position south of Port George mission on mudflats.'

'When we saw the machine gliding towards us,' Smithy recalled, 'Litch and I, with tears in our eyes, hugged each other.'[3] In his memoirs Ulm said that Kingsford Smith and Litchfield broke down and cried. Four sacks of rations had thumped down on to the mudflat. 'We just tore open two tins of bully beef and ate it like animals.'

As the big biplane circled, too heavy to risk a landing on the mud, its wireless-operator, John Stannage, kept up the running Morse commentary that was being excitedly received in Sydney. Within minutes newspapers were rushing out special editions and newsboys were chorusing the glad tidings. At 'Kuranda' the relief and happiness spilled over. Catherine, who had begun to fear the worst, had become ill with anxiety as hope faded. Then had come the ecstatic phone call. 'Great day of rejoicing everywhere. Boys all alive and well.' The customary media army descended upon the house. William, bewildered by the invasion, kept pointing to the garden flagpole on which he had hoisted the Union Jack and the Australian flag the moment he'd heard the news.

In central Sydney car horns blared and harbour ferries cock-a-doodle-doed. 'NATION SIGHS WITH RELIEF', said the *Sun*. People in offices stopped work and cheered; in hospitals nurses spread the news through the wards. School lessons were abandoned as head-teachers summoned children to special assemblies to give thanks. Stanley Bruce, whose government had done virtually nothing to help the search, said: 'I share the great rejoicing which I know will resound throughout the Commonwealth. It is splendid to know that these gallant men have been found.'

16

'The Boys Sent Keith to Look for You'

1929

But not all the missing fliers were safe. In the middle of the Tanami Desert, as people were shouting the *Canberra*'s news across the streets throughout Australia, Keith Anderson and Bob Hitchcock were on their knees beside the stranded *Kookaburra*, tormented by thirst, clawing at the hot, red sand, digging desperately for water. This time the government acted more promptly – if ineffectively. On the day the *Southern Cross* was found, the RAAF had ordered two small aircraft to set off from Melbourne to search for the *Kookaburra*. Yet, after a whole week they had still not flown a single mission into the middle of the Tanami, where the Widgeon had been stranded for two days in the heat of the desert bush. The last people to see the aircraft had been some Aboriginal stockmen working on Morton's cattle station on the eastern edge of the desert. The little aeroplane was already well off course, to the south of its intended track. It should have passed at least 40 miles to the north-west. It seems that almost as soon as he left the reassuring guidance of the telegraph poles, Anderson had been overwhelmed, yet again, by navigation difficulties.

In Sydney the *Southern Cross* search committee refused at first to use its resources of donated funds to look for the *Kookaburra*. It adopted the inflexible view that, as the money had been raised to look for Smithy, it shouldn't automatically be made available for anything else. The truth was that the committee was peeved that Anderson had set off, like the lone ranger, in a clear attempt to find the *Southern Cross* before the *Canberra* did. They accused Jack Cantor of mounting a rival, covert operation and went as far as to allege that he had dispatched Anderson 'under sealed orders', instructing him to fly in one great hop direct from Alice Springs to Port George. However, not a shred of evidence was ever produced that Anderson intended to do this.

But from these quite groundless suspicions, a quite extraordinary belief was rapidly gaining currency: that the disappearance of the *Southern Cross* and the subsequent flight of the *Kookaburra* to find it were all part of a publicity stunt prearranged between Smithy, Ulm and Anderson. It was whispered that had the *Kookaburra* not disappeared, Anderson would have gone to the precise location where they had all agreed the Fokker would put down. However, as Kingsford Smith and Ulm, their sunburned faces swollen by infected mosquito bites, sat under the wing of the trimotor devouring their first real food in nearly two weeks, they were oblivious to the gathering storm. They were happily discussing their intention, once their strength returned, to have petrol delivered to enable them to fly the *Southern Cross* out to Derby and back to Sydney to resume their journey to England. Meanwhile, at the desolate mudflat, they began to receive daily visits from aircraft which showered down everything they needed: clothing, bedding, mosquito nets, sunhats, tins of cigarettes, food and heaps of supportive telegrams from well-wishers all over Australia.

The day after they were discovered a West Australian Airways DH50 flown by Bertie Heath landed beside them, bringing yet more food and – to Ulm's deep dismay – a reporter called Tonkin from the *West Australian*. The reporter, a huge scoop within his grasp, tried to interview them, but, conscious of their obligations to Sun Newspapers, they were sparing in what they said. They did agree to be photographed, re-enacting for Tonkin their attempts to crank the generator with the aircraft's wheel. For a group picture, they insisted on hoisting Heath on to their shoulders. They were later to regret this when, after the wide exposure the photograph got, it was cited as evidence that their privations had not weakened them to anything near the level Ulm had claimed in his diary. 'The photography suggests,' one Sydney newspaper commented cynically, 'that Kingsford Smith and his mates were happy and well nurtured and might well be members of a camping party.'[1]

Ulm entrusted Tonkin, whose Perth newspaper didn't compete with the *Sun*'s interests, with the precious record of their twelve-day experience. In return for rights to publish the diary in the *West Australian*, Tonkin agreed to send it all in huge telegrams to the Sydney *Sun* and its Melbourne associate, the *Herald*. But other rivals, embittered by the *Sun*'s monopoly on this international story, struck back. Prominent among them were the aggressive Sydney *Daily Guardian* and the virulent, scandal-seeking *Smith's Weekly*, both owned by Smith's Newspapers.

It all began when yet another enterprising reporter arrived at Coffee Royal. This, to Smithy's and Ulm's mild horror, was the *Guardian*'s West Australian correspondent, John Marshall, whom Smithy had flown from Perth to Sydney in his failed 1927 record attempt. Marshall arrived from Derby in a Bristol Tourer hired by Smith's Newspapers. Although they were friendly to the journalist, Smithy and Ulm told him as little as possible. Marshall was surprised to find that the *Southern Cross* crew were already entertaining some visitors. George Beard, the missionary from Port George, had arrived, accompanied by three Aboriginal trackers. Although their settlement was only a dozen miles away, the mission party had pitched up spattered from head to foot in blue slime, having endured the most appalling two-day journey through mangrove swamps and deep, stinking mud.

Listening to Beard's account of his trek, Marshall was puzzled that the aviators hadn't at least made some exploratory forays to look for the mission so close by, and that they seemed to be in relatively robust condition. Smithy was carrying a painfully infected sore on the edge of one eye, and McWilliams' legs were numb from an inflamed mass of insect bites, but this did not prevent Marshall from filing the provocative story expected of him. When he got back to Derby that afternoon he wired to the *Guardian* in Sydney a report which helped to reinforce the newspaper's decidedly more cynical view of the Coffee Royal affair than that being presented by Sun Newspapers.

Smith's Newspapers' spate of harsh stories, openly critical of the heroes, played heavily on the fact that, while the *Southern Cross* crew were being lavishly supplied on the mudflat, no aircraft had yet begun to search the Tanami Desert for Anderson and Hitchcock, who were already being described as martyrs. The two

harles aged three.
hn Oxley Library, Brisbane

Twelve-year-old chorister Charles Smith at
Sydney's St Andrew's Cathedral School in 1909.
He was known there as 'Pontiac' and 'Yank'.
Canon Melville Newth

The Kingsford Smith family's annual Christmas camp at Flint and Steel Bay in 1913.
From left, seated: Philip Kingsford, Jimmy Harricks, William, Godfrey Kingsford,
Rupert Swallow, Charles (aged nearly sixteen), Eric, Madoline Martin (Elfreda's sister).
Standing: Winifred, Elfreda Martin (Leofric's fiancée), Leofric, Catherine, Wilfrid.
Kingsford Smith family collection

Recovering from his foot wound, suffered in aerial combat, Smithy spent several weeks in a wheelchair in late 1917 at Ellerman's Hospital in Regent's Park, London.
Kingsford Smith family collection

London, 1919. Still in RAF uniform, the team who had hoped to fly the Blackburn Kangaroo in the England–Australia air race that year. From left: Smithy, Cyril Maddocks, Valdemar Rendle.
London Daily Mail

Smithy dangling by his legs from the undercarriage of an Avro 504K over the Californian desert in 1920, when he worked briefly as a stuntman for a Hollywood film company. *National Air and Space Museum, Smithsonian Institution*

The accident that followed the christening party at Riverslea Station – and cost Smithy his job. *Beau Sheil*

Norman Brearley (centre) poses beside one of Western Australian Airways Bristol Tourers in December 1921 with his first pilot team. From left: Smithy, Bob Fawcett (killed on his first trip), Len Taplin, Val Abbott. *Aviation Museum of Western Australia*

Thelma Corboy, the first Mrs Kingsford Smith. This 1928 Perth newspaper picture identified her as the co-respondent in the protracted Ives divorce proceedings. *Library and Information Service of Western Australia*

Captain Allan Hancock, the oil millionaire whose generosity made the 1928 trans-Pacific flight possible. *Hancock family collection*

The 1928 Pacific flight crew. From left: navigator Harry Lyon, Smithy, radio-operator Jim Warner, relief pilot Charles Ulm. The picture was taken at Oakland Airport shortly before departure. *Tom Warner*

on Hilliard, Keith Anderson's fiancée,
hom Smithy wanted to marry.
dney Daily Guardian

The flight deck of the Fokker trimotor *Southern Cross*,
showing the large control wheels and triple-throttle levers.
National Library of Australia

he Brisbane newspaper picture which unconsciously captured the extraordinary event that
llowed the landing of the *Southern Cross* at the end of the great Pacific flight. On enlargement the
litary figures who disembarked in mid-field are seen to be the American crewmen, Jim Warner,
ith his trademark white panama hat, and Harry Lyon. *Brisbane Sunday Mail*

The Pacific heroes are driven triumphantly into Brisbane on 9 June 1928. From left: Smithy, Harry Lyon, Jim Warner, with Charles Ulm seated. *Queensland Newspaper Pty Ltd*

American radio-operator Jim Warner in the cabin of the *Southern Cross*. His Pacific flight messages, tapped out in Morse code, made aviation wireless history. *National Library of Australia*

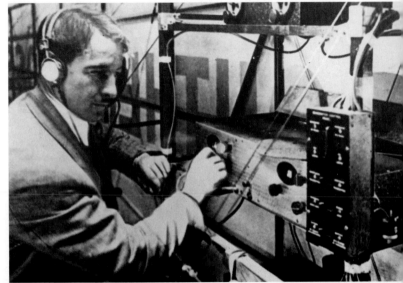

Smithy's mother and father, Catherine and William, pictured in their seventies at the peak of their son's fame in the late 1920s. *Sydney Morning Herald*

Wherever it landed in 1928, the *Southern Cross* was quickly engulfed in a sea of humanity – as here in Christchurch, New Zealand, after its first historic Tasman crossing. *Mitchell Library, Sydney*

The *Southern Cross* flies past Mount Taranaki on arrival in New Zealand for the 1933 joyriding tour – one of the few air-to-air photographs of the famous trimotor that has survived. *New Zealand Herald*

Each of the *Southern Cross*'s three engines had to be laboriously cranked into life. At Auckland in 1933 a mechanic winds up the starboard one. *NZ Truth*

The Kimberley wilderness of bush and mudflats where the *Southern Cross* remained undiscovered for twelve days. Visible are the aircraft's landing tracks which have baked into the mud. *Australian Archives*

Keith Anderson (right) and Bob Hitchcock photographed during the *Kookaburra* mission which ended in tragedy in the Tanami Desert. *Gwen Bliss*

The Coffee Royal survivors on the Gairdner River mudflat soon after they were found in April 1929. From left: Litchfield, Ulm, Smithy, McWilliams. *Australian Archives*

Smithy and his Avro Avian *Southern Cross Junior* in which, in 1930, he broke Bert Hinkler's England–Australia solo record. *Melbourne Age*

The flight team whose 1930 Atlantic journey was the first wholly successfully to cross the ocean from east to west. From left: navigator Paddy Saul, Smithy, co-pilot Evert van Dijk, radio-operator John Stannage. *Sydney Morning Herald*

At Smithy and Mary's 1930 Melbourne wedding Charles Ulm (right with bridesmaid Molly McBride) was best man. *Melbourne Age*

At Croydon Smithy delivers the 1931 Australian Christmas mail on to carts of Imperial Airways, the airline that was to thwart all his ambitions to operate his own services on the Empire routes. *Queensland Museum*

Scotty Allan: a pilot as brilliant as Smithy, and one of his sternest critics. *Allan family collection*

The strain shows behind Smithy's grin on arrival in Brisbane in his Percival Gull in October 1933 at the end of a record solo flight from England. His journey had been plagued by a succession of crippling panic attacks. *Brisbane Courier-Mail*

The Lockheed Altair *Lady Southern Cross* in which Smithy had hoped to win the 1934 England–Australia air race. Shortly after this picture was taken in Sydney he was ordered to remove the name ANZAC. *Mitchell Library, Sydney*

Smithy and some of the members of his exclusive 'magic circle'. From left: Tommy Pethybridge, Wilfrid Kingsford-Smith, Harold Affleck, Smithy's chief aircraftsman, and Harry Purvis. *Queensland Museum*

Two-year-old Charles Arthur Kingsford Smith with Smithy and Mary at their home at 27 Greenoaks Avenue early in 1935. *Queensland Museum*

Smithy and Bill Taylor, the man who saved his life on the Tasman. The picture was taken in Honolulu in 1934 during the eastbound Pacific crossing on which they twice came close to finishing up in the sea.
US Air Force

With the fractured starboard propeller (inset) stopped, Smithy brings the crippled *Southern Cross* back to Mascot on 15 May 1935 after Bill Taylor's heroic mid-Tasman oil transfer. *Melbourne Age*

A rare photograph of Smithy in flight in the *Lady Southern Cross*, taken somewhere over Hawaii on 29 October 1934. *US Air Force*

Nov. 4, 1934

SIR CHARLES KINGSFORD-SMITH AND CAPT. P.G. TAYLOR ARRIVE AT OAKLAND MUNICIPAL AIRPORT TO COMPLETE FIRST AUSTRALIA – AMERICA FLIGHT

Smithy and Bill Taylor are besieged by radio reporters on landing after the 1934 Pacific crossing. The toll taken by fame and flying on Smithy shows in his gaunt appearance. *National Air and Space Museum, Smithsonian Institution*

One of the last pictures ever taken of Smithy, as he and Tommy Pethybridge left Lympne Aerodrome in England in the dark before dawn on 6 November 1935. *Melbourne Age*

Aye Island, where Burmese fishermen from the mainland (visible in the distance) found the Altair's wheel eighteen months after Smithy and Pethybridge disappeared. *Dick Smith*

The *Lady Southern Cross*'s starboard undercarriage leg, found at Aye Island off the coast of southern Burma in 1937. It resides today in this storeroom at Sydney's Power House Museum. *Author*

At Maungmagan on the Andaman Sea coast of Myanmar (Burma), the author asks a Burmese fisherman about the 1935 crash of the *Lady Southern Cross*. Ninety-year-old U Aye Dun describes another aeroplane, from which the villagers fled into the forest.

RAAF aircraft, beset by mechanical problems, were still on their slow way up to Alice Springs. What the *Guardian* had taken upon itself was the unthinkable: publicly questioning the belief that Kingsford Smith could do no wrong. It not only challenged the level of their suffering so colourfully logged by Ulm, but questioned the whole 'fiasco' of the *Southern Cross*'s flight:

ULM'S TALE: THEY LIVED ON SNAILS AND GRASS
ONLY 25 MILES AWAY FROM MISSION
TOO WEAK TO MAKE SMOKE SIGNALS, THOUGH PLANES
PASSING OVERHEAD
SIMPLY WAITED FOR 12 DAYS
HEARD EVERYTHING ON WIRELESS; MADE SMITHY GRIN

A startling, but happily not tragic, jest has been played on public emotion by circumstances and by the failure or inability of the four missing men to show signals to searching planes . . . From Pilot Heath, who visited the marooned party with a hundredweight of commodities, comes the sardonic story of how Smithy grinned when the wireless related the acute fears of all Australia, and the activity of the prolonged search . . . Many a grim chuckle went round when these messages came through. Smithy would grin and say: 'It's beginning to get everybody guessing, and no one is able to pick the answer.' . . . he knew it was only a matter of sticking around the plane to be relieved . . . They listened to the Sydney radio and played tunes on a mouth organ . . . Why they did not light a huge signal bonfire remains unexplained.[2]

The Sydney *Bulletin* described Kingsford Smith and Ulm as 'private adventurers taking foolhardly risks.' It called the flight a stunt and 'a public nuisance – however gallant the stunters'. In London *The Times* criticised Smithy's flight-management. 'The question remains whether to venture on such a voyage at a bad season, without tools and without provisions, was altogether justifiable. It seems imprudent to set out without equipment to repair the wireless. A few sandwiches and a fortuitous supply of gruel was hardly enough for the quartet on such a flight.' Gleefully

reprinting *The Times*' strictures, the *Guardian* in Sydney returned
to the attack, demanding now that a royal commission, no less, be
set up to 'inquire into the fiasco'. The newspaper demanded to
know why the crew hadn't converted their radio receiver to transmit. It was to be several days before Smithy and Ulm, still camped
on the mudflat 2,000 miles away, read of these hostile allegations.
So they were puzzled to hear on the radio that their solicitor, Eric
Campbell, had taken it upon himself to issue writs for libel seeking £10,000 damages each (around £250,000 today) for Kingsford
Smith and Ulm.

Although his name did not appear on the *Guardian* stories,
Smithy and Ulm, when they eventually read them, were in no
doubt that they had been written by Smith's air correspondent,
Norman Ellison. Although Ellison denied this he was, as the
group's aviation specialist, the logical candidate: he understood
the technicalities of it all. Indeed, he was to admit at the inquiry
that he had spent time at the Custom House Hotel researching
the background to both the *Southern Cross* and *Kookaburra* flights.
Meanwhile, the damaging publicity had already begun to turn the
tide of public opinion. Only a few days earlier, people had been
cheering the news of the *Southern Cross*'s discovery; now many
started to wonder if they had been duped by the great pilot, and
angry letters began to arrive at newspaper offices.

The *Southern Cross* crew spent six days after they were found
recovering on the mudflat, rapidly regaining their lost weight.
Although some of the wing's plywood cover had been badly
warped and rotted by the sun, the Fokker still appeared airworthy.
Had Smithy known about the fracture in the wooden spar, the
wing's most vital structure, he said later, he would have left the
plane at Coffee Royal. Instead, on Thursday 18 April, eighteen
days after they had landed, he decided that he was now strong
enough, and the mud had sufficiently dried out, to attempt to fly
out. The plane lifted off the claypan in less than 200yds and
Smithy flew her south to Derby. The tiny port's normal population
of fifty had been swollen by search pilots and journalists. Here
their fears about Anderson and Hitchcock were confirmed: they
had been missing now for eight days, and there was still no word.
They were deeply affected by a telegram from Jack Cantor: 'THE
BOYS SENT KEITH TO LOOK FOR YOU. FOR GOD'S SAKE LOOK FOR HIM AND

BOB.' They wanted to go out in the 'old bus' and begin searching immediately, but they were still too weak for sustained flying.

During the miserable forty-eight hours they spent in Derby, they became aware that, despite the superficially warm expressions of delight at their survival, they were under a cloud. To their consternation, they learned that they were accused of being party to a stunt, that their integrity was being openly questioned, their flight-planning criticised. Their shining images of probity and infallibility were disintegrating around them. They were hurt and bewildered. A long telegram from Eric Campbell brought news of the libel writs he had slapped on Smith's Newspapers and urged them, before leaving Derby, to get signed statements from the pilots who had visited them at Coffee Royal to confirm the hardships they had suffered and that the forced landing had been genuine. Ulm hurriedly drafted a statement which he asked Bertie Heath and another pilot, Tommy O'Dea, to sign. Heath rewrote his; O'Dea refused to sign.

Back in Sydney, the disappearance of the *Kookaburra* had displaced the *Southern Cross* from the billboards. The gallantry of Anderson and Hitchcock in setting off across the desert in a tiny aeroplane to look for their mates touched the nation. Surprisingly, no newspaper added to the poignancy of the story by reminding people that the two missing men had so recently been defeated by Smithy and Ulm in their bitter courtroom battle.

The ineptitude and lack of urgency that dogged every phase of the efforts to find both missing crews is hard to comprehend today. Now that the *Southern Cross* was safe, the 'citizens' committee', still holding surplus funds from a generous public, appears to have become a small bureaucracy in its own right, immensely concerned with meetings and correspondence and growing steadily more inflexible. Once the Giant Moth *Canberra* had located the Fokker, it could have been dispatched to search the *Kookaburra's* intended route across the Tanami Desert, less than 500 miles away. Instead the aeroplane was allowed to sit on the ground at Wyndham while arguments went on in Sydney about what it should be permitted to do.

The ancient air force DH9As, the only other aircraft then on their way to hunt for Anderson and Hitchcock, had still not even reached Alice Springs. They were beset by a plague of fuel leaks, their water-cooled engines boiled in the heat and almost every time they landed they punctured their tyres. The *Kookaburra* had been missing for days when the prime minister, reacting to criticism of his government's inertia, sent a personal rocket to John Garlick, founder of the committee, instructing him to send the *Canberra* immediately using the public-subscription money. Flung into the search at last, the Giant Moth set off from Wyndham on 16 April, only to run out of fuel. Forced to land at a remote cattle station it was stranded there helplessly for four days waiting for petrol to be trucked out. Meanwhile the Ministry of Defence, its DH9As grounded at Oodnadatta, decided to charter a plane from Qantas. Unfortunately, the only suitable aircraft, a DH50J cabin biplane, the *Atalanta*, was at that moment on the opposite side of the country in Brisbane. By the time it set off, on 19 April, nine days had elapsed since the *Kookaburra*'s disappearance. Given the pitiful quantity of water it was known Anderson had taken from Alice Springs, few who knew the Tanami believed that the two men could have survived.

In Sydney, Bon Hilliard, angry at the lack of urgency with which the search was being handled and convinced that the *Kookaburra* had come down in the Port George area, demanded that the family hire an aircraft of their own. When the citizens' committee blocked her efforts, she went, bursting with exasperation, over everybody's heads and telephoned the defence minister, Sir William Glasgow, in Melbourne, beseeching him to use his authority to extend the search. But Glasgow merely passed the buck. He told her to go back to the citizens' committee. Still it failed to respond: its members had decided that it was 'inappropriate' to deal with a woman. They called Arthur Hilliard to appear before them. He made such a persuasive case that, ironically, they decided to ask Charles Kingsford Smith, recovering in Derby, to take the *Southern Cross* back into the area from which he had just been rescued. On 20 April, 'although we were completely worn out and in poor health and required medical attention,' Smithy wrote, he flew to Wyndham across the Kimberley on the very route he had attempted so disastrously three weeks earlier. There was no sign of the *Kookaburra*.

On the morning of Sunday 21 April, the *Atalanta*, flown by a young Qantas pilot, Lester Brain, finally left Newcastle Waters to

cross the northern Tanami heading for Wave Hill, a large cattle station on the desert's north-west edge. On the way he decided to
investigate some smoke that had been reported by Aborigines the
previous day. He soon spotted the brown column on the horizon
away to the south-west and turned towards it. A large area of the
desert was smouldering. On the edge of the blackened scrub, he
saw a silver shape on the pink, sandy ground. It was the
Kookaburra. While his radio-operator signalled the grim news to
the world, Brain circled the Widgeon, which was sitting there
undamaged. A desiccated body with sun-blackened face, clad only
in underpants and shirt, lay in the shade under the starboard wing.

For some reason Brain decided, mistakenly, that it was Keith
Anderson. There was no sign of another body and, for five days,
the hope was sustained that Hitchcock might have found water
and be alive somewhere. Although the *Atalanta* circled at low
level for nearly an hour, the crew saw no sign of the second man.
Brain could not find a clearing in which he could land and be sure
of getting off again, so, having dropped a can of water just in case,
they flew on to Wave Hill homestead.

Smithy and Ulm were at Wyndham, preparing to set off in the
Cross to join the search, when the terrible news reached them.
They were utterly devastated. Smithy's was the sharpest, most
deeply personal of their grief. He was so upset that he refused to
take the 'old bus' into the air for twenty-four hours as a mark of
respect for the men he knew must both be dead.

Smithy, Ulm, Litchfield and McWilliams left Wyndham to fly
back to Sydney on Tuesday 23 April, diverting into the middle of
the northern Tanami to pay their last respects to their old mates.
'We saw the machine lying there,' Smithy wrote. 'Ulm and I took
turns at circling low down, within 15 feet of her, and we surveyed
the awful ground on which they had been forced to land . . . We
caught sight of a body lying under the wing . . . The sight of the
Kookaburra and the dead body lying there affected us deeply.' For
a moment they considered trying to land to search for the other
man, but although they swooped low over the desert for miles
looking for a clearing or a claypan on which the Fokker could
safely alight and rise again, there was nowhere remotely suitable in
this endless carpet of wiry scrub. 'There was nothing we could do,'
Smithy said, 'except drop food and water on the remote chance

that the other was alive, and we continued on our course to
Newcastle Waters. I look back on that day as one of the saddest of
my life.'

Anderson and Hitchcock had paid a terrible price for haste and
negligence. Their martyrdom unleashed a barrage of violent criticism even from previously sympathetic newspapers, which were
now baying for a full investigation of the *Southern Cross*'s calamitous flight. 'INQUIRY INTO TRAGEDY IS BRUCE'S IMPERATIVE DUTY',
shouted the *Guardian*'s headlines. 'PLANE WENT OUT WITH BAD MAPS,
BAD FOOD, BAD TOOLS, BAD WIRELESS AND BAD WEATHER . . . Nobody yet
knows the full degree of tragedy and horror which may have arisen
from the original flight of the *Southern Cross*.' But Australia was
soon to hear it all.

When the party on horseback from Wave Hill, led by the commander of the RAAF's search flight, Flight Lieutenant Charles
Eaton, eventually reached the virtually undamaged *Kookaburra*, a
pitiful scene greeted them. The bandage on the leg of the body
under the wing identified it as Hitchcock. Anderson's decomposed
corpse was in the scrub about 400yds away. He had crawled off in
search of water, leaving a trail of possessions and personal papers,
including his last telegram from Bon Hilliard. Beside it was a business card, a reminder of happier days, bearing the names of the
three men who had set out to fly the Pacific together. Hitchcock's
only possession was his Bible, which lay beside his body. Eaton had
planned to take the bodies back to Wave Hill, but the horses,
demented by thirst, had become unreliable. Running out of water
and fearful for their own lives, they hurriedly buried the men in
shallow graves where they had been found. There wasn't even
time to make the simplest crosses.

A poignant record of the desperate events that had so swiftly
ended in tragedy in this godforsaken, fly-sizzling place was a diary
written remarkably neatly by Anderson, as his life ebbed away, on
the fabric of the aircraft's rudder:

DIARY 10/4/29 to –/4/1929
Force landed here at 2.35 pm 10 April 1929 thru push-rod
loosening. No 2 cylinder cutting out (as at Algebuckina SA
on 9/4/1929 but temporarily fixed – K.V.A.) exhaust valve
and 25% h.p. Cleared bit of runway here which turned out

just insufficient, or engine co-incidentally lost power. Since 12/4/1929 all efforts of course same next to nil, thru having no water to drink except solutions of urine [with oil, petrol, methylate from compass] directed on obtaining sufficient power from engine to permit a successful take-off.

No take-off able to be attempted since 11/4/29 due increased debility from thirst, heat, flies & dust.

Left Stuart [Alice Springs] 7.15 am local time & followed telegraph for 100 miles which was intention. Cut off then direct for point between Wave Hill & Ord River Downs. On a/c crosswind & inaccurate compass and having practically only sun for guidance as large map showed only featureless desert determined to above or nor'rard of course which am sure have done. As was in air for 7 hours and am pretty confident had 'Duckpond' on my starboard, I figure position now to be . . .

And here the diary stopped. At this point, probably on 12 April, their second full day in the desert, Anderson's faculties, dulled by severe dehydration, had begun to fade before he could wrestle with the geography of their location. In fact he had strayed more than 115 miles to the north-east of his intended track to Wyndham, finishing up travelling 22 degrees to starboard of his desired heading.

Many years later a myth persisted that Anderson had ended his agony by shooting himself, and that the returning burial party had found a pistol by his side. A member of the exhumation team, Stan Cawood, son of the Government Resident at Alice Springs, said in an Australian television programme that 'it was agreed not to say anything for fear of causing distress and trouble'. This was quite untrue. Eaton found no weapon anywhere at the site, and Anderson's body bore no evidence of gunshot wounds. Nor did Eaton find a Very pistol, which some writers later said that Anderson had used to start the desperate scrub fire. He appears simply to have used matches.

The *Kookaburra*'s engine was in perfect order. The wing tank was full of fuel and the loose tappet that, for the second time, had forced them down had been fixed. When the propeller was swung the engine sprang to life at the second pull. But the take-off path through the scrub, which had been crudely cleared by the two men with their bare hands and a pocket knife, wasn't long enough to get the plane off. Wheel tracks left in the sand from five or six desperate take-off attempts all terminated about 10yds before the end of the cleared area. It would be forty-nine years before the *Kookaburra* would be removed from the desert.[3] Both men had died by Saturday 13 April, if not sooner. Forty-five miles from the nearest water, they had survived barely three days, succumbing, it is likely, within hours of the discovery of the *Southern Cross* at Coffee Royal – eight or nine days before any search aircraft had flown into the Tanami. Anderson was nearly thirty-one, Hitchcock thirty-seven.

In the Nation's Dock

1929

When the details of the suffering of the *Kookaburra* crew were made public, sadness and horror swept the country. Their deaths brought an emotional outpouring of tributes in which Anderson's sacrifice was likened to some of the most famous in history – 'a gesture of mateship worthy to rank with that of Oates, who walked out blindly into a blizzard so that the Scott polar party might live'.[1] In London *The Times* devoted an editorial to the tragedy and King George V cabled messages of sympathy to the Anderson and Hitchcock families.

When Eaton's party returned to Wave Hill without the bodies there was a national outcry. Newspapers immediately set up memorial funds to have them recovered and money poured in from readers. The prime minister announced that they would be brought home for burial at government expense. News of the tragedy was received with distress at 'Kuranda', where Keith had been liked enormously by everyone, and especially Catherine. The Hilliard home in Cremorne was in deep shock. Arthur Hilliard told a reporter: 'It seems so hard and so cruel that Keith – the last man on whom the *Southern Cross* had any call – should have gone to his death.' Among those close to Anderson there was to be an enduring feeling that, in joining forces with the domineering Ulm, Smithy had turned his back on his old mate.

Bon Hilliard's cousin Jane Brooks said that after Keith's death, Bon had come down to stay with the Brooks family in Wollongong to escape the media and recuperate. 'She was broken-hearted and withdrawn. She didn't blame Kingsford Smith for Keith's death, rather for giving him too little credit for the things he contributed to the Pacific flight.'[2] The Hitchcock family were less reticent. Bob's niece, Gwen Bliss, described how they still feel today. 'We all believe that Uncle Bob was the innocent victim of a scheme hatched by Smithy, Ulm and Keith Anderson to get lost so Anderson could find them. Bob had just signed a contract for a good job he badly needed, and he actually abandoned it to go off in the *Kookaburra*. It's quite amazing that he was willing to do that after Smithy and Ulm had kicked him off the Pacific flight.'

At the time neither the Anderson, Hilliard nor Hitchcock families ever questioned the airmanship that had caused the tragedy. To have done so when the two men were being virtually canonised would have seemed churlish. But there can be no doubt that the catalogue of carelessness that marked every stage of their flight guaranteed that death stalked it all the way. Indeed, Anderson's culpability was seized upon by the Sydney *Sun* in an attempt to deflect attention from the major errors of judgement made by the *Southern Cross* crew. The newspaper called for a full investigation into the *Kookaburra*'s mission and the way it was sponsored. The *Guardian* retaliated with a demand for a public inquiry into the *Southern Cross*'s flight.

As the *Sun* and Smith's Newspapers locked horns on an almost daily basis, Stanley Bruce announced that there would be an inquiry. To the dismay of the *Sun* and Smithy, top of the terms of reference was to 'inquire into and report' on the *Southern Cross*'s flight. Also for investigation was why the position of the *Southern Cross* after its forced landing on 31 March was not ascertained until 12 April. In addition there was to be an inquiry into the deaths of Anderson and Hitchcock and the adequacy of their preparation. It was all started, Ulm said in his memoirs, by 'irresponsible newspaper writers and fostered by vicious gossip. The canard was floated that Kingsford Smith and I could have made contact with the world sooner than we did. The originators of the slur persisted in their uncompromising attitude.' The originators were, of course, the scurrilous Smith's Newspapers, owned by the rich cockney former Lord Mayor of Sydney, Sir Joynton Smith, and managed by the dynamic Robert Packer, founder of the Packer media dynasty, who drove his staff into every subterfuge to beat the opposition with provocative, competitive journalism.

In stark contrast to the euphoria that only two weeks earlier had greeted the joyful news of the crew's survival, the *Southern Cross* arrived back in Sydney on 27 April to a distinctly subdued reception. Only a handful of people went to the Richmond air base to meet them, the atmosphere was strained and the public was firmly kept away. Smithy, in dungarees, his face stubbled and sporting the moustache he had grown at Coffee Royal, climbed out clutching one of the snail shells from the mudflat. He looked tense and was not his usual forthcoming self. 'I have nothing to say,' he declared with untypical curtness to the reporters who crowded round him. 'As all the papers seem to misinterpret what we say, I will say nothing in future.' However, a few minutes later, 'behind closed doors', he and Ulm gave the *Sun* a long exclusive interview. *Smith's Weekly* hit back by grotesquely adorning its front page with a begoggled aviator's death's head hovering above a sketch of the *Kookaburra*, a body slumped beside it.

But with two writs already outstanding, Robert Packer stopped short of printing the dangerous and persistent rumour being spread that the whole affair had been a cynical conspiracy between Smithy and Anderson. Not so the reckless Edward Hart, whose Scottish sensibility was constantly offended by the Pacific heroes' nonchalant, adventuring style. He enjoyed living dangerously. 'The whole thing was a put-up job – the crew had lost themselves deliberately,' he quoted in *Aircraft*, adding that the magazine emphatically dissociated itself from the allegation. The attempted flight to England was a publicity stunt, and an ill-advised one at that, he agreed, but while it would have been of little value if it had succeeded, it would have been of no value at all if it had failed. Another publication, *Plain Talk*, was even less cautious, declaring boldly that 'it had been arranged that Smith and Ulm should lose themselves where they did and that Keith Anderson should find them and be given public reward'.[3]

The public inquiry began in the Darlinghurst courthouse in Sydney on 14 May 1929. It was conducted by a government-appointed committee of three: Brigadier-General Lachlan Wilson, a much-decorated Brisbane lawyer who had served in the South African and First World wars, enjoying a reputation for skill in the conduct of court-martials; Cecil McKay, a young businessman and private pilot, who was president of the Aero Club of Victoria; and

Captain Geoffrey Hughes, a Sydney solicitor and president of the Aero Club of New South Wales. None of them was supposed to have a shred of vested interest in the outcome, but the choice of Hughes, who was to prove a relentless inquisitor, deeply dismayed both Smithy and Ulm. He had voiced some criticism of their actions in persisting with the Pacific venture when the funds had dried up, and they believed he had little sympathy with long-distance flying and was prejudiced against them.

The committee was surrounded by a phalanx of lawyers hired by the crown solicitor, by Smithy and Ulm, by Constance Anderson, and by other interested parties. The proceedings, which heard evidence from seventy-four witnesses, had about them the ponderous majesty of a high-court criminal trial. It was not, of course, a court of law, but transcripts reveal that both Smithy and Ulm were firmly in the nation's dock. For the moment, doubts surrounded their integrity, which Australia had always taken for granted, and both were fighting for their reputations. For Smithy it was a shameful and humiliating experience. His skill, judgement and credibility, lauded internationally, had never before been queried or challenged.

When the investigation began that autumn Tuesday morning it didn't get very far. Mr Jack Cassidy, counsel for Smithy and Ulm, immediately stood up to plead for a postponement as his clients were due in the Supreme Court for preliminary arguments to be heard in their libel action against Smith's Newspapers and Robert Packer. They were reluctantly granted a two-day adjournment. In the other court Smith's Newspapers' counsel gruffly demanded the withdrawal of some of the statements they had made in their suit for damages. These centred on Smithy's formal claim that he had become 'famous as a pilot and aviator of great courage, skill and resource' and that 'after encountering bad weather, in wild and unknown country', he had been 'compelled to remain there without practicable means of communication . . . and without adequate food . . . in country abounding in flies and mosquitos'. The newspaper claimed that these were matters that should be adduced in evidence and refused to accept them as fact. In response, the doughty Richard Windeyer – the KC who had lacerated Bob Hitchcock – accused the defence of delaying tactics. 'We attach great importance,' he said, 'to the fact that these men were in a position which they won for themselves by gallantry in the past.' Windeyer lost his argument. Mr Justice Halse-Rogers ruled that the laudatory claims about Smithy's aviation brilliance and the representation of his Coffee Royal woes should be removed from the plaintiffs' statement. Smith's Newspapers had won the first skirmish. Both sides now prepared for a battle royal. But did it ever take place? Extraordinarily, in view of Kingsford Smith's and Ulm's anger, there is no record that it ever did.

The files of the *Sydney Morning Herald* contain no report of a hearing in any year up to Smithy's death; nor do the Supreme Court records in the New South Wales state archives, or even the notebooks of Judge Halse-Rogers and the court 'process books', which recorded verdicts and damages. Smithy's second wife, Mary Noldin, said: 'I have absolutely no memory of a trial. I would certainly have remembered it if we'd won any money.' Perhaps Charles Ulm's son John, who also had no recollection of the result, was right: 'You know,' he wrote, 'in those days it could have been all washed up in a simple phone conversation in which each party said, "Forget it!" and agreed to tear up the papers, without record.'

The Coffee Royal inquiry, however, left on the record copious documentation of its grinding proceedings which resumed in mid-May 1929. Almost daily there were grim reminders of the reason for the inquiry as a new expedition set out from Adelaide for the Tanami Desert with lead-lined coffins in a six-wheeled Thorneycroft truck to recover the bodies of Anderson and Hitchcock. Through the witness box, day after day, passed a cavalcade of people whose evidence was considered relevant: the crew of the *Southern Cross*, search pilots, government officials, newspapermen, aircraft radio experts, the search committee, mechanics, oil-company executives, air force officers, and even Smithy's doctor, who was called to report on his health. In addition the head of the RAAF, Air Commodore Williams, Herbert Campbell-Jones, Norman Brearley, John Garlick, and Edward Hart were all summoned to appear. The committee assembled nearly 80 exhibits – a formidable record of almost every document and news story spawned by the disaster which, it had been revealed by the government, had cost the country £30,000 (around Aus$1.3 million in today's values).

First into the box was the glamorous and jaunty figure of the star of it all. Immaculate in his best suit, Smithy had shaved off his moustache and appeared to have completely recovered from his ordeal. He had spent most of the three weeks since his return closeted with Eric Campbell and barrister Jack Cassidy. At home he had been subjected to endless ribbing by his brothers. Wilfrid, in Sydney on a visit – he now lived in Albury – had scoured the garden for snails and presented Smithy with a plate of them, arranged on tufts of grass, at the dinner table. There was little levity, however, at Darlinghurst court. For several days he was ruthlessly examined and cross-examined, 'acquitting himself', wrote Catherine, who was in the public gallery throughout, 'splendidly'.

Although Smithy had left much of the detailed planning of the flight to Ulm, he had to accept, as captain, full responsibility for the crucial decision to leave Sydney on Easter Saturday. On this matter he was persistently questioned by the piercing Geoffrey Hughes, who made it clear that, in his view, everything else flowed from that one exceedingly bad judgement. Hughes demanded to see the original of every telegram which had passed between Smithy and Ulm and Chateau in Wyndham during the days of bad weather before they left. The committee's counsel, Mr J. H. Hammond KC, tried to extract from Smithy his reason for setting off without Chateau's final weather clearance, but he was never able satisfactorily to supply one. Ulm was to explain: 'We disregarded the advice telling us to delay the flight because, after all, it was only advice . . . he might never send the final OK, or might not send it for a long time.' Perhaps the truth lay in a later remark Smithy made to the committee: 'We were in the position of pioneers, and pioneers have to take risks. We don't pretend to be supermen, and we know we are not.'

Asked by Hammond why he hadn't dumped fuel and turned back to Sydney when they had lost their receiving aerial so soon, Smithy said: 'We regarded the risk of another take-off as not worth turning back.' He meant another grossly overladen take-off. It was pointed out to him that he could have avoided this by crossing the country in two hops, refuelling in central Australia. Pressed on this again, Smithy offered another justification. McWilliams, he claimed, would not after a few hours of deafness from engine noise have been able to hear a recall message. This reason was also given by McWilliams, yet he later admitted that he had been clearly receiving Sydney radio at the moment the vital wire dropped off. None of the committee reminded them that, on the first long sector of the Pacific flight, Jim Warner had been able to hear messages from ships and shore stations even after twenty-four hours.

Edging towards one of the most sensitive areas of the inquiry, the committee, near the end of their cross-examination of Smithy, raised the question of why it had taken so long for them to be found when search planes had been passing close by. Instead of creating white smoke from wood fires, why had they not burned some of the remaining gallons of engine oil to create dense black smoke? Smithy replied that they had decided 'it wasn't worth trying'. He insisted that white smoke was more conspicuous in dark green terrain.

Of the four members of the crew, Tom McWilliams was subjected to the most rigorous cross-examination for his failure to convert the generator-driven transmitter to battery operation, which would have enabled the aircraft to have been located almost immediately. He insisted that his batteries had barely the power 'to light up a pocket torch lamp', and that the signals would not have been heard. Unfortunately for McWilliams, at that very moment his assertions were being emphatically disproved. Tests conducted by independent radio engineers on his transmitter unit showed that, when temporarily converted to transmission, the battery-powered signals could be clearly read 800 miles away. The negative and contradictory nature of McWilliams' evidence clearly worried the committee, who appeared unconvinced that the *Southern Cross* had been carrying either the most effective radio equipment available or the most resourceful operator.

The inquiry's most heated moments surrounded the committee's probing of the allegations that they had deliberately set out to get lost and found. When Smithy was asked about these, he gripped the edge of the witness box and, raising his voice for the first time, shouted: 'That is an absolute, deliberate and malicious lie, and I'm very glad you have given me the opportunity of saying that publicly.' Hammond went on to quote from the story which suggested that Keith Anderson would receive a 'public reward' for finding the *Southern Cross*. In response Smithy exploded: 'That is not only another malicious lie, but it is affecting a dead man's reputation, which I consider disgusting.' Counsel for the Anderson and Hitchcock families, Fred Myers, rose to ask him: 'It has also been suggested that, as you endorsed for Anderson a promissory note for £300, with which he partly purchased an aeroplane, that was part of the same arrangement?' Again Smithy snapped back: 'It is a malicious lie.' The gesture, he said, was 'purely a matter of friendship between myself and Anderson'.

But the suspicion that the *Southern Cross* crew may have been anxious not to be found too quickly had now been sown in the investigators' minds, and it began to germinate when search pilots described how invisible the aircraft had been from the air. Pilot Jim Woods claimed that he had passed within a mile of the mud-flat without seeing either the Fokker or signal smoke. This led the committee to explore the preposterous rumour that the plane had been deliberately covered up to delay detection.

Although outwardly Smithy seemed calmly unaffected by the rigours of the hearing, as the investigators began to dissect and analyse every single decision he had made on the fatal flight, it soon took its toll. Few people knew that the strain brought him down with reactive flu. Catherine was on her way to the court to hear Ulm's evidence when she met him coming home ill. 'Returned with him and doctored him,' she wrote, for Chilla was still her little boy. It was a stressful time for Catherine, too. She had been shocked by the arrival of a steady stream of hate mail. 'I cannot forget how certain of my countrymen turned from adulants to defaments almost overnight,' Smithy wrote. 'Scurrilous letters, unsigned, of course, were written to me, to my mother, and to other members of my family. The public which had been 100 per cent "Smithy" when we took off now began tossing mud and rocking the pedestal upon which they had placed me.'[4]

It was Ulm's evidence which dominated the inquiry. He had been the organiser of the flight and his widely published diary had purported to describe the crew's day-to-day hardships at Coffee Royal. Whereas Smithy answered the cascading questions in brief, rapid sentences, Ulm delivered long-winded, somewhat pompous speeches that would sometimes go on for five or six minutes. He was often prickly, defensive and brusque, refusing, to counsel's irritation, to answer yes or no. 'I'm afraid I'd have to go

into conference with you for two or three days upon the matter,'
he replied loftily to one question. He astounded the committee
by saying: 'Any reasonably minded person would say that our last
flight was probably our greatest achievement and the greatest
proof of the safety of aviation in that we had a forced landing in
what has been described as the worst flying country anywhere.'
Possibly having in mind the Kingsford Smith–Ulm airline about
to begin scheduled operations around eastern Australia,
Hammond asked icily: 'But does not the man in the street need
to be convinced first that not only will he not be killed, but that
he will get where he is going with reasonable certainty?' To
which Ulm, to general amazement, replied: 'And we have proved
that pretty well.'

Ulm's diary was constantly quoted back to him. It was suggested that he may have set out to dramatise his narrative and that
some of it may not even have been written on the mudflat. 'Is the
committee to take this diary as a somewhat graphic account of
your adventures written in retrospect, or as an absolutely accurate
statement of what occurred at Coffee Royal?' he was asked by the
steely Geoffrey Hughes.

'I don't quite understand what you mean by "graphic account".
That diary is true.'

The investigators were not, however, convinced. They suspected
that Ulm's record had been colourfully embellished for the titilla-
tion of the *Sun*'s readers. They were confirmed in this view when
some of the men who had landed at Coffee Royal after the Fokker
had been found said that they had seen none of the hordes of flies
so vividly described and had been surprised how chirpy the four
had appeared considering their privations. They clearly regarded
with a degree of scepticism Ulm's assertion that they were only
'three or four days from painful death' when discovered.

But this paled into insignificance compared with the sensation
that was to erupt around Ulm when, as he had feared, his worst
nightmare came back to haunt him. To his horror, not one but
three witnesses came forward to declare, on oath, that he had
described to them a money-making scheme for getting lost and
found in the back of beyond. The fall-out from this embarrassing
evidence was to shadow him and Kingsford Smith for the rest of
their lives.

In its determination to winkle out the truth behind the allegations of a dark plot between Anderson and the *Southern Cross* crew, the committee called some of the journalists who had published the stories, but all said they had merely made public the rumours. None of them could produce a scrap of substance. The author of the most scathing denunciations, the mildly eccentric Edward Hart, proved a voluble and slippery witness. His personal animus toward Ulm had clearly motivated his published attacks, and one is left with the feeling that the trail of debris created by Coffee Royal had presented him with the opportunity he had long sought to discredit Ulm. Hart was quick to remind the committee that his article had made it clear that *Aircraft* dissociated itself from the allegations. In his mind 'there was not the slightest suggestion that it was a disreputable flight, in any sense reprehensible'.[5]

But the enormous publicity the allegations received brought, in the final days of the proceedings, some new witnesses who had decided at last to tell what they knew. They provided damning evidence that Ulm had undoubtedly once suggested to a number of people that a good way to attract public sympathy and money would be to get lost in the middle of Australia and then, when the news coverage was at its height, to be found safe and sound. The fact that he had floated this idea in 1927, before the Pacific flight had brought them acclaim and brief riches, didn't stop people wondering whether he might have resuscitated it.

The first of the new witnesses was a well-known aviation-industry figure, Jim Porteus, the advertising manger in Sydney for Shell Oil, a member of the Custom House Hotel drinking fraternity. He said that in May 1927 Ulm had tried to interest Shell in sponsoring the round-Australia flight. 'He suggested that there were other ways of focusing attention for publicity on the plane and one was to instal a wireless on the machine and get lost in central Australia. I treated it more or less as a joke. I said we weren't interested in anything like that.'

Porteus had mentioned Ulm's suggestion to several other people, but all of them appear to have forgotten about it until the *Southern Cross* did disappear two years later. During the twelve-day search the story had begun to circulate again in the Custom House bars, and one of those to hear it was, unhappily, Norman Ellison, the

Guardian's air correspondent, who, Smithy was convinced, had been instrumental in turning the tide of public opinion with his brutal, anonymous stream of Coffee Royal insinuations. Ellison told the inquiry that, when the news of Anderson's and Hitchcock's deaths had reached the *Guardian*, he had gone immediately to interview Jack Cantor at his hotel. 'Mr Cantor told me: "In my bar the other day, Mr Porteus said in my hearing that Ulm had offered to get lost in the centre of Australia for a week for £600."'

Seizing the moment, Cassidy now leaped to his feet and demanded accusingly of Ellison: 'Did you write the articles in the *Guardian* as to Ulm's tale that they lived on snails and grass?'

'No, I did not,' Ellison replied.

Smithy and Ulm did not believe him for one moment. Indeed, some days later, according to John Kingsford-Smith, 'Smithy met Ellison in the long bar of the Hotel Australia and openly accused him of writing those articles. He became so angry he had to be restrained from punching Ellison on the nose.'[6]

Another witness at the hearing, Studley Lush, the New South Wales manager of the Neptune Oil Company, said that Ulm, seeking fuel and funding for the 1927 circumnavigation of Australia, had told him: 'There are lots of stunts we could bring off for publicity. One would be to get lost in the wilds somewhere or other. That would be a good stunt.' According to Lush he had replied: 'It wouldn't be much of a stunt if you were using my oil.' He insisted that Ulm meant it seriously.

The hearing took four weeks. When all seventy-four witnesses had been heard the committee went off to write their report. But Ulm's ordeal was not over yet. In Wellington, New Zealand, the ship's officer and navigator William Todd, whom Smithy and Ulm had dropped from their Pacific operation in 1927, had been avidly following the unfolding evidence. He had taken a ship to Sydney and went to see Arthur Hilliard to offer his evidence supporting that of Porteus and Lush, only to be told that the inquiry had concluded its sittings two days earlier. But when Hilliard realised the significance of what Todd had to say he phoned the federal crown solicitor's office in Canberra. As a result, on 12 June, amid furious speculation, the inquiry was reopened especially to hear Todd's evidence.

In an atmosphere of hushed expectancy at the reconvened

hearing, Todd recounted a conversation in the Roosevelt Hotel in San Francisco in which, he maintained, Ulm had described exactly the same scheme in the presence of Keith Anderson. Todd said he wanted to give evidence because he had read that Ulm had denied ever suggesting the idea. When Ulm returned to the stand to answer the allegations now made by three witnesses, he became extremely heated. 'Todd is a deliberate liar of the lowest order, and that statement is malice,' he declared fiercely. He also described the evidence of Porteus and Lush as 'deliberate fabrication'. As for Todd, he was a 'great big lump of a fellow very much given to drunkenness'. Brigadier General Wilson asked Ulm whether he could possibly have made the suggestion as a joke.

'Never,' Ulm replied. 'Not even in a joking manner.'

'Can you have forgotten it, even if it was a casual joke?'

'It is possible,' Ulm said, conceding for the first time that he may have made the remark. 'But I cannot think of any possible reason why I should mention it, even as a joke.'

'The whole question,' the general said, 'is one of the credibility of Ulm.'

Counsel Fred Myers agreed. 'It is important,' he said, 'for the committee to decide whether Ulm is a credible witness.'

Unfortunately for Ulm the committee was to decide that he wasn't. In its fifteen-page report, issued by Prime Minister Bruce on 24 June 1929, Smithy and Ulm were completely cleared of the accusations of conspiracy with Anderson to get lost in the Kimberley. However, the committee concluded that there was evidence that Ulm's remarks had been uttered, 'but were probably not made as serious business proposals'.

This opinion, together with the misleading evidence regarding wireless reception in the air, cause the Committee to regard the evidence of Flight Lieutenant Ulm with some suspicion, and particularly so in the matter of his diary, which contains internal evidence that it was not a daily record, but was obviously written for publication . . . His account of the weakness of the crew during the first few days after the landing is exaggerated. There is, however, no evidence that the crew of the *Southern Cross* took any steps to conceal their position, or to avoid being found.

The report criticised the casual attitudes of Smithy, Ulm and McWilliams to the loss of the receiving aerial and their attempts to hoodwink the committee into believing that radio reception was unimportant. It emphatically rejected the hopelessly untenable argument that McWilliams would have been too deaf to hear a recall message while they were still in sight of Sydney. With two lawyer pilots on the committee, they had perhaps been foolish to push this desperate argument. Also criticised were their reliance on day-old newspaper weather reports instead of those of the Sydney Weather Bureau; their failure to carry an emergency light-weight battery radio-transmitter; Ulm's failure to check that the emergency rations were on board; their failure to use the remaining 18 gallons of the aircraft's engine oil to create black smoke.[7] The committee considered that the long delay in finding the *Southern Cross* was the fault of the crew. They had confused searchers, first by their failure to mention in their radio messages that they had passed over two separate mission stations, an omission that wasted days. Then they had failed to convert their radio receiver to a transmitter. The latter censure was directed most harshly at McWilliams, who, in the committee's view, could have had them all speedily rescued.

Of the subsequent *Kookaburra* tragedy, the committee found that the Widgeon was too hurriedly prepared and, as an aircraft, unsuited to the task. Moreover, Hitchcock was not in a fit state to have undertaken the venture. The primary cause was 'the inaccuracy of the compass through which Lieutenant Anderson lost his direction and bore to the north of his intended course'. This was a curious conclusion, given that the compass had steered him accurately from Sydney to Blayney immediately after it had been swung, and that he had had the opportunity to check its accuracy – with the replacement tools – between Alice Springs and Woodforde Crossing before setting out into the Tanami. The report made no reference to his lack of navigation skill, but observed that, with another ninety minutes flying, he could have safely avoided the Tanami altogether. It absolved the government from any blame, even adding that there was 'no responsibility attaching to it to search for them'.

There were mixed reactions from the *Southern Cross* crew. Smithy, although privately mortified by the whole cruel, public

examination of his judgement and competence, appeared philosophical. The national hero, now seen to have feet of clay, said in
an interview: 'I'm sorry that our errors were exaggerated. They
were only human faults. If we had been successful nothing would
have been said.' His greatest relief was that he had been exoner-
ated from any suggestion of a plot to get lost. 'These rumours
spread throughout Australia and I believe linger even now,' he
wrote in his autobiography three years later. 'It is difficult indeed
to understand a mentality which could conceive such a despicable
and ridiculous idea.' Would he, he asked, have 'risked a machine
worth £10,000 in a forced landing which was very nearly a crash;
or risked three lives, besides my own, by attempting a landing in
that dreadful country? What motive had we – what prospect of
reward or gain?'

Ulm, protesting that he had been 'unnecessarily pilloried' by
the committee, told the newspapers that the evidence of his now
hugely publicised remarks was outside the scope of the inquiry
and should not have been admitted. But in his memoirs, written
five years later, he did finally concede 'the faint possibility that I
may have made a whimsical remark of some such character'.

The three wise men who sat in judgement on the Coffee Royal
aviators are not on record anywhere subsequently revealing their
private views of the events they were asked to examine. The most
formidable of them, the perspicacious Geoffrey Hughes, died in
1951. His son, Tom Hughes QC, a Sydney barrister, wrote to me:
'From conversations between my father and myself I gathered
that he had formed an unfavourable impression about the conduct
of Kingsford Smith and Ulm in the Coffee Royal saga. However,
my brother, Geoffrey, tells me that, on his deathbed in Sydney, our
father said that he was not sure that he had been altogether fair in
the judgement he formed of Kingsford Smith.' Fred Myers, the
barrister who had represented Keith Anderson's and Bob
Hitchcock's families, became a New South Wales Supreme Court
judge. In his retirement he told his nephew, John Myers, that he
'had formed the opinion that Ulm's business probity was suspect
and that Kingsford Smith's honesty and competency were flawed
by a larrikin streak'.[8]

Coffee Royal had been Smithy's and Ulm's first experience of
the tall poppy syndrome, a destructive national tendency to cut

down heroes perceived to have grown too big for their boots. The inquiry had cost them thousands of pounds in legal fees. They pleaded to no avail with the government to pay. Moreover, on the brink of the launch of their own airline, the significant damage it had done to their reputations as aviation stars couldn't have come at a worse time. Nor did it help their aspirations to extend their operation to the prestigious overseas route between Australia and England. In the eyes of the conservative British interests that dominated the Imperial route, Smithy and Ulm, although admired for their enterprise and courage, were beginning to be seen as adventurers prepared to take excessively high risks for headlines. It was an image that was to cling to both men for the remainder of their lives. It also, to some extent, clung to their families. 'We all suffered from that episode,' Leofric's daughter, Shirley Miller, said. 'I was at a small private school at Hunters Hill in Sydney at the time. The other kids taunted me. It was really unkind. I didn't even know what it was about.'

Airline
1929

As the Coffee Royal inquiry was hearing its last witness on Friday 14 June, the body-recovery expedition had reached the *Kookaburra* after an appalling eight-day journey into the Tanami, this time from Newcastle Waters to the east. They were so low on fuel that they had to take most of the Widgeon's petrol to get them back. From the railhead near Alice Springs, the coffins travelled by train, Hitchcock's to Perth, where he was buried in the Karrakatta Cemetery, and Anderson's to Sydney. Hitchcock's funeral was a small family affair; Anderson's obsequies, conducted with full military honours, assumed the scale and pomp of a royal passing. For several days he lay in state at various sites around Sydney, where tens of thousands came to pay their respects to the dead aviator, now exalted and deified by the media. The state funeral on Saturday 6 July 1929 remains one of the biggest in Sydney's history. Six thousand mourners, including a coterie of Cabinet ministers, followed the cortège through the streets of Mosman to Anderson's final resting place in Rawson Park, overlooking the entrance to Sydney Harbour. Preceded by a military band, the coffin travelled on a gun carriage pulled by six horses ridden by men of the Royal Australian Artillery. A Westland Widgeon identical to the *Kookaburra* circled the grave and dropped a wreath of red flowers on to the coffin.

The orchestrated praise for Anderson's actions and the grief at his death did not, at the time, allow for much objectivity around this paragon of Australian aviation. There can be no doubt that he was a kind and decent man, inspired by worthy motives, but he remains a

sad figure. The most charitable conclusion that can be drawn about
the utter recklessness of the *Kookaburra* expedition is that his judgement and competence must, like his personality, have been impaired
by the mental wounds caused by the traumas of war.

There was no wreath at his funeral from Kingsford Smith or
from Ulm. Nor were they among the mourners. In the repaired
Southern Cross, they had flown out of Sydney the day after the
Coffee Royal report had been issued to resume their record attempt
and were now halfway to England. Yet Smithy had been more
deeply affected by the whole appalling affair than he ever revealed.
'He never, ever got over Keith's death,' said John Kingsford-Smith.
'Nor the way fellow Australians had tried to blacken his name.' Said
Smithy's wife Mary: 'The hurt of Coffee Royal never left him. It was
a rotten thing to drag him through the courts like that.'

In Sydney, where she had been sharing her grief with the
Hilliards, Constance Anderson had privately begun to vilify
Smithy. The intensity of her feelings was laid bare in a letter she
wrote in the second week of June to her sister-in-law, Ethel
Willdridge.

Redcourt
8 Cremorne Road
Cremorne NSW

12 June 1929

Dear Ethel
    This boarding house is exactly opposite the Hilliards'
home. I spend all my spare time with them. Poor little Bon
keeps up bravely most of the time, breaking down utterly
every now and then.
    Just think, Ethel dear, of our beautiful boy sacrificing his
life for that 'scum of the earth'. Bad man in every way that
he is, even *he* has a conscience. Since his return he has been
under the influence of liquor more or less all the time, trying
to drown his conscience. I am not troubling about him and
his evil deeds – his punishment has already started – think
what his conscience must be when he is sober.[1]
    Yours, with love
    Constance

On their resumed flight to England Smithy had taken the same crew. Notwithstanding the inquiry's damning criticism of McWilliams, he told reporters that he still trusted the New Zealander. Despite a plague of engine problems all the way, they made it to London via India in a record twelve days eighteen hours, beating Hinkler's opposite journey time by three days. Coffee Royal might have cast a long shadow over their reputations in Australia, but in England their lustre was undiminished. They were heartened by a message of congratulation from the King, and to be greeted at the newly opened Croydon terminal by the under-secretary of state for air, Frederick Montague, and the director of civil aviation, the monocled and personable Air Vice Marshal Sir Sefton Brancker. After a celebration dinner at Romano's in London, Smithy was swept up in a social whirl which culminated in his being presented to the Prince of Wales at the Hendon Air Display. Leaving the *Southern Cross* at Croydon, he and Ulm went up to Manchester to discuss with the Avro company their order for the Fokker trimotors they needed to get Australian National Airways up and running. Designed to carry eight passengers and two pilots, the Avro 10s looked almost indistinguishable from the 'old bus', except for their 225hp British Armstrong Siddeley Lynx engines, which made them around 5mph faster than the *Southern Cross*. It was arranged that the aircraft would be shipped to Sydney before the end of the year in time for scheduled services to begin in January 1930. The crew then flew the *Southern Cross* to the Fokker works in Amsterdam for a complete overhaul, which Anthony Fokker insisted on doing free of charge.

In Europe that summer Smithy began to grow restless again. While Ulm was dashing about England, sorting out the Avro 10 contracts, interviewing pilots and engineers and discussing with Air Vice Marshal Brancker a bold plan for the new ANA to operate from Australia to India to connect with a new Imperial Airways London–Karachi service, Smithy startled the ANA board in Sydney by announcing in London that he planned to fly the Atlantic, and then to attack Hinkler's England–Australia solo record. Not only that, but it seemed that Ulm was intending to accompany him as his Atlantic co-pilot. The ANA's chairman, and major shareholder, Frederick Stewart, was horrified. He couldn't believe that both managing directors would simultaneously desert the vulnerable new airline in its infancy. He curtly instructed them to abandon their plans forthwith.[2] However, he had reckoned without the doggedness of Kingsford Smith, who was now such an internationally free spirit that he had become a law unto himself. When he challenged the instruction, the board reluctantly climbed down – on condition that Ulm took no part in the Atlantic flight and continued to devote all his energies to the company.

Meanwhile, in London, the ANA pilot interviews were continuing – without Smithy. Even though he was responsible for the airline's flight operations, he appears to have been as uninterested in the recruiting process as he was in the company's management. He left the vital interviews entirely to Ulm, booked a passage on the *Amsterdam* and sailed to New York to make arrangements for his arrival there the following year. After the heavy financial drain of the Coffee Royal affair he was no longer flush with money. So in New York he went to see Anthony Fokker, now president of the Fokker Aircraft Corporation of America. The two had much in common. Fokker, a small, ruddy-faced, boyish-looking man, fond of pranks and showing off, generous with money but unable to manage it, had, like Smithy in some respects, never really grown up. The wealthy Dutchman was delighted to see Smithy, whose flights had made his trimotor famous, and swiftly solved the cash problem with a cheque for £1,000 towards the Atlantic venture.

In no great hurry to return to Australia, Smithy took the train in early October to California, where he spent a leisurely few weeks staying with his brother Harold in Oakland and with Allan Hancock at Santa Maria, where the captain had now opened a college of aeronautics. He sampled some of the school's aircraft, adding five new types to take his tally to over fifty in a logbook of nearly 3,700 hours. Towards the end of the month, as the world began to plunge into recession, he reluctantly decided that it was time to return to Australia. He booked a passage on the *Aorangi*, sailing from Vancouver, buying a second ticket for Harold's glamorous twenty-five-year-old daughter, Beris, whom he had invited to Sydney for a holiday.

The ship had been due to sail at noon, but such was the status of their distinguished guest that its departure was delayed to enable him to give a lunch address to the Canadian Club. When, at long last, Smithy and Beris came hurrying up the gangway, watched by hundreds of impatient passengers, there were mutterings of disapproval. 'I was conscious of many black looks directed towards me,' he wrote, 'one young lady being evidently very annoyed at this unwarranted privilege bestowed on my humble self.' The young lady in question was Mary Powell, the daughter of an affluent Melbourne businessman, on her way back to Australia with her parents after a leisurely nine-month tour of Europe and North America.

The first feeling Smithy stirred in Mary Powell as he boarded the *Aorangi* in Vancouver that afternoon – apart from irritation that he'd delayed the ship – was surprise at how small he was. 'We were on deck and Daddy called me to the rail, saying, "Here's Kingsford Smith at last." It was a bit like saying. "Here's the King." I went over to look. I remember my absolute amazement that, in the flesh, he was such a little man. I said, "How insignificant he looks to have done all those things."' She hadn't taken much interest in his great Pacific flight the previous year, and when he'd flown down to Melbourne, she had declined to go with her parents to the airport. 'I had a tennis party at home that day,' she said. 'Tennis was much more important than aviators – even famous ones.'

But within twenty-four hours, as the *Aorangi* steamed towards Honolulu, aviation was thrust into her life. On the first night at sea Smithy's roving eye soon alighted on Mary. She was petite and very pretty, with honey-brown hair and arrestingly bright blue eyes, and spoke, he noticed, with an attractively modified Australian accent. He was instantly taken by her elegance, poise and good looks. The Powells were having a drink before dinner with a party of friends on the balcony above the first-class lounge. Several tables away sat Smithy with Beris. Mary said:

> Beris later told me that Chill was sitting there, as was apparently his custom on first nights at sea, assessing the female talent he planned to cultivate on the voyage. After sizing up all the apparently unattached women, he turned to Beris and said: 'The one in red will do me. I wouldn't mind practising on her.'
>
> Next morning he arranged to be introduced to me and from that moment on he pursued me quite relentlessly. Of

course I was flattered, for he was the biggest VIP on the ship, dining at the captain's table, and the centre of enormous attention. But he was so informal and such fun to be with it was impossible not to enjoy his company. He had such a magic personality. I wasn't yet nineteen, fresh out of school, naïve as they come, and here was this man of the world, this god person, coming up to thirty-three, who was staking me out. It was all a bit daunting.

There were a number of my friends on the ship and Chill simply invited himself into the contingent. We'd all gather round him and he'd regale us with priceless stories, with brilliantly mimicked foreign accents, and we'd sing to his ukulele. The lovely thing about him was his total lack of conceit. He didn't have a shred of self-importance. As for his great flights, you had to drag the details out of him.

About the fourth day out he suddenly said he'd like to meet Mummy and Daddy, so it was arranged that he would join us formally for coffee after dinner one evening. He turned up in all his gold braid, in full air force mess dress, in the rank of squadron leader, looking very splendid, but very conspicuous among all the other men in tuxedos. He had one, of course, but he explained to Daddy, in an elaborate story, that he'd accidentally spilt water over it in his cabin. It wasn't true. He just wanted to impress them with his uniform.

Smithy immediately hit it off with Arthur and Mary Florence Powell, known as Floss. They couldn't believe he was such an ordinary Australian bloke. The Powells belonged in the upper stratum of Melbourne society. At one stage Arthur had been an internationally renowned horse breeder, working in India and supplying polo ponies for the Prince of Wales. By the time Smithy came into his life he was a man of independent means with what seemed like infinite leisure. Some years the family would be abroad sightseeing for more months than they were at home. They had just been driven round England and Scotland in style in a chauffeured limousine, and Mary had been presented at court to George V. She had grown up with a retinue of servants, wanting for nothing, in Glenferrie Road in the upmarket Melbourne suburb of Hawthorn. She had been educated at the Hermitage in Geelong, one of Australia's most exclusive private girls' schools, and had recently emerged from a Melbourne finishing school, where she had been prepared for the task of running a house and managing servants.

Out of the blue, one night on deck in mid-Pacific, Smithy asked Mary to marry him. The proposal, she said, was totally un-expected. 'He'd kissed me several times, but had done nothing to frighten me off. He must have seen how absurdly innocent and ingenuous I was. I think it was my artlessness, my naturalness, that he found appealing. Anyway, I was stunned. I hadn't planned to get married for years. And here was a man who could have had almost any woman in the world, and he'd chosen me.'

Yet when, a few days later, she found herself agreeing to marry him, it was in the knowledge that it was all rather academic. She was certain her father wouldn't for one moment allow it. 'Chill said, "We'll see about that," and went to ask his permission. I can still see Daddy's shocked face. There was a moment's awful silence before he said, "You've got a damned cheek. You're much too old for her." More to the point, I'm sure, was his concern at exposing me to a man of the world with such a reputation for womanising, about which then I knew absolutely nothing.'

In spite of Arthur's misgivings, as he and Floss got to know Smithy better they soon succumbed to his winning ways. 'The truth was they were both immensely honoured,' Mary said. By the time the ship neared Sydney, Smithy had persuaded Arthur to relent. He agreed to an engagement on condition that they waited twelve months before announcing it. 'He told Chill, "If, after you've done the Atlantic flight, you and Mary still feel the same way, I suppose you can go ahead." But he added very sternly, "Not before."'

When the *Aorangi* docked on 9 November 1929, the customary large welcoming party of Kingsford Smiths was waiting on the wharf. 'He told his mother, "I've met the girl I want to marry." And she said, "Oh dear, not an American, Chill." He said, "No worries, she's a little Australian girl and I want you to meet her." Within no time he'd whisked me out to "Kuranda" and proudly introduced me to the whole family.' Mary recalled that what she immediately liked about the Kingsford Smith home was the laughter. 'It was so

full of fun, a relaxed, happy-go-lucky place with such a good feeling about it.'

'Mary was delightful,' said Smithy's niece Catherine Robinson.
'To us children she seemed awfully sophisticated, yet she had the
marvellous ability to relate to others, regardless of their social
background. She was a sweet person and very good for Chill.'
Molly Hudson, one of Mary's closest schoolfriends at the
Hermitage, came to know Smithy well in the early 1930s.

> For the Powells, meeting Chilla must have been quite a cul-
> ture shock. He was a very good and kind man, but of course
> his background was very different from the Powells'. If you
> were over-educated as Mary and I were you were immedi-
> ately aware of it. You could tell from his voice that, despite
> his fame, he was a very ordinary man, certainly not the sort
> of person her family would have been expecting her to
> marry. She told me that he put enormous pressure on her.
> He just swept her off her feet.

The Powells went home to Melbourne and Smithy, for the first
time in several months, reimmersed himself, if only half-heart-
edly, in the affairs of Australian National Airways. In his partner's
absence Ulm had virtually created the airline on his own, master-
minding every detail, from schedules and the livery of the
trimotors, which were beginning to arrive by sea, to the pilots' uniforms and the passengers' sick bags. He had recruited a staff of
forty-three and ran the business with a rod of iron. The company
had built a large corrugated-iron hangar and workshop at its
Mascot flying base, where Smithy test-flew the Avros – which
were named as sisters of the *Southern Cross*: *Southern Cloud*,
Southern Star, *Southern Sky*, *Southern Moon* and *Southern Sun* –
and gave public joyrides over Sydney to publicise the airline.

Yet at this time Smithy's mind was almost entirely on Mary
Powell. Impatient to marry her, he decided to force Arthur's hand.
Ordering an expensive diamond solitaire ring, he flew down to
Melbourne to present it to her at a dinner party on her nineteenth
birthday, 28 November. The wedding was fixed for September
the following year. Within hours the media had the story, and
overnight Mary became one of the most famous women in

Australia. 'I lost my privacy for ever that day. I had no idea what it was about to do to my life.'

In the few days of December that Smithy actually spent at Mascot, he checked out, somewhat perfunctorily, the pilots who were to serve as captains on the Avro 10s. One of them, recruited by Ulm from the Royal Air Force, where he was rated as exceptional, was George Urquhart Allan. 'Scotty' brought to the airline 1,000 hours' experience, much of it on multi-engined bombers, but he had never flown a trimotor. In 1992, I went to see him at his Sydney home overlooking the Pittwater. He was then ninety-two, a small, bald man with the impish features of a genial gnome beneath wings of white hair that floated above his ears. The most immediately remarkable thing about him was his perfectly preserved pugnacious Scottish brogue. He had retired in 1961 from Qantas, where he had become assistant general manager. With more than 13,000 flying hours, Scotty had become a legend in his own right, the last surviving pioneer aviator of Kingsford Smith's momentous era. Although he had suffered a stroke some years earlier, his mind was still alert and he displayed surprisingly few errors of memory. Recalling his test flight with Smithy, he said:

> I'd never seen an Avro 10 before. I met Kingsford Smith out at Mascot. He was taking six passengers for a joyride in the *Southern Star* and the engines were already running. He didn't bother to walk me round the aeroplane or brief me on the way it handled; he just said, 'Hop in.' I went up into the co-pilot's seat and off we went. He didn't even talk me through the controls. There was no intercom and it was too noisy to hear anything anyway. But as soon as we were in the air he handed the whole thing over to me. We did one wide circuit over Sydney and he indicated I should land it, which I did. We'd been in the air for less than twenty-five minutes. That was all the instruction I got. I think he just assumed that, like himself, I could get into any aeroplane and fly it. Two days later he sent me off solo with six fare-paying passengers aboard. He never checked me out again. Less than one hour's experience on the type and I was an ANA captain.'

Australian National Airways began its operations on New Year's Day 1930 with daily flights to and from Brisbane. Their reputations somewhat sullied by Coffee Royal, it was crucial for Smithy and Ulm that the airline should demonstrate reliability, punctuality and absolute safety. Alas, it could not have had a more disastrous start. The first northbound service, with seven of its eight seats filled, departed for Brisbane on the stroke of 8 am. The *Southern Cloud* was flown by Smithy himself with Scotty Allan as co-pilot. The passengers, dressed against the cold in overcoats, hats, scarves and gloves, sat in the draughty cabin with blankets drawn over their knees, wads of cotton wool stuffed in their ears, on wicker chairs anchored to the floor but with no seatbelts. They could, if they wished, slide the windows open in flight. At the back of the cabin was a primitive toilet bearing the warning: 'PLEASE DO NOT USE OVER POPULATED AREAS' – as somebody explained, 'What went in went out.'

The inaugural southbound service which left Brisbane at the same time was commanded by another ex-RAF pilot, an Englishman, Paddy Sheppard. Ulm, though unlicensed, flew with him as co-pilot. Over the MacPherson Ranges on the southern Queensland border, they flew into bad weather. Trapped by cloud in a densely wooded valley, they force-landed on a tiny farm paddock far too small for the trimotor. The *Southern Sky* careered through tree stumps and logs before being arrested by a barbed-wire fence. Amazingly, no one was hurt, but the undercarriage had been torn off the aircraft. The company's engineers arrived from Mascot, took one look at the 90yd paddock and announced that the aircraft would have to be dismantled and trucked back in sections. But Smithy had another idea: once the machine had been repaired he would fly it out.

This event, which took place two weeks later, joined his folklore alongside his historic landing in Suva's Albert Park.

A thick hempen rope was tied to the tail, thence over a log with the other end firmly attached to the stump of a felled forest giant. Kingsford Smith climbed on board. Motors started. He advanced the craft until the rope was fiddle tight. Revving the engines until the valley echoed with their roar, the plane literally bounding, he flung one arm up in a prearranged signal to Jack McKee, a local axeman of repute. With one fell swoop the rope was severed and *Southern Sky* catapulted into the air. Breaths were held as she maintained height and slowly climbed, barely clearing the trees. With a farewell dip of the wings, Smithy was gone. There are still folk in the area who remember seeing the aircraft winging away with remnants of rope dangling from its tail.[3]

The crash highlighted the inability of most of ANA's pilots to navigate and fly competently in cloud. 'Some were positively unsafe when they were forced to fly blind,' Scotty Allan said. 'Even the chief pilot, an ex-British Army officer, Travis Shortridge, didn't have the right experience. He was probably the most experienced light-aircraft pilot in Australia, but he had no idea about flying in cloud.' If the passengers had understood the risks they were running, most would have thought twice about booking a seat. They certainly needed strong stomachs. Said John Kingsford-Smith, who flew as a co-pilot: 'On some flights every passenger would be sick. We'd have to close the cockpit door against the stench.' The sick bags provided were simply tossed out of the aircraft. Qantas's managing director, Hudson (later Sir Hudson) Fysh, wrote: 'I remember on one trip . . . a passenger in a front seat was very sick into the usual container, which he then tried to throw out of his window. I got the full blast in the back seat.'[4]

Another of the early captains was ex-RAF test pilot Jim Mollison, a small, cocky Scot from Glasgow who, deceptively, had acquired a polished Oxford accent. He later married Amy Johnson, the darling of British aviation, and his own long-distance flights made him equally famous. But in Australia in 1930 he was better known as a remorseless womaniser, a drunkard and a man who, on the slightest provocation, delighted in meting out sadistic punishment with his bare fists. In a long drinking session with Smithy one night Mollison had talked him into giving him a job with ANA. Within days he was in command of an Avro 10 service, trying to survive in all manner of frightening weather with only rudimentary instrument experience. 'I learned it,' he said, 'as many learn to swim, by being thrown in. I often wondered what my passengers would have said had they known that the pilot who hoped to see them through was teaching himself blind flying by experience.'[5]

Later he came close to flying a planeload of these unsuspecting customers straight into the 7,300ft Kosciusko Range in the Australian Alps. His airspeed indicator froze up in cloud and he nearly stalled the aircraft. His passengers were hurled off their seats. 'Suddenly I saw the dark shape of a hillside looming through the mist. My heart gave a bound. I turned steeply and just managed to avoid it. It was a nasty shock.'[6]

Smithy himself piloted regular services to Brisbane for only two months. He quickly became disenchanted with the tedium of route-flying. March saw him bound for Holland to collect the refurbished *Southern Cross* for his Atlantic venture. He and Ulm had had no success with a new attempt to persuade the ANA board to grant them five months' leave to make the flight together, so instead they made a deal: Ulm would sell Smithy his half share in the *Southern Cross* in return for a parcel of his partner's ANA shares, an arrangement that would take effect once Smithy became airborne over the Atlantic. In Amsterdam in the third week of May, Smithy was reunited with the 'old bus', lovingly reconditioned at the Fokker factory. 'It was with exultation,' he said, 'that I once again climbed into the cockpit and took the air over Schipol to put my new beauty through her paces.' He is said to have climbed high above the aerodrome, put the trimotor into a steep dive and, to the excitement of the watching Fokker staff, completed a full loop. He had been dying to try out the manoeuvre ever since he had seen one of A. V. Roe's test pilots looping an ANA Avro 10 over the outskirts of Manchester.

With the longest days of summer now approaching, he was anxious to start his Atlantic flight. In Holland he turned to the national airline, KLM, for a co-pilot, eventually deciding upon the tall, ruggedly good-looking Evert van Dijk. A reserved, politely aloof man who did not suffer fools lightly, Van Dijk was not an easy person to get to know, and was regarded by his fellow pilots as a little dour and conceited. But at the age of thirty-seven he was recognised as a brilliant aviator with a unique ability in instrument flight. It was said that once, while he was being checked out on a new type, a younger training captain had gently corrected a minor fault on his final approach. Legend in KLM had it that Van Dijk had snapped back irritably: 'Hans, please don't try to teach your father how to pee.'

Van Dijk wanted very badly to make history with the man he regarded as the supreme master of his profession. When Smithy finally selected him he was over the moon. 'A mighty chap, Kingsford Smith,' he wrote. 'I feel so proud that he has chosen me from so many to be his mate.'[7]

Smithy signed up as his wireless-operator John Stannage, a ship's radio man.[8] Their paths had crossed before: two years earlier, Stannage had declined to join the Pacific flight, viewing it as a suicide mission. More recently he had been the wireless-operator aboard the *Canberra* on the Coffee Royal search. By this time, it seems, he was prepared to serve anywhere with Smithy for the sheer honour, and as luck would have it he was in England on holiday. 'In addition to being one of the best operators and technicians I have met,' said Smithy, 'he weighed under 9 stone (57kg), an additional recommendation where every pound avoirdupois means an extra available pint of petrol.'[9] For Stannage, slightly built, rather shy and very serious, and even shorter than Smithy, of whom, it was said, he stood in utter awe, it was to be the beginning of a long and warm association.

A navigator Smithy left to the last moment: as he planned to begin the flight from Dublin, he decided to look for one in Ireland. The commanding officer of the Irish Army Air Corps, Colonel Charles Russell, put him in touch with a former sea captain, Jonathan Patrick Saul, the son of a Dublin coal merchant. Saul had gone to sea at fourteen and had learned his navigation in windjammers. In the First World War he'd seen action with both the Australian and British armies before transferring to the Royal Flying Corps, where he flew twin-engined Vickers Vimy bombers. After the war, he returned to sea, gaining his master's certificate and his first command by the age of twenty-five. In 1924 he came ashore to join the family coal business, but what he was doing in 1930 is not clear. Whatever it was, he leaped at the chance to navigate Kingsford Smith across the Atlantic.

Some sentimental reasons, Smithy discovered when he met Saul in Dublin, underlay the navigator's interest in this Australian expedition. Not only had he served at Gallipoli with the AIF, but his wife – who had drowned on a voyage with him in 1922 when his ship had been wrecked – had been Australian. Saul appears in all the photographs sporting a prominent bushy moustache and a permanent scowl, but Smithy's first impression was of 'a genial and ebullient Celt, who was not only a master mariner and experienced navigator, but a practical airman'. He offered Saul the job; he felt, he said, that 'the best return I could make to the Irish people was to take an Irish navigator'.

Most of the numerous successful Atlantic crossings since Alcock and Brown had first achieved the feat – non-stop from Newfoundland to Ireland in a Vimy in 1919 – had been made from west to east with the aid of the strong prevailing westerly winds. Punching the wind in the opposite direction would mean a much slower, longer and more fuel-critical flight. All previous non-stop westbound attempts had ended in disaster until, in April 1928, a single-engined German aircraft, the *Bremen*, had made it from Dublin to Canada.[10] Over Labrador it had run into fog, which had forced a landing on Greenly Island off the Quebec coast. The aeroplane had been damaged and the crew stranded for several weeks. Smithy therefore decided to rate the attempt as unsuccessful. He announced that he would make the first non-stop flight from Europe 'to land on United States territory'.

19

Atlantic Ordeal

1930

For the long Atlantic take-off run Smithy found a beach at Portmarnock on the coast of the Irish Sea, 10 miles north of Dublin. In the three-week wait for suitable weather, he and his crew became the guests of the Irish Army Air Corps. The commandant of the army's staff college, Major General Hugo MacNeill, took Smithy under his wing, making a great fuss of him, introducing him to the aristocracy of County Kildare and driving him on sightseeing tours of Dublin. While Smithy was basking in Irish hospitality, his partner back in Sydney was growing distinctly unhappy about his protracted absence from ANA. The airline had had to inaugurate its Melbourne services without its megastar and Ulm was carrying the entire burden of the struggling enterprise. One of the Irish Army Air Corps officers recalled in 1980 that Kingsford Smith began to receive cables from Ulm 'saying that their mutually owned airline was facing problems which required his attention at home'. Predictably, Ulm's pleas fell on deaf ears.

When at last, on Tuesday 24 June, Smithy was preparing to take off from Portmarnock, he was handed an urgent cable from the US Weather Bureau. From Newfoundland for hundreds of miles south the North American coast was deeply fogbound and, even more worrying, 30mph south-westerly headwinds were blowing across the Atlantic. The bureau urged him to postpone his departure. It was a bit like Coffee Royal all over again, but this time there was another reason to spurn such advice: two French pilots were on the point of leaving Paris in an attempt to be the first to fly non-stop from Europe to New York. Smithy decided to take his chance with the fog and the wind.[1]

The *Southern Cross* took off in a pale yellow dawn. Photographs show the aircraft rising past a crowd which had waited all night in the sand dunes, the men raising their hats in salute. From Dublin to New York Saul had plotted a great-circle course which had a landfall – after 1,900 miles and more than twenty-four hours in the air – at Cape Race on the south-west corner of Newfoundland. It soon became obvious, as they crawled out across the grey, forbidding ocean, that the relentless westerly was going to slow them down so badly that they would be lucky to get any further than this. Despite a groundspeed of less than 70mph, the flight at first went smoothly. The faithful Wright Whirlwinds didn't miss a beat and a big anticyclone had, unusually, calmed the Atlantic into a millpond. About two hours out they saw the last of the sun, and from here on Saul was prevented by high cloud from getting any further sextant readings for a long time. This wasn't as serious as it might have been, for Stannage began to harvest some very accurate radio bearings from a multitude of ships which passed up their own latitude and longitude. The position plot this gave Saul made fresh aviation radio history: for the first time an aircraft was being steered accurately across an ocean quite independently of astro-navigation.

A third of the way to Newfoundland, they flew into a giant belt of fog which sat on the sea and rose to merge with an impenetrable woolly mass of stratus thousands of feet high. Smithy tried at first to get above it, but this took them into an even stronger headwind. When he then tried to go underneath he gave the crew one of the worst frights of the journey. Their trailing aerial began to drag in the sea. 'For God's sake no lower – aerial touched twice,' Stannage scrawled frantically to the pilots, whose altimeter was still showing 600ft. They had moved into a zone of lower atmospheric pressure and their instruments were now badly overreading. 'After this nasty jolt,' Smithy wrote, 'we decided to remain flying blind – in preference to a watery grave.'

Almost immediately they encountered another problem. 'Why can't you keep on course?' asked Saul. 'My compass shows up to 90 degrees divergence from course – and Stannage has two radio bearings which I find inexplicable.' The bearings indicated that the *Southern Cross* had begun to fly round in huge, imperfect circles. 'I shall never forget the numb feeling when I began to realise that all the compasses were being affected in some mysterious way, and that we were lost in the fog,' Stannage said. 'I felt completely helpless. My limbs felt heavy and useless, my brain dull and confused.'

The cockpit magnetic compass had vibrated out of its mount on to the floor, and Smithy was trying to steer by the electromagnetic one controlled by Saul, whose own purely magnetic compass showed that they were slowly circling over the Atlantic 400 miles east of Newfoundland. From what is now known of Smithy's fear of the sea he must have been close to panic. 'I began to have visions of our possible fate. My thoughts went to our predecessors – those who, like us, had attempted pioneer flights across the Atlantic. I knew some of those men – Hinchliffe, Minchin, Nungesser.[2] They were accomplished pilots. What had brought about their unknown end? Was it the same as this – some mysterious, uncanny, horrifying factor which disturbed their compasses, leading them to fly round aimlessly until, petrol exhausted, they had come to the end?' For three hours Smithy and Van Dijk blundered about in the maw of the fog. For three hours they made not a single mile of progress westward. 'My God – how long is this going to last?' the stoical Van Dijk wrote. 'If he and I don't make it then no one will ever make it.'[3]

How close they came to disaster was never to be publicly admitted by either pilot, but from Saul we know that they were extremely lucky not to have finished up in the Atlantic. He first set about dismantling the large master magnetic compass in the rear cabin, using the aircraft's engine starting handle to subject the needle to some 'vigorous hammering' to try to magnetise it. When this failed he turned his attention to the earth inductor system, on which Smithy relied as his primary directional aid. The electrically powered wind-driven unit was located inaccessibly far back in the fuselage, necessitating a dangerous scramble through a lacework of bracing wires along the unfloored rear cabin, where only thin fabric would separate Saul from the sea. As he worked there with frozen hands, vomiting from the petrol fumes, he was suddenly startled by a series of brilliant blue flashes. He turned to see that their wireless had now packed up, denying them the crucial radio bearings. Stannage was frantically taking it apart amid bursts of exploding valves.

It took Saul several hours to fix the electromagnetic compass. Its lubricating oil had thickened in the cold and clogged the bearings. When the radio was working again it confirmed that they were still flying round in circles. In desperation Smithy now decided, however strong the winds, to climb up out of the fog. They emerged into clear air between the fog and a mass of higher cloud. Dawn was breaking. And at this moment, he wrote, 'to our unbounded joy, the three compasses returned to normal. They all began to indicate the same direction. But our hopes of reaching American territory had now vanished. We could only hope to make the nearest land – Newfoundland.' Finding it was another matter: the whole of Newfoundland lay under an unbroken blanket of fog.

It was the liner *Transylvania* that saved them. Its radio officer collected bearings from the aircraft's transmissions passed to him by other ships. The information showed that they had drifted over 100 miles south of their intended course, and that they were now about 200 miles south-east of Cape Race, from whose radio station presently came the bad news that St John's was hopelessly fogbound. So they set course for another landing ground about 25 miles to the north-west, at the fishing town of Harbour Grace on Conception Bay, which was reported to be clear. Minutes later Smithy found a hole in the fog through which they spiralled down to find, by some divine providence, a lighthouse which Saul immediately recognised as Bull Point on the Avelon Peninsula.

'Shouting with hysterical joy,' Van Dijk said, they found themselves over a bleak landscape of lakes, forests and bare rock. Soon a clutch of houses and fishing boats appeared below a hill bearing a windsock. A handful of people, waving white sheets and sending up a friendly column of smoke, were waiting there. At 8 am local time they touched down.

The flight from Dublin had taken thirty-one and a half hours. When they checked the tanks they were surprised to discover that they still had fuel for another four hours. It was not the first westbound non-stop crossing – and indeed the *Bremen* had landed further west than the *Southern Cross* – but at least Smithy had arrived with his aeroplane intact and, unlike the Germans, he had managed to find an aerodrome. Yet only by great good luck had he conquered another ocean.

What had gone wrong with their compasses? Smithy advanced the unlikely theory that the magnetism had been affected by the fog. 'It is now believed,' he wrote, 'that each particle of moisture in the fog belt off Newfoundland is, for some unknown reason, charged with electricity. It is my belief that our continuous flight through this moisture-laden atmosphere had so charged the steel components of the plane that they had become magnetised. This directly affected the magnetic needles of our compasses, causing them to deviate from normal.' He offered the further improbable explanation that it might have been caused by their proximity to the North Magnetic Pole, more than 2,500 miles away in the far north of Canada. Perhaps the truth was just human error. Later that week Smithy admitted to the *New York Times*: 'It may be that we were tired and were not holding the *Southern Cross* up to her work as we did earlier in the flight . . . It was all blind flying and this condition, if a pilot keeps it up long enough, isn't conducive to accurate piloting.'[4]

'He said the compasses were going round in circles,' remembered Scotty Allan. 'Of course, that was nonsense. In any case he went on circling with his electric instrument. Compasses don't behave like that. It's quite obvious what was wrong: he was simply flying the aeroplane round the compass.' Someone else with an opinion was a former Second World War bomber pilot, Colin Watt of Adelaide, who, fifty years later, was still flying – at the controls of a replica of the *Southern Cross*, faithfully recreated in Australia.[5] 'I suspect his wandering heading was quite simply the result of sheer fatigue,' he said. 'Some of those early aviators who disappeared may well have just fallen asleep and flown into the sea.'

Smithy was so relieved to be alive that he promised himself it would be the last time he would risk his life on a long ocean hop. Four years later he broke that vow, but when he talked later that morning to the Newfoundland correspondent of United Press his nerves were still badly shaken. 'Flying the Atlantic from east to west is a most uninviting adventure, trying human courage and endurance,' he said. 'I doubt it will ever become a practical commercial venture. The route is beset with inconceivable dangers.' Once again he had pushed long-distance aviation beyond all safe limits. Not for sixteen years would sustained and reliable transatlantic air travel become a reality. At Harbour Grace the four slept for twenty hours. According to Saul, it had been the 'severest test of both our mental and physical stamina'. He described how residual terror had them constantly waking up and reliving the nightmare 'bringing me back again to nights during the war when we slept in such a manner'.[6]

In an uneventful sixteen-and-a-half-hour hop they flew on to New York, where, on 26 June, they were welcomed with a fervour even Smithy had never before experienced. As the aircraft, flanked by police motorcycle outriders, came to a stop at Roosevelt Field on Long Island, it was stormed by a crowd of frightening power and determination. When Van Dijk jumped down to supervise the parking arrangements his place in the cockpit was immediately taken by a pretty young woman clutching an enormous square microphone. Smithy recognised her as Elinor Smith, whom he'd met in California the year before. She proceeded to interview him for NBC in a live coast-to-coast broadcast. 'It was a scoop beyond the wildest dreams of any reporter in the field,' she wrote in her autobiography.[7] As a pilot herself, helping to finance her flying with freelance radio work, she regarded Smithy as an aviation superman. Smith, who was later to become a flying celebrity in her own right, establishing American women's endurance and altitude records, told me in 1992:

> I only knew him professionally as a fellow pilot – I was never romantically involved – but I was, of course, aware of his wicked reputation. We all used to be warned about him and Jimmy Doolittle.[8] The advice was not to be left alone with either of them. Actually, Smithy was a funny little guy in many ways. Afraid of nothing, always short of money. I got the impression that he wasn't capable of ever being seriously in love with anybody. The only enduring commitment I suspect he was capable of was to flying. Yet he was very kind to me. We met several times and he would always go out of his way to share little bits of aviation wisdom with me.[9]

Smithy, Van Dijk, Stannage and Saul were whisked away in a siren-screaming convoy to Manhattan, where they were installed in huge luxury suites at the Roosevelt Hotel. For five days they lost control of their lives as New York's hospitality machine ingested them. They roared about the city accompanied by police motor-cyclists; they were treated to a tickertape drive down Broadway, presented with medals, flown to Washington to meet President Hoover. A cable came from Australia to say that the government had promoted Smithy in his honorary RAAF rank from squadron leader to wing commander. Nowhere was there sanctuary from the intrusions of the press and the crowds of fans, many of them young women, who camped outside the hotel. Smithy, still affected by his Atlantic ordeal, began to wilt under the ferocity of it all.

When the *Southern Cross* landed at Oakland, San Francisco on 4 July 1930, it had completed, over two years and in a series of unrelated journeys, a circumnavigation of the world. As for her pilot, after two more days of pitiless adulation, he was close to cracking up. It was Allan Hancock who came to Smithy's rescue. The millionaire took one look at him and spirited them all off to his latest luxury ocean-cruiser, the 125ft diesel *Velero II*. They sailed out from Los Angeles to Santa Catalina Island where, for two days, all they did was swim and sleep. Hancock then arranged for them to unwind for several more days at the fabulous home of his friend William Randolph Hearst, the newspaper baron, at San Simeon on the Californian coast. Back in Los Angeles they were caught up in a whirl of Hollywood parties where they were photographed with Myrna Loy, Charles Laughton and Mae West.

'Saturated with pleasure and enjoyment', they stayed on in California until the third week of June. Here Smithy decided that the time had come to return the *Southern Cross* to its rightful owner. 'Now that she had completed the Pacific task I naturally felt that I should offer Captain Hancock the dear old machine back.' Hancock wouldn't hear of it. 'With his wonderful tact he realised that I could ill afford such a sacrifice. He insisted the plane should remain mine.' What Smithy didn't add was that he was so broke that he had promptly put the aircraft up for sale. Rival interest quickly came from the cities of Oakland, San Francisco and New York, but when it came to it he couldn't yet bear to part with the 'old bus'. Instead he had it shipped back to Australia. Despite his financial problems he turned down an offer of a tempting £10,000 a year – around £250,000 today – to make some major flights for the state of California. The sticking point was that the deal required him to become an American citizen.

Although Ulm was again pressing him to hurry back to the airline, Smithy appears by this time to have become quite remote from his company. Fame had sucked him into another world. To Ulm's annoyance he and Stannage now sailed to Bremerhaven in Germany, where they were collected by Fokker and flown to Amsterdam to be formally applauded for their Atlantic feat. In Holland the pressure finally caught up with Smithy. He was gripped by acute stomach pains. Instead of consulting a doctor he insisted that a holiday away from the ballyhoo would put him right. So he and Stannage set off together on an extensive tour of Europe, travelling anonymously from country to country on what seems to have become an aimless attempt at escape. But the abdominal pains grew progressively worse. Alarmed, they hurried back to Holland, where Smithy turned for help to an eminent historian and author, Dr Hendrik Willem van Loon, whom he had met on the voyage from Australia. Despite the cultural gulf that separated them, he and Smithy, both charismatic personalities, had struck up a warm friendship.

Shocked by Smithy's condition, Van Loon took him to a doctor who diagnosed acute appendicitis. He was in hospital for ten days. The surgeon removed not only his appendix but his tonsils as well. Photographs show him, pyjama-clad and with a moustache, looking uncharacteristically drawn and unsmiling. It was now early August and he was anxious to end his protracted sabbatical. The invitations for his September wedding had been sent out, and he was in a hurry to get back to England, take delivery of a new biplane he had ordered and fly it home to Australia. There was another, less happy reason for urgency: he had learned that his father was dying of bowel cancer. The Dutch doctors urged him to return by sea, forbidding him to go near an aeroplane for at least six weeks. But his new Avro Avian was waiting at A. V. Roe's Manchester factory, and the thought of abandoning the opportunity to smash Hinkler's England–Australia record was unthinkable. In view of all these uncertainties Smithy and Mary, in some shouted phone conversations on the bad long-distance lines, decided to postpone their wedding until December.

On 15 August he left hospital and went to Van Loon's home in rural Veere in the far south-west of Holland to convalesce and plan his first long-distance solo flight. The England–Australia route had now been flown many times – most spectacularly, in May that year, in nineteen and a half days by Amy Johnson, the first woman pilot to do it alone. But no one had yet bettered Bert Hinkler's 1928 time of fifteen and a half days, and to do so now seemed the most important thing in the world. His first problem was paying for the new aeroplane. In desperation be cabled ANA, offering to sell the company the *Southern Cross* for £5,000, but the board wasn't interested. He must have raised the money from somewhere else, because in mid-September he left Van Loon's home and went to England at last to collect the Avian, G-ABCF, which he had named *Southern Cross Junior*. He was impatient to be off, because four other contenders in three aircraft were already on their way to Australia, bent on smashing Hinkler's record. Yet, as so often when poised for a long and dangerous flight, he was struck by a sudden severe attack of flu which put him to bed for nearly a week. By the time he took off from Heston on Thursday 9 October, a few days after logging his 4,000th flying hour, his formidable vitality had been sapped by the Atlantic adventure, the surgery and the flu.

For the first time in his long-distance career he was alone. There was no co-pilot, no navigator, no radio; no helpful headings would be thrust into the cockpit on the end of a stick. He would have to map-read his way to Darwin. Planning to get there in ten daily hops of around 1,000 miles each, he set a cracking pace and, despite his debilitated state, appears not to have been seriously crippled by over-water panic, for he carried no lifejacket or dinghy, only an inner tube and a pump. Over the Bay of Bengal he was spared the destructive monsoonal weather he most feared: the inter-tropical front had retreated. He missed the 'old bus's' three engines: 'Over the open sea the airman experiences a curious and entirely imaginery suspicion that his engine is not running as well as usual. One hears all kinds of noises – a psychological reaction to the fear of a forced landing.'

He overtook all his rival pilots to reach Darwin on 19 October 1930, in a new absolute record time for an England–Australia flight of nine days twenty-one hours and forty minutes. He had lowered Hinkler's record by five and a half days and had made the journey in around half Amy Johnson's time. The familiar telegrams poured into Darwin, including one from King George V and another from the British prime minister, Ramsay MacDonald. At that moment, Smithy was the world's greatest-achieving aviator of the era. What purpose had his latest flight served beyond satisfying his now insatiable need for further accomplishment and acclaim? In his autobiography he claimed: 'It had shown that Hinkler's time of 15½ days, which two short years before, had astonished the world, would now be a comparatively leisurely journey. It had demonstrated the absolute reliability of the modern British-made light aircraft. It had shown that what I had done could be equalled and improved upon by regular established services.' But this last truth had been self-evident for a long time; indeed, scheduled airline services operating from Europe to the Dutch East Indies on Australia's doorstep had begun that very month. It was no longer necessary for brave solo fliers in open cockpits to stimulate the development of the long-haul airways, even if the public appetite for the adventures of colossi like Kingsford Smith remained as voracious as ever.

Smithy arrived in Sydney on 22 October, less than 13 days from London. Twenty aircraft flew out from Mascot in a noisy swarm to welcome him and he and Mary were driven through central Sydney to cheering throngs. He had only just got home in time. At 'Kuranda' his father was already fading away and Smithy was shocked to see how ill he was. In the last week of October, William was moved into a hospital in Longueville, where, on 2 November, with Smithy, Leofric and Eric at his bedside, he died peacefully.

Smithy made no mention of his father's death in his autobiography. He had always enjoyed a warm and affectionate relationship with William, but the deeper bond was unquestionably with his doting, spoiling mother. William, it seems, had remained a secondary figure in his life, an amiable but rather sad man, happy to leave the management of the family to the hyper-competent Catherine. His productive life, and with it his vigour and self-esteem, had ended thirty-one years earlier on that disastrous January Thursday in 1899. From this deep disgrace, as he regarded it, he had never, people said, fully recovered. Nor, sadly, had he ever managed to find the money he had sworn to repay. 'But,' said Catherine Robinson, 'he had remained a good husband and father – he was a model to be proud of in both roles, a man of high integrity but neither physically strong nor worldly wise. He was a more sympathetic and gentle person than Catherine. The soft side of Chilla's nature would certainly have come from him.'

William's ashes were scattered over the Pacific from the *Southern Moon*, piloted by Smithy with Catherine on board. 'Although Catherine became sick and lonely,' said Catherine Robinson, 'she never demonstrated any obvious grief for Will. She just wasn't given to that sort of emotion. I remember her deeply shocking Elsie after he'd gone by saying, "I was never in love with your father, you know."'

In recognition of his latest flight the government had again promoted Smithy, for the second time in four months, in his honorary air force rank. This dramatic elevation – from wing commander, bypassing group captain, to air commodore, the highest rank in the RAAF – was not greeted with much enthusiasm in the higher echelons of the air force itself. There was renewed indignation among its long-serving senior officers that rewards of honorary commissions for private record-breaking ventures were making a mockery of the system. Most affronted was the chief of the air force, Richard Williams, whose own rank Smithy now shared. He was angry that the promotion hadn't been referred to the Air Board. 'I considered it wrong in principle,' he wrote in his autobiography, still simmering, nearly fifty years later. Of Kingsford Smith and Ulm he declared: 'These men had never been members of the RAAF. Other appropriate honours should have been awarded to them.'[10] In 1930, however, he had wisely chosen not to voice these views in public, for no reward was seen as too good for Australia's icon. Smithy himself was not in the least embarrassed by the extravagance of the honour. He lost no time in having his uniform upgraded into the full regalia of air commodore and being photographed in it.

The airline, now struggling in the face of massive recession, saw little of him during November. He was either giving joyrides at Mascot, competing in air races in *Southern Cross Junior*, or making lengthy trips in her to Melbourne to visit Mary and to finalise the arrangements for their imminent marriage.

The wedding, on Wednesday 10 December, was the society event of the year. The groom and the best man, Charles Ulm, turned out in their air force formal dress uniforms supported by a contingent of RAAF officers. There were four bridesmaids, among them Mary's closest friend, Molly McBride (later Hudson) and Smithy's niece Beris, and 200 guests. Because Smithy had been divorced the Church of England had refused to marry him, so the ceremony took place at Scots Presbyterian Church in Melbourne's Collins Street, attracting a crowd of 10,000 which disrupted traffic for hours. As the couple left the church through lines of police battling to hold back a wall of cheering humanity, the weight of people toppled the wooden barriers and Smithy and Mary were mobbed as they tried to get into the car. Two bridesmaids were crushed and their bouquets trampled underfoot. For Mary it was a frightening moment. The day before, she had received an anonymous letter threatening to throw acid in her face at the church. Ever since Coffee Royal Smithy had been receiving a stream of hate mail which now extended to Mary. 'From the day of our engagement I was never free of cranks,' she said. 'Nor was my morale helped by newspapers describing me as Chill's "child bride".'

They went to Tasmania for their honeymoon. 'He was a very physical but gentle and endlessly patient person,' Mary said.

He taught me to smoke, to drink and introduced me to highly risqué stories. 'A dirty mind is a perpetual solace,' he would often say. And he loved to announce outrageously: 'My greatest ambition is to be hanged for rape when I'm ninety-two!' As I was soon to discover, the honeymoon was to be one of the rare times when I would have him to myself. He had this deep need to be surrounded by people. He hardly ever read and had very few books.

Back on spasmodic duty with ANA in January 1931, Smithy involved himself for a time with the extension of their operations from Melbourne to Tasmania. He decided to command the inaugural flight, on 16 January, taking Jim Mollison as his co-pilot in the *Southern Cloud*. They were given a civic welcome in Launceston and wined and dined for two days. On the night before the first northbound service back to Melbourne, Mollison wrote, Smithy said to him at the hotel: 'Jim, we must impress the Tasmanians with our steadiness and sobriety. In the company's interest we'll spend a quiet evening and be early in bed, say about eleven o'clock.' Mollison claimed that he took the instruction seriously.

By eleven thirty I drowsed among the sheets, the reputation of Australian National Airways secure in my keeping. Hours later, I awoke to a thunderous 'Ssh!' that shook the rafters. Staggering slightly and wild of eye, Smithy tiptoed towards the twin beds, noiseless as a battery of horse artillery at the canter, finger to his lips. A slightly rumpled blonde behind him made shaky efforts to bolt the door on the inside. Between them they made clatter enough to bring the ceiling down. We all drank and made merry together until the smallest hours.[11]

Mollison, himself a notorious philanderer, applauded Kingsford Smith's style. 'On the ground,' he wrote, 'Smithy could do and did all the damn silly things that show the great man is human after all.'

Smithy's burst of flying activity did not last long. In the last week of January he began a three-week rest to enable him and Mary to settle into a flat in Sydney which Catherine had found for them at the top of a small block at 74 Drumalbyn Road, on Bellevue Hill, overlooking Rose Bay. 'As a married man,' said John Stannage, 'Smithy now determined to settle down to routine work. He was honour-bound to help his company weather the financial crisis that had overtaken the world of business.' However, the move to Drumalbyn Road unleashed a spasm of social activity, and at ANA's head office in Martin Place they saw less of him than ever. Ernest Aldis, a retired engineering director of Qantas who was then a sixteen-year-old apprentice mechanic with ANA, said:

We rarely saw Kingsford Smith – he was just a sleeping partner. He would come out to Mascot and take the odd service up to Brisbane or down to Melbourne. Or he'd just climb into one of the company's training Moths and go off and do some aerobatics. He just came and went as the spirit moved him, never seeming to worry about anything. But because he was so universally worshipped and the most famous man in the country, everyone just accepted it. He was totally beyond reach of life's routines. Without Ulm that airline wouldn't have operated for more than a day.

The minutes of ANA's board meetings show that Kingsford Smith rarely bothered to attend them. 'He still only came in to read and dictate answers to his constant fan mail, a large proportion of it from children. He would sometimes sit in the outer office and fire paperclips from elastic bands at my bottom while I was taking dictation from Mr Ulm,' the prim and proper Ellen Rogers was later to tell John Ulm. 'ANA wasn't important to him,' said Scotty Allan. 'He was only interested in his own flying. He was quite heedless, really – unbelievably unreliable and unpunctual if it didn't concern his own interests. If a meeting were arranged for ten o'clock he'd turn up at eleven – or he mightn't appear at all. Ulm was the boss as far as I was concerned. He may have lived in Smithy's shadow, but he had more integrity.'

With his RAF background of safe, precision all-weather flying, Allan felt uneasy about the airline's safety standards, for which Smithy was responsible. All too soon his concerns proved to be well founded.

20

Grounded
1931

On Saturday 21 March, 1931 ANA's *Southern Cloud* left Sydney a few minutes after 8 am on the daily five-hour flight to Melbourne, commanded by the chief pilot, Travis Shortridge, an experienced and cautious captain. Near Canberra the Avro 10 flew into a cyclonic storm of which he had been given no warning on departure from Mascot. Having no radio, the plane could not be recalled. It never arrived at its destination. ANA immediately suspended all services to divert aircraft to search for it. For eighteen days they scoured the huge area of uninhabited mountain country lying between the Sydney–Melbourne railway and the Tasman Sea coast. Reports that the Avro had been seen and heard as far south as Melbourne poured in for weeks, but none led to its discovery. The plane, with its crew of two and six passengers, had vanished. Despite the lessons of Coffee Royal, Australia still had no national search-and-rescue service, and the financial burden fell cripplingly on ANA, already in serious financial trouble with falling load factors.

In the *Southern Cross* Smithy flew out every day for two weeks until he was on the verge of collapse. He based himself mainly in Melbourne, where Mary joined him. 'They were terrible weeks,' she said. 'I'd never seen his famous sense of fun disappear like that before. He stopped smiling, he stopped joking, he couldn't sleep. The worry began to make him physically ill. He flew from dawn to dusk, and every time he landed back at Essendon there were these relatives waiting for news. It was quite hideous.'

The mystery of the *Southern Cloud* was not solved for twenty-seven years. It was not until October 1958 that a young carpenter out for a bush walk with his camera in the Australian Alps stumbled on the burned-out wreckage lying on a ridge, concealed by mountain ash. There had been no survivors. One of the passengers' watches had stopped at 1.15: in the five hours the plane had been in the air it had averaged barely 44mph.[1]

On the day of the *Southern Cloud*'s disappearance, Scotty Allan had flown the Melbourne–Sydney service at the safe terrain clearance height of 9,000ft. 'The tail wind was approaching an incredible 100mph,' he recalled. 'It drifted me so powerfully to the east I had to offset my heading by 55 degrees. Going in the opposite direction in cloud, Shortridge obviously wasn't aware that he was probably going backwards at at least 10mph. When he'd been in the air for five hours, he probably reasoned that he must have reached Melbourne and began his fatal let-down.'

In the second week of April, after thirty aircraft had failed to find any trace of the Avro, a civil aviation inquiry was begun. Most of the evidence was heard in Melbourne. As the head of ANA's flight operations and one of the most tireless of the search pilots, Kingsford Smith was a central witness, but he had been so deeply affected by the tragedy that he wasn't well enough to return to Melbourne. He sent the committee a telegram to say that 'unless he was particularly required, he preferred to stay in Sydney and rest'.[2] Instead it was Ulm who went to explain the company's operating procedures – and its frustrations at being refused permission by the government to introduce its own aircraft radio direction-finding network on the Melbourne route.

The disappearance of the *Southern Cloud* was a catastrophic turning point in the ephemeral life of Australian National Airways.

Although the company resumed operations, it was now doomed. In the worsening depression, fewer people were travelling by train or ship, let alone by air. Nor was the airline's business helped by public concern about its safety standards: with no aircraft radio, people asked what was to prevent a recurrence of the disaster. Bookings began to fade away and flights to leave empty. Smithy's own finances were again in a parlous state. To his anguish, the NSW State Savings Bank had collapsed, taking with it much of his and Mary's savings.

ANA was to remain in notional existence, with a tiny staff, for another year and a half, as Ulm struggled singlehandedly to get it back on its feet. When he tried to persuade the government to bail them out, federal prime minister James Scullin was besieged by the powerfully orchestrated railway lobby, which opposed even a penny of subsidy for what it called an elitist service for an insignificant fragment of the population. There was also a belief in some quarters that Scullin's reluctance to help might have been subtly influenced by something else.

As his personality and interests would suggest, Smithy was not a political animal. Except where it touched on aviation matters, politics bored him. But his attitudes, shaped by his background and military service as an officer, tended instinctively towards the right. Whether in a reaction to the loss of his savings, or because he was attracted to the prospect of some action to counter his restlessness, he had joined, along with Ulm and his young nephew, John, an extreme right-wing organisation called the New Guard, inspired by the flourishing European fascist movements and founded by Eric Campbell, their solicitor and a prominent member of ANA's board. Alarmed at what he perceived as Premier Lang's Labour state government's mishandling of the recession – which had brought massive unemployment, bank closures, bankruptcies, strikes and an upsurge in militant trade-unionism – Campbell, a First World War colonel who kept portraits of Hitler and Mussolini on his desk, declared that the state was on the verge of anarchy and revolution and promised that his New Guard would destroy communism, maintain law and order and run strike-bound services. A veritable army of ex-servicemen rushed to join this secret paramilitary movement, which quickly grew to a strength of 100,000 men. The New Guard acquired arms and began to clash with police, give fascist salutes at its rallies, and to allow its members to conceal their identities with Ku Klux Klan-style hoods.

Since Scullin's federal government was also a Labour administration, it can hardly have welcomed the appearance of the New Guard, and it may not have been altogether wise of Smithy and Ulm, or of ANA's chairman, Frederick Stewart, to have joined this fascist outfit. What Smithy possibly didn't know was that the state police were regularly recording in their files the presence of his car parked outside locations where the organisation's clandestine meetings were taking place. 'The police records show,' said an Australian historian, Dr Andrew Moore, 'that Smithy was actually to have commanded an air squadron in the event of the Guard staging a coup. At a dinner party in Woollahra a servant heard him say: "If the Lang government doesn't come to its senses, perhaps a bit of bombing might persuade them." There was even a far-fetched plan to seize Lang and some of his ministers, fly them down to Berrima in the southern highlands and hold them captive there.'[3]

Although Smithy remained a passive member of the New Guard, his prestigious name helped to boost its image as the saviour of the state. However, his nephew John, then twenty and jobless, became an active participant. 'We were actually issued with arms and practised rifle drill and marching, and groups of us were sent out to harass the so-called "Reds" who preached on street corners,' he recalled. 'We would seize them, drive out into the country, strip them and leave them naked in the bush. It all sounds a bit extreme today, but at the time it was considered rather harmless. Certainly Chilla's association with Campbell and that whole movement can't have helped persuade the government to save the airline.'[4]

Smithy's lack of income led to other desperate measures. John described how he entered into a dubious scheme, kept secret from the family, to help Uncle Chilla financially.

I hit on the bright idea of destroying his speedboat, which he was now hardly using, so he could claim the insurance. A friend and I set fire to it, trying to make it look like an accident. After we'd towed the blackened mess back to the ramp at Longueville, I told Chilla, who winked and thanked me. He claimed the engine had backfired and the insurance company paid up £300. He told me it had helped to clear some of his debts. I've always been a little ashamed of what we did, but I would have done anything for that man.

While Ulm continued the hopeless fight to revive the airline, Smithy was forced to take the 'old bus' joyriding into the country to keep the wolf from the door. He never again worked from his ANA office, of which he had in any case been an infrequent occupant, and from this point until the company's eventual demise, his connection with the failed airline seems to have been informal at best. He began to cast around for a new spectacular enterprise. His England–Australia record of the previous year had now been reduced to nine days and four hours by the English pilot Charles Scott. And Jim Mollison, seeing his ANA job about to disappear, had flown back to England in eight days nineteen and a half hours. Smithy decided to attack both records. He bought himself a new Avian, naming it *Southern Cross Minor* (VH-UQG). Of how he paid for it there is no record, but a £1,000 cheque from his father-in-law to replace the lost savings bank funds may have helped.

Smithy took off from Melbourne on 21 September. Off the north-west coast of Malaya he flew into a terrifying monsoonal storm. Low on fuel as night approached, and with his destination, Victoria Point in southern Burma, still 80 miles away, he put down in blinding rain on a beach for the night. As he sat there in the cockpit, tired, hungry and wet, listening to the rain drumming on the wing, the tide began to rise round the aircraft. Worried that the wheels would sink into the sand, he hurried into the jungle to search for branches to lay under the tyres. But the roar of a tiger close by sent him crashing back to the safety of the cockpit. He huddled there nervously for the rest of the night, emerging only briefly to jam some driftwood under the wheels. At dawn he flew on to Victoria Point, where he learned that his temporary disappearance had already begun to cause concern round the world and that now, at the beginning of the third day from Australia, he had slipped behind Mollison's time. He flew on to Rangoon, snatched a few hours' sleep and pushed on again at 3 am, determined to make Jhansi in India the same night. Cautiously he followed the Burma coast north to Cox's Bazar, where the sea crossing to the Ganges delta narrowed to 120 miles. Setting a compass course for Calcutta, he headed gingerly out to sea.

For the first 50 miles everything went smoothly. The weather was perfect, the sea calm, the engine purred contentedly. But then, without warning, the familiar debilitating symptoms of panic began to grip him. 'It was halfway across the bay, with 60 miles of open sea on either side, that I was stricken. I remember thinking that the midday sun on the back of my head was not very good for me. My head seemed to be getting heavy . . . I ought to have obtained a proper solar topee in Rangoon.' In fact it was only 8 o'clock in the morning and the sun was still quite weak: what he was experiencing had little to do with the heat. The sense of dread, the disorientation, the awful feeling of unreality, were all of psychological origin, the same manifestations of distress he had experienced on the Pacific, the Tasman and the Atlantic. But then he'd had three engines and a crew around him; now he was out of sight of land on one vulnerable engine. This time the fear seemed to paralyse his entire being.

'Suddenly I had a horrible feeling that I didn't know who I was or what I was doing. I knew that I was flying the plane, and that I had to reach land which was out of sight. But who I was, or why I was there, I didn't know! This curious attack lasted a minute or so. I was in a peculiar condition of half consciousness. The next moment I was diving at a fairly steep angle for the sea. In a sweat of apprehension I gained control of myself.' In fact he had stalled and flicked into a spin from which he managed to recover only a few hundred feet from the water. As his head swam he began to vomit over the cockpit side. Yet it all seemed to be happening to someone else. It was as if some mood-changing drug had disconnected his brain from his body, as if he was observing his own suffering from a vague and great distance. All reality – the cockpit, the sea, the roar of the engine, the slipstream on his face – had receded. So divorced were his senses from his airborne environment that he worried he mightn't be capable of controlling the aircraft long enough to make land. 'I felt that my only chance was to pancake the machine on the water. It would float for some time and I might drift ashore on it.'[5]

Somehow he managed to avoid this extreme solution and reach the verdant islands of the Ganges delta, from where he headed straight for Dum Dum Aerodrome outside Calcutta. Here he borrowed a sun hat and gulped down 'some emergency brandy'. The terrible panic fell away and the world began to swing gently back into focus. For an hour he sat in the shade, with a violent headache, in a serene alcohol-induced haze.

Late that morning he felt up to resuming the flight. 'I had only one idea – to push on, to keep ahead of Mollison.' But as he flew west across northern India, the soothing effect of the raw spirit wore off and the panic began to creep back. Prudently he had taken on board at Calcutta a whole bottle of brandy. Unlike Mollison who, on his long-distance flights, became chronically dependent on cockpit alcohol, Smithy had hitherto managed without. Now, suddenly, it was the only thing that would keep him together. A medicinal swig at judicious intervals 'fixed me up'. Assailed by waves of fear and nausea, and constantly vomiting over the side, even in the cool of dawn, he pressed on to Aleppo, arriving at 11 pm on the sixth day, so exhausted that he had to be lifted from the cockpit. Although he was almost a day ahead of Mollison, when he set out on the seventh morning for Rome, he was nearing the end of his tether.

Almost immediately he made a bad navigation error, setting a south-westerly heading instead of west and hitting the Mediterranean coast far south of the Gulf of Alexandretta, where he should have been. To reach the southern coast of Turkey on the other side of the gulf, he had to make another dreaded long sea crossing. For more than an hour he prayed that the panic and nausea wouldn't return, because he was now out of brandy. Following the Turkish coast westward he was soon overwhelmed by fresh waves of anxiety and an even more alarming symptom: a 'light-headed feeling' which filled him with a compulsive urge to 'jump out of the machine'. For a moment he seriously wondered if he was going mad. The desire to undo his straps and leap over-board was so pressing that he knew it was not safe for him to remain in the air any longer. He pointed the nose down and dived towards a beach, 'determined to get to earth as soon as possible', but as he circled the deserted coast the agitation receded. He abandoned the landing, intent on keeping going a little longer.

Passing over the town of Antalya and turning south to avoid high mountains, he prepared to leave the Turkish coast and set out across the Aegean Sea for Greece. But as he looked towards the far horizon he knew that he couldn't again risk going out of sight of land. He hadn't arranged permission to overfly Turkey, and if he put down there he would be in trouble, but he had no option. He flew inland and, near the town of Milas, found a safe spot. 'More dead than alive, I brought *Southern Cross Minor* to earth, my idea being to persuade the villagers to procure me some brandy and to rest in the shade of the wing before continuing to Rome.'

The Avian was quickly surrounded by a crowd of Turkish peas-ants. Smithy climbed out and promptly fainted. When he came to he was surrounded by armed soldiers and under arrest. He had landed in a Turkish military area and permission to leave would have to come, he was told, from Turkish army headquarters in Angora (Ankara). He was locked up under an armed guard for the night. His second disappearance in the space of a few days made anxious headlines in London and Australia and was soon creating ripples of diplomatic activity. When news of his whereabouts finally reached the Australian High Commission in London, the Turkish ambassador was pressed to urge his government to release the famous pilot. The High Commission was told that if Air Commodore Kingsford Smith had landed without authority, then the matter would take some time to resolve. It took three days.

When, on the afternoon of 2 October, Smithy took off and flew out over the Aegean Sea, the familiar numbing terror immediately surged back. He had acquired more brandy and took long swigs, but though it contained the panic, he felt his sanity was still poised on the brink of a dark abyss. Not even the alcohol, he now knew, would supply the confidence he needed to cross the open Aegean. Instead he took a cautious route to the Greek mainland, nervously zig-zagging through the Dodecanese, feeling his way from island to island, everywhere anxiously on the look-out for landing places.

When he arrived in Athens he was so patently unwell that he was persuaded to see an American psychiatrist practising there. The consultant declared him in no fit state to carry on to England. Yet even in his stricken condition and after his terrifying experiences, Smithy was not prepared to abandon the flight. After three days' rest, he flew on to Rome and London, arriving, shattered, on 7 October at Heston, where Mollison came to greet him. 'Bad luck, old man,' reporters heard him say.

Smithy did not fly back to Australia. He was forced to abandon his attempt on Scott's record. In an interview with *The Times* he was foolish enough to criticise the Turkish authorities for spoiling his Australia–England bid. The Turks responded by permanently banning him from their airspace, denying him the most direct route through southern Europe. Moreover, there was now such deep concern for his health that he was instructed by the Australian civil-aviation controller to submit himself to examination at the RAF's Central Medical Establishment in London.

I consulted a nerve specialist who, after a thorough examination, completely disorganised my plans. Not satisfied with his own diagnosis, he called in a heart specialist and, between the two of them, I was soon thoroughly convinced that a return flight was out of the question . . . I was forced to the realisation that my detention in Turkey might have been all for the best. The doctors were emphatic that, in my low condition, a continuation of the flight from Milas might have ended in disaster. What appeared to be a cruel blow of fate was doubtless a merciful dispensation of Providence.

Agitated cables flew between Horace Brinsmead, the civil-aviation controller, and the military attaché at the Australian High Commission in London as Brinsmead tried to get to the bottom of the dramatic breakdown that had led to the illegal landing. Smithy had told reporters in London that he had had sunstroke; Brinsmead, however, had another theory. 'KINGSFORD SMITH MACHINE PROVIDED WITH STUB EXHAUSTS INVOLVING POSSIBILITY MONOXIDE INSPIRATION FOR LONG PERIODS. ENQUIRE RAF MEDICAL SPECIALIST CONSULTED BY SMITH WHETHER HIS CONDITION INDICATES SUCH POSSIBILITY RATHER THAN THROUGH SUNSTROKE.'[6] The attaché cabled Brinsmead in response: 'SPECIALIST CONSULTED BY KINGSFORD SMITH ATTRIBUTES UNFITNESS TO NERVE DISORDER FOLLOWING GREAT FATIGUE AND ACCENTUATED BY SUNSTROKE. NO INDICATIONS OF EFFECTS OF MONOXIDE.'[7]

Nonetheless, the seed of another Kingsford Smith myth had been sown. The carbon-monoxide explanation was rubbish, of course: the poisonous gases from the Avian's engine would have been completely dispersed in the 80mph slipstream. Nor was the equally convenient alternative of sunstroke a likely cause. Yet because 'nerve disorder' was, in the 1930s, seen as a mild disgrace, as human weakness with implications of lack of moral fibre, no one was prepared to accept that one of aviation's most intrepid pioneers was, beneath his aura of superhuman stamina, just another vulnerable human being. The legend of Charles Kingsford Smith had no room for the effects of fear and fame upon his mind. Even Mary, witness to the slow process of his decay, still sincerely believed that it was carbon-monoxide poisoning which changed his life. 'He was never the same again after that 1931 flight,' she insisted. 'The dizzy spells went on for weeks after he got to England. He always blamed it on carbon monoxide. Whatever it was, his health just seemed to go permanently downhill from then on.'

What, then, had led the RAF doctors to the opinion that Smithy was suffering from a nervous disorder? In 1993, the RAF's consultant adviser in psychiatry, Wing Commander Ken Craig – attached to the same unit, the Central Medical Establishment, which arranged Smithy's 1931 medical – very helpfully agreed to discuss with me the condition that Kingsford Smith had described so vividly. The discreet brick building in Cleveland Street, near Regent's Park in London, hadn't changed much since the day Smithy walked in, bewildered by what was happening in his mind. The creaking lift to the second floor looked as if it might easily have been the one that took him up to the consultation that was so drastically to clip his wings. Ken Craig was a friendly, softly spoken Ulsterman, patient and attentive. He listened closely as I summarised the events of Smithy's life: the emotionally secure and happy childhood; the horrors of war; the happy-go-lucky sometimes irresponsible attitude to life thereafter; the rise to superstar fame. He made careful notes, then paused for thought. 'What an interesting person he must have been,' he said eventually.

I suspect, from all the evidence, that the strong likelihood is that he was an alcoholic. Sunstroke wasn't a factor, I'm sure, nor carbon-monoxide poisoning. They were, I imagine, just smokescreens for things that were much more complex and deep-seated. Lots of things about him suggest that it could have been a combination of factors, but with an underlying alcohol-dependency.

Several significant life events must have affected him quite deeply. First the near-drowning in the surf when he was ten. It could certainly have left him phobic about open water. Add to that his childhood fear of heights and you have another. Then the traumas of war. He may have been seen as a gung-ho extrovert killer, but that wasn't the real him. It was a façade. Machine-gunning men from the air he clearly didn't enjoy at all. The war would have left him psychologically damaged, suffering, whether people recognised it or not, from some degree of post-traumatic stress disorder.

The war would also have introduced him to heavy drinking. It was seen as part of squadron life that guys should get drunk together. They'd even fly drunk, which wasn't that critical at 80mph. So alcohol became one of the staples of his life, leading him to imbibe at air shows and fly under the influence. Then suddenly comes great fame and everywhere he goes people are throwing booze at him. It would be amazing if it hadn't all created a degree of dependency. Yet one suspects he wouldn't have known it. He wouldn't have known on those long flights that what was actually hitting him worst were bad withdrawal symptoms. All the horrors he described are quite classically those. No one probably ever thought of him as an alcoholic because he was routinely satisfying the habit without necessarily being seen in any obvious way to be drunk. That is very common: only sudden deprivation shows it up so painfully.

There were other things, too, about him that are very common to alcoholics: his promiscuity, the constant need for fresh conquests, seeking reassurance about his potency; his chronic restlessness; his earlier flighty irresponsibility as a pilot with the Diggers outfit; his inability to handle money, the great generosity – ready to give away his last penny, always broke. And the evidence from the photographs that show how rapidly he aged – another consequence of alcoholism.

Why, if he had such a deep dread of drowning, would Smithy have set out so often to expose himself to oceanic flying? There was, said Wing Commander Craig, a psychological explanation: counter-phobia.

He sounds like a textbook example: the man who drives himself to conquer his phobias by setting out to do, quite obsessively, the very things that terrify him, and, quite paradoxically, derives pleasure from them. The way fear of heights drives some people to become mountaineers, tackling the most dangerous climbs they can find. Here was a man who nearly drowns in the sea. So he spends much of his adult life trying to conquer large oceans, constantly becoming panic-stricken in the process. His worst attacks always occurred out of sight of land. Yet he goes on doing the thing he hates again and again. Add the aggravating symptoms of withdrawal and you have a very good explanation for those awful feelings he described. It surely wasn't coincidence that, when it was available, he was always able to control things with a swig of brandy.

On top of all this we have the significant pattern of illness immediately before major stressful flights. The sudden incapacitating flu, invariably on the eve of departure. That was no coincidence, either. Those bouts of flu weren't viral, they were psychological in origin, a postponement of imminent danger.

Subsequently I sent Wing Commander Craig some of Smithy's own detailed accounts of his illnesses in flight. 'They have simply reinforced my hypotheses about him,' he wrote back: 'His panics are explicable in purely psychological terms with alcohol-withdrawal aggravating the condition. He was clearly a man, one suspects, who was tortured by his early experiences.'[8]

It is unlikely that in 1931 any of this psychological insight would have been communicated to Smithy himself. He clung, it seems, to the simple view that his breakdown had been caused by nothing more complicated than the exhaust from his engine. But there is evidence that his apparent steely confidence had been badly shaken by the cracks which were appearing in his legendary physical endurance. Parking the Avian at Heston with instructions for it to be sold, he went back to Australia by sea. Reporters heard him give the news on the phone to Mary in Sydney. 'Hello, kiddy, it's all up,' he said. 'The doctors have turned me down. They warned me I could collapse over the sea.'[9]

On the voyage some of his fellow passengers noticed how uncharacteristically unsociable he had become. He kept himself to himself, avoiding contact with returning Australians anxious to chat to him. He had a lot on his mind: he was not only depressed by the disastrous end to his record attempts and by worries about the health he'd always taken for granted, he was also seriously concerned, for the first time, about his future. With the airline virtually defunct, the only prospect of a livelihood, it seemed, was a resumption of circus life – barnstorming around country towns.

21

Parting of the Ways
1931–2

Smithy arrived back in Australia in November 1931 to face the disintegration of his celebrated partnership with Charles Ulm. In public they had maintained the façade of immutable friendship, but it is clear that their once-cherished relationship had been souring for some time. 'It was hardly surprising they drifted apart,' Scotty Allan said.

The newspapers may have created them as a close partnership, but the truth was they actually had very little in common. Temperamentally they were poles apart. In many ways I used to think they were strangers. I do know very definitely that during the ANA days Ulm became extremely resentful that Smithy wasn't playing fair. It was pretty disgusting the way he left everything to Ulm, then cleared off for months to fly the Atlantic in search of more glory. Ulm used to complain that Smithy was just a passenger, but although there were lots of rumours, there wasn't, to my knowledge, any culminating row. They just began to go their separate ways.

Ulm's smouldering feelings had been brought to the surface by the content of parts of Smithy's autobiography, *The Old Bus*, on which he had been working with Melbourne *Herald* journalist Geoffrey Rawson. Smithy had left the manuscript behind when he had flown off to England without bothering to show it to Ulm. While he had been away the story had begun to appear in serial form in the *Herald*, and Ulm had been angered by what he saw as a lack of recognition of his contribution to the joint flights they had made. He decided that his objections couldn't wait for Smithy's return. He put the matter in the hands of his solicitor, Eric Campbell, who was left to sort it out with Leofric, Smithy's unofficial business manager.

Ulm's demands, characteristically terse and detailed, reveal the extent of his sensitivity to what he saw as his relegation to a role in Smithy's shadow – and his belief that he had a right to censor his colleague's book. He insisted that no further episodes be published in the *Herald* until the amendments he stipulated had been made, and that the changes should be submitted to him for approval. Claiming that he was entitled, under their partnership agreement, to share in any revenue resulting from their flights, he left it to Campbell to negotiate a satisfactory slice of the fee the *Herald* had paid Smithy. Ulm's list began with the point that rankled the most: 'Acknowledgement in each section of the serial . . . that I was co-commander jointly with Kingsford Smith on all flights of the *Southern Cross* up to and including the flight from Australia to England, and later from England to Holland.'

There is no record of whether Eric Campbell and Leofric were able to relay the demands to Smithy in England. With or without his knowledge, Campbell (who was in the invidious position of being solicitor to both men) and Leofric were forced to act quickly to avoid the serialisation being stopped if Ulm applied for an injunction. While Smithy was cruising dispiritedly home to Australia, someone began hurriedly to revise the text. The new material, carefully vetted by Ulm, went overboard in its anxiety to please him. 'It is fitting,' Smithy's story now read, 'that I should acknowledge how much of the success of the [Pacific] flight was due to the ability and untiring efforts of my friend and present co-director, Charles Ulm. From the time he wrote the first letter to a Sydney newspaper setting out our plans, his organising ability was mainly responsible for our eventually commencing the flight.' There followed a reference to Ulm's 'co-commander' role on many flights and an elaborate explanation as to why he had not been permitted to fulfil it also on the Atlantic trip. To crown it all the book now bore a new, prominent dedication: 'To my old flying colleague, Charles T. P. Ulm, without whose genius for organisation and courageous spirit many flights in the *Southern Cross* could never have been achieved.'

So it was that Smithy came home to find, to his amazement, that these paeans to Ulm had suddenly appeared in his text. Yet, having seen Ulm in ruthless action over four years, he can have been in little doubt that his partner wouldn't have hesitated to take his grievance before a judge. A few generous words in print was a small price to pay to avoid yet another expensive and sordid public squabble in court.

However, this solution merely papered over the ever-widening rift between the two men. 'Something did go wrong between them,' Mary said. 'I never knew what it was. It happened around the time of ANA's collapse. Chill refused to discuss it. All I know is that something occurred that left him feeling that someone he'd trusted and liked had let him down. Whatever it was, it hurt Chill very deeply.' Bruce Cowan, the first apprentice mechanic to join ANA in 1929, told me: 'I can remember Hal Litchfield often saying, "I don't know what happened between those two, but there was definitely something." It never came out. All I know is that after ANA folded we never saw Smithy and Ulm together at Mascot again.'

Smithy left no record of his true feelings; however, in Percy Cogger's unpublished biography of Ulm's life, *Wings and the Man*,[1] there are several references to his slow-burning bitterness. Kingsford Smith 'is regarded as a hero and the greatest of the world's pilots . . . in Australia as almost an immortal', Cogger wrote, but he went on to say that Smithy would not have attained his godlike status but for Ulm, who was 'forced to assume the role of second fiddle . . . Because the part played by Ulm lacked the elements of spectacularism, the greater glory fell upon his colleague.' Ulm's contribution 'did not fire the public imagination as did Kingsford Smith's cheerful grin, nonchalant manner and superb pilotage. Ulm lacked the knack of popular appeal . . . he felt he had had to take all the knocks and much less than half the glory.' However the partnership ended, Smithy and Ulm were never to make another flight together.

Most of ANA's staff had now moved on to new jobs or the dole queue, but still Ulm battled to get the airline back on its feet. To demonstrate its international potential, he decided to mount a publicity exercise in which one of the company's Avro 10s would fly the 1931 Christmas mail both ways between Sydney and London. The *Southern Sun* was prepared for the flight and, because Smithy was still not fully fit, Scotty Allan, who had taken a job as a flying-club instructor, agreed to return to pilot her. The Avro set off on 19 November, carrying two passengers including the civil-aviation controller, Horace Brinsmead, bound for London on business. It got no further than Alor Star (now Alur Setar) in northern Malaya. On take-off from the small, waterlogged aerodrome there, its wheels hit a perimeter embankment and the aircraft bounced into the air and crashed into a ricefield, so badly damaged that it never flew again. Miraculously, the four occupants clambered out into the water unhurt.[2]

It was now the last week of November. To get a plane to London and back to Australia by Christmas, Smithy, even though he had still not recovered from his last flight and was beginning to suffer from nagging back pain, insisted on mounting a relief mission in the *Southern Star*. Landing at Darwin in a thunderstorm, he hit the top of a telegraph pole, punching a hole in the wing and nearly writing off his engineer and himself. Pressing on to London in the repaired machine with Scotty Allan as his co-pilot, he was once again overwhelmed by claustrophobic panic. This time there was both a witness and salvation. 'It began almost the moment we were out of sight of the Burma coast, heading out across the Bay of Bengal,' Allan told me. 'A strained, anxious expression came over him. He got more and more agitated and presently grabbed the pad and scribbled a note saying that he was feeling ill and asking me to take over while he went back to rest.

'Somewhere I may still have the notes – I seem to remember there was more than one.' He shuffled off into a back room and was gone for some time. When he returned he was clutching two small, faded scraps of paper. 'I knew it had happened more than once,' he said, waving the little messages he had preserved for sixty-two years. 'Can you carry on for a while Jock. I feel a bit sick and will try and sleep for a bit,' one of them said, in Smithy's unmistakable writing. 'That was on the way over,' Allan explained. 'The other note was coming back. Both times we were over the Bay of Bengal. It seemed to happen every time we got into that area.' The second message simply read: 'I want to vomit. Will be back in 10 minutes.'

'Both times he left the cockpit looking quite dreadful and went back to be sick in the cabin,' Allan recalled. 'He would lie on the mailbags, trying to recover. The monsoon had retreated and we were in beautiful clear weather.' It wasn't Allan's first experience of Smithy's phobia. 'I'd seen it earlier in the year in the Gulf of Martaban, just south of Rangoon, when we'd been flying up to Akyab together through solid walls of rain, black as coal, right down on the water. He'd then written similar notes asking me to take over. On each occasion, once we were over land again, he would come back to the cockpit and brightly resume control.'

Smithy never discussed the panic attacks, Allan said.

Our relationship was never that close. I think he saw me as air crew rather than a mate. We didn't really have a lot in common out of the cockpit. When we arrived anywhere people would fuss over him, and after eight or nine hours flying I'd just want to go to bed, so we seldom even had dinner together. When we did all he really wanted to talk about was flying. It was the only thing in the world that interested him. That and women, of course. I suspected that his education had been quite limited. I don't believe he ever read very much. I remember I once quoted a famous Shakespearean character and he just looked blankly at me. Behind all that magic he was quite a simple guy, really.

Later on their flight to England Smithy and Allan were grounded by fog in Lyons. After Scotty had retired to his hotel room, he was surprised by a knock on the door. 'I opened it and standing there was this very attractive young French woman. To my amazement she said she'd been sent to my room by Kingsford Smith. Her friend was already with him. Smithy, she explained, had paid her in advance to come to me.' The puritan in Scotty Allan was outraged. 'I had to indicate rather forcefully that I wanted her to clear off. I never told Smithy. I guess I was too embarrassed. As he saw it, he'd merely been doing me a favour – he would never have understood.'

They delivered the mail at Croydon Airport on 15 December

amid a blaze of publicity. At a time when a letter from Sydney to London took over six weeks, fourteen days was sensational. The headlines called Smithy the 'Flying Father Christmas'. The festive season was not, however, a happy one. On 23 December Scotty Allan collected the *Southern Star* from the A. V. Roe factory at Hamble near Southampton. Low on fuel, and finding Croydon Airport fogbound, he bravely attempted a forced landing through a carpet of fog in rural Kent. The site turned out to be an orchard, and the aircraft ploughed through a thicket of apple trees. Happily, Scotty and three passengers – two of whom were stowaways, who ran off into the dark – were unharmed, but the *Southern Star* was extensively damaged.

The third accident to befall the Christmas mail expedition plunged Smithy into a fresh financial crisis from which ANA's long-suffering chairman, Frederick Stewart, had to rescue him. The *Southern Star* wasn't ready to fly again until the New Year, and then the return flight was delayed yet again when Smithy went down with a severe attack of pre-flight psychosomatic flu.

Eventually he and Allan made a fast flight of eleven days to Darwin, during which Smithy clocked up his 5,000th flying hour.[3] The major sea crossings brought on more panic attacks, the first, as Allan had described, over the Bay of Bengal and the second over the Timor Sea between Kupang and Darwin. 'Smithy never enjoyed the Timor,' Allan said. 'On this occasion I was flying. The weather was bad with walls of dark rain squatting on the sea. He didn't like those conditions one wee bit, even though he wasn't flying. The tension came back into his face. About two hours out he'd had enough. He told me to turn back to Kupang. He'd never done that before. But he was in charge, so we returned and flew across next day.'

Scotty Allan was the only person still alive in the 1990s who had witnessed Kingsford Smith's attacks at first hand. 'I'm quite convinced,' he said, 'that he should never have flown again on stressful long-distance flights. Whatever the psychological problem was, regardless of his technical skill, he had in my view ceased to be safe over the sea.' But, impelled by the demons of fame, he was to do it again and again.

In spite of the mishaps which dogged the mail flights, 'we had demonstrated that the empire air mail was a practical possibility,' wrote Smithy. 'We had the plant, the organisation and personnel. We were ready to take our part in establishing a regular air service. What, then, prevented a fulfilment of our hopes and expectations?' The painful truth was that although Smithy and Ulm were seen as trail-blazers, they were unable to convince the cautious aviation establishment that these triumphs automatically fitted them to run an Australian international airline. Although idolised as a pilot, Smithy could never become an organisation man. And Ulm, despite his business abilities, political nous, entrepreneurial thrust and highly developed vision, was tainted with a reputation as someone around whom controversy and acrimony perpetually swirled. Nevertheless, in the early months of 1932, Ulm, in competition with Qantas and West Australian Airways, doggedly pursued on behalf of ANA the route between Australia and Singapore, with which Imperial Airways was planning to extend its UK–India services. He mounted his bid with minimal help from Kingsford Smith.

Yet it was Smithy for whom the media clamoured, calling for him to be rewarded with a plum route of some kind as a grace-and-favour gesture or, at the least, a major government aviation job. The latter was always to be denied him because the defence establishment, which still controlled civil aviation, was only too aware of his temperamental unsuitability, his patent lack of gravitas. All he contributed to the early bids for air routes was his celebrated name, and a loose understanding that, when the time came, he would be prepared to be involved with one of the contenders. Meanwhile, with no employment and no immediate prospect of a route, he was reduced, as he'd feared, to taking the 'old bus' joyriding again around country towns. But because he was still believed to be associated with Ulm's pitch for the Brisbane–Singapore route, he had become, along with Ulm, the target of some powerful forces behind the scenes.

The most deadly was the Imperial Airways representative in Sydney, a prosperous and influential businessman in his mid-sixties called Albert Rudder, best known by his initials, 'A. E.' Rudder owned a shipping and travel agency in Pitt Street and, by early 1932, had come under immense pressure from the British airline to lobby the Australian government on its behalf for a share of the Singapore route. A dapper formidable man whose vision of an

England–Australia air service dated back to the mid-1920s, Rudder was said to combine integrity with a messianic belief in the power and goodness of empire. He was dictatorial, well connected and had the ear of the new prime minister, Joseph Lyons. Early on he set out successfully to cultivate a warm friendship with Qantas's managing director, Hudson Fysh, and chairman, Fergus McMaster, with a view to shutting out Smithy, Ulm and Norman Brearley, whose West Australian Airways had also thrown its hat into the ring.

It is unlikely that Smithy or Ulm ever knew the extent to which Albert Rudder worked so assiduously to denigrate and undermine them in order to guarantee that Ulm, at least, would be excluded from any significant role in any partnership on the Singapore route with Imperial. In the Imperial Airways archives in London, the fading correspondence reveals the stream of hostile criticism of Ulm, and disparaging comments about Smithy, that Rudder was privately feeding Imperial's managing director, George Woods Humphery.

In one of his most damaging letters, written in July 1932, Rudder sent Woods Humphery a summary of Ulm's business activities 'over the past ten or twelve years . . . which seem to provide evidence of a most appalling record justifying some of the evil reports in circulation'.[4] Dramatically, he offered to send his managing director details of this 'sinister record', which clearly came from the Ulm dossier collected over the years by the journalist Edward Hart. Although there is no evidence that Woods Humphery ever asked to see the offered details, the damage done to the aspirations of Ulm – and indirectly of Kingsford Smith – by this letter alone must have been immense. Meanwhile, in parallel correspondence, Rudder was busy extolling the virtues of Qantas. 'The chairman, Mr Fergus McMaster, is a shrewd and very likeable man . . . Mr Hudson Fysh knows his job and is an able and practical executive . . . as straight as a die.'[5] In another letter he wrote: 'We certainly do not want to carry the dead weight of ANA, or bring them into the picture in any form.' Imperial Airways agreed. With Rudder's help they set out to create a subsidiary airline, jointly owned with Qantas, to exclude all other contenders for the Singapore–Brisbane route.

It is not clear how far Smithy realised that the reputation of the colleague whose publicity and planning skills had helped to create his illustrious image was damaging his own imprecise aspirations. 'I don't think Chilla ever knew how far the knives were out for Ulm,' said John Kingsford-Smith. 'The trouble was, people always overestimated the closeness of their relationship. Despite all their joint triumphs, they were never very intimate friends.'

Early in 1932 both Smithy and Ulm came close to being killed in separate flying accidents. Ulm's occurred on 21 February, as he was on his way back with a friend from a bibulous reunion of the Australian Flying Corps Association at the RAAF station at Laverton, near Melbourne. Ulm, piloting his friend's Avro Avian back to Essendon Airport, flew, with a blinding flash, into a 132,000-volt power line alongside the Geelong Road. Although the aircraft plunged down in a tangle of wreckage, both men, amazingly, survived without major injury. Smithy's crash came a month later on 19 March. He had interrupted his barnstorming tour to fly back to Sydney for the official opening of the harbour bridge, over which he proceeded to give joyrides. At one of the many celebration parties, resplendent in his air commodore's mess dress, he created a stir by announcing that he was going to make a night flight over the bridge to view a water carnival. A group of guests, all in evening dress, among them his mother-in-law, Floss Powell, went out to Mascot to join the night adventure. The 'old bus' was wheeled out and Smithy, in mellow mood, took off with the aid of a handful of flickering oil flares. By the end of the short flight, undetected by Smithy, the gentle night breeze had veered. Bowled along by a tailwind, the plane touched down so fast and heavily that the entire undercarriage collapsed. Amid the terrified screams of his passengers, the Fokker slithered out of control across the pitch-black landing ground on its frail tubular and fabric fuselage. The port wing struck the ground and broke off. As the *Southern Cross* finally slewed to a halt, he shouted to everybody to get out and run. Men in dinner jackets and women in long dresses scrambled out on to the grass and stumbled clear. Thankfully the aircraft didn't burn, and astonishingly nobody was injured, though according to Catherine's diary, Floss Powell was 'bruised and shaken'.

It was the worst crash ever to befall the *Southern Cross*, but few people ever knew about it. Presumably, as no one was hurt and because it must have been an acutely embarrassing incident, Smithy did not submit an accident report to the Civil Aviation Department. There is no trace of it in the 1930s files of the Bureau of Air Safety Investigation, and somehow the newspapers never got hold of the story. Instead, after arranging for the aircraft to be dismantled, Kingsford Smith, still in air commodore's regalia, calmly collected Mary and drove her to a charity ball which he had been invited to declare open. 'Sorry, ladies and gentlemen, for being late,' he is reported to have said. 'I had a slight accident with the old bus at Mascot.' Later he confided that 'as the aircraft was grinding to a halt, making dreadful noises', he was counting the cost of the damage in his head: '£500 . . . £800 . . . £1,000 . . . £2,000.'[6] But behind his practised jocularity, he was devasted. It would be more than two months before the *Southern Cross* would fly again, and until then, he had lost his only remaining source of income.

Smithy hadn't the least idea how he was going to find the £1,500 needed for the massive repairs to the aeroplane. As ever, most of the cash he had earned joyriding had been absorbed by staff, fuel, hotels and booze. In desperation he appealed to Prime Minister Lyons to allow the work to be done at the navy dockyard on Cockatoo Island in Sydney Harbour under a delayed-payment arrangement. Lyons, aware that helping the national hero out of a jam, even one not widely known about, would work to his advantage, agreed, and in the first week of April the wrecked trimotor was dismantled and shipped on a barge out to the island.

While the 'old bus' was out of action Smithy decided to teach Mary to fly. 'I wasn't in the least enthusiastic, but he was insistent. I thought one pilot in the family was enough. He taught me at Mascot on a Gipsy Moth. But I never enjoyed it, and after about three hours solo I gave it up.' Another reason was that she was pregnant. 'The news absolutely delighted him and he became very protective, spoiling me more than ever.'

At the end of May 1932 the repaired *Southern Cross*, with 50 per cent of her structure replaced, was shipped back to Mascot. With his brother Wilfrid as his manager, Smithy immediately resumed his barnstorming tour. The combination of his personal magic and his celebrated aeroplane drew large crowds in every town, in spite of the chronic shortage of money everywhere, presenting him once

again with the twin temptations of an endless flow of alcohol and a
ready supply of women. The latter, it seems, were often willing to
form brief liaisons in return for the honour of a free flight in the
Cross – an arrangement which became known as 'a ride for a ride'.
Marge McGrath, who, the following year, was to become Smithy's
secretary at Mascot, was filled with awe and curiosity when she
heard the expression repeated, with winks and relish, by the men in
the joyriding team. Many years later she told Nancy-Bird Walton, a
prominent Australian pilot of the 1930s, about it. 'I must say,'
Nancy-Bird recalled, 'that at that time I wouldn't have had the
remotest idea what this code was all about.' However, later on,
when she was learning to fly at Mascot and watched this barter in
action, the scales fell from her eyes.

As the circus travelled from South Australia to Queensland,
two more aircraft joined it: a DH37 three-seater open-cockpit
biplane, flown by a young pilot, Pat Hall, and an Avro Avian. Two
members of the team – the chief engineer, Tommy Pethybridge,
who had bought himself out of the RAAF for £18 to join
Kingsford Smith, and a mechanic, Harry Purvis – had clubbed
together to buy the Avian from Charles Ulm. It soon acquired the
name *Southern Cross Pup* (VH-UOE). Purvis, later a distinguished
airline pilot and Second World War wing commander, had been
taken on as a nightwatchman after convincing Smithy that 'I knew
how to use my fists.' He had abandoned his own motor engineering business in Griffith to join the 'old bus' and 'the godlike beings
who flew her'. Along with Pethybridge and Hall, Purvis eventually
became a member of the small elite permitted by Smithy to fly
the *Cross*. He was also a close observer of the Peter Pan traits
which were never far from the surface of Kingsford Smith's
character:

> You never knew what was coming next. I remember one
> frosty morning at a Victorian town, we were in a large grass
> paddock in calm air with take-off possible in any direction.
> Smithy faced the *Southern Cross* straight at a large ditch only
> a few hundred metres away and said, 'Ever do a hedgehop in
> a large aircraft, Harry?' He then proceeded to open the
> throttles and rush at what seemed certain disaster. Fresh
> from three prangs, I was starting to rise in my seat, scalp

prickling. Then I saw what he was about. We reached the ditch with nothing like flying speed (about 35 to 40 knots), and then he yanked the stick back and we hopped the ditch and settled gently on the grass the other side, where we gathered up the required speed for normal take-off. I later discovered that he was often given to it – 'Let's have a bit of a gutter hop this morning!'

At the small towns they visited, flying sixteen people at a time, many of them with children on their knees, the locals were amazed by Smithy's laid-back accessibility. Although Wilfrid sometimes tried to shoo hangers-on away from hotel dining rooms to let him eat in peace, almost anyone could approach him to shake his hand, get his autograph, talk to him, or join him while he held court in the bar, spicing his stories with his vast repertoire of unprintable jokes. He also became a legend for constant small acts of kindness: taking poor schoolchildren and unemployed men for free rides, lending people money, giving up his evenings to make the speeches he hated.

In the first week of June 1932 it was announced that Charles Kingsford Smith had at last been knighted for his services to aviation. Mary hurried to join him and they flew in the *Southern Cross* to Canberra, where they were guests of the governor-general, Sir Isaac Isaacs, at a Government House King's birthday banquet. Few of Smithy's private reactions to the honour – he became a knight bachelor – have survived. In his autobiography he referred to it only briefly in the context of criticism 'that this new honour accorded ill with my barnstorming performances in which I was plying the *Southern Cross* for hire'. He couldn't understand 'why attempts to earn an honest, if strenuous livelihood should be regarded as inconsistent with knighthood'. Certainly he didn't allow his new status to affect either his lifestyle or his celebrated informality. He made it clear that he didn't want to be addressed as Sir Charles. 'Just call me Smithy,' he told everyone. Nonetheless, back on the barnstorming circuit, the speeches of welcome became even longer and more elaborate to reflect his elevation to Air Commodore Sir Charles Kingsford Smith, and embarrassingly, he even began to hear himself addressed on occasions as 'Lord Smith'.

One of the penalties of his exalted rank was the need to be less casual about his clothes. 'He had no dress sense at all,' Mary recalled. 'He'd go about in baggy trousers with two-tone white and tan shoes, ill-fitting sports jackets straining at the buttons, pockets bulging with stuff, and think nothing of wearing white sandshoes with a suit. Having clothes made to measure had never entered his head. I marched him off to a good tailor and insisted he order a couple of really decent suits.'

His proclivity for practical jokes, however, remained unsubdued. One day at Mascot he taxied a Moth into soft ground outside a hangar. To his shame the aircraft tipped up on its nose. Before anyone noticed, he had jumped out, scuttled round the back of the hangar and removed his helmet and goggles. Walking unconcernedly out of the front again, and surveying the damaged Moth, he exclaimed, 'Good heavens, who did that?' It was some time before anyone realised who had. 'I was always afraid he would embarrass me in public with one of his coarser stories,' said Mary, 'but he never did – he left all that to the all-male gatherings. At one of these, a Flying Corps reunion where the speakers had to stand up on the table, he created an uproar. Zip fasteners had not yet arrived on men's trousers in Australia, so, having acquired a pair with one overseas, he leaped up and demonstrated it, whipping the zip up and down to everyone's amazement. He could get away with almost anything.'

On 22 December Mary gave birth to a boy, Charles Arthur. 'Chill fixed me up with a nurse and early in the New Year he'd gone,' Mary recalled. 'I knew by then that this was going to be the pattern of our marriage – that his son and I weren't going to see very much of him, ever.' Having run out of Australian business for the barnstorming tour, Smithy had decided to try his luck in New Zealand. He flew the *Southern Cross* across the Tasman on 11 January 1933, taking with him as co-pilot and navigator an ex-Royal Flying Corps pilot, Bill Taylor, and John Stannage – who had recently become part of the Kingsford Smith clan on marrying Smithy's niece, Beris – as wireless-operator. Now that Ulm was no longer involved, the Fokker could be operated on long ocean crossings by a crew of three.

Patrick Gordon Taylor was more famously known as P. G. Taylor, but insisted on being called Bill. He had been one of ANA's

Avro 10 pilots and was engaged for the sea crossing only. Although, like Smithy, he had won a Military Cross as a First World War fighter pilot, he was not of the gregarious, roistering breed that typified the Kingsford Smith circle of pilots and mechanics. A small, lean, rather aloof and unassuming figure, prematurely bald with a neat moustache, he looked more like a diffident academic than a pilot. Educated at public school and a man of independent means, he had his own 35ft sloop and a Gipsy Moth floatplane. Indeed, Taylor was many of the things that Smithy was not: a fastidious dresser whose suits and shoes were expensively made for him in London, an abstemious character who shrank from showmanship and dodged the raucous, boozy sessions at the Mascot Hotel in favour of the sanctuary of Sydney's exclusive Union Club. Yet he enjoyed enormous respect. He was also a writer, and later communicated his deep love of flying in an affectingly poetic series of books which were compared to the work of the famous French writer and pilot Antoine de Saint-Exupéry. What had brought this totally opposite personality into Kingsford Smith's orbit was Taylor's burning desire to complement Smithy's flying skills. Just as Charles Ulm had capitalised on his partner's lack of business flair, Taylor had seen an opening to create a long-term role for himself as the *Southern Cross*'s navigator. Smithy's decision to take a chance on this elegant tyro was to launch a significant partnership.

The flight to New Plymouth in New Zealand was made in fine weather and appears to have been a panic-free trip for Smithy. It was the first of his major oceanic crossings in which he dispensed with the big 800-gallon auxiliary fuel tank. The message stick became redundant, since the reserve fuel was now carried in a rectangular tank that sat on the floor behind the cockpit door, over which the crew could scramble to and fro with their notes or to shout and gesticulate. It was four and a half years since Smithy had been in New Zealand and he was welcomed back with huge enthusiasm. Families drove all night to reach the landing places on paddocks and beaches and queued up to pay for a few deafening minutes in the air. Special trains were laid on; schools were closed to allow children a glimpse of the aviator and his magic aeroplane. Near Palmerston North, a local man challenged him to a race between the *Southern Cross* and his Austin 7. Smithy flew the 'old bus' at full throttle so low that, overtaking the small car as it passed under a railway bridge rigged with repair scaffolding, the blast from the trimotor's engines blew down the flimsy frame-work. Later, in a personally desperate situation, trapped with a load of passengers in a deep ravine in the Kaikoura Mountains, he was, to the horror of all on board, forced to stall-turn the aircraft, intuitively hauling up the nose until she was standing on her tail, then cartwheeling her back in the opposite direction out of the gorge. By day the charismatic showman pilot, he could swiftly regress at night into the moving spirit in bawdy sing-songs and uninhibited games in which chairs were routinely smashed up.

Despite the financial success of the tour, it became clear that, beneath Smithy's bouncy exterior, all was not well. He had come to New Zealand not to be fêted but to make money – it was a commercial operation, he kept repeating. He didn't expect to be welcomed with civic formality by the mayor of every town. But the balls, the receptions, the plague of speeches, the ritual dinners, went on remorselessly. Poems in his praise were recited and lauda-tory songs sung by choirs. Towards the end of January, less than three weeks into the tour, he warned Wilfrid that the strain was becoming unbearable; he feared he was grinding to a halt. They agreed that he would take a week's complete rest when they reached the South Island the following week. But before that came a blessing in disguise. The *Southern Cross* met with a serious taxiing accident at Palmerston North when an underground drain caved in under its weight. The port undercarriage assembly col-lapsed and the wing tip hit the ground, breaking the main spar 6ft from the tip. Although it was a terrible financial blow, it couldn't have come at a more timely moment to preserve Smithy's sanity. During the three weeks it took to repair the aeroplane, he went home to Sydney for a break.

In late February he forced himself to resume the tour with the patched-up 'old bus', but he was still far from fit. Indeed, he felt so ill that he agreed to go into the Catholic Mater Misericordia hos-pital in Auckland to be treated for severe nervous exhaustion. An uncaptioned photograph shows him during his convalescence, in pyjamas and dressing gown, standing in the sun, looking thin-faced and unhappy, surrounded by a group of visitors. 'He'd simply col-lapsed under the strain,' John Kingsford-Smith said. 'He couldn't go on. Not many knew that his stress limits were actually quite low.'

When the New Zealand tour ended in the last week of March 1933, Smithy was still unwell. Although the daylight flight back to Sydney with Bill Taylor was another uneventful journey in clear weather, it precipitated another oceanic trauma. In mid-Tasman, Taylor was stunned to see the man whom he held in awe and envied for his legendary stamina succumbing helplessly to a panic attack. Overwhelmed by nausea and too disorientated to remain at the controls, he scrawled a note to Taylor and reeled back to the cabin, where he passed out. 'He was so sick he had to lie on the mail-bags for a couple of hours,' Taylor recalled.[7] The stresses triggered by flying out of land's sight had conspired with the exhaustion of the tour to crumple him. But, as always, as they neared the coast, he revived and returned wanly to the cockpit to make the landing at Mascot in the late afternoon. When he stepped out of the aeroplane, with forced grin and automatic wisecracks, allowing himself to be carried off shoulder-high, no one, apart from the crew, knew the truth.

Sad news awaited him in Sydney. Australian National Airways had finally gone into voluntary liquidation in the last week of February and all its aircraft were up for sale. But Smithy's emotional involvement with the ill-starred venture to which he had contributed so little had long ago ceased. All that concerned him now was his own survival and, as he entered his thirty-seventh year, his worryingly declining health. Advised by his doctor to take a long holiday, in the middle of April 1933, he drove with Mary and the baby to Melbourne to go to earth for a month.

Aquaphobia
1933

Back in Sydney in better health in the middle of May, Smithy decided to form his own aviation business with the money he had made in New Zealand. He built a big iron hangar at Mascot as a new home for the 'old bus', which was soon to be joined by three Gipsy Moths, an Avian, and a DH50 cabin biplane, *Southern Cross Midget*. Just a few hundred yards away, as if to underline their now separate existences, Charles Ulm had taken over the old ANA hangar. Kingsford Smith Air Service Ltd was planned as a charter-flying, pilot-training and aircraft-maintenance business. It also provided badly needed work for a number of pilot and mechanic mates hit by the continuing Depression. John Stannage became manager; Tommy Pethybridge was appointed chief engineer and Harry Purvis and Pat Hall became two of three resident pilots. Smithy even found casual work for Wilfrid, whose life had temporarily lost direction.

From the outset the company, finally registered in October, floundered. As at ANA, Smith was rarely seen in the office. His generosity as an employer was not matched by their income, and although they soon had a few pupil pilots on their books, the business struggled to feed too many mouths and soon ran out of money. To make ends meet Marge McGrath, Smithy's secretary, was forced to take a second job working almost every night until the small hours at a nightclub in King's Cross. 'She also had to keep the little cash there was firmly out of Chill's reach,' said John Kingsford-Smith. 'If she didn't lock it up he would just help himself. Of course, one of the reasons he never had any money was that he was always giving it away. He was permanently surrounded by bludgers trading on his incredible generosity. He would lend nine of his last ten pounds even though he knew he'd never see it again.'

There were rumours that Smithy had hand-picked Marge, a tall, attractive, slender young woman whom the staff nicknamed 'Split Pin', from 300 applicants for her looks, and that she had become romantically involved with him. This she was always to deny. Nonetheless, 'She told me,' Scotty Allan said, 'that she wanted to work for him so badly that, to impress him, she had forged her references. I don't think there's any doubt they were strongly attracted. Certainly she endured a great deal of sexual harassment.'

Smithy kept a ukulele in his office, and when they were bored or had been drinking, he and Stannage would sit on Marge's desk, serenading her with impromptu songs praising her physical attributes. At other times they would converse in front of her in Morse code, using a practice key and buzzer on Stannage's desk in the same room. According to Norman Ellison, through these coded exchanges they discussed her desirability in language he described as 'flagrantly ungenteel'. But, he said, she endured it for 'the honour of working for such a demi-god'. Marge McGrath, however, learned to give as good as she got. 'She was more than a match for them. She became one of the boys,' Nancy-Bird Walton said. 'She was flippant and witty – and the only woman Smithy would ever take at the end of the day into the bar at the Mascot Hotel. Marge belonged in that magic circle in her own right. She was privy to all their hangar talk, their dirty stories, their gossip. She shared all their secrets.'

Some of those secrets inevitably concerned Smithy's private life. At the height of his fame he could get away with almost any indiscretion. In one of them, Nancy-Bird Walton unwittingly found herself involved as a decoy. 'This exotic young thing, heavily made up and beautifully dressed, arrived one day at Mascot,' she said.

She was what I'd describe as a bit of a flapper – a lady of the night. I was just about to go off for some dual with a pilot called Harold Durrant. It was decided, for some reason that

wasn't immediately clear to me, that we'd go in formation
with Smithy and the girl, out west toward the Blue
Mountains. About half an hour out, nearing Wallacia, Smithy
pointed to a big paddock beside a river. He'd obviously been
here before, because he quickly circled it and landed. I'd no
idea what was going on and was amazed when Harold closed
the throttle and we glided down to land beside him. It would
have made a lovely picnic spot, but of course that was not
what we'd come for.

Smithy and this lass almost immediately set off together
down towards some trees beside the river. I said to Harold,
'Aren't we going to join them?' and he shook his head,
saying, 'No, no, I wouldn't do that – they won't be very long.'
Nonetheless, they were gone quite some time. But I was so
innocent I hadn't the least idea what Smithy was up to.
When, at last, they returned, the first thing I noticed was the
lipstick on his cheek, and that puzzled me, but I still didn't
twig. I was nineteen and he was the great Sir Charles, the god
of Australian aviation, and you didn't question what he did.
What's more, he was married. But I didn't then know a lot
about the ways of the world.

The two pilots swung each other's props and the Moths took off to
fly back to Sydney. But things now went embarrassingly wrong.

Near Bankstown Smithy's engine stopped and he had to
force-land in open country. We circled to check that the
plane was undamaged, then flew quickly on to Mascot
where, in the office, all hell was let loose as everyone went
frantically into damage control. John Stannage and Marge
were terrified the newspapers would get hold of the story
and Mary would hear about it, so they rushed Tommy
Pethybridge out to Bankstown to fix the engine and get
Smithy and the girl away from the scene. Luckily, the media
never picked it up.

Out of sheer respect for his image, few of Sir Charles's indiscre-
tions were ever reported in his lifetime. Only his close mates knew
about another of his proclivities: his compulsion for recklessness in

the air when relaxed by drink. John Kingsford-Smith remembered one late-night incident at Mascot.

Chilla had been to a reception. Obviously he'd had quite a few grogs and was in a happy, devilish mood, ready for mischief. Suddenly he said to a group of us, 'Anyone for a flight?' No one wanted to risk it in the state he was in, so he turned to me. 'You coming?' I didn't want to appear chicken, so, rather unenthusiastically, I nodded.

One of the Moths was wheeled out and started up. He got into the back and I clambered into the front. It was a pitch-black night – there was no airfield lighting, no moon – and as we roared off he called cheerfully through the voice tube, 'Let's go over and wake Mary up.' So off we flew to the eastern suburbs. It was very dark out there, but he managed to find the street and, to my horror, began, on this really black night, to do aerobatics right over the house. The place was on the side of a hill and I was terrified that we'd hit the top of it. He dived and looped at unbelievably low level and the noise must have woken up the whole district. I just kept praying that his judgement was still intact, because at the bottom of the loops he was pulling up with barely 100ft between us and the ground. I was fervently willing him to stop. When eventually he did and we headed back to Mascot, I was shaking. God knows how he landed without any runway lighting – the only chink of light came through the doors of the hangar. Yet he made a perfect three-pointer, ending the landing run, with this aircraft with no brakes, just 10ft from the hangar door. It was an amazing demonstration, as if the wings were part of his body.

By the middle of 1933, Smithy's company was desperate for income and he was casting around for a new record to break. He settled for a fresh attack on the England–Australia solo time, in the false belief that to smash it might see him rewarded with a prominent role in the operation of the Darwin–Singapore leg of the Brisbane–Singapore route. But flying the England route was no longer a novelty, and as quickly as records were made they were being broken. The fastest time then stood at eight days twenty-one hours, flown in a Gipsy Moth by Charles Scott.

Turning his back on the faltering business in the third week of August, Smithy went to England where a brand new Gull 4 was waiting for him. 'God knows how he paid for it,' John Kingsford-Smith said. 'What I do remember, though, is that there was, at that time, a balance of around £300 in the company account. Chill blithely drew it all out and just sailed off, leaving the company absolutely skint. I can still hear John Stannage loudly protesting: "The bugger just went to the bank and drew out the lot. Until someone hires an aeroplane we can't pay the wages." It almost certainly went towards the Gull and his first-class boat fare.' It is likely that the expedition was also helped by his father-in-law, Arthur Powell, whose own wealth had been boosted by a recent investment in a Melbourne company, Diecasters, which made moulded components for the motor industry.

On his arrival in England in mid-September, Smithy had a large, cylindrical auxiliary fuel tank fitted behind the pilot's seat in the cabin of the Gull, which he had named *Miss Southern Cross* (G-ACJV, later personalised as VH-CKS). This small, neat-looking monoplane was the thirty-ninth Gull designed and built by the expatriate Australian Edgar Percival. It was powered by a 130hp Gipsy Major engine, the same that drove the Tiger Moth. But, in the aerodynamically sleek Gull, Smithy hoped to cruise at 120mph, a far brisker pace than Scott's Gipsy Moth had been capable of. In London he caught up with a disillusioned Charles Ulm who, a few weeks earlier, had tried to fly the Atlantic. The venture had ended in disaster in Ireland even before it had started. On Portmarnock Beach near Dublin, his aircraft, *Faith in Australia* (converted from ANA's *Southern Moon* and piloted by Scotty Allan), had suffered a devastating structural failure – fortunately, while stationary – collapsing under a mammoth fuel load into the sand as the tide came in to swamp it. The aircraft was being rebuilt and Ulm was now planning an attack on the England–Australia absolute record.

In his own bid to break the 'one-week barrier' as well as the solo record, to Australia, Smithy left from Lympne in Kent in the early morning dark of 4 October 1933 and flew non-stop to Brindisi. He took with him a bottle of sal volatile – spirits of ammonia – to shave the raw edge off his fear in case of a panic attack. He was soon in need of it, for the familiar phobia of drowning and the awful nausea began to arrive early on the second day, on the 1,600-mile leg to Baghdad, as the sun rose over the Ionian Sea. From here on his log recorded the distress that was to demoralise and terrify him all the way to Australia.[1]

THURS 5 OCT

5.10 am. Dawn breaking off coast of Greece. Feeling bit rotten and nervy . . .

9.30 am. Now on Turkish coast and bad luck for me if I have a forced landing. The Turkish government will not let me land in their territory any more.

10.45 am. In the middle of the Bay of Angels – about 100 miles over water . . . will be glad to reach land again as the water looks very wet.

1.15 pm. Another recurrence of nervousness. Nasty feeling as if I was going to faint. Hope I can get through.

3 pm. Very much better now [he was reassuringly over land again, flying across Syria]. A couple of big doses of sal volatile seemed to fix me up. At present flying south of Euphrates River, about 275 miles from Baghdad. I will be there long after dark but asked Brindisi to wire for flares.

Once more, with his body denied alcohol for up to twelve hours at a stretch, withdrawal symptoms were aggravating the over-water phobia. Instead of brandy, his prop had become the medicine bottle – but although Smithy probably didn't know it, the alcohol base to the sal volatile made it far more potent than brandy. 'Every time he took a swig he was actually getting a mighty kick of pure alcohol – it would have represented seventy-five per cent of the volume of that stuff,' a pharmacist explained. 'On top of that, the ammonia, nicely flavoured with nutmeg and lemon, would have given some added shots to his nervous system, artificially stimulating his whole aerobic function.'

FRI 6 OCT

7 am. Landed by flares at Baghdad last night. Couldn't sleep for nerves and had bad night. Felt pretty rotten today. Left Baghdad at 4.5 am. Now at head of Persian Gulf.

9.15 am. 300 miles from Jask [on the southern coast of Iran]. I feel terribly sick and wonder if I can make it.

10.25 am. Had very bad turn and had to come down to 200 feet. Thought I was fainting. Will try and make Bandar Abbas.

Terrified of leaving the desert coast, he now clung to the shoreline in a long detour to avoid having to cross the open sea in the Strait of Hormuz. He was wobbling between consciousness and oblivion, connected only tenuously with reality. He knew that he might at any moment have to put the Gull down on this rocky desert coast in a landing which would certainly destroy it, but each time he reached the point of looking for somewhere, he managed to regain just enough equilibrium to carry on.

Over the Arabian Sea, flying east past the lunar landscape of Baluchistan in what today is Pakistan – a slate-grey, lifeless terrain of dried-up water courses and eroded cliffs hundreds of feet high – the only place to put down was in the water. But somehow, in the late afternoon, he managed to drag the Gull on to the small coastal desert airstrip at Gwadar, where he climbed out, retching uncontrollably into the sand. He wanted to go on to Karachi, but he was too ill.

SAT 7 OCT

Landed Gwadar terribly sick at 4.15 yesterday. Couldn't sleep until 2 am. Got some medicine, but couldn't eat. No food now for 36 hours. Left at 7.15 this morning. Beautiful morning but fail to appreciate it.

9 am. 125 miles from Karachi and not feeling too good, but better than yesterday. It is strange that there have been hardly any following winds on this trip. Possibly they are blowing up high – but I'm afraid to go up there in case of feeling suddenly faint and not being able to reach ground before passing out. I wish I was as reliable as this machine and engine.

At Karachi he rested for four hours, trying unsuccessfully to get the sleep he craved, 'But can't sleep. That is what is killing me. Got some bromide here and will take a stiff dose tonight. Now in

air again for Jodhpur and feeling slightly better . . . thanks to a
doctor chappie at Karachi who gave me some nerve pills.' The
next day, his fifth, he flew across India to Akyab in Burma. With
the aid of stiff doses of sal volatile, the tranquillisers the Karachi
doctor had given him and masses of bromine sedatives, he kept
the panic suppressed to cross the Bay of Bengal, the cause of so
much incapacitating fear in the past. After a night in Akyab,
where he knocked himself out with another large dose of bromide, he flew on the sixth day to Alor Star, and on the seventh he
reached Surabaya in Java. Only a few hours now separated him
from Wyndham in north-west Australia and the record. But there
still remained the biggest water hop of all: the Timor Sea. The
three-hour crossing brought a final surge of panic so overwhelming that he briefly passed out. He didn't record this in his
log, probably because he was overtaken by euphoria at the eventual sight of land: 'Hooray, Australia ahoy, dead ahead . . . Grand
little plane, grand little motor. You never faltered in anything I set
you and got poor old Smithy the record again for Australia. Stout
fellows.'

When he landed at Wyndham on 11 October, it was confirmed
that his seven days four and a half hours had cut around forty
hours off Scott's time. Here he revealed to reporters, the final
horror of the Timor Sea. At noon, he said, 'I was too ill even to
write in my diary.' For the first time he confessed publicly that a
flight had left him 'a bundle of nerves'. The newspapermen were
staggered to hear him say that on the journey down the Persian
Gulf 'I went to pieces and had to go to bed for half a day . . . It has
been a pretty constant fight against sleeplessness and that extraordinary sickness and nervousness I get over water. I suppose
doctors would call it aquaphobia. At one stage over the Timor Sea
I felt I would have to break out of the cabin. I'm afraid I'm getting
too old for these stunts.'[2]

The only one of Kingsford Smith's first five biographers to
touch on his little-known flight phobias was the New Zealander
Beau Sheil. 'In all the annals of record flights it is doubtful if there
is any document more remarkable than the logbook of Smithy's
solo flight from England in 1933,' he wrote in *Caesar of the Skies*.
'Some eminent medico and psychiatrist could, and perhaps
should, write a treatise on it. Whatever other analyses may be

made of it, this was something more than the spirit being willing
and the flesh weak. His mind itself was sick, in a sick body.'

'It was a classic counter-phobic condition,' said the RAF's chief
psychiatrist, Wing Commander Ken Craig, when he read the 1933
log. 'Compulsively engaging in activity that was dangerous and
frightening – and deriving pleasure from it. What one needs to
understand about the disorder is that the panic attacks could occur
even when there was actually nothing to fear – during moments in
the air when there was time for him to dwell upon what *might*
happen.'

More revealing even than the log is a photograph of him sitting
in the cockpit soon after his arrival in Australia. He has aged visibly
and looks thin, wasted and ill. His sandy-brown hair has receded,
his face has acquired more premature lines and large crow's feet
have spread around his eyes. He is so desperate for a fix of nicotine
that he is drawing heavily on two cigarettes simultaneously. The
famous grin, formed around both jutting butts, has retreated into
a sad, tight-lipped grimace. It is but a ghost of the man who flew
the Pacific only five years before. Yet, even though his log, published in newspapers throughout Australia, finally laid bare the
private hell into which he was being plunged with every new
long-distance flight, nobody, it appears, was able to bring themselves to comment on it. It was as if neither the media, nor the
government, nor his friends and close family could accept that
the physical and mental health of the country's idol was beginning
to fail. Frailty was the antithesis of the Kingsford Smith myth; it
was unthinkable. Everyone much preferred to go on believing that
Smithy was indestructible. And he reinforced this belief by skilfully masking his collapsing health with brave words and jokes –
although the nonchalance was steadily becoming more difficult to
sustain. 'Oddly enough,' said Catherine Robinson, 'his declining
health, as far as I can recall, just wasn't discussed within the
family.' Even John Kingsford-Smith, who was old enough to relate
to his uncle as an adult, couldn't remember it being a subject of
concern. 'But looking back now,' he said, 'I suppose all the evidence was there had we wanted to face up to it. Clearly he was
slowly destroying himself.'

Around the world his latest record journey was applauded.
Australian headlines proclaimed: 'ACE BIRDMAN', 'UNCONQUERABLE

SMITHY', 'WORLD'S SUPREME AIRMAN'. King George V had the news phoned through to him at Sandringham and immediately cabled Smithy. For bringing Australia within reach of a week's journey from the mother country, Prime Minister Lyons announced that the government was to award him a tax-free grant of £3,000. Vacuum Oil hurried to offer him a job as its aviation adviser, with a big desk and a large prestigious office at its Sydney headquarters. Smithy leaped at the chance of this well-paid sinecure. John Kingsford-Smith's future wife, Betty Quinlin, was then working at Vacuum Oil as a clerk. 'I was taken up to be introduced to the great airman. What struck me most was the powerful presence he emanated. It was so strong you could actually *feel* it. But there was also something very elusive about him – a rather hard to define quality – that of a dreamer divorced from this world.' Wilfrid's daughter, Margaret Harricks, said: 'His blue eyes were always looking beyond you, as if you weren't there and he was totally preoccupied with distant thoughts ticking round in his brain, planning something that had nothing to do with you. He was a being apart.'

When Smithy flew on to Melbourne he was met by 100,000 people. But so visibly demolished was he that doctors ordered two weeks' complete rest. He and Mary, with the baby and Nurse Haselick – known as 'Nurnie', Charles Arthur's first rendering of her name – went to the Powell family seaside cottage at Sorrento on Phillip Bay to escape the media. It was here, to add to his unhappiness, that he learned that *Faith in Australia*, flown by Scotty Allan with Ulm and Bill Taylor, had shattered both the 'one-week barrier' and his England–Australia record of barely a week's standing, reaching Derby in the North-West in six days eighteen hours.[3]

At the Qantas head office in Brisbane these spectacular new flights were viewed through jaundiced eyes. The company's secretary, George Harman, wrote sourly to Albert Rudder: 'The Sydney papers I believe are absolutely full of Kingsford Smith and his flight and are insistent upon his being granted the Air Mail tenders . . . But the majority of us know that the mere ability to smash records . . . does not necessarily qualify a man to run a regular service.'[4] Nonetheless, Imperial Airways, now more conscious than ever of the value of Smithy's prestige, had begun to explore ways of taking him on board. George Woods Humphery asked Rudder for suggestions. The idea, Rudder replied, 'has been tickling my mind for some time . . . Kingsford Smith is a difficult man to place in any fixed position – or to nail down to anything definite. If any suggestion of an offer from our side were made . . . it might be looked upon as buying him for his sentimental worth and be seen in the nature of a bribe to secure the [Singapore] contract.'[5]

The battle for the Brisbane–Singapore route was about to enter its final stages. Imperial Airways and Qantas had now formally created the powerful partnership of Qantas Empire Airways and Ulm and Brearley had united in another syndicate, Commonwealth Airways, to tender for the route. Both these rival alliances were consumed with curiosity to know what aircraft were being proposed by the man they saw as their greatest competition for the prize – Smithy, they assumed, as the country's most celebrated long-distance pilot, must himself have entered a formidable bid. Although the Australian Defence Department had stipulated that only British planes would be acceptable, it was widely known that Smithy, regarding the latter as obsoletely locked into the trundling wooden biplane era, would only contemplate the new, much faster, more sophisticated all-metal American airliners. How, they were all asking, could his tender ever succeed? But, incredible as it may seem, it appears that, in the end, he didn't bother to apply for a route at all. As this conclusion flew in the face of family belief, in 1995, one of Smithy's nephews, Rollo Kingsford-Smith,[6] the youngest of Wilfrid's four children, went to try to find his uncle's Singapore tender in the sixty-year-old government aviation files in Canberra and Melbourne. In Canberra he found the March 1934 report of the Defence Department Air Contracts Committee, which considered the applications.[7] It showed that, for what was to become Australia's first scheduled overseas airline operation, from Brisbane to Singapore, the only submissions were those of the Imperial–Qantas partnership and the Ulm–Brearley syndicate.

Where, then, in all this, had Smithy involved himself? Like a will-o'-the-wisp, it seems he made the surprising decision to join forces, informally and at the eleventh hour, with an up-country road-transport operator, George Robinson, who had started a tiny airline based in the small northern New South Wales town of Lismore, running services to Brisbane and Sydney. His company,

New England Airways, had made a bid, but only for some of the connecting services within Australia. It had, unhappily, proposed operating them with slow and noisy Avro 10s. People were surprised that Smithy hadn't tendered in his own right for the entire length of the Singapore route he had done so much to pioneer. But then, few were aware of his chronic inability and disinclination to run such an operation.

During the early months of 1934, while the contracts committee was pondering the Singapore applications and an expectant hush had fallen upon the Australian aviation scene, Smithy, his bank balance at zero, had decided to try his luck barnstorming again in New Zealand. He took the 'old bus' across in January, only to find himself, to his surprise, competing for business with Charles Ulm, who had been flown over ahead of him by Scotty Allan in *Faith in Australia*. This new rivalry gave rise to renewed speculation about the true state of their friendship. They refused in interviews to be drawn on the subject; nor do they appear to have met. Quite separately, each had informal discussions with New Zealand cabinet ministers, before whom they put forward competing schemes for trans-Tasman and internal services. Smithy and Wilfrid had created a company called Dominion Airways for the internal services, using a brand-new six-passenger airliner, the Codock, which was being designed and built by the ubiquitous Lawrence Wackett. But the prototype quickly acquired a bad reputation among Smithy's mechanics and never got to New Zealand. Dominion Airways never took to the air.[8]

At the end of March Smithy flew back to Sydney, having clocked up his 6,000th flying hour during the tour, to await the Singapore route decisions. He and Mary had moved nearer the city to the upmarket suburb of Darling Point where, at 27 Greenoaks Avenue, they were renting their first house, a Spanish-style two-level home with white stucco walls and terracotta tiled roof. Today tourist buses pause in what is now a busy street for guides to point to the bronze *Southern Cross* plaque on the wall, but in 1934, it was a sleepy corner of suburban Sydney. Here Smithy and Mary, despite their perennially uncertain income, lived comfortably with three servants – the nurse, a cook and a gardener – amid a never-ending flow of visiting pilots and mechanics who daily followed Chilla home as if he were the Pied Piper.

It was at Greenoaks Avenue, on 19 April, that Smithy learned that the New England Airways tender, with which, in some vague way, he had thrown in his lot, had failed in its bid for the key routes connecting the Darwin gateway with Australia's main cities. Commonwealth Airways had not been awarded anything, either. The coveted Brisbane–Singapore all-through service had been offered to the Qantas–Imperial company, QEA, which had clinched the deal by agreeing to buy a small, unproven four-engined British aircraft, the de Havilland DH86, which was being built for the purpose. Overnight the little outback flying company Qantas had become Australia's first international airline.

Although he had contributed little more than his name to the New England Airways application, it seems that this news came as a numbingly bitter blow to Smithy. Besieged by reporters who had assumed he would be given a significant role in the country's first overseas commercial operation, he denounced the decision, with unusual heat, as a 'serious injustice'. Airmen 'who have been primarily responsible for the development of aviation in Australia have been overlooked', he complained.[9] 'He was heartbroken,' Mary said. 'He just kept repeating over and over again, "Nothing – absolutely nothing – is working for me."'

'I don't think he ever understood what he was up against,' said Rollo Kingsford-Smith. 'They were formidable forces, dominated by the British aviation establishment, which regarded him quite simply as a bloody nuisance. I remember de Havilland's marketing director, Francis St Barbe, telling me in the 1950s that they saw him as nothing more than an 'adventurer' – and he didn't mean it in the nicest sense, either. To the manufacturers the record-breakers were absolute anathema, people who flew aircraft dangerously overloaded for their personal glory. Their frequent disappearances and crashes served only to give air transport a bad name.'

Fortuitously for Smithy, a ready-made escape from this latest disappointment was waiting. The Titans of international aviation were about to compete in a high-speed race from England to Melbourne with the aim of reaching the Australian coast, sensationally, in just two days. To bury his sorrows he decided to enter. If he won, it would, he wrote, 'crown my flying career'.

23

A Nation's Whipping Boy
1934

The air race, conceived as part of the 1934 Melbourne centenary celebrations, was due to start from Mildenhall in Suffolk on 20 October. Presenting aircraft manufacturers with the opportunity to demonstrate their latest machines, it was creating wide international interest. Many of aviation's most celebrated pilots had entered and, from the moment the competition was announced by the Lord Mayor of Melbourne, Australians took it for granted that Smithy would enter it – and win. Only one thing stood in the way: he had no suitable aeroplane. Nor, as ever, the money to buy one.

The race was to be run in both speed and handicap categories. Smithy was only interested in the former, for which, to be a serious contender, he needed a 200mph aeroplane with 3,000-mile range. He wanted to make the trip spectacularly in a previously never-attempted forty-eight hours from England to Darwin. There weren't many aeroplanes able to do this, and certainly not a British one. But the Australian government still expected him to use a British-built aircraft out of loyalty to the mother country. One was, however, in the process of being frantically designed and built by de Havilland. Its DH88 Comet, a slender, wooden, cigar-shaped machine with twin engines and retractable undercarriage, would cruise at over 200mph carrying enough fuel to reach Baghdad in one hop from England. Three orders had already been received, and the aircraft had to be built in just nine months if the race was to be prevented from going to an American plane.

Smithy's first choice was the American Gamma, an all-metal, single-engined single-seat cargo plane built by Northrop. He wanted to fill the freight space with enough fuel to reach Australia in a couple of stops. But no one was willing to sponsor even some-one of his great repute in an American aeroplane. He then had a phone call from a Melbourne chocolate millionaire and philan-thropist, Sir Macpherson Robertson, a shrewd Scot who liked to be known as 'MacRobertson' and whom the newspapers were fond of calling 'Australia's Carnegie'. Robertson had put up the £15,000 prize money for the race, £10,000 of it for the winner of the speed section. He told Smithy he would like to buy him an air-craft in which to win the event for Australia. He was prepared, he said, to find £5,000, provided the plane was British. It would have to be one of the new Comets.

Of the first three, one had been ordered by Amy Johnson, who planned to fly it with Jim Mollison, now her husband. The second was earmarked for a rich Englishman, Bernard Rubin, and the third for Mr A. O. Edwards, managing director of London's Grosvenor House Hotel, to be flown by the record-breaking Charles Scott and Tom Campbell Black.[1] One of the technical features that would allow the Comet to fly economically over great distances was its state-of-the-art variable-pitch propellers. Few of these units were yet available in England. Smithy was told by de Havilland that they could build a fourth Comet in time for the race, but it would have to be fitted with the much less efficient fixed-pitch propellers. Rejecting this out of hand, he went down to Melbourne early in May 1934 to try to persuade Sir Macpherson to fund an American plane.

To keep him in the race Robertson reluctantly agreed. The Northrop Gamma, however, was too expensive, so Robertson sug-gested that he go to America to look for something cheaper second-hand. Smithy now had in mind a Lockheed, one of a new breed of fast single-engined machines. Feeling guilty that he could-n't satisfy Robertson's wish for a British aircraft he agreed to accept only half the offered £5,000, which forced him to look for more backers. The extra money came mainly from Arthur Powell and the Melbourne store magnate Sidney Myer.

On 2 May Smithy and Mary, leaving Charles Arthur, now eight-een months old, with Nurnie, sailed on the *Monterey* for San Francisco to find a plane to beat the Comets. Within days of arriv-ing in America he found what he was looking for at a small aircraft factory at Burbank on the northern outskirts of Los Angeles. It was a single-engined Lockheed two-seater racing machine that had begun life as a Sirius, *Richmond Virginia*, with a fixed undercarriage. This wooden, low-winged aeroplane had been built in 1930 for a Baltimore pilot, Captain George Hutchinson, to fly the Atlantic. He had experienced problems handling the lively machine and had crashed it at Los Angeles. After being rebuilt it had been acquired by two famous Hollywood figures, actor Douglas Fairbanks and film director Victor Fleming, who had flown it around California for a couple of years before selling it back to Lockheed early in 1934. Now, at Smithy's request, the company upgraded it to an Altair, replacing the Sirius's wing with one carrying flaps and a retractable undercarriage to make it aerodynamically cleaner and much faster.[2] Fitted with a 550hp 9-cylinder Pratt and Whitney Wasp engine which developed almost as much power as the *Southern Cross*'s three engines combined, she was a formidable-looking craft. What was more, she had a variable-pitch propeller.

With its big radial engine and small tandem cockpits under a sliding hood, the Altair had about it the menacing appearance of a Second World War fighter. The supercharged engine enabled it to cruise economically at 15,000ft, above the worst of the weather, at around 205mph. Here was a plane, more than twice as fast as the 'old bus' which could cross the world at over 3 miles a minute. For US$25,000, then worth just over £5,000, Smithy decided to buy her. He got Lockheed to instal extra fuel tanks and to paint the name ANZAC[3] on the fuselage.

However, by adding extra tanks and raising the aircraft's load when fully fuelled, he had grossly exceeded the weight limits permitted by the American certificate of airworthiness. The restrictions were imposed for safety reasons to limit the stresses on the aircraft's structure – particularly on the undercarriage during take-off or landing with heavy fuel loads. The vital certificate required for the aircraft's operation in Australia had been cancelled. Although Smithy had twice been warned by the Australian controller of civil aviation, Edgar Johnston, that his department would insist on a current certificate of airworthiness from the country of origin, he blithely ignored the advice, raised his fuel tankage from around 150 to 418 gallons, and shipped the

uncertificated Altair back to Australia, impatient to show off this
remarkable aeroplane at home before flying her to England for
the start of the race.

With the Altair stowed on the tennis deck of the *Mariposa*, he
and Mary steamed proudly through Sydney Heads on 16 July to
be greeted by a joyous formation of Kingsford Smith Air Service
aircraft wheeling like a flock of seagulls over the ship. Within
minutes, however, customs officers had hurried aboard, examined
the US Commerce Department's already expired experimental
registration certificate and sternly pronounced the Altair a
prohibited item which could not be imported. It would have to
be impounded and on no account flown in Australia. Smithy
stood accused of illegally trying to import a banned non-British
aeroplane. 'I'm British and proud of the fact,' he protested.
'English manufacturers haven't had time to develop an aircraft of
this type. What's more, most of my critics here own American
cars or refrigerators anyway. There was no howl of protest in
England when Malcolm Campbell raced a French car. Nor by
anyone in Holland when KLM chose the American Douglas DC2
for its air-race entry.'

The import breach in itself would not have been fatal to his
plans – he could have applied for temporary importation. Much
more disastrous was the aircraft's lack of a valid airworthiness
certificate. The documentation niceties of the crisis were scarcely
understood by most Australians as the story hit the front pages
and Prime Minister Lyons demanded from the defence minister,
Sir George Pearce, an explanation of the bewildering mess
Smithy had got himself into. The official in the eye of the storm
was, of course, Edgar Johnston. All he could tell his minister
was that Kingsford Smith's failure to heed his advice 'was
incomprehensible'.

Nobody could credit that such an experienced aviator as
Smithy could be so foolish, but he assured them in a lengthy interview that he'd simply 'botched things up'. He said: 'Quite frankly,
I admit to the thought that "Johnno" knew I was rather careless in
matters of routine. And yes, he did warn me – and later on, when
I was in America, he repeated the warning to John Stannage, my
manager at Mascot, who passed it on to me.'[4] Yet he had done
nothing about the essential documentation. The stalemate was to

continue for weeks. To get the embarrassing aircraft off the *Mariposa*, the Civil Aviation Department, as a concession, agreed that it could be unloaded and carried by barge across the harbour to Anderson's Park at the head of Neutral Bay. First, though, the Defence Ministry, responding to complaints from the vocal Returned Soldiers' League that the word ANZAC was 'too sacred to be commercialised', ordered Smithy to remove the offending acronym from the plane. The lettering was concealed with patches of hurriedly pasted-on brown paper and the aircraft was swung over the side. From the tiny park, sandwiched between hills, thick with houses, and watched by 5,000 people, Smithy, joined by Bill Taylor, who had agreed to go as co-pilot and navigator in the race, roared off in 150yds and flew the aircraft to Mascot.

Here customs and civil-aviation officials promptly immobilised it. Smithy was now at loggerheads with his own government and, because he was who he was, the prime minister and the federal Cabinet were soon involved again. The air race was only three months away, and Smithy pleaded unsuccessfully with the defence minister to waive the rules. Prime Minister Lyons told reporters, 'It is not directly a Cabinet concern.' Indeed, some ministers felt the problem really belonged firmly with Sir Charles; that it was his responsibility to cable the American Commerce Department for his certificates. When he did so the Commerce Department merely asked how could it certificate an aeroplane that, after major modification, had not been presented to it for stress- and load-testing.

As if this wasn't depressing enough, it now became clear that the uncertificated Altair was equally unacceptable to the race organisers, a committee in Melbourne and the Royal Aero Club in London. His only hope now was that the Australian Civil Aviation Department would issue him with some temporary dispensation that would satisfy the race management. They agreed, provided that the aircraft underwent some rigorous local flight tests. A heavy price was attached to the gesture: the Customs Department demanded a bond of £2,000. Somehow he raised the money – probably the bountiful Arthur Powell wrote another cheque.

Issued with the Australian registration VH-USB, and renamed, in Mary's honour, *Lady Southern Cross*, the controversial aeroplane successfully completed a series of take-off and climb-out tests, with all tanks filled, at the RAAF station at Richmond. Yet it was still not cleared to enter the race. While Edgar Johnston, anxious to avoid going down in history as the man who prevented one of the world's most popular aviators from starting in the most prestigious and lucrative flying event of all time, began a frustrating cabled dialogue with the US Department of Commerce, Smithy was given permission to make some major flights within Australia. In late July he and Taylor flew the *Lady Southern Cross* from Sydney to Melbourne in the then staggering time of two hours twenty-three minutes. Through August and September 1934, they proceeded to shatter record upon record, covering the distance between Melbourne and Perth in ten hours twenty minutes at the revolutionary speed of 229mph.

Despite all this evidence of its potency, the Altair's essential documents still did not arrive. Day after day, into early September, the cliff-hanger ran in the newspapers like a soap opera. And such was the media-fostered belief that Smithy could do no wrong, the stories cast blame in every quarter but his. There were allegations that it was all a dark British plot to let the Comets win; that it was part of a campaign to discredit American aircraft. From the huge correspondence in the files of the Australian archives it is clear that it was none of these things. Every other American aircraft entered in the race, some with huge fuel tankages, was accepted without drama, their pilots having had their machines structurally approved and certificated before they left America.

Smithy and Taylor were now running out of time. If they were to get to England for the October start of the race they had to leave Australia by the last day of September. But now another crisis was looming. Since his unscheduled landing in Turkey in 1931, Smithy had been banned from entering the country's airspace, which he now needed to fly straight across if he was to have a chance of beating the Comets. The Turks had agreed to allow all the competitors to overfly the country with one emphatic exception – Sir Charles Kingsford Smith. His criticism of the Turkish government had not been forgiven. There was even less sympathy for his predicament when it began to involve the Australian High Commission in London, the British Dominions Office, and the Air Ministry. Indeed, the director of civil aviation in England, Colonel Francis (later Sir Francis) Shelmerdine, took the drastic view that, given the danger of another diplomatic incident, Smithy's entry should now be refused. 'A further landing by Kingsford Smith in Turkish territory,' Shelmerdine wrote to the High Commission, 'would have far-reaching and disastrous effects on future aviation relations with Turkey. The risk involved in his participation seems hardly worthwhile.'[5]

It was beginning to look like 1919 all over again. Smithy, determined that history would not repeat itself, came up with an enterprising solution: on his flight to England he would, if the Turks agreed, land in Angora and personally make his peace with the aggrieved government. While this was being considered by the Turkish Foreign Office, the Australian government began to grow nervous about the entire messy business. Its foreign relations were more important than the flights of one man, even if that man was Smithy. Reluctantly, the prime minister decided that the time had come to sacrifice the aviator's latest ambitions in the interests of Australia's reputation abroad. He wrote to the premier of Victoria urging his government to discuss with the race committee in Melbourne the wisdom of allowing Kingsford Smith to compete at all. But in the end the matter was decided for them.

First came a bombshell from Lockheed. In the third week of September they reported that their structural calculations showed the aircraft's shock-absorbers, with all Smithy's tanks filled, were 'inadequate'. This was all Edgar Johnston needed. He decided to get the Altair off his back once and for all and park the crisis somewhere else. He issued Smithy with a restricted Australian certificate of airworthiness to enable him to fly to England and fight his own battles from there. The certificate put the *Lady Southern Cross* into a 'special/racing' category and, reflecting Lockheed's concerns, cautiously limited the fuel to less than 300 of the Altair's 418-gallon capacity. Regardless of what the Turks decided, Smithy would not be able to fly from England to Baghdad in one hop. By this time, however, he was grateful for any certificate at all.

The protracted anxiety had brought on one of his terrible flu attacks, which had put him to bed for a week. When, at last, he insisted on getting up, groggy and decidedly unwell, he still did not know if the race committee would allow him to enter. But as time had now almost run out, he and Taylor decided to prepare the

Altair for the flight to England in the hope that they would. On Friday 28 September Smithy sent an urgent telegram to the Royal Aero Club in London asking them to telephone their decision directly to him. Later that day, at Mascot, he watched civil-aviation officials, under instructions from Johnston, seal his auxiliary tanks to ensure that his fuel did not exceed the approved limit.

He was never to know that behind the scenes another attempt had been made to persuade the Royal Aero Club to refuse his entry. It had come from de Havilland's manager in Australia, Allan Murray Jones. Worried that the Altair might outpace the Comet, he had decided to put the boot in. He had cabled the company's marketing director, Francis St Barbe, to inform him, not without pleasure, of the Altair's seizure as a prohibited import. In a subsequent letter he added: 'I thought I should advise you by cable of the situation, both for your information and for that of the Royal Aero Club . . . that some little assistance from your end would go a long way towards ensuring that no special case was made of Kingsford Smith on account of his name.'[6]

Smithy, taut and edgy, spent that Friday on tenterhooks in the hangar, surrounded by a knot of reporters, waiting for the verdict. He and Taylor had set themselves a deadline of 6 o'clock the following morning. At last at 2.15 am in a phone call to his home, a Royal Aero Club official told him that, subject to the fuel limit set by the Australian certificate, the Altair would be accepted for the race. At 6 am he and Taylor roared off into the sunrise, hoping to reach Darwin by evening. All the fun had long gone out of the venture for both of them. They knew that, with the extra refuelling stops, they didn't stand a chance against the Comets.

The fuel restriction compelled them to cross Australia in short hops. Reaching Cloncurry in north-west Queensland in the late afternoon in a raging duststorm, they decided to stay the night. At the airfield they were amazed to see a familiar sight – 'battlescarred and showing signs of her advancing old age,' wrote Taylor – approaching through the pink dust haze. It was the *Southern Cross*, flown by Harry Purvis and Pat Hall, taking a party of government geologists on a survey of remote parts of northern Australia. Exhausted by the day's flying, Smithy used this fortuitous encounter to ask Purvis to check the Altair over. Purvis was rather peeved. 'Smithy was so obsessed with the task ahead of him he didn't even stop to ask how long we'd been flying the old bus that day.' Nonetheless he dutifully climbed up to remove the sections of the Altair's large circular engine cowling. He was shocked by what he found. Numerous bad cracks, some of them up to 6ins long, had appeared in the aluminium covers. The implications were all too obvious: with the vibration of flight, the cracks would rapidly enlarge. The aircraft could not safely continue to England.

It was the last day of September. The race was still three weeks away. Even allowing for a stopover in Turkey, which had at last been arranged, there was still just a chance they might make it. But the repair work could not be done in Cloncurry. They had to fly the Altair back to Sydney at slow speed lest the weakened cover peel off. There they were told that a complete new cowling would have to be spun – a week's work. Smithy knew that he was beaten. On 4 October he announced that he was withdrawing from the race.

The news was received everywhere with dismay. In London the secretary of the Royal Aero Club, Commander Harold Perrin, reluctant to see so distinguished an aviator pull out, offered to extend the deadline. Jim Mollison, with Amy Johnson another favourite in the Comet *Black Magic*, publicly urged him to change his mind and hurry to Mildenhall. But with the stop in Turkey, and the need to have the plane overhauled in England, there wouldn't be time to rest before setting off on the sleepless marathon back to Australia. 'We would both be goosed,' he said.

In Melbourne the race committee did not exactly go into mourning. Its deputy chairman, Wing Commander (later Air Vice-Marshal) Adrian Cole, reflecting a little of its growing impatience with Smithy's cool irresponsibility and his utter naïvety over the paperwork, commented with what sounded like less than genuine disappointment: 'While sincerely regretting Sir Charles's withdrawal, the committee feels that Australia is still well represented by Melrose, Penny, and Woods and that the many other competent men, women and machines that remain in the race will provide a unique contest.' In other quarters in Australia his withdrawal unleashed overt hostility. It was as if Don Bradman had wilfully refused to play in a cricket Test. He was, quite extraordinarily, accused of cowardice; of being afraid to fly merely, as one critic put it, because he'd found 'a few cracks in the bonnet'. He was called a 'gutless squib'. He was censured in some newspapers for his lack of patriotism in choosing an American aircraft and for his carelessness with its documentation. To his disgust, he began to receive white feathers in anonymous envelopes. Five arrived in the space of a week. 'It was suggested,' he wrote, 'that I had lost confidence in myself . . . that I was no sportsman . . . A nation's hero may often become a nation's whipping boy overnight.'

To repair his reputation, he knew he would have to make a major flight somewhere else – one that would silence his detractors and put him back on his pedestal. It would need to be a spectacular and dangerous 'first'. He decided to fly the Pacific again, this time from west to east, from Australia to California: a distance of more than 7,000 miles over the sea, and on one engine. To raise the funds to repay those who had put money into the Altair, he said he would sell the aircraft on his arrival in America.

Sir Macpherson Robertson was appalled. In no circumstances, he said, should Kingsford Smith risk his life flying the plane to America just to sell it on his account. But for Smithy there was much more at stake. He wanted to show Australia what this officially despised aeroplane could do, and he was determined in the process to deflect the world's attention from the England to Melbourne race. He would start from Brisbane, he said, on 20 October – the very day the flag was due to fall at Mildenhall. There was now another major Pacific flight competing for the headlines – Charles Ulm, with a hired pilot and navigator, was about to cross the ocean in the opposite direction on a proving flight for a paper airline, Great Pacific Airways, he had formed. He hoped the venture would be a forerunner of regular commercial services. To make the flight Ulm had mortgaged virtually everything he owned: his bungalow at Dover Heights, his car, his yacht, his aeroplane *Faith in Australia* – even his life-insurance policy. The newspapers speculated that he and his old partner might pass in mid-Pacific.

The route Smithy planned was the reverse of his 1928 flight: Brisbane–Suva–Honolulu–San Francisco. The critical sector, as before, was the 3,150-mile middle leg from Fiji to Hawaii. To provide the range for this he threw caution to the winds. He got Lawrence Wackett to secretly cram in even more fuel tanks in contravention of the permitted weight. Mechanic Bruce Cowan recalled this hasty engineering work: 'Civil Aviation had only a tiny administration then – just one aircraft inspector at Mascot. While old Wack was putting all those tanks in the guy conveniently looked the other way.' According to Taylor they could now carry 514 gallons – 'nearly 200 more than we were permitted'.

As the departure date approached, Catherine noted that Smithy had developed the now reflex pre-flight heavy cold. 'Chill had to go early to bed and be dosed,' she logged two days beforehand. But as always, on the day he dragged himself from his bed and, however rotten he felt, presented to the world the grin and the quips that everyone expected of him. 'In the old *Southern Cross*,' he joked to reporters at the aerodrome, 'there were three blasted engines to go wrong. This time there's only one – a third of the worry, lads.'[7] But as twenty assorted aircraft, ranging from the world's latest metal airliners to ancient wooden biplanes, were lining up for the race start at Mildenhall on 20 October, the *Lady Southern Cross* crew were, mercifully unknown to the media, in Brisbane facing a new crisis. At the eleventh hour they'd discovered that, notwithstanding the enormous load of fuel, the Altair might still lack the range to make it safely from Fiji to Hawaii.

What had gone wrong? On the flight up to Brisbane, repeating earlier tests in Sydney in which they had run one tank dry, they had been shattered to discover that their first figures had been dangerously over-optimistic. When they allowed for a mid-Pacific average headwind of 25mph, their likely groundspeed dropped to something like 140. 'We had,' wrote the cautious and meticulous Taylor, 'fuel for 21.4 hours at 1,700 revs, enough to take us 3,000 miles – about 150 miles short of Honolulu.' At Archerfield Aerodrome that Friday afternoon, they confided in only two people – their old friend and unofficial publicity adviser, the Sydney journalist Jack Percival, and the works manager of the newly formed Qantas Empire Airways, Arthur Baird. 'The position boiled down to one of two things,' said Taylor. 'We had to find out how to go farther with 514 gallons, or not go at all.'

Abandoning the project, they knew, would mean another shower of white feathers. Smithy's reputation could not have survived it. So he and Taylor, escaping from the press to a secluded Qantas office provided by Baird, began a long conference, filling sheets of paper with fresh range calculations. Around mid-afternoon they decided to make some more air tests. They filled the Altair to capacity and, telling no one what they were doing, flew out over Moreton Bay. Along a measured course they nervously observed the consumption yet again. On the flight up from Sydney it had been a suicidal 24 gallons an hour. This time the results were more cheering. By cutting back the power to 1,600rpm, at which they could still maintain 150mph, they reduced the hourly consumption to a comfortable 18 gallons. Even against a continuous headwind this would – with very accurate navigation – get them to Hawaii with 400 miles to spare.

Although a huge relief, it was not the end of their problems. Smithy's health had begun to cause Taylor deep concern. His atrocious cold, compounded by the stress of the previous weeks and the subconscious fears that beset him on the eve of every oceanic flight, had returned with a vengeance which, Taylor said, 'would have put any ordinary individual to bed for days. I suggested we wait for a day or so as he was really not fit enough to go.' Taylor was justifiably worried for his own safety, but Smithy was adamant. He was still smarting from the white feathers, three of which he had kept in his wallet and had shown to a Brisbane journalist who had questioned the need for the flight. 'I think,' said Taylor, 'that little short of the sheer physical inability to raise hand or foot would have prevented him from leaving the next morning. The battle was on.'

Collapse in LA

1934

Of the 1934 eastward Pacific crossing, one of the greatest of all Kingsford Smith's feats and certainly the most dangerous, he left little record. In his autobiography he dealt with it surprisingly briefly, dismissing it as 'just another hop' in which 'I was rather bored by the prospect of sitting in the pilot's seat for over 20 long hours'. It is Bill Taylor we have to thank for the only detailed account of the hair-raising journey which they very nearly didn't survive at all.

Smithy and Taylor left Brisbane in the dark at 4 am on 20 October, exactly twelve hours ahead of the first of the air-race competitors departing from Mildenhall, Amy Johnson and Jim Mollison. Smithy flew from the front cockpit, in which he had installed a transmit-only wireless set which enabled him to tap out hourly position and news reports. He had replaced the dog-eared picture of Nellie Stewart with a snapshot of Mary and Charles Arthur, which had joined a St Christopher medallion, a rabbit's foot and a pair of dice. They flew to Fiji in twelve hours, only just making it to Albert Park, Suva as darkness was falling. While waiting for suitable weather to continue they heard, on 23 October, that the Comet *Grosvenor House*, flown by Charles Scott and Tom Campbell Black, had arrived in Melbourne to win the air race.[1] Landing to refuel only three times – at Baghdad, Allahabad and Singapore – they had made it from England to Darwin in a staggering two days, four and a half hours. There was no way, Smithy knew, that the Altair, compelled by its load restriction to land twice as frequently, could have beaten that. He made a private

vow at that moment that he would smash the record at the very
first opportunity.

It was not until 29 October that the Altair set off on the long
leg to Hawaii. For the first 1,500 miles up to the equator the flight
was largely uneventful. Thanks to Taylor's immaculate navigation,
they passed within sight of several of the Phoenix atolls, which
reassuringly fixed their position right on course in mid-Pacific.
But that night, a few hundred miles north of the equator to the
west of the Line Islands, they encountered Smithy's greatest dread:
the inter-tropical convergence zone.

Plunging into the middle of this dark, Himalayan-sized mael-
strom of cumulo-nimbus at 15,000ft, they were snatched into the
familiar, frightening world of turbulence and explosive rain. Their
biggest fear was that the high-speed shock of the rain would
damage the fabric-covered wooden leading edge of the wing. This
had already happened once, between Brisbane and Fiji, when the
fabric had been ripped off and the exposed wood scoured and
weakened by the sheer, drilling force of the water at the Altair's
high speed. Smithy was afraid to take his eyes off the leading edge.
In the blinding rain, he began nervously to switch his landing lights
on and off. Despite the punishment it was taking, the wing surface
appeared to be holding up. But slowly they became aware that
something else was not quite right. Taylor, attuned to the aircraft's
every sound and vibration, was the first to detect it. 'I stiffen in my
seat and listen. The sound of the motor is different; less revs.' His
eyes shot straight to the engine rev-counter. Ever so subtly the
needle had dropped from its normal 1600 to under 1500. He saw,
too, that their airspeed had fallen back from 140 to barely 90mph,
yet the throttle lever was at full power.

His nerves tingling, he watched the altimeter. They were
steadily losing height. They had left 15,000ft and were passing
14,500. Anxiously he called to Smithy, 'What's wrong?'

'I don't know. She won't give any more power, that's all.'

The engine temperature gauges showed normal. Neither of
them could think of any explanation. As they sank through
14,000ft Taylor hurriedly spread out his chart to see how far they
were from the nearest land. This was the lonely Pacific radio outpost of Fanning Island, which was keeping lights on for them all
night, just in case. But the island was 500 miles to the south-east

of their position. At their present relentless rate of descent they would be in the sea long before they could get there. They were now reduced to only 1400rpm. 'The machine seems balanced on a knife-edge. Smithy has to juggle with the slack controls to keep her flying, just above stalling . . . I feel it can't go on like this.' Suddenly, in one swift movement, the airspeed needle swung to zero and the Altair stalled. In the black of the night cloud and hammering rain it dropped a wing and pitched down into a giddying spin, winding its way rapidly toward the sea with the closed-throttle undercarriage-warning klaxon wailing. 'The whole world is waving about and there is a tightness in my head. It is a fantastic whirling madness in the centre of black infinity. The turn indicator needle is hard over and the altimeter winding its way round the dial.'

Taylor said he could 'feel Smithy all out on the controls', but she didn't respond. 'You have a go at her,' he shouted in despair to Taylor. 'I ram on hard opposite rudder and shove the stick forward. It makes no difference at all. The klaxon screams and whirls in my ears and the black nightmare drums at my brain. I saw at the controls and try to throw her out of the spin. I feel him at it again, so let go the stick and hold my feet back clear of the rudder bar.' At 8,000ft there came through the tube into Taylor's helmet a forlorn voice. '"Look, Bill, I'm terribly sorry, but I can't get her out." You know, sort of apologising for the fact that we were going into the drink, which seemed inevitable.'[2]

'The instinct to fight was so great,' Smithy recalled, 'that I pressed both feet on one rudder pedal, braced my back against the seat – and pushed. Either the controls were going to break, or the machine *had* to come out of that spin. I kept this agonising pressure up until my back ached.'

At around 6,000ft Taylor felt the aircraft twitch, then steady as the nauseous autorotation stopped. They were now in a straight, unspinning dive. 'I think I've got her,' Smithy called hoarsely. Gradually he eased the Altair out of the dive and as they resumed level flight, still in darkness, rain and cloud, Taylor heard the engine roar back into life. By some miracle Smithy had saved them. But at full throttle he still couldn't get the engine revolutions back. They were continuing their seemingly unstoppable descent to the sea. And still neither of them realised what was wrong.

Whereas moments earlier they had had only seconds of life left, now it was minutes – maybe twenty, if they were lucky. It was the breathing space Smithy needed. For the first time he was able to make a systematic check of all the controls and instruments. Almost at once he found the problem. The flaps were fully extended. They had been acting as a brake, creating enormous drag against which the engine could not efficiently drive the propeller in the high, coarse pitch of cruising flight. He flicked the flap switch off and at long last their airspeed crept back to normal. 'It was,' Taylor said, 'like rowing a boat, towing a bucket.' But how had this near-disaster occurred? All too easily, according to Smithy: while flicking the landing lights on and off he had accidentally knocked down the switch that lowered the electrically operated flaps. The port and starboard landing-light controls and the single flap switch were mounted on the same console on the right-hand wall of the cockpit. The flaps were activated by a small toggle switch, whereas the landing lights were controlled by much bigger, knobbed levers some distance away which needed to be swung up and down. Normally there would have been little risk of confusion, but, under the high stress of instrument flight in dark, cloud, and rain, heightened by his fear that the wing was being weakened, Smithy had mixed them up. Moreover, flying at 15,000ft without oxygen, his faculties were dulled.

Around midnight, as their adrenaline surges melted, they broke free of the convergence zone into a calm, clear, moonlit night. Taylor, using Sirius and the North Star, got his first fix for 1,000 miles, and rechecked their drift from self-igniting flares dropped into the sea. With only 980 miles to run to Hawaii, they were less than 30 miles off course. His early morning landfall in the Hawaiian islands on 29 October was a triumph of astronavigation. They arrived, as he intended, exactly in the middle of the group at Lanai with what he described as 'colossal satisfaction and thankfulness'. They landed at 8.40 am at the US Army Air Corps Base at Wheeler Field outside Honolulu. The 3,150-mile journey from Suva had taken exactly twenty-five hours at an average speed of 126mph. The *Lady Southern Cross* was the first aircraft ever to arrive in Hawaii from Australia. 'In our tanks,' Smithy wrote with pride, 'we had sufficient fuel left for a further 2½ hours flying.' He was mistaken: in fact, they were extremely lucky to have reached Hawaii at all.

The next day, refreshed by sleep and made 'benevolent', as Taylor delicately put it, by endless stiff cocktails, Smithy invited the city's mayor to join him for a flight in the Altair. For this brief circuit of Honolulu city he didn't bother to refuel. Three minutes after take-off, passing through 2,000ft, the engine stopped. Silently he glided back to Wheeler Field, reaching it with barely yards to spare. 'The tank was dipped,' said Taylor. 'No fuel. The significance began to creep up my spine. Notwithstanding our careful fuel checks at Brisbane, estimating two hours' fuel remaining at Honolulu, we had landed with about five minutes' petrol.'

Army Air Corps mechanics discovered that a 90-gallon gravity tank which sat in the fuselage between the two cockpits had sprung a large crack. Two hours' fuel had leaked out in flight, draining away through the bottom of the aircraft. Highly dangerous as it seems today, in the absence of gauges, their practice was simply to fill all eleven tanks to the brim and hope that there would be enough fuel to get them there. Once airborne, they had no means of measuring consumption or detecting leakage. Nonetheless they decided not to go to the trouble of having the gravity tank repaired for the last leg to San Francisco. The 2,450-mile hop didn't require a full fuel load. But when they went out to Wheeler Field to board the Altair they learned that the mechanics had now found a serious leak in the aircraft's oil tank. This was a major repair job. To remove and weld the fracture, the entire fuselage, from engine to tail, had to be completely separated from the wing.

While this complex two-day job went ahead Smithy and Taylor returned to the hotel to re-immerse themselves in the seductive Hawaiian lifestyle. Smithy bought a ukulele so that he could accompany the serenading groups that seemed to appear every-where. Grinning, swaying and swinging his hips, he infiltrated the ranks of the young Hawaiian women and tried to sing along with them. The island had never welcomed a VIP so disconcertingly informal and uninhibited. The abstemious Taylor had not previously spent much time in Smithy's company on the ground, but now he saw for himself his partner's inordinate capacity for pleasure. A woman who knew Taylor well recalled:

That stopover in Honolulu was a real eye-opener for him. He told me that women just couldn't keep their hands off

Smithy. Those luxury hotel suites made it so easy. And the inevitable gossip followed him about – you know, women boasting that their babies were his.[3] The more Bill saw of him in action, the more he felt he shouldn't have been married at all. He was just not capable of being pinned down. Too many women loved him, and he just loved women. And because he was Smithy he got away with it. It all somehow added to the romance of his image. Larrikin that he was, Bill absolutely worshipped him. He used to envy his fantastic charisma.

The oil-tank repair had almost been completed when, unbelievably, the technicians stumbled on yet another serious leak. This one was in the biggest petrol tank of all, which had been worn almost all the way through by a protruding bolt. A mid-flight burst would have put them in the ocean between Hawaii and the American mainland. The plague of leaking tanks delayed them in Hawaii for nearly a week. Finally, with the help of a tailwind they reached San Francisco in fifteen hours on the morning of 4 November 1934. The flight from Australia had taken sixteen days: their flying time of fifty-two hours was thirty-two hours faster than the time the 'old bus' had taken in the opposite direction six years earlier.

As a small crowd swarmed round the aircraft at Oakland, Taylor and Smithy heard a voice calling excitedly, 'Smitty! Smitty!' They turned to see Harry Lyon and Jim Warner waving from the ground. Lyon, who had fallen on hard times and had recently been declared bankrupt, had come all the way across America from his home in Maine specially to see Smithy again. But the two Americans who had contributed so much to his fame were swept away in the crush. Standing up in their cockpits amid a forest of microphones, the heroes were trapped for some time aboard the plane. Swaying with exhaustion Smithy, gulping a bottle of ice-cold beer and greedily inhaling a cigarette, stood in a deafened daze, trying to respond to the volley of reporters' questions. No one knew that the terrifying flight had once more reduced him to the verge of emotional collapse. The photographs that caught him off guard as he stood on the wing that morning show how ill he was. Here again are the sunken cheeks and the sad and haunted expression. He looks fifteen years older than his thirty-seven years.

Harold Kingsford-Smith and John Stannage, who had come over to handle the post-flight publicity, were shocked by his haggard appearance. Harold and Elsie whisked him off to their house on Leimert Boulevard. It had already been staked out by reporters and photographers demanding more pictures and interviews, and Smithy was forced to go out and talk to them. He was tired and unusually irritable. After a few minutes, he cut it all short, abruptly turned his back on the reporters, retreated into the house and firmly shut the door.

Harold and Stannage were aghast when Smithy told them that he and Taylor intended to fly on to Los Angeles that same day. He was so nervous and jumpy that they begged him to postpone the journey, but he refused. According to the *San Francisco Examiner*, he and Taylor were in a hurry to get to Los Angeles because of 'a business deal that awaited them there,' but nowhere is there any record of a deal requiring such urgency.

In Los Angeles the fêting rituals began again. But it was apparent that the flight, overshadowed by Scott and Black's stunning air-race performance, had failed to catch the world's imagination in the way Smithy's earlier epic journeys had done. There was no customary cable from the King; in an ominous sign of the times, the first world leaders to send congratulations were, wrote Smithy respectfully, 'Herr Hitler and Signor Mussolini'. Although the *New York Times* praised his achievement in a leading article, the London newspapers reported it in subdued fashion, buried at the foot of the news pages. And while it must, by any standards, rank as his most desperate and courageous flight, there was a feeling in some quarters that it had served no worthwhile purpose; indeed, that it had been foolhardy. The influential British aeronautical magazine *The Aeroplane* – whose editor, the acerbic C. G. Grey, regarded Smithy as a self-seeking daredevil – declared harshly: 'Two good aviators made an extremely dangerous flight for nothing. If they had been lost, their deaths would have done harm to aviation. By surviving they have done it no good.'

Smithy never claimed that the flight had helped to prove the route for airline operations, for nobody would have contemplated operating a Pacific service with a single-engined racing aircraft. In any case, the large, comfortable, four-engined Sikorsky and Martin passenger flying boats already in existence were capable of serving the route – indeed, they were undergoing trials with PanAmerican Airways. The Altair flight had no relevance at all to commercial aviation. It had merely shown that a brilliant navigator could steer an aircraft across the huge ocean accurately without radio aids. In the wake of his air-race fiasco, Smithy had undertaken the venture purely for his own ego, to restore his damaged public image and to get rid of the *Lady Southern Cross*. He never tried to imbue it with any higher, nobler purpose.

Suffering from the post-traumatic effects of the flight, he stubbornly refused to take any part in the customary money-making activities – the newspaper articles, product-endorsements and lectures. 'I simply couldn't get Smithy to work,' said John Stannage. 'His nerves were shot to pieces.' It did not help his state of mind when the Altair was seized in LA by a deputy marshal in an unhappy echo of his penniless days in California six years earlier. A promotions consultant, Thomas Catton, commissioned by Smithy and Ulm in 1928 to help raise money to equip the *Southern Cross*, had had him served with an attachment order for fees he insisted he was owed. The Altair had been taken hostage, wheeled into a hangar and the uniformed deputy sat on a chair guarding it, his arms folded intimidatingly. Smithy was forced to hire a lawyer, and it was soon established that he and Ulm did owe Catton money. The case was settled out of court for what Catton described as 'a satisfactory sum', but which Smithy preferred to call 'nominal'.

Parking the Altair at Lockheed's Burbank factory with instructions for its sale, Smithy moved into his favourite LA bolthole, the Hotel Clark on 4th Street, whose manager, 'Bud' Morriss, tried to cheer him up by taking him off to party with film stars James Cagney and George Raft and then on a two-week holiday yachting, swimming and sightseeing. But Smithy soon lapsed back into melancholy, pessimism and uncharacteristic mood swings. One moment he was immersed in silent introspection, the next he was planning to refly the Pacific to Australia. One day he would declare that he had to sell the plane to cover his debts, the next that he was about to fly it back to Australia in time for his son's second birthday on 22 December and was looking for a navigator to take him across the Pacific. Stannage, presumably trying to humour him, is reported as saying gaily: 'Everything is ready for the flight. It is a toss-up between philanthropists and the oil companies who will put up the necessary money.'

Just as quickly as it was announced to an eager press, the risky Pacific journey was abandoned in favour of a flight home the long way round. 'I would much prefer to make my way home by boat in leisurely fashion,' Smithy said now. 'However, I think that plans have just about materialised for me to fly from Los Angeles to New York, across to London, then on to Australia.' He still didn't have a firm backer for a flight of any description. By mid-November his plans had been modified again. He had decided, he said, to form a new airline in Australia. He would swap the *Lady Southern Cross* for a larger Lockheed Orion, a cabin-plane version of the Altair. With a fleet of these six-passenger aircraft he would introduce fast intercity services. But he was no longer well enough either to create a new business or to attempt another fearsome flight across the world in any direction. Had he set out at this time, it is almost certain that he would have killed himself and whoever he persuaded to go with him.

At the Hotel Clark Stannage grew more worried by the day. Autograph-hunters, whom Smithy had always goodnaturedly taken in his stride, had begun for the first time to rattle him. 'He locked himself in his hotel suite and sent out word by his manager, Mr Stannage, that his nerves were ragged and he was determined to get some rest. "Sir Charles must have rest and quiet," said Stannage. "If need be I'll take him away to some remote spot in the hills. He has been pestered no end and he's tired of it all."'[4] This was not the approachable, laid-back, accessible Smithy the world held in such affection. He was by this stage so overwhelmed by sadness, despondency and revolving bouts of high agitation that Bud Morriss and Stannage decided to summon a doctor. The doctor called in a psychiatrist, who gently but firmly declared him unfit to fly for a very long time.

No record exists of the clinical diagnosis, or how he was treated, apart from bed rest and sedatives. As he lay in bed in the Hotel Clark, his room barred to all except Stannage and Morriss, Smithy's depression was aggravated by two pieces of bad news which arrived within days of each other. In the last week of November he was distressed to hear that his prized Gull, *Miss Southern Cross*, had crashed in the Blue Mountains south-west of

Sydney and was a complete write-off. It was being flown by Pat Hall, who had been lucky to escape with a broken leg. His passenger had been killed. On Tuesday 4 December he got up to meet the actor Will Rogers for lunch with Stannage at the Fox Studios. It was here that he learned of a tragedy even more shattering. Charles Ulm and his two companions in a twin-engined Airspeed Envoy, *Stella Australis*, had disappeared between San Francisco and Hawaii on the first leg of their trans-Pacific flight to Australia. Smithy was devastated. Whatever the circumstances of his split with Ulm, the two had maintained, in public at least, a civil, if distant, relationship. The 1928 Pacific flight that had catapulted them both to such prominence had woven bonds that major disputes, deep philosophical divides and their inherently different personalities could never quite dissolve.

With pilot George Littlejohn, a Sydney flying-club instructor, at the controls, *Stella Australis* (VH-UXY) had left Oakland on the Monday afternoon.[5] It had been due to arrive at Wheeler Field at around 8 am next day. In the vicinity of the islands, despite an onboard radio direction-finder and a shore-based beam on which to home, they had become hopelessly lost. It was clear to those listening to the flow of signals from the aircraft that the navigator and wireless-operator, Leon Skilling, had not been able to tune his receiver properly. He never heard any of the messages that would have helped him. Their fuel had run out and they had gone into the sea. Three heartbreaking Morse messages had come from the aircraft. 'We are just going to the water,' then, as they apparently lined up for ditching, 'We are turning into the wind.' Three minutes later Skilling called: 'Come and pick us up. The plane will float for two days.' There followed a six-minute stream of SOS signals. Then, as the trailing aerial cable touched the sea, silence. Ulm had refused to carry a liferaft, preferring to take the weight in fuel. Within hours the US Navy in Hawaii had begun a big search operation. More than twenty ships, submarines and many aircraft began to scour the area, soon augmented by Japanese fishing boats, but no one knew where they had actually gone down.

At the Fox Studios, Smithy's instant reaction was to join the search. 'I watched his face,' Stannage remembered. 'It went white. All he said was, "Let's go." We drove back to our hotel and I was ordered to go immediately and arrange to make ready his machine.'[6] Bill Taylor having returned to Australia to join the new QEA as a pilot, Smithy asked Stannage to approach the US Navy in Los Angeles to provide a navigator for the eighteen-hour flight across a stretch of the Pacific in which there was not a single rock or reef to help him check his position. Stannage and Morriss, convinced that Smithy was about to fly to his death, hurriedly recalled the doctors. They listened incredulously as their patient tried to explain the emotional imperative to go in search of the *Stella Australis*. It was clear that all rationality had deserted him. He could not appreciate how insane a plan it was to fly, with a leaking tank, across 2,600 miles of open sea that was guaranteed to terrify him, when a large force of military pilots was already scouring the area. Even when Mary's voice, crackling and distorted, came on the phone from Sydney to plead with him to abandon the idea, he remained obdurate. 'Certain forceful means had to be taken to restrain him,' said Stannage. 'He was invited to have a farewell drink,' said Bill Taylor. 'Bud Morriss mixed a fearful potion and after he drank it he was absolutely knocked out for about twenty-four hours. Then, and only then, they managed to make him see reason. Of course, if he had gone out he would have been lost, but he hadn't thought about that. He just thought, Charles Ulm is missing and I'm going out to look for him. That was Smithy.'[7]

The hunt for the *Stella Australis* continued for over a week, but the aeroplane and its crew were never found. When, at the end of the second week in December, the search was finally abandoned, Smithy was said to have been in great distress. He turned for emotional support to Mary. According to Catherine's diary, he began to bombard her with cables and phone calls pleading with her to come and join him. The Kingsford Smith family network began to hum with anxiety for his welfare, and Catherine sent him a loving cable urging him to get on the next ship home. At last he capitulated, but with one final petulant proviso. He insisted that Mary must join him and accompany him back to Australia. Only after a further spate of cables and phone calls, in which his anxiety became all too apparent, did she agree to go. Leaving Charles Arthur with Nurnie, she sailed for America on the *Monterey* on Saturday 15 December.

25

The Tasman Dream

1935

When Mary arrived in Los Angeles in the first week of 1935 Chilla went to some pains to present the appearance of jaunty normality. Sixty years later she couldn't recall having been shocked by the state in which she found him. 'I lacked the perception then to see that things were going badly wrong with him and that he was covering it up, afraid I'd see it as weakness. He must have been doing it for years, right through all those disabling episodes which his mates knew about, but which he deliberately kept from me and the family.' Charles Arthur, who has few clear memories of his father, speculated:

> It's possible that he'd learned to compartmentalise his life in such a way that the psychological traumas were short-lived and specific to the flights themselves; that they erupted with those bouts of pre-departure nervous flu and then subsided in the euphoria of safe arrival. On the other hand, it may have been much more evident than Mother can now remember. She could be repressing the buried memories which might still be too painful to resurrect. My own theory is that she and his home environment played a big part in restoring him. I suspect he didn't want to complicate all that by spilling every fear and fright to her.

At the Hotel Clark Mary found Chilla still absorbed by the shocking news of the *Stella Australis*. 'Because he hated speaking ill of people, he'd always been very guarded about his true feelings towards Charles Ulm,' she said. 'Yet when Ulm went it was still a terrible blow. Then he could only recall the good times and all the triumphs they'd shared. I think it brought home at last just how appallingly risky those big flights were. Certainly it helped dissuade him from flying the Altair back to Australia.'

Leaving the *Lady Southern Cross* at the Lockheed factory, he and Mary travelled up to San Francisco to rejoin the *Monterey*. En route the ship called in at Honolulu, passing through the very waters in which Ulm and his crew had disappeared. Smithy read the outpourings of praise for Ulm's courage and his contribution to the development of aviation. Although he'd lacked Kingsford Smith's beguiling personal magnetism and had lived deeply in his shadow, he had, at an intellectual, political and business level, done a great deal more to aid the advance of the country's airline industry than the partner who lived only to fly the aeroplanes. Obituaries lauded his genius for organisation and his vision of a world in which air transport would become a vast and viable industry – one in which he had fought so unsuccessfully for a significant role. But his pugnacious and often pompous style had alienated many who saw him, as did Qantas and Imperial Airways, as a threatening figure. He'd made too many enemies for comfort, and despite the brilliant way he had almost single-handedly created Australian National Airways, he had never wholly overcome the loss of trust that had followed the damaging events of Coffee Royal. Nor had he ever quite succeeded in escaping the unglamorous truth that, on all his great flights, he had been flown virtually as a passenger. Smithy, arriving in Sydney at the end of January, paid generous public tribute to the architect of his fame. In his 'unusual character and temperament', Charles Ulm had possessed, he wrote, 'many of the qualities of greatness'. He was 'ruthless and tough,' said Bill Taylor, 'but there was something good about him.'[1]

Ulm's death at the age of thirty-six cast a brief shadow over Australian aviation. More than ever Smithy was convinced that the small, slow, wooden British planes, like Ulm's Envoy, were dangerously inadequate for airline operations. Indeed, Qantas Empire Airways was already having major trouble with the new de Havilland aircraft thrust upon it for the Australia–Singapore route. The fin was too small, rendering it dangerously unstable, and the much-publicised DH86 flagships had been grounded following two disastrous crashes in quick succession. It was a blow to both the Qantas–Imperial alliance and to public confidence in the safety of flying to England.

Smithy now planned to challenge the British-only policy and create his own trans-Tasman airline using much more advanced American aircraft. But persuading backers to finance him was to prove difficult. Meanwhile, in the early months of 1935, depleted in health, restless and frustrated, he was hopelessly broke again. Nevertheless, on a plot of land near his rented home, he was having a sumptuous new four-bedroomed house built for the family. How it was all paid for Mary couldn't recall: 'As Chill never had a bean, I'm sure Daddy must have had something to do with it.' Certainly the money didn't come from Kingsford Smith Air Service, whose overheads were still exceeding its uncertain trickle of income. Early in February he was forced to take the 'old bus' on yet another joyriding tour of rural New South Wales. But flying had become less of a novelty and money was even scarcer. Business was so bad that within a few weeks he was back in Sydney casting about 'for some other method of "raising the wind"'.

While the grand new house at 33 Greenoaks Avenue rose, a stream of family, friends and flying acquaintances floated through the villa. Among the visitors at this time was a glamorous, dark-haired young woman pilot from New Zealand. The previous year Jean Batten had become a world celebrity overnight with a solo flight from England to Australia which had broken the women's record set in 1930 by Amy Johnson. Her achievement had been inspired by Smithy's feats in the *Southern Cross*, in which, a few years earlier, she had made her first flight. She had set out to cultivate his friendship and a warm relationship had sprung up between them. In London, where she had gone to learn to fly, he had made a point, she wrote in her memoirs, of unfailingly visiting her and her mother every time he came to England, giving her hours of his time to plan her record attempt and even lending her some of his own precious maps. Whether or not they had a sporadic affair is not recorded, but people who knew them both believed it was highly likely, given Smithy's opportunism and her own habit of rewarding men who assisted her with favours.

Now that she had become an aviation star in her own right, Jean Batten's head had been more than a little turned by fame. 'We put on a specially nice dinner party for her,' Mary said, 'but she was so full of her own achievement, so busy flirting with Chill and trying to impress him with her one single flight I don't think she noticed the rest of us.' Batten later wrote that Smithy had given her that evening two pieces of well-meant if sexist advice: don't attempt to break men's records, and don't fly at night. 'I made a point of ignoring them both,' she declared.[2]

In the first week of March staff at the tottering Kingsford Smith Air Service were shocked to learn that their boss had sold the business to another small company, Eastern Air Transport, which planned to run air services into rural New South Wales. Smithy had decided to direct his energies into bigger things. At his Vacuum Oil Company office his only interest now was the creation of his own Tasman airline. 'It seemed to me that we'd earned the right to have a first claim over this service . . . We had blazed the trail . . . had risked not only our money but our lives. We deserved at least some encouragement.' Encouragement from both the Australian and New Zealand governments was minimal. Neither country had yet freed itself from the tentacles of empire. Their dependence on Britain as their main export market forced them to heed Imperial Airways' determination that it, too, should have a stake in the operation of a Tasman service. Although Imperial's management privately dismissed Kingsford Smith as a reckless soldier of fortune, they were concerned about the way he was using his household name to promote the superiority of American aircraft for the route. Smithy was proposing to buy either the new Sikorsky flying boats or Douglas DC2 landplanes to offer great passenger comfort in a crossing of seven or eight hours.

When he went to Canberra to try to persuade the defence minister, now Sir Archdale Parkhill, to support his proposal with a government subsidy, Parkhill was outraged at the very suggestion of foreign aircraft and accused him of lack of patriotism. So Smithy took a ship to Wellington to make a direct appeal to the New Zealand prime minister, George Forbes. His approaches to both governments seem to have been both informal and haphazard. He had not yet formed a Tasman operating company, and nowhere in the preserved official correspondence about the development of the route did he appear to have lodged any costed proposals in even the briefest outline. Apparently he still assumed he could win the day with the sheer power of his name, his public popularity and the access he enjoyed to the highest in the land, who were always prepared to humour him.

Although Forbes and his Cabinet received Smithy warmly, he met the same reluctance in New Zealand as he'd encountered in Canberra. The ministers listened patiently as he outlined his proposal for a permanent twice-weekly Sydney–New Plymouth operation flown by DC2s and financially guaranteed by the two governments. But neither government could take his proposals seriously in the face of an imminent Imperial Airways plan to extend the empire route to New Zealand in a partnership venture with Qantas and a New Zealand airline yet to be formed. At the heart of this scheme was a luxurious new four-engined flying boat of which Imperial had already ordered from Short Brothers a large number direct from the drawing board.[3] Smithy's American DC2s would never be allowed to compete with this new pride of British long-haul aviation.

Still unaware of the power of the forces ranged against him, Smithy, back in Sydney, decided to expedite matters with a spectacular gesture which he hoped would convince the two governments of his operating expertise: a one-off return mail flight to New Zealand. Jack Percival, with whom he discussed the idea, said that a much more newsworthy stunt would be to take two aeroplanes – the 'old bus' and Charles Ulm's *Faith in Australia* – fill them with freight as well as mail, and fly them across in formation. Enthusiastically Smithy agreed. He asked Percival to manage the operation.

At first the Australian government refused to allow the flights, but Smithy successfully appealed to the acting prime minister, Dr Earle Page, to allow him to fly 'official mail' to New Zealand. It was proclaimed as the Jubilee Air Mail to coincide with the celebration of the twenty-fifth year of George V's reign. Smithy was to pilot the *Southern Cross*, with Tommy Pethybridge (on loan from Eastern Air Transport) as his co-pilot and engineer and John Stannage as wireless-operator. Also joining the flight were a marine navigator, Commander Bennett, and Beau Sheil, as a sort of travelling organiser. Sheil, who became Smithy's first biographer, had fallen under his spell. He had left his job as an official in Vacuum Oil's aviation department, where he'd often arranged fuel for the *Southern Cross*, to throw in his lot precariously with the exclusive

Kingsford Smith club. He was also a pilot, having qualified for Air Force wings in New Zealand. *Faith in Australia* was to be flown by Bill Taylor – who, having refused to fly Qantas's unstable DH86s, was back in Sydney at a loose end – with a mechanic, Bob Boulton as co-pilot, wireless-operator Syd Colville and Jack Percival as flight publicist. Taylor summed up the mission: 'I think we liked to feel it had some counterpart to the privateers of the sixteenth century capturing a couple of galleons for Queen Elizabeth's birthday.'

Such romantic notions may have persuaded him to join the flight, but Taylor soon had major misgivings about the mechanical state of the two aeroplanes. He knew that the engines in the 'old bus' were now 'long past their prime', and that *Faith in Australia* had developed major fuel leaks in all her tanks. These were patched up, but the condition of the *Cross*'s engines continued to make him nervous. Not only was its starboard motor devouring oil at the alarming rate of a full gallon per hour, requiring it to be changed, but the centre engine had developed a problem in its exhaust system. A new manifold was having to be built by a metal-working firm and welded on at the eleventh hour. But Smithy assured him that the aircraft was in good shape. 'I believe he felt,' Taylor said, 'that once he got his hands and feet on the controls she would stay in the air for him in any circumstances.' Stannage, too, was also privately worried by the condition of the weary trimotor. He had a premonition that the famous plane was about to let them down. 'I had a sneaking fear, at the thought of that trip, that something horrible would happen.' Yet Stannage's diffidence, and the singular awe in which he held Smithy, would not have allowed him for one moment to question his judgement.

On Monday 13 May, the day before they were due to go, Commander Bennett went down with severe flu. There was no civilian available to replace him, so Taylor was now the only navigator between the two planes – as well as the pilot of *Faith in Australia*. Both aircraft were air-tested. On the *Southern Cross* the oil consumption of the centre and port engines, which hadn't been changed, was checked as a precaution. The centre motor was burning three pints, and the port engine half a gallon an hour, sufficient to keep it running for twenty-two hours – more than enough to get to New Zealand. After the test flights the aircraft were flown out to Richmond where, that evening, the eight remaining crew members gathered at the Carrington Hotel in the nearby township of Windsor for dinner and a pre-flight briefing. The whole operation had about it, Taylor wrote, something of the 'wartime spirit'.

Yet his anxieties had begun to keep Taylor awake at night. 'There was some stalking presence, heavy with dread of nothing in particular.' He pleaded with Smithy to take *Faith* instead of the *Cross*, but again Smithy brushed aside his fears. However, Taylor's sombre, edgy mood had spread like a virus to the others as they sat down to dinner that night. Always slightly aloof, Taylor had chosen to eat with a group of friends in a separate dining room. If one is to believe the depth of his recorded concern, the meal must have had about it something of the atmosphere of the last supper. In the main restaurant Smithy hosted the remainder of the two crews, all neatly dressed in their best suits and ties. Whatever private worries he may have had, he masked them as usual. But his mind was wrestling with an eleventh-hour decision he had to make. He had just learned that the final load of freight was pitifully small: the total revenue would scarcely fund the trip for one aeroplane.

For the last time in that heroic era of Australian flying, nearly every member of Kingsford Smith's inner circle was gathered in the Carrington Hotel with their beloved boss. After dinner he announced that only the *Southern Cross* would make the flight. Only two of them would now be going with him: Taylor to navigate and relieve him at the controls, and Stannage as radio-operator. The news was received in dreadful silence. Taylor was still not sure he wanted to go at all.

He walked out across the aerodrome on that bitterly cold night to think over what he was certain would be 'as good as walking the plank into the Tasman Sea'. Yet he decided at last that he couldn't let Smithy and Stannage go off without a navigator. 'I had no feeling of heroics . . . something just said clearly and without doubt: "Go in the *Cross*."' Over in the RAAF officers' mess he found Smithy sitting by the fire, sipping coffee and eating a sandwich. He was explaining the change of plan to reporters. According to the Sydney *Sun*, he gazed into the fire for some time, lost in thought. 'Quite suddenly he looked up and said: "Here am I, thirty-eight, apparently sane and sensible, and I'm going out over an ocean again in the middle of the night."'

Out on the tarmac, where *Faith*'s engines had been switched off and a cold mist was beginning to drift in, Mary, Catherine and Beris, swathed in overcoats and fox furs, had arrived to say good-bye. Smithy, in his flying suit and helmet, walked out to the plane with his arms around them.

As the *Cross* roared off along the flarepath of flickering oil lamps, Mary told a *Sun* reporter: 'I'm glad that Captain Taylor is going with him. With John Stannage it makes the perfect combi-nation.' She had not the least idea that both these very special mates were privately convinced that they were going to their deaths.

Six Hours Out,
Nine Hours Back
1935

'Smithy started the motors and life awakened in the machine . . .
She seemed to rouse herself from sleep, like some splendid beast,
and stand erect, calling to the winds. I take my place by Smithy, in
the starboard pilot's seat, and hear the tearing snarl of each motor
as he runs it up . . . Called to the hunt again she faces the night
with a steady bellowing roar and slowly moves away, gathers
speed, and floats into the air.' Thus Bill Taylor lyrically described
the departure of the *Southern Cross* from RAAF Richmond, at
12.20 am on Wednesday 15 May 1935. For the first six hours or so
everything went smoothly. The weather was good, the engines
thundered faultlessly through the night. Taylor concentrated on
navigation in between relieving Smithy on the flight deck, accessible to the cabin over the big, flat floor tank. Stannage sat at his
wireless rack, revelling in the novelty of a radio telephone as well
as Morse.

At around 5 o'clock Smithy handed over to Taylor and went
back into the cabin to send some personal radio messages. Alone in
the cockpit, flying from the co-pilot's seat, Taylor gazed out over
the top of the centre engine ahead into the dark. As the sky began
to lighten he found his attention drawn, with a frisson of concern,
to a small spot on the top of the manifold that seemed to be glowing brighter than the rest of the big exhaust-collector ring that
encircled the engine. It began to assume the appearance of a small
brazier, slowly spreading before his eyes. With full daylight he saw
the reason for the glow.

The newly welded edge of the centre motor's exhaust pipe had come away and a crack was creeping up behind the top cylinder. The blow of the flaming exhaust was bursting open the entire top of the manifold. Smithy returned to the cockpit and climbed back into the left-hand seat. Almost immediately, the glowing, disintegrating top of the manifold bulged out, broke off and was flicked away in the slipstream. Instantly a violent vibration seized the whole aircraft. The fractured chunk of metal had flown into the starboard propeller, shattering one of its wooden blades. Flung out of balance, the motor 'leapt and struggled in its mounting as though it had gone mad and was trying to break from the machine', said Taylor. The threshing, destabilised engine threatened the whole aircraft with structural failure. Smithy swiftly shut it down. 'As we finally saw the blades come to rest, one stuck out towards us in broken splintered wood – a jagged stump, like a lightning-struck tree.' About a foot of the blade had gone.

To stop the shattered propeller spinning in the airflow Smithy was forced to cut its ignition, raise the nose and sit the aircraft on her tail, flying at barely 60mph, dangerously near stalling speed. The moment he let the nose drop the propeller would begin to revolve and the awful shuddering returned. 'This was a terrific strain for a pilot,' Taylor said.

It wasn't the only strain. Flying on the remaining two engines, now at full power, the aircraft was in a permanently asymmetric state, continuously struggling to turn to starboard. There was no rudder-trimming device. The only way Smithy could hold her straight was by applying constant pressure on the left rudder, an action that soon began to cause him a good deal of pain in his mutilated left foot. 'I don't think any pilot was ever expected to fly for hours in an asymmetric aircraft as Smithy did that day,' said Colin Watt. 'The more I've flown the replica and realise what he did with the Cross, the more I appreciate what a magnificent pilot he must have been.'

The moment he'd stopped the propeller, Smithy had turned back to Australia. Although they were almost halfway to New Zealand, it was, at 590 miles away, a little closer. Taylor estimated it would take ten hours to get home – if they could stay aloft on two engines that long. They had been at 3,000ft below cloud when disaster had struck at 7 am. They had already begun to lose height, and the only way to arrest a long, slow descent into the sea

was to lighten the load. They dumped as much fuel as they dared
and threw out the cargo. This slowed down their rate of descent,
but they were still losing height. As usual, they carried neither lifejackets nor raft.

Stannage had begun an anxious running commentary by radio
telephone and Morse to Sydney and to a station at Bluff in the far
south of New Zealand. News of their plight had quickly been
passed to newspapers and radio stations, but people could only
listen powerlessly. There was no search-and-rescue service to come
to their aid.

Stannage's Morse key conveyed his every hope and fear.

7.15 am. Looks like we're going in. Gee! It's cold. Get that?
Just climbing 100 feet. Get that? Fifty knot destroyer
ready? . . . Of course it would happen when we are right in
the middle of it. Wonder what splintered the propeller . . .
Smithy says, no, don't dump mails. We have dumped much
gas though.

7.21 am. Cripes! One of the others spluttered.

7.25 am. Lovely isn't it? The first Tasman freight has to be
dumped at sea . . . Don't let them worry our wives unnecessarily. Thank God we have this marvellous radio set. My
antenna must be nearly in the drink now. The sea's going to
be cold when we go in.

7.45 am. Smithy says we will try and hang onto the mail,
but if the Post Office says dump it, we would be very glad
to.

At 8.26 the director-general of Posts and Telegraphs, who had
been phoned at his home, agreed that the mail could be jettisoned – as if he had any option. But Smithy, unaware that his
colleagues feared he was merely prolonging the agony and deep-
ening the risk to their lives, refused to part with it just yet –
refused to concede that his expedition had been a total commercial failure. Yet they were now down to 500ft. In Australia
radio programmes were interrupted by breathless newsflashes as
the live drama gripped the nation. At Richmond, *Faith in
Australia* was prepared for flight and stocked with flotation gear,
and a cruiser, *HMS Sussex*, in Sydney, was ordered to raise steam.

But her engines were undergoing maintenance work and most of the crew were ashore. The RAAF was unable to assist: none of its aircraft had the range to fly more than 100 miles out from the coast.

Aboard the *Southern Cross* no one expected to survive. They knew that the two engines couldn't possibly withstand the punishment of running at full power for ten hours. Taylor tried to even up the blades so that the dead propeller would idle with less vibration. He reached out with a hacksaw while Smithy, with extraordinary skill, semi-stalling the aircraft, nudged the damaged blade towards him. But every time he tried to cut the metal leading edge it slipped away in the air blast.

The events of this awful day, played out as they occurred before the world's media, were later to be fully chronicled by Taylor and Stannage. But there is no record of Smithy's own feelings as his life hung in the balance. The other two predictably portrayed him as a cool flying genius whose masterly handling of the aircraft kept them in the air against all the odds, when lesser aviators would have had them in the water. How did the constant fear of imminent drowning affect him? If his phobia at any point threatened his composure, neither he nor the others ever mentioned it. Yet Taylor had already seen him overwhelmed by it on this very same sea in the course of a quite normal flight. 'I'm not at all surprised that he coped that day,' said aviation psychiatrist Ken Craig. 'Paradoxically, people with panic disorders can often do miraculous things in extremis, as Kingsford Smith demonstrated during that potentially fatal spin at night in the middle of the Pacific. On the Tasman he obviously rose above the stress of the moment and what you might call his personal autopilot just took over. He was, after all, a most unusual man.'

Smithy never revealed the full horror of it to Mary or his family. He knew, of course, that Taylor was competent to take over the controls, but the reassuring presence of a co-pilot hadn't always been enough to quell his inner terrors. However, on this occasion it seems that he was able to hide them from the others with his standard aplomb. Stannage, who admitted, 'I was afraid, horribly afraid – not of death, but of the painful manner of it,' described how Smithy's unflappable presence at the controls encouraged him. Looking back over his hunched shoulders from time to time, he would grin through the door. 'His smile and wink from the cockpit helped tremendously.'

Two hours after they'd turned back they had crawled barely 120 miles toward the coast. With 480 miles to go, their pitiful progress was hampered even further by a stiff north-west wind. Under the strain and reduced cooling at slow speed, the port engine began to overheat and vibrate.

9.27 am. . . . Hell that port motor keeps spitting. Every time I feel she's going to quit and we'll go straight down. Smithy would drop her in, and we shall be able to float OK.

9.37 am. Going down, I think . . . Wait . . .

9.38 am. . . . No! She's right! Picked up again.

9.43 am. Smithy says he expects port motor to go any moment. The wind is rising and the sea is nasty. I would hate to go down in that. Could you please get a steamer to come out on our course and send up a big smoke.

The engines were fighting a losing battle. They were losing height again. By noon, when Smithy had been nursing the wounded plane for five hours, Taylor relieved him at the controls for the first time. They were still 300 miles from home. Their greatest concern was the port motor which was beginning to run out of oil. If it seized, the centre motor alone wouldn't keep them in the air for long. Back in the cabin Smithy appeared resigned to the inevitable. Stannage recalled that he came through, grim-faced, from the cockpit, making a thumbs-down gesture of despair. He shouted: 'Looks like we've collected it this time, old son. The port motor won't last another hour.' To underline the depressing finality of their situation, he began to take off his heavy flying suit. He then collected together in a pile, beneath the roof escape hatch, the tools – woodsaw, hacksaw and a small axe – he fondly believed were all they would need to saw off one of the wings to make a raft. He stuffed a rag into the vent of the cabin floor tank to limit flooding on ditching. 'These actions were a startling reminder,' Stannage said, 'that in a very short time we should probably be floating about on a wing – if we were lucky.' Yet, he added, 'it was good to be near Smithy. His very presence inspired confidence'. Smithy, cupping his hands round Stannage's ear, bellowed: 'Let's have a spot.'

I reached for a miniature bottle of whisky that some friends had given me as a joke, labelled 'Radio Operator's Moaning Fluid', and we drank a silent toast to each other – and to Bill's hardworking back.

'Now,' Smithy said, 'just one cigarette. It doesn't really matter any more if she does blow up, does it?' And, although smoking in flight was strictly *verboten*, we smoked.

I wouldn't have minded the least little bit dying with a man like that. It would have been an honour. I think that (what we thought) last smoke with Smithy was the most intensely dramatic moment of my life.

Before returning to the cockpit, Smithy briefed Stannage on the ditching drill. They would have to escape through the roof hatch, taking the tools for cutting off engines and wingtip. His parting words were: 'Take your boots off, Johnny. It's bad luck. But, we've had fun, haven't we?' Stannage added: 'Lots of people would think I was lucky, I suppose, being able to die in such exalted company.'

And die they almost certainly would have done. The notion that one half of the *Southern Cross*'s wing, free of its quarter-ton engine, would provide a temporary liferaft, which was first blandly mooted by Smithy on his 1928 Pacific flight, was hopelessly optimistic. 'The machine would lie in the sea, wing-deep, both outboard motors and the structure attaching them well and truly under the sea and under the wing, which would be awash,' said Taylor. 'I can think of more amusing occupations than diving under the wing with a hacksaw.'[1]

The thirty minutes which followed Smithy's farewell rites were the worst. The port motor, rapidly running out of oil, was spluttering badly.

12.12 pm. Port motor only last quarter of an hour. Going . . .
going . . . going—
    12.15 pm. She's going fast—
    12.16 pm Wait a sec . . . going down any minute.

For eight long minutes the operators ashore waited for a further tremor of Morse. They had almost begun to accept that there wouldn't be one when, at 12.24, they were puzzled to hear

Stannage report: 'Bill is trying to get oil out of the other engine. Stand by.' Then, at 12.54, 'Still in the air. Bill, the hero, climbed out and got oil for the dud motor.'

As the oil pressure of the smoking port engine had begun to drop below its normal 63lb per square inch to 35, Taylor had pulled off his heavy flying boots and tightly belted his leather flying coat. 'If we happened to survive the ditching . . . we would stay afloat just as long as we could go on swimming in a rough sea without lifejackets. There was a strong incentive to do something about oil for the port engine,' he recalled. There was only one source of spare oil: the dead starboard engine. He reckoned there must have been at least 9 gallons left in its tank. 'The obsession drives me with a strange confidence and the decision is a fixture in my mind. I have no idea how I'm going to get it, but just that if I can reach the tank behind the motor there must be a way.'[2]

Ignoring Smithy's attempts to dissuade him, Taylor tied one end of the slender mail cord round his waist and the other to a vertical steel tube in the cockpit. Then, in his stockinged feet, he climbed out through the right-hand opening immediately under the wing, aft of the windscreen. The cord was so thin that, had he fallen, it would never have held his weight. He found, however, that if he pressed his upper back against the wing the airflow helped to pin him there. In a huge effort of courage, he finally let go of the cockpit wall and, in a semi-crouch, facing the blast, began to edge his way towards the motor. The oil was in a tank in a cylindrical housing behind the engine. Hanging on with one arm, Taylor squatted on his haunches and set about wrenching free the side cover of the metal nacelle. The whole panel flew away in the airstream. There, in front of him, was his objective: the hexagonal-headed brass oil-drain plug. But he hadn't brought a tool to turn it. He looked hopefully towards the cockpit, and there was Stannage in anticipation, leaning out holding the one shifting spanner that had not been jettisoned.

Taylor stood up and, without releasing his hold on the strut, reached across and just managed to grasp it. He then sat astride the strut. Putting his left arm round one of the engine supports, he was able to attack the drain plug with both hands. To his relief it yielded to the first twist, which broke the wire seal, and he speedily unthreaded it with his fingers. All he needed now was a receptacle. The only two suitable things Stannage had been able to find were the small leather suitcase in which he carried his radio tools and spares and a Thermos flask. He banged the flask to smash and shake out the glass, and handed it out to Taylor, taking back the spanner. Hooked round the vertical strut, Taylor hung on with his legs, leaving both hands free to hold the flask and unscrew the plug. It was not difficult, but the airstream blew the oil away as soon as it emerged from the plughole. He jammed the container tightly up to the drain hole, filled it, then reinserted the plug, but the moment he passed the Thermos out from the shelter of his body to Stannage's waiting hands the slipstream whipped nearly half the oil away.

In the cockpit Stannage poured what remained into his case and handed the container back. Taylor squeezed in the top of the flask to reduce the wastage and repeated the collection procedure several times. But the job was still only half done. Now he had to get the half gallon of vital fluid out to the dying port motor. Splattered in oil, his neck pressed against the front of the wing and his feet inching sideways, he made his cautious way back to the fuselage along the now dangerously slippery beam. 'I watched aghast,' said Stannage. 'It was the bravest thing I had ever seen done.'

Back inside the plane Taylor was so paralysed by cold and exhaustion that he was unable to move. The port oil pressure was now down to 10lb and Smithy, worried that Taylor was too shattered to complete the transfer, moved over from the left to the right-hand seat and motioned Stannage to complete the operation. Few accounts of the events of that day acknowledged Stannage's own bravery in attempting to get the oil out to the ailing motor. He was too modest to mention it publicly himself, until nine years later, when he privately published his memoirs, *High Adventure*. At the time, he was in no doubt that he was going to his death.

As Taylor lay on the cabin fuel tank struggling for breath like a stranded fish, the terrified Stannage pulled off his boots and forced himself to climb out of the port cockpit opening and lower his feet on to the spar. The blast nearly swept him off his perch. Taylor, on the starboard side, had had only the backwash from the centre engine to contend with; Stannage was faced with the full fury of two motors. Flattened against the side of the fuselage, he was quite unable to move. He just clung, petrified, to the edge of the cockpit. A smaller man than Taylor, his neck didn't reach up to the front of the wing. 'I had nothing to hold me for that two-foot shuffle between handgrips and the plain truth of it was I hadn't the courage to try it even if I'd been tall enough. So I crawled back into the cockpit.'

Taylor had now recovered sufficiently to have a go himself, but he fared no better than Stannage. As the pressure needle twitched down to zero, Smithy hit upon a new strategy. He signalled to Taylor that he would alternately climb and descend to allow him to get out while the port engine was briefly throttled back in the glide. It worked. In the moments of descent, when the Fokker dropped so low that it was almost skimming the waves, Taylor poured in the oil, passed out to him in the Thermos by Stannage. 'We lose a lot as the airstream sucks it out – but there is still more than half in the tin when I shepherd it in behind the motor, cup my hand to the filler opening, squeeze the top of the tin and upend its contents into the tank.' A moment later there came 'shouts and waving from the cockpit. Pressure! Oil pressure on the gauge. John Stannage holds his hands out with his thumbs up.'

For the time being the transfusion had given the port engine a new lease of life, but in accomplishing it, they had almost dropped to the sea and Smithy had to climb again. 'I feel,' wrote Taylor, 'a magnificent exhilaration . . . There comes a reckless enjoyment of the situation, something which makes me want to stand and shout and laugh at the roaring mass of air that tears at everything around me.' In several more switchbacks, as the aircraft clawed for height then sank back almost to the wavetops, he emptied the entire gallon from the suitcase. Stannage's radio messages told Sydney: 'Bill Taylor is world's greatest hero.' Although no one fully understood why, the signal prompted fresh billboards to be rushed on to the streets declaring 'TAYLOR'S HEROIC ACT'.

But Taylor's heroism had only temporarily relieved their perilous situation. Nearly half of the gallon of oil had blown away and they were still over 180 miles from the coast. The faltering motor would need to be supplied again if it was to last three more hours. The engine at full power was devouring oil at the rate of a full gallon an hour. Taylor knew that he would soon have to repeat the whole frightening exercise. And the Thermos had begun to split down one of its seams. Stannage tore up one of his shirts and secured it round the flask with his tie.

By this time the centre engine, their one constant source of power, was at last rebelling. Its steady note had started to flutter and quiver; it, too, was getting low on oil. There was no possible means of reaching it in flight. All Taylor could do, sitting beside Smithy, oozing oil from his helmet to his feet and looking like some science-fiction swamp creature, was continue to keep the port motor alive. In all he made six round trips, twelve awesome journeys into the slipstream. After the second, when it became obvious that oil alone would not be enough to keep them in the air, Smithy finally ordered Stannage to jettison the mail. The wireless-operator couldn't get back to the cabin fast enough to hurl the bags out. They began to creep back to 500ft. Although he was far too loyal to have dreamed of saying so at the time, Taylor privately believed that Smithy had quite unnecessarily imperilled their lives by stubbornly hanging on to the mail for more than six hours. 'I consider that Kingsford Smith would have been perfectly justified in dumping it all immediately . . . Instead he held it at the expense of extra fuel which would have simplified our return passage,' he commented later. 'When the trouble first happened I was in favour of casting everything overboard. I asked Sir Charles for instructions and he said, "Everything except the mail – under no circumstances must the mail go." That shook me up rather.'[3]

The mail bags weighed over 100lbs (nearly 50kg). Although the port engine probably wouldn't have lasted to Sydney even if Smithy had got rid of the mail as soon as the crisis struck, certainly fewer hazardous oil replacements would have been needed.

Through the afternoon, the 'old bus' limped painfully towards Sydney. The prime minister, Joseph Lyons, away in London, instructed that progress reports be telephoned to his hotel regularly during the northern hemisphere night. Mary, fearful of the state in which Chilla would return, asked his GP, Dr Matthew Banks, to go with her to the aerodrome to meet the aircraft.[4] As they approached the coast, Taylor climbed out to complete his final oil transfer. 'Smithy was against my making this last passage,' he wrote, 'and said that rescue would now be certain if we went into the sea. I wasn't sufficiently convinced of this to consider the risk worthwhile.' He made no mention of what Stannage

afterwards told investigators: that Smithy had decided that, if
Taylor had fallen into the Tasman on any of his oil excursions, he
would immediately have ditched the *Southern Cross* in the water
beside him. But the likelihood of Taylor, with no lifejacket and
encumbered by his heavy flying coat, being able to reach the
briefly floating, disintegrating aeroplane would have been
extremely small, as indeed would the chances of the other two.
Smithy may have reasoned that, if Taylor went, all hope of keeping the port engine functioning would go with him and they
would end up in the sea anyway.

With the centre motor almost out of oil and the port engine
threatening to seize at any moment, they crossed the coast at
Cronulla, south of Botany Bay, and flew north to Mascot for a textbook three-point landing. It was four o'clock, and they had been in
the air for more than fifteen hours. The last nine none of them had
expected to survive. In all the punishing experiences of his life,
Smithy had never before been poised for so long on the brink of
the death he most feared. But nowhere did he ever write about
what it did to him. All he said, casually, in his autobiography, of
their safe return was: 'Never did Mother Earth seem so sweet.' As
he taxied the oil-streaked 'old bus', with its smashed propeller, up
to the hangar, the plane was rushed by a crowd of reporters and
newsreel cameramen. When the engines had fallen silent there
was an awed hush. The three aviators had to be physically helped
from the aircraft. Smeared in oil, they filed out like automatons.
They couldn't hear the clapping and shouted congratulations.
Kingsford Smith 'emerged from the plane,' said one reporter, 'like
a man from the dead. His face was expressionless.' Beau Sheil
went up to him and, grasping his hands affectionately, said, 'Great
work, Smithy,' but 'Sir Charles just stared blankly' at him. For the
first time at the end of a flight, he was for some moments quite
unable to speak. When words eventually came, he was heard to say
grimly, 'That old Tasman tried to kill me – but it can't.' He was,
Stannage wrote, 'tired almost to his very soul'. Mary and Dr Banks
took him in their arms and gently steered him to a waiting car.
Banks firmly forbade any interviews.

Back at Greenoaks Avenue someone poured Smithy a drink
and Mary ran a bath for him. Some time later, aware that the
sounds of splashing had died away, she went in to see if he was all

right. 'It was just as well,' she recalled. 'He had slid down and was fast asleep with his mouth under the water. What an irony to have finished that day drowning at home!' In Longueville Catherine hadn't left the radio until she heard that they had crossed the coast. 'They were very near to death,' she wrote. 'Southern Cross arrived about 4 pm crippled and done. She brought them home safely though.'

It was to be the Fokker's last long-distance flight. In the aftermath some newspapers began a campaign for greater tangible recognition of Smithy's achievements. The government was urged to buy the *Southern Cross* for preservation as a national treasure, paying him enough to buy a modern airliner to operate a reliable Tasman service. But the reality was that another of Kingsford Smith's highly publicised expeditions had come close to calamity. The fact that thousands of people's letters had been dropped into the ocean, and shippers had lost their cargo, had been a poor advertisement for a Kingsford Smith Tasman airline.

Taylor and Stannage were up and about next day, but Smithy, ill, exhausted and depressed, stayed in bed, receiving no visitors, on the orders of Dr Banks. The disaster had left him £1,000 out of pocket, and dismayed that he had let down his customers. He offered to take the seven surviving mail bags to New Zealand the following day in *Faith in Australia*, but the Postal Department declined his gesture. Instead, while the newspapers published sentimental poems expressing public relief, Smithy made a broadcast to the nation which was followed by a special thanksgiving service at St Mark's Church at the top of Greenoaks Avenue. Obligingly, he went along. But he was, at heart, despite – or perhaps because of – his enforced indoctrination at St Andrew's, not a religious man. 'Mother told me,' said Charles Arthur, 'that he was pretty indifferent to any organised practice. She believes that he would never have been moved to pray, even under "foxhole" conditions of mortal danger. Religious belief of any sort, affecting behaviour and decisions, was never central to his life. To me that seems profoundly sad – I have been an evangelical Christian most of my adult life.'

Defence minister Parkhill, who had opposed the Tasman flight in the first place, instructed the civil-aviation controller to order a full inquiry. The three-man group, headed by an RAAF wing commander, was mainly concerned with the cause of the incident and devoted most of its time to the maintenance history of the engines and the failed exhaust-pipe welding.

At the end of May 1935 Smithy was, at thirty-eight, almost back where he had started before the Pacific flight had made him famous. He no longer had a company, he had no air-route licence, no job, an aircraft that was no longer safe for oceanic flight – and he was again in debt. To make matters worse, in an echo of Coffee Royal, there were whispers that the Tasman fiasco had been a stunt contrived for personal publicity. The allegations this time were so absurd that no newspaper dared take them seriously, yet the unkind accusations lived on. In the early 1990s, when I appealed in Australian newspapers for people who knew Kingsford Smith to contact me, a letter came from a retired airline captain in Melbourne to say that the legendary oil transfer, which eventually earned Taylor the George Cross,[5] was physically impossible and could never have been made. He cited an attempt that was made to recreate Taylor's feat in 1985, during the filming of *A Thousand Skies*, the TV mini-series about Smithy's life. The production company had simulated the event on the ground, using a full-sized model of the *Southern Cross*, realistic in major detail, and a fan to reproduce the effects of the slipstream. It had proved impossible, according to the former captain, either to collect or to pour the smallest drop of oil in a Thermos flask. The wind had blown it away at every attempt. He said that a number of pilots of his generation, trained in the 1930s, had believed that the whole episode had been a hoax perpetrated for publicity.

The pilot of the *Southern Cross* model – which, unlike the flying replica later built in Adelaide, was capable only of taxiing – was a distinguished Second World War and former airline captain with over 23,000 hours. He preferred not to be named, but wrote to explain his doubts: 'The wind machine generated a strength of approximately 30–35mph and we found it impossible to pour any oil at all into the tank. It was blown all over the actor, the wing and the tarmac. It was just as bad with the engine idling and no wind machine.'

The uncertainty this raised bothered me. It was as if the veracity of the first ascent of Everest by Hillary and Tenzing was being queried forty years after the event. In fairness to Taylor's memory,

I decided to seek the opinions of John Kingsford-Smith, who had flown out to meet the *Cross* that afternoon, and Bruce Cowan, who had worked on her engines both immediately before and after the unhappy flight. John said:

I've never heard anything so preposterous. Of course the oil was transferred. It's irrelevant what happened during filming. The simple fact is that if Taylor hadn't succeeded in doing it they just wouldn't have got back. I went into the cabin immediately after they landed. There was oil all over the place – on the floor, in the cockpit, along the sides of the fuselage. Are people to believe they went to all that trouble, including showering Taylor from head to foot with the stuff, just to make a story? It defies understanding.

Bruce Cowan agreed.

I knew those engines well. The port certainly wouldn't have lasted way over fifteen hours, ten of them running flat out, on its original 11 gallons. On the simple arithmetic of consumption it would have burned over 9 gallons coming back alone. Some oil *must* have been added in flight. I can tell you that when I checked it over after they got back there was damn all left. What's also pretty relevant was the amount left in the starboard tank. It normally burned around half a gallon an hour at cruising revs and had been running less than seven hours when it was stopped. It should therefore have arrived back with seven or eight gallons unconsumed. When I looked there was barely a couple of gallons. So where did it all go?

So incensed was Bruce Cowan that he got his wife to drive him down the Gold Coast to Elanora to visit Taylor's widow, Lady Taylor, and took a photograph for me of the famous Thermos, which the family had kept all these years. The picture shows the holy grail still wrapped in Stannage's shirt, dyed completely brown by oil, tied up like a bouquet with his blue patterned tie. 'And would you believe it, after all those years it still reeked of oil,' Cowan said.[6]

'It's important to remember,' wrote a prominent 'Early Bird', Bill Booth, of Perth, 'that we are looking at the Scotts and Shackletons of aviation exploration – men larger than modern experience allows us to understand.' Booth, a retired airline captain with a formidable 28,000 hours, went on to say that the perils that lurked on every major flight Smithy made were beyond the comprehension of today's long-haul captains, to whom, in an entire career in the cockpit, 'the worst thing that may happen is getting cold coffee'. He concluded with a significant piece of information. For many years, he said, he had faithfully preserved within the pages of a book a sliver of glass, one of a number of fragments from the famous flask. They had been found in 1945 by RAAF mechanics working on the *Southern Cross*'s engines at the air force's Canberra base, where the 'old bus' was then stored. The tiny shards had lain for ten years in the sludge of the port engine, silent proof of Taylor's bravery.[7]

27

Final Flight
1935

The near-disaster over the Tasman forced Smithy to accept that the aeroplane which was so intimately woven into his own legend had become a liability. 'She had flown 300,000 miles and, like me, was getting old. That last gruelling experience . . . was, I felt, the last service I could expect from her. She was now definitely worn-out, and out-of-date – but I was strongly averse to sending her to the scrap-heap.' Because he badly needed the money he hoped that the government would buy her for the National Museum. After some haggling, he accepted £3,000, on condition that she should never be flown again. It was agreed that she would be stored at the RAAF's Richmond base outside Sydney until space could be found at the Canberra air station. Smithy pleaded for a cheque urgently, but when officials came to draw up the purchase agreement they had difficulty establishing to their total satisfaction that he actually owned the aircraft. It took more than half a year for the money to be paid.

But despite mounting financial worries and the mental scars of the Jubilee mail nightmare, he stubbornly turned his attention yet again to the Tasman. 'I was quite confident that the failure had been due to a simple and trifling circumstance which really had no bearing whatever on the feasibility of a regular service,' he said cheerfully. 'After all it was one chance in a thousand that one of our propeller blades should have been damaged in mid-ocean.' In the first week of June he registered a new company, the Trans-Tasman Air Service Development Company Ltd, to capitalise a Tasman airline and seek operating licences from the

two governments. It was formed with the modest share capital of
£75.

The founding shareholders were Smithy and the small circle of
close mates who still worshipped at his feet: Bill Taylor, John
Stannage, and Beau Sheil. It was agreed that Sheil would act as
their business manager. The company was launched from Smithy's
office at the Vacuum Oil Company with an operating loan of
£500. Frustrated by the delay in payment for the *Southern Cross*,
he even discussed with Catherine selling 'Kuranda' to produce
some ready cash. In the end he couldn't quite bring himself to do
this, for it was now also the roof over Leofric's family, and managed to borrow the £500 from somewhere.

The company planned a twice-weekly Tasman service using
Sikorsky S-42 flying boats. To overcome the American aircraft
objection, Smithy this time offered to have them built under
licence in Britain. He announced that if the two governments
would subsidise the operations, his company would find its own
capital of £150,000 for two flying boats. The proposal created
immediate shockwaves at Qantas and Imperial, still planning their
own Tasman service with a New Zealand partner. Once again they
were afraid that Kingsford Smith's megastar status might win over
the respective governments. Imperial Airways appealed to the
British director-general of civil aviation to help them fight off this
new threat, and the Australian and New Zealand governments
were virtually instructed to look at the new British flying boat
'before seriously considering Sir Charles Kingsford Smith's offer'.[1]

In Sydney Albert Rudder began once more to stir his poisoned
chalice. He wrote to the New Zealand postmaster-general, Adam
Hamilton, describing the Trans-Tasman Development Company's
proposals as 'hysterical nonsense' and an attempt 'to have a finger
in the pie'. He concluded: 'This great Empire service will not be a
complete success unless selfish interests are entirely excluded.'[2]
Meanwhile, Smithy, unaware of the consternation his Tasman proposals were creating, was privately becoming increasingly
depressed by the setbacks he was suffering. 'His whole temperament seemed to change,' Mary said. 'His nerves became stretched
to the point where he would explode at a touch. This wasn't the
Chill I'd known. Neither were the long withdrawn silences or the
rows we found ourselves having for the first time. He was getting

really desperate, for he saw the Tasman as his last chance for a financially secure future.'

There was something else eating Smithy at this time, according to Mary's friend Molly Hudson. Molly, now married to a tea-planter in Ceylon, had earlier in the year come back to Melbourne on holiday. She was surprised to get a phone call from Smithy, who had come down from Sydney on business and was staying at Menzies Hotel.

> He sounded a bit tense and asked if we could meet. So I went along to Menzies and we sat in one of the lounges for tea. He looked terribly strained. He said he suspected that Mary had been unfaithful during his absences from Sydney. Tongues had been wagging about her relationship with one of her tennis partners. I was flabbergasted. This was not Mary's style at all. I had known her almost all my life and she was definitely not the type who ever played around. I told him so, saying it was ridiculous because I knew that Mary loved only him. I think it helped, but he'd obviously become very jealous and unhappy. He seemed to have lost all his old *joie de vivre*. I didn't think he looked at all well.[3]

Mary was well aware of the rumours. 'I know who started the whole preposterous thing. This one woman spread stories about me when Chill wasn't in town. I believe it was jealousy. It was absurd, of course. Chill knew full well I wasn't capable of doing a thing like that. If he hadn't been away so constantly there'd have been nothing for him to brood about.' On the contrary there was, together with the impending completion of their luxurious new house, something else to induce Smithy to spend more time at home: in July 1935 Mary was pregnant again, a particular joy, since she had suffered a miscarriage in 1933. 'But almost as soon as he'd heard the good news he was starting to pack his bags again.'

Exasperated by the lack of response from either government to his proposals, he announced that he was off to London to try to raise the capital for the first Sikorsky there. He planned to go via Los Angeles to collect the unsold *Lady Southern Cross*, fly her to New York, ship her to London, obtain a British registration and certificate of airworthiness acceptable in Australia – and make a record flight home, lowering Scott and Black's time to Darwin to less than two days. He was sure that such a resounding achievement would guarantee the Tasman licence.

For the record attempt he'd chosen Tom Pethybridge as his co-pilot. Pethybridge didn't have the Lockheed on his licence and had never flown the England–Australia route, but Smithy wanted him for his skill and devotion as a mechanic. A small, amiable, wiry young man with curly hair, he had a fondness for women that, like his permanently cheerful expression, rivalled Smithy's, and was a hugely popular figure at Mascot. Unlike his boss, however, he did not smoke or drink. He is said to have venerated Kingsford Smith to a degree described by several people as touching. Pethybridge and his fellow mechanic, Bob Boulton, had already sailed for Los Angeles to prepare the Altair for the flight. Smithy booked his own passage for Thursday 18 July. Although he was still waiting for his £3,000, he arranged to deliver the 'old bus' to the government before joining his ship.

For this final emotional flight from Mascot to Richmond he donned his air commodore's uniform, climbing aboard with a hand-picked group of passengers drawn from his magic circle: Mary, Bill Taylor, John Stannage, Beau Sheil, the Reverend Colin Scrimgeour, an old New Zealand friend, and, in memory of the man who had made him a celebrity, Charles Ulm's fourteen-year-old son, John, who sat in the co-pilot's seat his father had so often occupied in the turbulent days of the famous partnership. Escorted by six RAAF Hawker Demons, Smithy flew via Georges Heights, where he circled and dipped in salute over Keith Anderson's grave, then to Longueville, where, banking steeply over Arabella Street, he looked down at 'Kuranda' to see the small figure of Catherine standing outside waving. At Richmond the defence minister declared: 'The *Southern Cross* now becomes the property of every Australian.' Smithy, fighting back the tears, replied that, as she 'couldn't express her appreciation of being acquired by the nation, I will answer for her'. He took a step back, looked up at the cockpit and saluted. 'To you, old friend, farewell.'[4]

It was the end of a truly Olympian era. He knew that his own flying days, too, were coming to an end, hastened by his declining health. The Jubilee mail flight had damaged him more than he would admit, leaving him even more restless, insecure and nervous than before. There were persistent rumours that he had a stomach ulcer. Mary cannot remember him complaining of this, but he may have wished not to alarm her. All she can recall is that around this time he put himself, unprecedentedly, on a strict diet. But he didn't always tell her when something took him to the doctor.

In the early afternoon he drove away from the Cross for the last time, bound for the Sydney docks, where he boarded the *Aorangi*, the ship on which he had first set eyes on Mary five years earlier. She stood now on the wharf with Catherine, amid the fluttering paper streamers, holding Charles Arthur's hand, watching her husband recede down the harbour. It was to be the last time she would ever see him.

Breaking his journey in New Zealand, Smithy went to meet the acting prime minister, Sir Alfred Ransom, and his Cabinet to make a further plea for his Tasman service. It was rejected. New Zealand, Ransom was to say in a press statement, could not, 'without embarrassing' the British plans, 'become prematurely committed to a separate Tasman scheme at this stage'. On 16 August, as Smithy's ship neared San Francisco, Archdale Parkhill announced the Australian verdict: Sir Charles' Tasman scheme was 'both very expensive and unnecessary'. Cabinet had decided to go with the Imperial Airways plan. With two stunning blows every one of Smithy's Tasman aspirations had been killed stone dead.

Still refusing to give up, he now resolved to launch an independent Tasman service without government help. He arranged to meet Sheil in London to raise the capital. But, reunited with the *Lady Southern Cross* at Burbank, it seems that his objectives became confused. The sight of the Altair had him immediately torn between the task of funding a major airline and the whim of seeking yet more personal glory by smashing the England–Australia record – despite the nightmare consequences that the Australian import ban would create on arrival. It seemed that he had come to live his life desperately from day to day, his mind and his enthusiasms leaping with erratic abandon from one project to another. For he now tried to get the *Lady Southern Cross* converted at Lockheed into an Orion – an equally embargoed Australian import. As he had no money to pay Lockheed for the six-seat cabin, the company offered him one for half-price. But when he cabled Stannage to expedite the government's £3,000 payment for the 'old bus', the latter replied that there was still a major hitch in completing the purchase. The crown law officials had not yet established the history of the aircraft's legal ownership from its acquisition from Hubert Wilkins, through its various mortgagings, its gifting by Allan Hancock, and the share deal by which Smithy had acquired her from Ulm. As there was clearly no immediately foreseeable money from this source, he cancelled the Orion conversion.

'I am seriously tempted,' he wrote dejectedly to Beau Sheil in Sydney that month, 'to sell at a colossal sacrifice – about 10,000 dollars (£2,500).' So disenchanted was he, he added, that he was considering abandoning the record attempt and shipping the machine home by the next boat. However, when he called Stannage to inquire whether the civil aviation department would allow him to fly the aircraft in Australia, the answer was a firm no. Once again the Altair had become an expensive liability.

Yet there was a way round the impasse: ship the Altair to Britain, where American aircraft were permitted, and apply there for a British registration and airworthiness certificate – which would be recognised in Australia. Although he barely had the £200 Atlantic freightage, he knew that this was now his only option if he wanted to attack the record.

The Altair left New York for London on a Swedish freighter, the *Dalhem*, on 21 September. Pethybridge and Boulton travelled with the aircraft while Smithy went ahead on the liner *Britannic* to meet Sheil. At the London docks the *Lady Southern Cross* was lowered by a floating crane on to two Thames barges lashed together and towed down the river to a beach near the tiny village of Allhallows on the Isle of Grain on the north Kent coast. Here, at low tide, it was manhandled ashore on planks and pulled on ropes a few yards inland across the marshes to a rough, grassy field, from which Smithy flew her the 35 miles across south-east London to Croydon Airport. He hurried from Croydon to the Air Ministry in Kingsway to apply for the vital British certificates.

The *Lady Southern Cross* had arrived in England still fitted with the eleven fuel tanks providing the 514-gallon illegal capacity with which he and Taylor had flown the Pacific. This huge petrol weight had, of course, been approved by no one. The American certificate of airworthiness firmly limited the all-up weight to its original at the time of purchase before the addition of a single tank. Without bothering to request any load tests to satisfy the authorities that the aircraft was safe to fly at the much higher weights he would need to match Scott and Black's giant hops to Australia, he had blithely taken it to England. The madness of the air-race formalities was about to begin all over again.

At the Air Ministry Smithy was politely told that the Altair could become a British-registered aircraft – it was quickly issued with the letters G-ADUS – but that the certificate of airworthiness could only perpetuate the American fuel-weight limits. He was granted a dismal 145 gallons. Moreover, this limit was subject to the drastic condition that all the long-range tanks were blanked off or removed and the rear cockpit sealed to eliminate any possibility of adding the weight of a second occupant. Smithy – who, according to Sheil, was now in a highly testy and reactive state – flew into a rage and demanded that he be certificated, as a special concession, at least to 300 gallons, to allow him to fly non-stop from London to Baghdad as the Comets had done. The officials wouldn't budge. If there was to be any chance of raising the authorised fuel load, he was told, he would need to fly the Altair the short distance to the Royal Aircraft Establishment at Farnborough in Hampshire for undercarriage stress and structural tests. It was not an altogether unreasonable condition, but Smithy, fearing that the *Lady Southern Cross* might fail such clinical examination, declined this invitation.

Both he and Sheil refused to see it as an issue of safety. Rather they appear to have viewed it, in almost paranoid fashion, as a British conspiracy to prevent a colonial pilot in an American aircraft breaking the British-built Comet's record. 'Smithy felt this kind of thing,' Sheil said. 'Not only was this pin-pricking humiliating to a man who knew more about flying an aircraft than these petty officials could ever hope to know, but it was making him irritable and nervy.'

When the Air Ministry cabled the Department of Aeronautics in Washington seeking a one-off special certificate for the flight with all tanks full, the American officials replied that at that weight the aircraft's airworthiness could not be guaranteed. On 12 October, he was again offered load tests at the Royal Aircraft Establishment. Astoundingly he still refused. After days of argument, during which he grew visibly greyer and more unwell, the Air Ministry agreed that his long-range tanks could remain on board unfilled and that the rear cockpit could be left open. At least Pethybridge could now go with him, and although Air Ministry inspectors would prevent him from contravening the fuel ban, once out of their jurisdiction he could fill the long-range tanks. Secretly he devised a plan to fly to Marseilles and take on all he needed there.

While all this was going on Smithy and Sheil had been talking to a potential fairy godmother. The British Pacific Trust was a London investment company with a finger in a host of aviation pies around the world. With elegant offices in St James's Square and a board bristling with peers and knights – including Lord Southborough, Sir Maurice Bonham Carter and a well-known long-distance aviator, Lord Sempill – the firm had acquired interests in both aircraft-manufacturing and airlines. To realise its ambitious plans to operate long-haul air services in competition with Imperial Airways, it had arranged with Sikorsky to build its thirty-passenger S-42 flying boats under licence in England. The company offered to underwrite £125,000 of the Trans-Tasman Air Service Development Company's capital on condition that it bought two of their British Sikorskys. The deal seemed to Smithy almost too good to be true. Not only would he have half the capital but the very airliner he wanted for the Tasman. But when he and Sheil went to see the flying boat's English manufacturer, they were in for a bitter disappointment. The factory had yet to be built – there wouldn't be a Sikorsky available for at least two years.

After this setback Smithy decided to set off with Pethybridge on the Australia record attempt, leaving Sheil to go on to America and try to float the Tasman company there. One cannot help but admire his unquenchable fortitude and persistence in the face of the overwhelming odds stacked against him. It must have been patently clear that the Tasman route would now be flown with the new Empire flying boats, once they were built, by an airline created by the three governments and operating as an extension of the Imperial–Qantas route. But beyond his native brilliance in the cockpit and his understanding of the sort of aircraft that airline operations now demanded, he was, by all accounts, at heart a simple and unsophisticated man. His interest in air routes still lay entirely in the aeroplanes that flew them. His office, Scotty Allan said, would undoubtedly 'quickly have become a place, as in the past, to answer his fan mail, play the ukulele and flirt with the secretaries while being late for appointments and passing most of the executive paperwork on to someone else'.

During that English autumn of 1935 Smithy's health was going further downhill. There is no longer any record of his precise medical condition, but from every description it would seem that he was heading for another nervous collapse. He had become depressed and anxious and, most unusually, he had begun to confide to Sheil that he didn't feel at all well. One of those seriously concerned about him was Freddie Kent, the Rollason Aircraft Company's technical director, who was responsible for the *Lady Southern Cross* at Croydon. 'Whenever he came into the hangar I was struck by how very nervous he always was, like a cat permanently on hot bricks. He seemed to do everything in such an excessively quick, nervous way, always fussing round the aircraft and getting in the way of Tommy Pethybridge, who didn't need any help. I remember thinking that he was definitely getting too old to fly such a fast and demanding machine as the Altair. He was certainly in no shape to tackle a 12,000-mile flight in one.'[5]

Bob Boulton was also worried. During the first half of October, he said, 'as a result of fatigue and illness, Smithy spent almost two weeks in hospital in London'.[6] This proved impossible to verify so long after the event. Mary, to whom he regularly spoke on the phone, had no memory of it. But it would have been typical of him not to have told her, she said, to avoid worrying her on the eve of a taxing flight.

He set Sunday 20 October as his departure date. By then the south-west monsoon would have retreated from the Bay of Bengal, the scene of some of his worst panic attacks. On the Saturday evening he and Pethybridge checked into the Croydon Airport Hotel, where they had a farewell dinner with Sheil and Boulton. The mood was subdued. Smithy was not his usual jolly eve-of-departure self. He was visibly in the grip of the pre-flight nerves he normally kept out of public view, which disturbed his colleagues. The familiar 'flu', triggered by the imminence of a stressful flight, struck suddenly, in the middle of dinner, and with such speed that he had difficulty finishing his meal. Sheil recalled:

He went to bed immediately after dining. About 2 am the night porter called me, saying Sir Charles was very ill. I went to Smithy's room. He was definitely a sick man. He had a temperature and was concerned about the people coming to the aerodrome to see him off. I told him that he would be all right if he had a few hours' sleep and gave him a hot drink and some aspirin. As soon as he was asleep I left him and sent a cable informing the Australian Broadcasting Commission, which had arranged to purchase exclusive progress reports, that the flight was postponed. His instructions, that he should be called early that morning to take off, I cancelled. It was unthinkable that he should fly.

Smithy didn't wake up until two o'clock in the afternoon. He was horrified that the flight had been cancelled, but was too ill to argue and allowed Sheil to call a doctor. The doctor, as all the others had done over the years at the point of Smithy's departures, diagnosed a 'severe chill' and ordered him to remain in bed for at least two days. Smithy didn't fight the decision. He knew he was too sick to fly safely. Indeed, in his heart, he no longer wished to make the journey at all. It didn't take Sheil long to persuade him to abandon the flight and take the Altair home by sea.

Unfortunately, they didn't have the passage money. Smithy asked Sheil to cable Stannage in Sydney to approach the Defence Department for a £300 advance on the £3,000, still, after nearly three months, owed for the *Southern Cross*. Stannage made an urgent phone call to Melbourne, raising the figure to £500. He didn't meet with much success. The department, he was told, was still seeking documentary evidence of ownership and was unable to commit government funds to a loan. It was, however, prepared to advance £500 if Sir Charles would agree to a lien on all his household furniture. When this suggestion reached Smithy he was livid. He refused point-blank. Sick or not, he told Sheil, he was now determined to fly home. He would leave within forty-eight hours.

He called Mary, who begged him to come home by sea. Now four months' pregnant, she worried that she mightn't see him again.

It was absurd, I told him, that for the sake of a few hundred pounds he should have to risk a flight he wasn't fit to make. That *Southern Cross* money wasn't the only source. In England there was Lord Nuffield, one of his great admirers, who'd just presented him with a brand new Wolseley car. He would have helped him out straight away. So would Daddy. He would've cabled the money and just debited it in his little black book. Chill knew this. But Daddy had helped him out so often and he was too proud to ask. He just kept saying, 'If only they'd pay up for the old bus I wouldn't need to do this.'

On Wednesday morning, 23 October, Charles Scott, whose seventy-one-hour record to Melbourne Smithy was bent on breaking, turned up at Croydon at dawn to wish him luck. So did two Australian pilots, Jimmy Broadbent and Jimmy Melrose, both also about to fly home, each in a Percival Gull, the former's being delivered to Bill Taylor. Melrose, a tall, debonair twenty-two-year-old with long lanks of flaxen hair, was that rare Australian phenomenon, a young man of well-financed leisure. He had already covered himself in glory the previous year when, in a Puss Moth, he had taken third place in the handicap section of the great air race.

As the *Lady Southern Cross* was rolled out of the hangar, Smithy talked with perceptive vision to reporters about the future of aviation. 'Within ten years,' he predicted, 'airliners carrying a hundred passengers will be flashing through the stratosphere, between 40,000 and 60,000 feet up, at 500 to 750 miles an hour. Sky giants of the future will have a range of 6,000 miles, able to reach almost any part of the earth non-stop. The internal combustion engine may have gone – it has too many moving parts.'[7] As he and Pethybridge climbed aboard, he called to the reporters: 'My kiddy in Australia is three. By the time he's old enough to pilot a machine, I shall be flitting over to England for the weekend. I'll be the passenger in the back. I'm now thirty-eight and, win or lose, this is my last record attempt – really my last.'

'As the first stroke of seven boomed out from the clock,' wrote Sheil, 'he opened the throttle. Before the last stroke had sounded he was off the ground, banking steeply round the control tower

and heading for Australia.' To defeat the Air Ministry's load limit
he went straight to Marseilles to take on enough fuel – 360 gallons – to go non-stop to Baghdad. But over the mountains of
Greece, north of the Gulf of Corinth, they flew into a violent
storm. They were hosed by frightening deluges of hail; ice built up
on the wings, blocking the pitot head and swinging their airspeed
needles to zero. Although he wasn't far from Athens, when Smithy
saw the hail carving into the plywood wing, he decided to turn
back. He diverted to Brindisi in Italy and later limped back to
Croydon.

He was now less enthusiastic than ever about 'the job', as he
called it. The near-miss over Greece had shaken his confidence in
his ability to go on surviving these endless skirmishes with death.
But, whatever his instincts were telling him, he insisted on having
another go. As soon as Pethybridge and Boulton had overhauled
the Altair, he said, he would be off again.

It is no longer easy to disinter the concerns for his safety felt by
his mates in England in that last week of October. Tom
Pethybridge wrote about it to his two brothers in Sydney. One of
them, Horrie, recalled a letter, which hasn't survived, written that
week from London. 'It was a cheerful note, full of excitement for
the big flight. But what sticks in my mind was the nagging worry
he said he had about Smithy's health. He hadn't seen him as crook
as this before. It was naturally making him a bit anxious.' Scotty
Allan's wife, Barbara, met Smithy in England around the end of
October. Her family's company, Tozer Kemsley Millbourn, had
been ANA's London agents, and she was at her parents' house in
Purley when her brother, Cecil, brought Smithy home from
Croydon Airport. 'I can still see him with what to me was such a
typical Australian face. I can't remember how well he looked that
day he was on the point of flying off, but what I do recall very
clearly is that he definitely did *not* want to go. We all just knew it.
I expect he'd told Cecil and that's how I heard.'[8]

Someone else who knew was the New Zealand pilot Jean
Batten, who was preparing to fly to South America. Whether or
not Smithy looked her up to seek solace, they certainly met in
London that October and it seems that he poured his heart out to
her. 'I thought he looked tired and rather frail,' she wrote.
'Although I wouldn't have dreamt of trying to dissuade him from

his latest record attempt, I did ask him why he needed to do it when he had already achieved so much. "I've got to do it, Jean," he told me, "I desperately need some money." But I sensed that he was not really at all happy about it.'[9]

'He most certainly wasn't,' Freddie Kent remembered. 'When he got back to Croydon after that first attempt, he looked quite terrible, so old and drawn you wouldn't have believed he was only thirty-eight. He was more twitchy than ever. In the hangar, while we repaired his damaged wing, he was openly admitting to dreading the second attempt.'

Of all those close to Kingsford Smith at this time, including his family, the only person with the insight to understand exactly what flying had done to him appears to have been Beau Sheil. He was the first publicly to draw attention to the fact that so many of the rigorous flights Smithy had undertaken over the previous five years had made him ill. 'Yet he had still made records . . . The "physical Smith" had cried a warning to the mind and spirit, "Give it up!" – but he had not given up and had gone on and conquered. He would do it again.' Sheil shared the popular view among Smithy's disciples that this very special man lived his life on a higher plane than average mortals could comprehend. 'Don't call this rashness or foolhardiness. There was something magnificent about this willingness of the spirit scorning the weakness of the flesh. It was the spirit of Smithy.' No suggestion was ever made, it seems, that what they saw as Smithy's magnificence might also be construed as selfishness and irresponsibility; that in setting out, diminished in mind and body, to satisfy his obsessive need for a new record, he was risking the life of a loving colleague.

On Sunday 3 November Sheil sailed from Southampton for New York. The Cord Tyre Company had shown some interest in the Tasman airline and the backers of Pan-American Airways had agreed to talk to them. Sheil badly wanted Smithy's enthusiasm and expertise at his elbow in New York. 'I told him that I couldn't accomplish much capital-raising in the US on my own and that Pan-Am would want to see him as well,' Sheil said later. 'But he was adamant that if he took off and broke the record, everyone interested would open their chequebooks while I was in the US. To me breaking records and trying to start an international airline were two totally unrelated things. His record attempt was totally unnecessary.'[10]

Smithy went down to the ship to say goodbye. At the dockside Sheil tried one last time to persuade him to abandon the flight, but he had made up his mind. 'I don't feel fit enough for the job,' he said, 'but I'm going to see it through.' Sheil knew that Smithy wasn't merely struggling to throw off a bout of flu. It was, he wrote, the catalogue of setbacks and disappointments that had destroyed his happiness from the day he was forced to retire from the Melbourne air race: the public criticism of his choice of American aircraft; the rejection of his Tasman proposals; the endless certification battles and futile wrangling with the Air Ministry.

No one knows for sure where he stayed in London during the first few days of November 1935, probably at the Royal Aero Club. He was seen on his last day in England lunching at the Athenaeum in Pall Mall with Lord Sempill, no doubt discussing the British Pacific Trust's involvement in the Tasman operation. Later that day he called Mary in Melbourne to tell her he'd received a good weather forecast and the moon was right; he would be starting from Lympne the next morning.

I tried again, on a very bad line, to stop him. His voice came through roars of static like the waves of the sea. I pleaded with him to get on the boat. I said I would come to Ceylon and meet him halfway. He admitted he was ill, but I knew that nothing I said would stop him. He just kept saying he wanted very desperately to get home to be with me. There was a sense of panic about the urgency, as if he couldn't hold out much longer.

In the late afternoon, to escape the London morning fog belt, Smithy and Pethybridge flew the *Lady Southern Cross* from Croydon to Lympne in Kent and spent the night at the Hythe Hotel nearby. At 5 am on Wednesday 6 November, a civil-aviation inspector checked the quantity of fuel they were taking and Pethybridge stowed in the locker a set of silk tyres he'd bought for his brother Horrie, a British empire cycle-racing champion. How much fuel Smithy left with is unclear. One report quoted it as 118 gallons, another 138 and a third as 145. Whatever the load it was barely sufficient, at the brisk cruising speed he planned, to get them to Athens, let alone to Baghdad. He told reporters that over

central France he would decide whether to press on to Athens or
divert again to Marseilles, where he would have no compunction
about filling all the tanks. He would notify his decision by radio –
he was again carrying a transmit-only set. 'There will be no turning back this time,' he told *The Times* man. 'We shall plod on.' To
another journalist he said: 'I want to see the sunshine again, but
most important of all, get back to my family.'[11]

It was still dark on that frosty morning when he and
Pethybridge, in fur-collared flying suits, helmets and goggles,
climbed aboard. The final photographs that were taken of them
show Smithy in the cockpit, looking pale in the newsreel arc lights,
leaning out to shake hands with officials and being given rolls of
maps and the aircraft's journey logbook. Bob Boulton pulled away
the chocks and shouted up to Smithy: 'Cheerio! see you in
Sydney!' Smithy called back: 'Sorry we haven't a third seat, Bob.'
As he taxied off into the dark the very last picture of all caught
him with an arm high in the air, waving. At 6.28 the *Lady Southern
Cross* was airborne and heading for Paris.

Helped by a tailwind, and climbing to 15,000ft, the most efficient altitude for the supercharger-boosted Wasp engine, they
made fast time across France, bowling along at 220mph. At 8.40
they were seen passing over Lyons 'at a great height'. They had
burned so little fuel that Smithy decided he could safely reach
Athens. He sent out a message that he wouldn't be going into
Marseilles. 'Everything is going well,' he told newspapermen in
Athens on his arrival at 4.30, eight hours from England. But were
they really? While the aircraft was being refuelled he was surprised to bump into his Atlantic co-pilot, Evert van Dijk, bringing
a KLM service through from the Dutch East Indies. 'Usually
Kingsford Smith was cheerful and confident, but on Wednesday he
struck me as being somewhat reserved,' the Dutch airline captain
commented when he got to Amsterdam.[12]

Early that evening Smithy and Pethybridge left Athens to press
on through the night to Baghdad. Although the ban on overflying
Turkey had not been lifted for this flight, it seems probable that he
ignored it and crossed the south of the country undetected in the
dark. Around dawn they touched down in Baghdad. From England
they had taken only an hour and a half longer than Scott and
Black, who had travelled to Baghdad non-stop in a direct line

across central Europe and the Black Sea. During their thirty-five minutes on the ground Smithy sent a cryptically brief and unhelpfully vague cable to the Australian Broadcasting Commission: 'ARRIVED BAGHDAD ALL WELL AND MACHINE FUNCTIONING PERFECTLY. EXPECT ARRIVE THREE OR FOUR DAYS.'

It was around 3.30 in the morning when they rose from the desert airfield and headed east on the 2,300-mile leg to Allahabad in northern India. For some reason they didn't, as Scott and Black had done, fly directly across Iran, but took the longer route via the Persian Gulf and Karachi, where they were seen passing overhead at around one o'clock in the afternoon of Thursday 7 November. Confirmation that they were probably at their 15,000ft intended cruise level came from the airport controller, who reported that 'it looked like a speck, identifiable only through field glasses'.[13]

It took the Altair, now battling against a strong headwind, the rest of the day to cross the hot northern Indian plains to Allahabad. They had lost time against Scott and Black on this thirteen-hour leg and now needed around three hours to catch up, which Smithy planned to save by cutting out the Comet's Charleville stop in Australia and flying from Darwin to Melbourne in one hop. At Allahabad they learned that the two other Australia-bound pilots, Broadbent and Melrose, both trying to break Smithy's 1933 England–Australia solo record, had passed through not long before. Up to that point they had been more or less flying the route together, meeting up at the end of each sector, but Broadbent, in the more powerful 6-cylinder Gull, had decided to push on ahead and had left the previous night. Melrose, in his lower-powered Gull 4 *Westley* (VH-UVH), had taken off shortly before three that Thursday morning. Before leaving Allahabad, Melrose had noted in his diary: 'The Altair flown by Kingsford Smith is now on our tails. He's after Scott's record and we are out to beat Kingsford Smith's 7 days 4 hours to Darwin.'[14]

As with all the brief stops Smithy made on this desperate flight, very little is recorded of the *Lady Southern Cross*'s transit of Allahabad's Bamrauli Aerodrome as a golden sun was sinking that evening. 'After a perfect landing,' said India's *Statesman* newspaper, 'Sir Charles rushed to the aerodrome office for a wash and refreshment and left for Singapore at 6.28 pm, one hour after his landing.'[15] Subsequent news stories reported merely that he left

Pethybridge to supervise the refuelling and that on his brief mission to the hangar office he paused to sign a woman's autograph book. While the engine was warming on the tarmac, in a shouted conversation between the ground and the cockpit, he gave his last interview, to a reporter from the *Pioneer* in Lucknow. He spoke of his determination to reach Singapore in faster time than Scott and Black; otherwise, the reporter wrote, he had little to say. All that was offered by the Melbourne *Herald*'s correspondent in Allahabad was that 'he hurried back to the plane with refreshments, and the plane rose amid cheers'. Nowhere has any reliable reference to his state of health survived. Later, partly arising from his significant failure to send even the barest progress message to the ABC from Allahabad, there was speculation that Smithy had become too unwell to fly the aircraft, and that Pethybridge had taken her off. But this rumour was undoubtedly a misconception based on the fact that Pethybridge occupied the rear cockpit, from which people were used to seeing small biplanes flown. He had never made a take-off in the powerful and tricky-to-handle Altair, and Smithy would certainly not have risked asking him to do so at this critical juncture – on the verge of nightfall, with the plane heavily fuel-burdened for the 2,200-mile non-stop flight to Singapore and from a position in which forward visibility was dangerously restricted. Only in the air would Pethybridge have taken the controls to relieve Smithy in cruising flight in alternating spells.

As they headed eastwards towards Calcutta, 470 miles away, they would have climbed slowly, labouring under their great load, back to their optimum cruising level, which was probably again between 10,000 and 15,000ft. They made good time to Calcutta, where they were sighted by aerodrome staff over Dum Dum Airport shortly after 9 pm and correctly identified in the moonlight as 'a low-winged monoplane'. Then they headed south-east, out across the Bay of Bengal, to Akyab (now Sittwe) on the coast of north Burma. Happily, it was not the sort of night on that notorious stretch of sea to bring the terrors Smithy had previously experienced there. The drenching south-west monsoon had been succeeded by a dry, north-east airstream rolling down from the cooling interior of China. The night was fine and the moon, nearly full, was low in the west, an hour off setting.[16] The sea was almost dead calm.

Less than two hours from Calcutta they picked up the lights of Akyab. The aerodrome staff there had stayed on duty specially and kept the boundary lights on and a kerosene flarepath lit. They logged the Altair's time overhead as 11.50 pm. They saw a torch signalling from the aircraft as it turned to pick up the new south-east heading for Rangoon. Melrose, already in Rangoon, had spent several hours resting at Mingaladon Aerodrome that evening in the hope that Kingsford Smith might arrive. But when midnight came and there was still no sign of the *Lady Southern Cross*, he decided to press on through what remained of the night to Victoria Point (now Kawthaung) on the Burma–Siam border, or, fuel permitting, to Alor Star in northern Malaya. He left Rangoon at 12.45 on the morning of Friday 8 November. According to his diary, he flew out across the Gulf of Martaban into 'a clear moonlight night and ideal flying weather'.[17]

The Altair, which cruised at around a mile a minute faster than the Gull, soon caught up with him. Smithy, whose groundspeed was now approaching 190mph, had made fast time southward across Burma and was reported passing over Rangoon Airport at 1.30 am, forty-five minutes later. It appears that the Altair was not actually seen, but the aerodrome staff, who had lit a flarepath in case he wanted to land, heard it go over. Since the *Lady Southern Cross* and Melrose's Gull were the only aircraft airborne in Burma airspace that night, and the time coincided with the Altair's notional estimated time of arrival, there can be little doubt that it was Smithy.

On to which heading he turned over the lights of Rangoon will never be known for sure, but as all the evidence points to the fact that he was flying his big sectors from point to point at safe ter-rain-clearance heights of at least 10,000ft, he would not have been map-reading his way mile by mile along coastlines but, for effi-ciency, flying direct compass courses. To improve on Scott and Black's time to Singapore, and as the weather over the Gulf of Martaban was fine and cloudless, it is almost certain that he now flew more or less straight down the Malay Peninsula – a heading, in its early stages, quite close to Melrose's course to Alor Star or Victoria Point.

Aware of this, Melrose, for safety, switched on the Gull's navi-gation lights, which he didn't normally bother to do in remote areas. He was soon glad he had for, to his huge excitement, at what must have been about 2.50 am local time, around 250 miles from Rangoon, over the Andaman Sea off the coast of southern Burma, another aircraft overtook him.[18] As soon as he saw it go by, about 200ft above him, and at a much greater speed, he flashed his lights on and off in a frantic greeting. But the other plane was already ahead of him, and no answering signal came. As it receded rapidly southward, Melrose noticed the glow of its twin exhausts. There was not the least doubt in his mind that it was the *Lady Southern Cross*.

If it was, he was the last person capable of identifying the aircraft ever to see it. The Altair was due to reach Singapore soon after dawn. It did not arrive; nor was there the briefest crackle of a radio message from it. Somewhere in the jungle of the Malay Peninsula, or in the surrounding oceans, Charles Kingsford Smith and Tom Pethybridge, in the early-morning dark of Friday 8 November 1935, had vanished.

The Search and the Tributes
1935

The search went on for ten days. Every mile of the route between Rangoon and Singapore was combed by Royal Air Force aircraft sent out from Singapore. Showers of leaflets, offering in local languages a big reward for news of the Altair, were dropped on to every village, mine and plantation. The search was joined by a QEA DH86 airliner flown by Scotty Allan, and by Jimmy Melrose in his Gull.

On landing in Singapore that Friday morning Melrose had leaped out and demanded, 'Where's Kingsford Smith?' Surprised to find that Smithy hadn't passed through hours earlier, he had hurried to tell the senior air force officer that the *Lady Southern Cross* had overtaken him over the Andaman Sea. 'Smith was travelling at twice my own speed of 110mph. He disappeared into the darkness like a comet with a trail of brilliant flame behind him,' Melrose reported.[1] Beau Sheil was stunned on docking in New York to be greeted by billboards shouting: 'SMITHY DOWN IN FLAMES IN BAY OF BENGAL'. 'The shock was like a thunderbolt,' he said. 'Smithy, who had always beaten death, who had been so vitally alive. That there was now no Kingsford Smith seemed inconceivable.' It was several days before Sheil discovered that Melrose had not seen the Altair on fire, merely the hot gases of its exhausts. The *Lady Southern Cross*, wherever she was, was obviously south of the spot at which she had rushed past the Gull.

This position, off the southern coast of Burma, Melrose at first pinpointed as around 150 miles south-east of Rangoon. That would have put it over the Andaman Sea about 60 miles off the

Burma coast, immediately north-west of the Moscos group of islands. Later he recalculated the spot and moved it further south, to around 200 miles from Rangoon. It was from this area that another relevant report had come. Aboard the *Sir Harvey Adamson*, a ship steaming through the Moscos in the early hours of 8 November, the officer of the watch had seen the lights of an aircraft go by at 2.50 am Burma time. The ship was then in the vicinity of the Middle (Maungmagan) Moscos Islands, about 25 miles off the Burma coast. The aircraft could, however, have been Melrose, for both the Altair and the Gull must have been in the area at that time.

Beyond the point where Melrose had seen the aeroplane, the searchers faced an immense tract of ocean and dense tropical rain-forest over which, in Malaya and southern Siam (now Thailand), the inter-tropical convergence zone was still daily deluging. Amid the vegetation that lay as a solid, olive green cloak around snaking yellow-brown rivers were trees reaching up to 150ft. 'The country,' wrote Melrose, 'made us shudder to look down – with rivers disappearing into the mountains, wild elephants in the jungle and drifting cloud over the trees.'[2]

In Australia the news of Smithy's disappearance was at first received with only mild concern. He had force-landed in remote places at least three times before and had always turned up. So universally credited was he with imperishable qualities that people just assumed that in a few days he and Pethybridge would re-appear somewhere unharmed. All that Catherine wrote soberly in her diary that evening was: 'Chilla and Tommy Pethybridge lost somewhere over or near Bay of Bengal. Many phone calls all day.' Mary recalled: 'The thought that he and Tommy might be dead just didn't enter our heads.' Scotty Allan, scouring the route in his DH86, wasn't so sanguine. 'I really believed he'd bought it this time,' he said. 'I wasn't surprised he'd met his end in this part of the world. He never had any confidence crossing the Bay of Bengal. It was very sad, especially when you think that the flight was to no vital purpose.'

In all the days of the search there was only one brief moment of hope. From a remote Siamese village came a report that an aircraft 'with broken wing' had been found deep in the jungle, its crew of two reportedly alive. The story was true: an aircraft with two pilots had indeed crashed in the jungle on the very morning that the *Lady Southern Cross* had flown into oblivion. By quite extraordinary coincidence, a Polish aircraft, a Lublin monoplane, also on its way to Australia, had been forced down by bad weather about 150 miles south of Bangkok. Within a few hours of the Altair's Singapore ETA, it had crashed near Prachuap while attempting to take off again. Neither pilot had been hurt.[3]

When, on 18 November, the RAF search was called off, there was an outcry in Australia. The man in charge, the air officer commanding the Far East Air Force, Air Commodore Sydney Smith, a stickler for procedure, had been irritated from the outset by the slapdash route information Smithy had supplied. When he had appealed to the Australian civil-aviation authorities, all they could find was a three-sentence letter dictated by Smithy from Menzies Hotel in Melbourne five months earlier. A masterpiece of vagueness, it gave no indication of the intended flightpath from Allahabad to Singapore. By mid-November, the air commodore believed that without more specific details, little more could usefully be done.

But Australia was in no mood to end the operation. As had happened with Coffee Royal six years earlier, a public search fund was swiftly opened. The incredible plan was for an independent search by a single aircraft sent all the way from Australia to Burma. The machine chosen was another Lawrence Wackett brainchild, the brand-new twin-engined Gannet, developed from the ill-starred Codock, which it closely resembled. Bill Taylor was to fly it to Singapore and re-comb the entire 1,200 miles from there to Rangoon, accompanied by Harry Purvis as co-pilot and mechanic and John Stannage as wireless-operator. The valiant expedition didn't get very far. The new aircraft, an untried prototype, proved difficult to fly and at Cloncurry Taylor, still haunted by the traumas of that punishing day on the Tasman, suffered a resounding nervous breakdown. Taking command from there, Purvis experienced a major aileron-control failure in mid-air which nearly killed him and Stannage, and the mission was abandoned. Its failure spelled the end of the air search for the *Lady Southern Cross*. Nowhere from Rangoon to Singapore, in sea or jungle, had the smallest piece of the Altair been found.

By early December 1935 the world was forced to accept that Sir Charles Kingsford Smith and Tommy Pethybridge had not survived. In both Houses of Parliament Smithy's death was, on 6 December, formally presumed. For hours the chambers rang with eulogies. One after another members rose to praise his achievements: his 'adventurous spirit', his 'indomitable courage', his 'high sense of chivalry'. He was described as 'gallant' and a 'martyr', as an 'aviation genius'. Inevitably there came from several MPs the familiar chorus of complaint that the country had not adequately rewarded its flying hero. Had it done so, he might still be alive. In a passionate burst of rhetoric a Melbourne MP, Dr Maloney, declared: 'Sir Charles and his companion have gone to their death together, like Leonidas and his fellow Spartans, dying, to the last man, in the service of their country.' The members of both houses stood in silence. No one referred to the £3,000 for the *Southern Cross* which would undoubtedly have allowed him to live to fly another day. The money was, however, speedily paid to Mary.

In London many of the newspapers headlined their obituaries 'A GREAT AIR PILOT'. *The Times* commented that he and Charles Ulm had sacrificed themselves in a cause they believed would establish their right to a share of the operation of the 'imperial communication chain'. 'Given even a modest measure of success in business he would not have found himself back on the old and still perilous trail of the record-breaker.' But while praising his unique skills, *Flight* magazine said he was reckless, citing his 1934 Pacific flight in a single-engined aircraft as evidence that his old principles of caution had been abandoned.[4] Nobody could quote the flying hours he had accumulated, for his final logbook, begun in the middle of 1932, had gone with him. The consensus among his mates was around 6,500.

In the wave of world grief his scarcely known mechanic and co-pilot was almost forgotten. Newspapers had difficulty even spelling his name. But in the Australian aviation fraternity twenty-eight-year-old Tommy Pethybridge was mourned as keenly as Smithy. In the 1990s there were still many people who remembered his unfailingly sunny disposition, his mechanical brilliance and his touching devotion to 'Sir Boss'. At his hosiery factory in the Sydney suburb of Newtown, sixty years after his brother's death, Horrie Pethybridge, by then in his mid-eighties, still kept a daily reminder of Tom on his office wall – a framed copy of a 1935 newspaper front page breaking the story of the missing Altair.

The growing certainty that Chilla was dead crept upon Mary slowly. It was as if, she said, continuing to deny it would eventually bring him home. During the empty Christmas of 1935 and through the early months of 1936, she still hoped for the joyous witty cable, or the phone call bringing his breezy distant voice crackling down the line. But, as the weeks became months, her hopes began to fade – and her life to crumble. 'First I lost the baby – a girl. After that I went steadily downhill. It was the most terrible year of my life. I teetered on the edge of emotional collapse for the whole twelve months, going out less and less, preferring my own company as I sat there in the big new house, answering the hundreds of letters of condolence. It all exploded finally in the most dreadful outbreak of shingles that spread over my entire back, leaving me scars to this day.'

Smithy's estate was valued at £17,611, but a catalogue of debts reduced it to £12,875. The largest was the £2,500 mortgage on the new house, followed by an £1,100 overdraft – money he'd borrowed to meet the full price of the Altair. He had also mortgaged 'Kuranda' for another desperately needed £500 and owed £753 in unpaid salary to the long-suffering Beau Sheil. It was clear from his estate file that for months past he had paid for very little. He owed hundreds for rates, gas, electricity, telephones and telegrams, printing, architect's fees, insurance, plumbing, clothing, petrol, medicine, cartage, cleaning and for a raft of miscellaneous purchases at Sydney department stores. And then there were the medical bills. There was one from St Luke's Hospital in Darlinghurst, another from an anaesthetist, and a third for nursing. Mary had no recollection of his having been in hospital in Sydney in the weeks immediately before his final departure from Australia, and the hospital's medical records were destroyed in a fire around 1970. Whatever operation he had, apparently it was arranged without Mary's knowledge.

Kingsford Smith's passing signalled the beginning of the end of the romantic age of Australian aviation. It also marked the last days of an imperial era in which the country had been compelled to use unsophisticated and uncompetitive British aeroplanes, for it was within only a few months of his death that the ban on foreign aircraft was lifted. The exclusive circle that had been held together by Smithy's magnetic power and thwarted visions began to break up. Bill Taylor, back from his enforced rest at Cloncurry, Beau Sheil and John Stannage tried, with little enthusiasm, to get the trans-Tasman airline into operation. Mary briefly took Chilla's seat on the board. But without his influential name and bewitching leadership, the token company, its hopes crushed by the forces of empire, soon collapsed as, one by one, the founders went off to make new lives for themselves.[5]

So sacred was Kingsford Smith's legend that it was with much trepidation that I began to explore his life. Because the media and biographers had said it so often, I had somehow accepted that he was, in his day, the 'world's greatest aviator'. Five years later I was still not sure what that meant. If it reflected the number of previously unflown intercontinental routes he conquered, in addition to his quite separate record-breaking solo performances, then he certainly must rank alongside Jim Mollison as one of the greatest of aviation's achievers, even though Mollison's tally was higher.[6] It is difficult any longer to appreciate what it was like on board the primitive aeroplanes on some of those frightening flights they hadn't always expected to survive, the true measure of the risks, the hours of cold fear and the breathtaking accomplishments in an era when the great oceans were still largely crossed by sea. As his profound fear of the sea and terror of drowning was slowly uncovered by the years of research, my admiration for Smithy soared. So did my amazement at his apparent perversity in driving himself to tackle flights of increasing risk that exposed him ever more acutely to the very condition he most dreaded.

Yet the more the evidence of his phobia accumulated, the more questions it raised about his conscious motives and his sense of responsibility to those whose lives depended on his emotional equilibrium. The revelation of his 'aquaphobia' may have increased hugely the measure of his courage, but, given the fine edge upon which his psyche wobbled on every flight over the sea, were these ventures unconscious acts of selfishness? Had he risked the lives of worshipping mates to prove that his legendary stamina would keep them safe? Had he in the end sacrificed the idolising Tommy Pethybridge in an utterly unnecessary flight in the face of an illness that was crying to him from his very soul to call it off? Some of his contemporaries believed that he had.

At the time, however, no one would have dreamed of suggesting such a thing. Not his friends, his family, nor the myth-making media which had trapped him within such a godlike image that the world all but lost sight of the human being. It was, above all, this persona of the superman that had both elevated him to international fame and sown the seeds of his downfall. Such towering expectations surrounded Smithy that he could never escape the desperate need, even as his powers declined, to go on proving that he could sustain the skills that supported the fantasy of his indestructibility. Yet behind the relentless adulation, the wisecracks and the protective grin, there resided a surprisingly humble person. His superb piloting gifts had never been complemented by the smallest business skill. He couldn't run an airline, and he didn't understand the politics of aviation. Had the opportunist Charles Ulm not seen in him a vehicle for his own ambitions and mounted the Pacific flight, Smithy would probably have spent his life in colourful obscurity.

Instead, in that one historic journey he had, overnight, become king of Australia. He had mortgaged his life to the media which had transformed him into a national phenomenon, fostering among a generation of people the belief that his deeds entitled him to significant reward. Yet the payback was always to elude him. Too many events in his life had marked him: the traumas of war, the near-drowning at Bondi, the jealousies and terrible squabbles that had soured his partnership with Ulm and Anderson. The private tensions with the American crew, acrimonious litigation from old mates, the airmanship blunders of Coffee Royal and the deaths of Anderson and Hitchcock. The hurtful accusations that had put him in the dock before all Australia. The failure of the only airline he was ever to see get off the ground. The furore that raged over his air-race entry with an American aircraft. The white feathers. The nightmare journey over the Tasman which hastened the failure of his air-route bids. The desperation that had led him, like a character in a Greek tragedy, through disillusionment and illness to his last flight, which he believed, as ever, would bring the security a spectacular career had never yielded. Yet although none of the virgin routes he flew ever became his to operate, his dashing pioneering activities, and the unglamorous barnstorming to which he was constantly reduced, helped to create among millions an acceptance of air travel that would launch one of the biggest industries of this century.

While history honours Sir Charles Kingsford Smith as a remarkable aviator, the dwindling handful of his colleagues who were still around in the middle of the 1990s remembered him affectionately for quite different reasons. For the entirety of what he was: a man untouched by fame who, through all the years of his apotheosis, remained the quintessential Australian good bloke – disarmingly approachable, devoid of a shred of pomp. Old mates, asked to describe him, spoke of his basic decency, his kindness, generosity and tolerance, his reluctance to speak unkindly of anybody. They remembered his total, indeed almost calculated informality, his preference for the oily, raunchy camaraderie of the hangar over lavish banquets held in his honour. They talked of his infectious enthusiasm, his contempt for officialdom, of the boyish immaturity he never outgrew. Of his endless pranks, inveterate beer-drinking, risqué jokes, larrikin ways and the dashing spirit of adventure he always brought to flying. He was, they said, stimulating company, radiating a spellbinding charm that was almost electric. His deeply appealing mixture of the heroic and the human inspired loyalty and devotion; they would all have followed him to the ends of the earth.

His only real interest in life had been flying. The wings of every aircraft he flew seemed almost, it was often said, to fuse with his own body to become a living extension of it. The compulsion took over his whole being, driving him, regardless of personal cost, to pile achievement upon achievement. But, sadly, the price of the fame it brought had been his own slow destruction. 'I hope,' he once declared, 'to win a reputation for being not the best aviator in the world, but the oldest.' One flight too many denied him this. He had always been philosophical about death. It was waiting for him, he used to say, on every flight.

'There was really nothing else left for him,' said his niece Margaret Harricks. 'He could never have been an old man. He was destined to die young.'

'The truth was,' said John Kingsford-Smith, 'that he had just burned himself out. But he went in a blaze of glory.'

The Mystery of the
Lady Southern Cross

On the first day of May 1937, eighteen months after the *Lady Southern Cross* disappeared, two Burmese fishermen found an aircraft wheel floating in the sea among the rocks of an uninhabited island called Kokunye Kyun, also known as Aye, about 150 miles south-east of Rangoon. The small jungle-covered hump that rose to 460ft above steep cliffs lay among a chain of scattered islands and sandbanks about a mile and a quarter off the Tenasserim coast near the small, sleepy south Burma river port of Ye.

The big black tyre, fully inflated, was still attached to its under-carriage leg, a heavy structure which dangled in the sea beneath the wheel, its tubular steel fork encased in a sheath of molluscs and marine growth. Lashing it to the side of their wooden boat, the fishermen took it back to their village on the mainland, where it was subsequently seized by the township officer at Ye. Beneath the heavy encrustation and weed, he found a manufacturer's serial number still embossed on the cylindrical oleo shock-absorber that had been torn from the aircraft's wing. But this vital information, and numbers stamped on the tyre and metal rim, were not immediately telegraphed to the civil aviation department in Rangoon. The wheel remained, unidentified, in the District Administration Office for several weeks.

While it lay there, news of its existence reached the Rangoon newspapers and, by the first week of June, the discovery was making headlines in Australia – and electrifying the Kingsford Smith family. It seems they allowed themselves to believe that it could mean Chilla might still be alive, subsisting on some remote island like Robinson Crusoe. For Mary, the resurgence of hope created something of a dilemma. She had begun to rebuild her life and was on the point of remarrying. Her fiancé was one of Chilla's close friends, an Englishman, Alan Tully, who had been posted to Melbourne in 1934 to manage the Ethyl Corporation's Australasian and Far East operations. The thought of Chilla re-appearing, like Enoch Arden, to find her married to one of his old mates was a risk she could not contemplate until this latest hope had been extinguished. It was a lengthy process.

On 2 July, a mysterious cable arrived out of the blue at the office of the New South Wales civil aviation district superintend-ent at Mascot. It came from an obscure place called Kanbauk near Tavoy in south Burma. 'FOUND WHEEL OF SMITHY'S LOCKHEED STOP DEFINITELY SMITHY'S.' The sender's name had not transmitted prop-erly and arrived as 'Studder', which meant nothing to the superintendent, Captain Bill Burgess. Puzzled, he dutifully sent the message to Edgar Johnston, now controller-general of civil avi-ation, in Melbourne, whose officials were equally baffled. The man who had sent it was Jack Hodder, an Australian motor mechanic working as chief engineer of a tin dredge in the Heinze Chaung estuary, about 45 miles south of Ye. A private pilot who had learned to fly at Mascot, he had known Smithy and had become specially chummy with Pethybridge. Such was his regard for Kingsford Smith that he kept his hero's photograph permanently attached to his flying licence. He was also familiar with the Altair. As soon as he had heard about the wheel he had hurried up to Ye to see it.

The instant he set eyes on it Hodder recognised the wheel as part of an Altair's retractable undercarriage. As, to his knowledge, no other Lockheed had ever gone missing over Burma, he was certain that it belonged to the *Lady Southern Cross*. He decided that at the first opportunity he would go out to Aye Island to search for more wreckage, and triumphantly cabled the only civil-aviation official he knew in Sydney with the news.

Meanwhile, by coincidence, another Australian pilot passing through Burma stumbled on a quite separate possible clue. Lores Bonney was en route in a Klemm monoplane from Australia to South Africa and had night-stopped at Tavoy, 40 miles south of Kanbauk, on the very day the fishermen claimed to have found the

wheel. Her host in Tavoy, an expatriate Englishman in the public-
works department, told her that eighteen months earlier a friend
of his Burmese house servant, night-fishing around the Middle
Moscos Islands, 'had heard a noise and then seen a big light in the
sky go down into the sea some distance off'. The Englishman had
set out to try to discover the exact date of the event. It turned out,
Lores Bonney later told her biographer, to have been the night of
7–8 November, exactly when the *Lady Southern Cross* disappeared.[1] Had the wheel floated north from the vicinity of the
Moscos Islands for 80 miles to Aye Island?

In Rangoon the Burma Civil Aviation Department's formal
inquiry was distinguished by an astonishing lack of urgency. The
official in charge, the acting director of civil aviation, was an Indian
government civil servant, an Irishman, Michael Doyle, an aeronautical engineer who had served as a pilot in the RFC. Obsessed
with economy, when the undercarriage leg was eventually delivered to him he chose the slow option of sending the serial
numbers to Lockheed in Los Angeles by seamail letter, unaware
that they had already been cabled direct by the impatient Hodder.
Doyle was taken aback when, on 8 July, long before his letter
could have reached America, a Lockheed vice-president, Carl
Squier, confirmed to the world that the numbers tallied, and the
wreckage definitely belonged to the *Lady Southern Cross*.

In Australia the news galvanised Wilfrid and Eric Kingsford
Smith, who had been bombarding the acting defence minister,
Harold Thorby, for weeks with phone calls and letters. Desperate
to believe that the wheel might have drifted from an island on
which Chilla and Tommy were still alive and well, they pressed
Thorby to demand that the Burma government urgently send a
ship to search again all the remote, uninhabited Andaman Sea
islands. But when the Rangoon officials told the Australian government they would have to pay for any search, Thorby quickly
declined. Instead the wheel was sent to Professor Meggitt, head of
Rangoon University's zoology department, to be analysed for
botanical clues which might indicate whence it had come.
Unfortunately, by the time it reached him, most of the seaweed
had been cleaned off. However, from the shellfish that remained,
Meggitt found that 'the salvaged wreckage, most probably while
still attached to the main portion of the aircraft, has been resting

for some considerable time motionless in seawater to a depth not exceeding 15 fathoms (90ft/27m) on a muddy bottom'.[2]

To this conclusion Doyle added another. At the top of the undercarriage leg, he said, there was still attached a small part of the metal structure that connected the landing gear to the wooden framework of the wing inside which the gear folded when retracted. He had studied the fracture surfaces where the metal had snapped and made an unscientific deduction that was to mislead searchers of the main wreckage for more than fifty years. 'The fractures,' he wrote in a preliminary report to the Australian government, 'are not straight clean fractures but appear to be the result of "working", indicating that the buoyant wheel must have been lying either in a comparatively strong current or at a depth not exceeding the depth of wave disturbance.'[3] With this well-intentioned guesswork Doyle had created a myth that subsequently embedded itself deeply into Smithy folklore: that the *Lady Southern Cross* had crashed close to Aye Island and that the wheel had only quite recently parted from the wreckage, bobbed to the surface and floated ashore on to the island's rocks.

Some further dramatic discoveries added credible weight to this belief. In January 1938, eight months after the wheel had been found, in the calm weather that came with the retreat of the stormy south-west monsoon, Jack Hodder had borrowed a launch and set out with a Burmese crew from the Heinze Chaung estuary to make the 50-mile voyage north to Aye. Cruising slowly round the island, he studied the rocky shoreline through binoculars for signs of wreckage. Quite quickly something caught his attention:

> Right at the highest point, about 1,000 feet, I noticed a very big tree with the top cut off it. Then further down the southern slope I saw a dozen other trees with the tops broken. These formed a path right down to the edge of the cliff. In my opinion these trees were actually broken by the Lockheed. Having hit the tree on the highest point, she would be out of control, and would go on down. The mountain slope is very steep, and would just about coincide with the path of the machine at about 200mph.[4]

At the eastern end of the island he anchored in a small, sandy bay.

Sending the boat across to the mainland to fetch Maung Du, one
of the fishermen who had found the wheel, Hodder went ashore
and climbed up through the jungle to the peak, which was actually
less than half the height of his 1,000ft estimate. Then he worked
his way down the steep southern slope, scrambling from tree to
tree, until his way was barred by the sea cliffs. Many of the trees
had indeed been 'lopped' from the summit downwards.

Quite why Hodder was so convinced that the destruction had
been caused by an aircraft, he never explained. Nor at the time did
he report a finding that the Aye Island legends subsequently
ascribed to him: some telling smudges of what he later claimed
was the Altair's blue paint on a tree.

Back in the eastern bay, Maung Du took him to the spot among
the rocks on the west side where he said he had first seen the
undercarriage leg.

Here I decided we should make a thorough search of the
foreshore. We removed about ten tons of driftwood and
bamboo and were rewarded by finding a piece of steel
moulding about 15 inches long, badly rusted, but unmistak-
ably part of the Lockheed. I would say it came from around
the cockpit, as it had been nickel-plated.

This caused us to redouble our efforts, and we soon
located a small piece of duralumin [aircraft light aluminium
alloy]. Another search of the small bay at low tide next day
brought to light another small piece of duralumin, jammed
between rocks which mostly were covered by water.

Then I decided to drag the bed of the bay. This I did
pretty thoroughly and, on two occasions, I thought I had
found the machine. Our grappling gear caught on something in about 18 feet of water, so I dived down each time,
only to be disappointed at finding nothing more than jagged
rocks.[5]

Sudden rough seas interrupted the dragging operation, and
although Hodder stayed on at Aye Island for several days the
choppy conditions prevented any further searches before he had
to return to Kanbauk. A letter he sent a few days later to the
Sydney *Sun* concluded with a confident statement which

remained unchallenged and was accepted by aviation historians as fact for the next half century, luring other searchers to Aye Island.

> I am of the opinion that the Lockheed and the men are in the water right at the foot of the cliff in front of where the trees were broken down, and I'll not be satisfied until I go there again and drag that ocean bed . . . My contract in Burma still has 18 months to run, and some time before then I'll finish this job. If they ARE there, I'll find them.[6]

This enthusiastic letter was the principal record of Jack Hodder's findings. He kept no diaries, took no photographs, made no notes or sketches.

It was not until the end of March 1939 that the matter was given another stir. Planning to make an air search of the Aye Island waters in an aircraft he had just bought, Hodder went along to the civil aviation office in Rangoon to meet the director who had taken over from Michael Doyle. Captain Alan Eadon, another ex-Royal Flying Corps pilot, had been India's deputy civil-aviation director and, like Doyle, was unfamiliar with the operation of the new generation of high-speed American aeroplanes. Quite uncritically he embraced the Hodder theory: that because the wheel had been found at Aye, it must therefore be the crash site; that Smithy had hit the island in the dark because it wasn't marked on his map. However, Eadon preferred an engine-failure explanation. Although he had never seen the impossibly steep terrain, he concluded that Smithy must have been trying to force-land on Aye – that he had lowered his undercarriage and the dangling wheels had hit the treetops, tipping the aircraft over the cliff into the sea. Unfortunately, Eadon lacked the technical knowledge that would have told him, from the appearance of the wheel, the true position of the landing gear at that moment. Having swallowed Hodder's theory, he was compelled to make the facts fit it. To do so it was necessary to rubbish Jimmy Melrose's claim to have sighted the *Lady Southern Cross* at a position which, given the respective speeds of the two aircraft that night, couldn't have been less than 200 miles south of Rangoon and thus, at the very least, 50 miles south of Aye Island. 'It is highly probable that Mr Melrose was mistaken, as meteors often occur in this part of the world, and he has not been consistent in his statements as to time and location,' said Eadon dismissively. Yet Melrose had, carefully logged the sighting, recorded it in his diary that evening, told the RAF in Singapore about it, and had described it clearly to numerous reporters.

Eadon disagreed with Doyle's hypothesis that the wheel had lain underwater for nearly eighteen months before metal fatigue allowed it to work loose and drift away. He believed it had broken off at the moment of impact and remained among the rocks ever since. In May 1939 he repeated these unproven suppositions in yet another report to what had become the Australian Civil Aviation Ministry. This was the last of the Burma government's attempts to explain, three and a half years after the event, the fate of the *Lady Southern Cross*. The Australians refused to pay for another sea search of the Aye Island waters and Hodder never flew out to investigate again – he crashed his aeroplane, a BA Eagle, near Rangoon in fog and, by the time it was repaired, the monsoon had muddied the Andaman Sea. Suddenly, with another world war looming, there were higher priorities for both governments.

In November Hodder flew home to Australia, where he met John Kingsford-Smith and his father Wilfrid. 'He didn't have a camera so he'd brought back no pictures of those mutilated branches,' John recalled. 'It was all anecdotal. We just accepted as fact everything the guy told us.' When Hodder voiced his belief that Smithy had hit the island because he didn't know it was there, Wilfrid wrote to the Royal Aero Club in London. 'They supplied his strip maps of the route. When they sent us the Burma section we saw that Aye Island wasn't on it.' And so another dubious theory – that Smithy had been map-reading his way in the dark using tiny island references rather than major geographic features – took root in the flowering legends of his death.

A few weeks before the outbreak of war, the Altair's wheel arrived back in Sydney. It was put on display for several years at the Kingsford Smith Aerodrome before being moved to Sydney's Power House Museum, where today it lies in a basement store. The Australian civil-aviation authorities made no attempt to conduct their own examination of it to confirm the conclusions arrived at in Burma. The assumption that the aircraft lay in the sea at Aye, tantalisingly awaiting a search expedition, came to be accepted as fact. It was to be nearly fifty years before anyone went to the island with the necessary equipment to test the Hodder theory.

The Australians who did so in 1983 were a well-equipped expedition whose leader was neither a pilot nor an underwater diver, but an enthusiastic human dynamo called Ted Wixted, a Queensland museum librarian in his mid-fifties. He had acquired a reputation for his passion for chronicling and tirelessly commemorating famous flights by Australian aviators, and believed that Australia owed it to Smithy's memory to find and bring home his aeroplane. If the government wouldn't do it, he would. He was convinced that Melrose had confused a meteorite with the Altair that night and that Smithy, with his landing gear lowered, had hit the island's summit treetops and plunged into the eastern bay. The Altair's gear was down, he claimed, 'to steady the aircraft to take a sextant reading'.[7] Yet lowering the gear would have made the plane less stable – and Smithy had not been carrying a sextant: pilots didn't use astro-navigation on this largely overland route, and in any case Smithy had never mastered the art. Nonetheless Wixted persuaded the RAAF to fly the Brisbane team to Rangoon and the Burmese Navy to take them to the island. They worked in atrocious conditions in fierce currents. The water was so muddy that the divers couldn't see their hands in front of their masks. A coral-encrusted engine found on the seabed brought a brief surge of excitement, but it turned out to belong to a sunken fishing boat. Of the *Lady Southern Cross* there was no trace. Wixted vowed to return, and at the end of 1997 he was still trying to raise money for a further attempt.

Is it likely that anyone will ever find the *Lady Southern Cross*? Does the aeroplane really lie at Aye Island? Or could Hodder have been wrong and Melrose right? Is it possible that what little remains of the Altair rests at the bottom of the Andaman Sea, far over the island's southern horizon? Setting out to research Smithy's life in the early 1990s I too at first accepted the Aye Island crash theory as historical fact. Yet the more I studied the original accident files in the Australian archives, the more questions began to form in my mind.

Why had no expert ever examined the central exhibit? Surely it could have revealed something technically pertinent. And the fragments of metal Hodder had found on the rocks: from what part of the Altair had they come? Indeed, did they belong to the *Lady Southern Cross* at all? Had anyone ever bothered to have them analysed? It seemed not. And what was known about Hodder himself? Was the man whose untested hunch had given birth to the hypothesis a dependable investigator who had objectively considered the whole range of scenarios before arriving at his conclusion? It seemed a good idea to start with him.

The few photographs that exist of Jack Hodder are remarkable in two ways: in all of them he bears a quite striking resemblance to Smithy, and in all of them he looks quite profoundly doleful and unhappy. A newspaper appeal in 1992 led me to Jack's son, Squadron Leader (now Wing Commander) John Hodder, an RAAF air-traffic control officer at Richmond air base. His father had died in 1979 leaving no written record of his Aye Island discoveries. 'The only evidence he ever showed me,' said John Hodder, 'were some bits of aluminium wreckage he'd brought back.'

More revealing was a call from Jack Hodder's former sister-in-law, an Australian in her late seventies now living in Auckland, who asked not to be named. She described a solitary, intensely lonely, introverted man whose life had been a battle to overcome a lack of education and a childhood of unbelievable cruelty.

His father remarried when he was quite small and the step-mother, for some terrible reason, just didn't want to know Jack. She refused to have him in the house. His father was made to build him a little dog house out in the garden, and he was pushed out there to live and sleep. They even took his food out to him. Then, when he was barely fourteen, they just kicked him out, took him out of school and told him to push off, find work – and never to come back. Not surprisingly, he became completely antisocial and grew up to be a loner, a sad, very private man who had difficulty all his life mixing with people. He was married twice, the second time to my sister. What a time she had of it! For a while he was a good and loving husband, but it didn't last.

Hodder, she said, had become mentally unstable, and suffered from such delusions of persecution that he began to sleep with a gun under his pillow. 'My sister was so terrified she left him, and soon afterwards poor Jack had to be taken into care.' Hodder's sister-in-law couldn't recall him ever talking about the *Lady Southern Cross*. 'He just wasn't the sort of person with whom you could sit down and have a long conversation. But I would imagine that once he'd got those crash theories into his head, nothing would ever have dislodged them.'

'He was utterly convinced that the aircraft had hit those trees,' his son John said. 'Yes, he was a shy and introspective man who didn't drink or socialise and kept himself to himself. But the aviation community and I respected him as a very competent engineer – some would have said brilliant.'

Within days of hearing all this I had a phone call from another elderly Australian living in New Zealand. Charlie Wardrop, the retired managing director of the Fijian company Burns Philp (South Sea), had been one of Hodder's closest friends. 'I've got something here that'll interest you,' he said. He told me that he had in his possession one of the pieces of metal Jack had picked up on Aye Island in 1938. In some excitement I drove next day to Whangarei, 100 miles north of Auckland, to see it. Wardrop, now in his eighties, told me that in the early 1930s he and Hodder had worked as young mechanics at a Sydney motor workshop. They had spent their weekends out at Mascot, where Tommy Pethybridge had taught them to fly. 'What amazed us all was that, with precious little education – barely two or three years in primary school – Jack was able to go on and take a commercial pilot's licence. His writing was always ungrammatical and he needed a lot of help from his friends to scrape through his written exams.'

The piece of jagged, wafer-thin metal was about 5ins square: it had originally been larger, but Wardrop had given half of it to a friend. It was pitted and corroded green-brown by its long immersion in the sea, and its outline didn't, apart from a few rivet holes, immediately suggest any obvious part of an aeroplane. Wardrop explained its history. 'Jack found just two bits like this. He never mentioned any nickel-plated steel or blue paint on the trees. He believed the metal had come from the engine cowling.' By the time Hodder returned to Australia, Wardrop had gone to live in Fiji. They were reunited in Sydney in the early 1950s. 'Jack showed me one of the fragments. As we were parting he thrust it into my hand and said, "You keep it – I've got the other." I was quite touched. It was the last time we ever met.'

As the metal had never been scientifically identified as aluminium alloy of the Altair's type, Wardrop agreed to let me have it analysed. Back in Auckland the weathered fragment sat on my desk and seemed to stare at me. Had it really been part of Smithy's tomb? To which part of the Altair had it belonged? Was it even part of an aircraft at all? Through the Lockheed Corporation at Calabasas in California, I traced a retired production engineer who had worked on the company's famous wooden aeroplanes at Burbank in the mid-1930s. Dr Herbert Boen had known the *Lady Southern Cross* well; indeed, his knowledge of the aircraft seemed encyclopaedic. The theory that Smithy had lowered his undercarriage that night puzzled him. 'No Altair pilot would ever have done that,' he told me over the telephone. 'If he was in trouble he would have gone for a belly landing. The ship could easily withstand that.' Dr Boen said that if ever a search expedition did get into the vicinity of the genuine crash site, its sonar equipment would have a helpful underwater target. 'We had a weight and balance problem with the *Lady Southern Cross*, I remember. She was tail-heavy. Behind the front instrument panel we had to bolt to the number three horsecollar something like fifty pounds of lead. It must still be there.'

He invited me to send him photographs of the fragment. Having studied them he sent them for a second opinion to another former Lockheed man, Harvey Christen, in Pasadena. Christen, in his early eighties, had been a Lockheed vice-president responsible for quality control and had, in the early 1990s, been making news around the world through his involvement with another great aviation mystery. He had voiced his disbelief that a piece of aircraft duralumin found by an expedition on Nikumaroro Island in the central Pacific was from the Lockheed Electra in which Amelia Earhart and her navigator had disappeared in 1937. The spacing of the rivet holes in the metal artifact, he claimed, did not match those of Earhart's aeroplane. Christen was clearly someone eminently qualified to venture an opinion on the Altair, and he did so. He disputed Hodder's view that it was part of the engine cowling.

'He is of the opinion,' Dr Boen wrote in May 1992, 'that it probably came from the final-closure panel of the retractable gear.'

This was significant information. The final-closure panel was a small door that shut flush with the underside of the wing to enclose the wheel in the final action of the retraction operation. If Christen was right, the possibility existed that the metal panel could have arrived at Aye Island from somewhere else, attached to the floating wheel; that it may have been broken off by waves as the wheel was pounded on the rocks.

Getting the metal accurately analysed in New Zealand proved impossible. To unlock the secret of its genetic heredity, I snipped off a sample and sent it to ALCOA – the Aluminum Company of America – in Pittsburgh, Pennsylvania, the company which, back in the 1930s, had manufactured it. A helpful technical consultant in the Alloy Division, Bernard Lifka, conducted an analysis on a quantometer, a spectrascopic device which fired a high-voltage spark at the metal to measure with great precision the wavelengths of the resulting light. The test positively identified the metal as a type then known as 24S, an alloy introduced by ALCOA in 1932 and used widely in aircraft during the Second World War. Although 24S hadn't come into general use until 1936, it had been available to Lockheed in 1934, when Smithy's Altair had been created from a Sirius by fitting the new wing with the retractable undercarriage.

The biggest challenge remained the wheel itself. The curator of the transport section of Sydney's Power House Museum, Ian Debenham, took me into the store room to see the long-forgotten structure, shrouded like a mummy under a dustcover. He confirmed that the wheel had never been examined by aeronautical engineers. As he lifted off the cover I found myself momentarily affected by an eerie sense of the proximity of a relic which had shared with Smithy the swift moment of his death. It was very much larger and heavier than I had expected. The long, tripod-shaped frame in which the shiny black tyre sat was of shoulder-height, its repainted tubular-steel assembly looking as new as the day it was built. Amazingly, given that it had spent eighteen months in the water, the hinged bell crank around which the leg rotated when lowered and retracted still moved freely.

It was not possible for the layman to tell whether the wheel had been up or down at the time of the crash, or indeed whether it was the right wheel or the left, as Captain Eadon had pronounced. Nor was it obvious to an untrained eye whether the raw fractures had been caused, as Eadon had declared, by the leg rocking about in the currents until metal fatigue had snapped it off. To answer these questions would once have been a simple and inexpensive matter, but in the market-driven 1990s technical expertise came at a price. The few organisations in Australia competent to do so expected fees of thousands of dollars. I would have to find one prepared to do it as a gesture to aviation history.

In the meantime, I faced the need for a radical reappraisal of the crash location. It arose from a meeting with a present-day Australian aviation folk hero, the larger-than-life self-made millionaire, publisher and explorer, Dick Smith. Smith is so widely admired for his philanthropy and aviation exploits that he was voted in the early 1990s the most popular choice as the country's first president. After selling his multinational electronics retail business in the 1980s, he embarked on a life of aviation adventure. An unashamed romantic who sometimes flew with a photograph of Kingsford Smith in his cockpit, he made the first-ever solo rotor-wing flight around the world, a helicopter journey to the North Pole and, in a Twin Otter, the first vertical circumnavigation of the world, landing at both Poles.

Kingsford Smith, he told me, had been one of his boyhood heroes, and he had set out to rediscover some of the landmarks of Smithy's life. He had gone into the Tanami Desert and recovered the remains of the *Kookaburra*, leaving a monument there to Keith Anderson and Bob Hitchcock. Later he had found the rusty cans and cartridge cases that identified the Coffee Royal site in the Kimberley, and left a plaque there as well. But most relevantly of all, in 1982 he had visited Aye Island, circling it for forty minutes – shooting film and taking photographs – in a new helicopter he was bringing from America to Australia. What he saw led him to dispute Hodder's tree-collision theory. 'I can afford to fund the entire cost of an expedition to bring that aeroplane home – and believe me, I'd do it like a shot,' he told me. 'But I'd need to be a great deal more convinced that it's actually there.'

To illustrate his doubts, Dick Smith showed me the film he had shot that day. There, rising above a grey hem of tidal rocks, was the familiar jungle-covered profile in the sea, towards which the camera tracked to simulate what Hodder believed was the Altair's fatal approach from the north. The screen began to fill with the jungle slopes as we rushed toward the highest point, scudding over it with only feet to spare. Then the island's southern face dropped away precipitously immediately below the summit – so steeply that it was clear why Hodder had had to scramble from tree to tree to make his way safely down to the clifftop below. 'You can see there's just no way an aircraft above stalling speed could have nosed down so quickly to chop off all those trees,' Dick Smith said. 'The notion is preposterous. Its momentum would simply have carried it clear of all vegetation, out over the cliffs and into the sea. The only way it could have ripped through the trees would have been at the end of a screaming, very steep dive. The chance of that coinciding precisely with the slope angle would be millions to one.'

The film showed the huge trees towering up into vast, profusely branched canopies. 'How on earth could a wooden aeroplane bore its way through branches like those without disintegrating and showering bits of itself all over the slope?' Smith went on. 'Yet Hodder tells us he went down and searched and found nothing. The truth is that what he surmised just wasn't physically possible. The Altair didn't hit that island, it went into the sea a long way south. Hodder and those inexperienced investigators all got themselves locked into a theory – a total mind-set – incapable of accepting any fact, like Melrose's sighting, that even slightly threatened their beliefs.'

A technical post-mortem of the wheel produced more evidence to suggest that the Altair had not flown into the island. In the spring of 1992, the Aeronautical Research Laboratory of the Ministry of Defence in Melbourne, intrigued by the historical significance of the assignment, offered to do a preliminary examination at no charge. The undercarriage leg yielded its secrets without the need for costly electronic fracture-analysis. Indeed, they were revealed within minutes to the expert eyes of one of ARL's structures engineers, Dr Graham Clark, who went to inspect the gear. 'It was quite an elementary bit of detective work,' he said. 'His gear was definitely up when he crashed. No question about it. It was the right leg, and it didn't break off slowly with fatigue, it parted violently at the moment of impact. If you know what to look for it's quite obvious.' It was clear to Dr Clark that the whole right-hand leg, attached to the largely wooden aeroplane by four separate metal components, had broken off for the simple reason that every one of these connections had failed in the split second of violent impact. The examination quickly disposed of the myth that the leg had lain underwater on a muddy bottom before breaking away from the aircraft. 'There is no obvious evidence to support the metal-fatigue theory,' Dr Clark said.

In collaboration with an ARL colleague, John Kepert – an accident investigator with thirty years' experience of reconstructing crash causes from wreckage dragged from the sea – Dr Clark produced a report for me, helpfully illustrated with photographs and diagrams.[8] It described the simple mechanical evidence which proved that the undercarriage could not have been down when the crash occurred. Still visible was a deep depression punched into the metal of one of the tubular legs by a large nut against which it had been slammed. 'It could only have happened with the leg in the fully retracted position. Furthermore, all the evidence indicates that the leg separated on sea impact.' The crucial piece of misinformation that the gear had been down, arrived at by the Burma civil-aviation director, which had helped to lure the 1983 expedition so frustratingly to Aye Island, had gone uncorrected for decades.

Graham Clark and John Kepert were certain that the *Lady Southern Cross* had dived into the sea out of control at a fairly steep angle. 'Where that happened there's no way of knowing,' Kepert said.

But what we can say is that it didn't hit those trees. The damage to the undercarriage, folded up in the wing at the time, is consistent with one quite substantial impact. It was severe enough to crack the wheel rim in several places, but it didn't reflect the destructive process of tearing through huge trees. It was, after all, quite a fragile aeroplane. No way could it have done that without breaking up in a shower of wreckage. There would have been bits of it everywhere on that hillside – certainly long-surviving pieces of metal from the engine, the cowling and the landing gear.

Why he was out of control there's no way now of telling. The two occupants, with that sort of deceleration, would have been flung forward through their instrument panels and would have died instantly of massive injuries. Their bodies would have quite quickly disappeared without trace, and so, in those tropical waters, would all the wooden components, followed eventually by the light alloy sections, which would include quite a bit of the engine. All that will eventually remain somewhere, probably spread across 200yds of the ocean floor, will be the few steel parts: the engine crankshaft, propeller-reduction gear, cylinder barrels, impeller drive gears, the port undercarriage leg and that chunk of lead ballast.[9]

So, if it was not the *Lady Southern Cross* which cut that swathe through the Aye Island jungle, what was it? Most probably a cyclonic storm, according to one of India's leading botanists, Professor P. S. Ramakrishnan, an expert in the jungle vegetation of south-east Asia. 'Mr Hodder may not have realised how common cyclonic storms are on the south Burma coast during the monsoon. They sweep in over the exposed offshore islands, snapping off large branches like twigs, even cracking whole trees in half. I'm sure what he saw was no more than one of these all-too-familiar patches in the forest. A crashing aircraft would have left a relatively small, narrow scar, masses of wreckage, and probably evidence, too, of a fire.'

From where, then, had the wheel arrived on the Aye Island rocks? If it was the Altair that passed over Melrose that night, then the wheel must have floated up from somewhere a long way south. I tried unsuccessfully for two years to locate Melrose's original 1935 diaries and logbooks. After Melrose was killed in an air crash in July 1936, his mother, Hilda, had acquired them. Extensive use had been made of them for a biography, published privately in Adelaide in 1990 by a retired accountant, Eric Gunton.[10] But to my surprise, Gunton told me that his book had actually been written forty-four years earlier. He had returned the diaries and flight logs to Mrs Melrose in the mid-1940s, and had no idea what had become of them after her death in 1968. However, there was not the least doubt in his mind that Melrose's sighting of the Altair had been real enough: 'He had noted it in the log he kept on a notepad on his knee, and again in the little diary he wrote up faithfully every evening on the ground.'[11]

It is possible to calculate the location of the sighting with some coarse degree of accuracy. The groundspeed that the Altair had made on its flight from Allahabad, over Calcutta and Akyab to overhead Rangoon had averaged 187mph, and it would probably have continued at least at that rate as it flew south-east over the Gulf of Martaban. The Gull's speed is more difficult to pinpoint, since two rates of progress need to be allowed for: the climb out of Rangoon with a heavy fuel load (Melrose was carrying enough for the 800 miles to Alor Star even though, in the event, he landed to refuel at Victoria Point) and the subsequent level-flight cruise speed at 2,500ft altitude. I was unable to find any surviving pilots with long-distance operating experience on Gipsy Major powered Gull 4s. Several theoretical sources came up with such widely different figures that it seemed wiser in the end to rely on Melrose's own publicly declared level-flight cruise value of 110mph, adjusted for the initial climb. I took these figures, together with both planes' departure times from Rangoon, to the University of Auckland, where an obliging mathematician calculated algebraically the overtake point off the south Burma coast. He estimated the encounter to have occurred at 0250 hours, 248 miles from Rangoon.

These calculations took no account of the wind which would have affected both aircraft that night. Over the years, reports of the Andaman Sea weather at the time of Smithy's disappearance have ranged from violent storms to clear moonlight. Archivists at the Meteorological Office at Bracknell in England were able to produce a digest of the actual weather for the morning of Friday 8 November 1935. The Indian daily weather report issued in Poona just a few hours after Melrose saw the Altair, showed that the day was dry and the skies over Burma 'lightly to moderately clouded'. No rain had fallen at nearby Tavoy in the previous twenty-four hours, the sky over the Tenasserim coast was partly cloudy, the sea was 'smooth' and the Tavoy surface wind was from the north-north-east at a gentle 2–3mph.

However the relative speeds are calculated, it seems probable that the *Lady Southern Cross* was still airborne roughly abeam Tavoy, more than 100 miles south of Aye Island. From that position, on any routing to Singapore, the aircraft had little more than 200 miles to run before its heading would have intersected the Kra Isthmus. It would therefore have had not much more than an hour to go before leaving the Andaman Sea. Somewhere in that stretch of water between the Moscos group and the islands of the Mergui Archipelago, it had dived into the ocean and disintegrated.

Would the winds, tides and currents have allowed the starboard wheel to float 200 miles or more north to Aye Island? I discovered from admiralty charts that the Andaman Sea coastal tides flowed in a north-south direction, flooding and ebbing at equal speed. If the wheel's voyage had been determined only by their daily rhythm, its northbound progress would theoretically have been neutralised by the flow in the reverse direction. Much more relevant were the currents. Had anyone ever reliably plotted them? For the first time I attempted to approach the Burma government. Since the Aye Island expedition of 1983, the country had been renamed Myanmar, and by the early 1990s was being ruled with an iron fist by a military junta which had attracted worldwide condemnation for its brutal suppression of a 1988 uprising, its refusal to recognise the outcome in 1990 of the country's first free elections in thirty years and its decision to confine to house arrest most of the leaders of the popularly elected opposition party, the National League for Democracy, led by the charismatic Nobel Peace Prize-winner Aung San Suu Kyi. Moreover, Myanmar was racked by ethnic strife and rebel armies were in control of some of the country's border areas. This nation of gentle Buddhist people was in economic stagnation, and its capital Rangoon – now renamed Yangon – still bore a shabby resemblance to the colonial city the British had left in 1948. The junta, intimidatingly named the State Law and Order Restoration Council, deeply suspicious of foreigners, had effectively isolated the country from the world.

At the country's embassy in London I was firmly told that my innocent request for information about the currents of the Andaman Sea could be considered only if it was formally presented to the Myanmar government 'through the correct channels' by the government of New Zealand. As New Zealand had no embassy in Yangon, this procedure declared itself immediately to be dauntingly tortuous. Happily, it turned out that the Indian Ocean current information was in fact already widely available.

Called 'ship-drift data', it had been supplied voluntarily for decades by ships' navigators in daily radio reports for collation by oceanographers.[12] From Florida, England and India, this international community of marine scientists, fascinated by the romantic purpose of my research, soon showered me with pages of revealing flow charts in which small current arrows swirled like magnified spermatozoa in a circle around the Bay of Bengal. Their unanimous view was that, in the month the *Lady Southern Cross* crashed, the wheel would quite definitely have been carried north.

From a research vessel at that moment fortuitously in the Indian Ocean on a sea circulation-measurement voyage using sophisticated electronic devices, a British oceanographer, Dr Harry Bryden of the Southampton Oceanography Centre, wrote: 'The large-scale circulation of the Bay of Bengal switches from clockwise to counterclockwise in October and then back to clockwise in January. Thus, for the months of November and December there are relatively strong northward flows along the coast of Myanmar. For the 50 or so days after the crash – from 8 November to 1 January – the wheel could have drifted hundreds of miles north at the rate of 10 to 15 miles per day.'[13] The circulation charts Dr Bryden enclosed illustrated vividly how the Myanmar coast currents flowed determinedly north during only four months – April, October, November and December.

Another ocean scientist, Dr Satish Shetye, at India's National Institute of Oceanography in Goa, agreed. 'Rather than floating about the Andaman Sea for eighteen months, going alternately north and south, I think it's much more likely that it did most of the northward journey in the weeks immediately after the crash. When it arrived at Aye Island we'll never know. Nor where it floated about for that year and a half gathering marine growth.'[14]

A marine biologist at the Goa institute, Dr Arun Parulekar, who had once been based in the Andaman Islands, said that the heavy weed and mollusc encrustation by no means indicated a lengthy sojourn on the seabed. 'In the tropical water temperatures, the fouling organisms settle equally on a drifting or submerged object. The mollusc and weed growth would have occurred whether the wheel was floating or trapped in rocks.'[15] As to the theory that it was delivered to Aye by the crashing Altair, Dr Shetye said: 'If it rose to the surface immediately after impact it most certainly wouldn't have hung about there. Tides, currents, not to mention the annual cyclones, would, within days, have taken it far away from the island.'

In July 1995 the Australian embassy in Yangon succeeded in locating for me Dr Tin Hlaing, an authority on the coastal tides and currents of the Andaman Sea and a former head of Burma's marine services. I had written to him in 1993 but it seemed my letter had never reached him. My first professional Burmese opinion on the northward-drift theory now came from Dr Tin Hlaing in the shape of a highly informative five-page report which confirmed the seasonal current flows the oceanographers had described and the powerful influence of revolving storms on surface-water movements. From weather records of the 1930s, he even sent a precise list of the storms – some of Force 10, 60 knots' strength or more – that had battered the Tenasserim coast month by month between November 1935 and May 1937. There had been no fewer than nineteen of them, any one of which, he said, could have caused the treetop havoc which had prompted Hodder to jump to his hasty conclusions.

Even more enlightening was the persuasive evidence of the northward journeys made over the years by other items of tragic flotsam. As recently as 1994, Dr Tin Hlaing said, a Singaporean ship, the *MV Jaya Pura*, on a voyage up to Yangon laden with drums of oil, had sunk near Simalan Island off the west coast of southern Thailand. Some of the drums, rolling north through the islands of the Mergui Archipelago, had been found near Aye Island. They had travelled over 400 miles up the Myanmar coast. And in a ghastly re-enactment of the Altair wheel journey, the wreckage of a Korean Airlines Boeing 707 which crashed into the sea off the far south of Myanmar on 29 November 1987 travelled more than 200 miles in a few weeks. 'It was on a flight from Abu Dhabi to Singapore. There was a mid-air explosion and wreckage showered into the sea. One of the aircraft's dinghies, along with some of its flotsam, was found floating about near Ye. It was all drifting north to the vicinity of Aye Island. Note that it was the same month as the crash of Sir Kingsford Smith.'[16]

If the *Lady Southern Cross* did go into the sea much further south than the tree-crashing legend had it, what disaster had overwhelmed Smithy and Pethybridge that calm moonlit night over the Andaman Sea? A dramatic engine-failure theory was, nearly forty years later, advanced by the fertile-minded Sir Lawrence Wackett. In a much-publicised lecture in Sydney in 1974,[17] he had given the *Lady Southern Cross* mystery a belated stir by claiming that the Altair's supercharger had failed. The Pratt and Whitney Wasp's supercharger impeller had, he said, been set by the manufacturer at a gear-speed ratio that was too high, causing it to collapse. As a safety measure, in later models of the motor, the ratio had been reduced from 12:1 to 8:1. 'It failed while being driven for record-breaking purposes,' he declared. Just like Hodder's Aye Island disaster explanation, this new scenario from the eminent aircraft-designer acquired a life of its own. Journalists provided fanciful descriptions of how, with the supercharger disintegrating, large quantities of oil flooded into the engine, seizing it and compelling Smithy to lower his undercarriage for a forced landing.

However, George Foster, the retired chief engines engineer of the Commonwealth Aircraft Corporation, which built hundreds of Wasps locally during the Second World War, wrote to me, after conferring with another retired CAC engineer, 'Neither of us has ever heard of a failure of the supercharger drive – or of the 8:1 ratio Lawrence Wackett described.' Nor had Kenneth Bird in Connecticut, a management engineer in the piston production days. 'I'd call it far-fetched,' he said. 'There are no facts that support Sir Lawrence's conclusion. I have no knowledge of a supercharger failure ever occurring anywhere in the world on a Wasp SE model engine. What's more, the company never, ever derated it as he suggested. In fact there were plenty in military service with blower ratios as high as 13:1 and there was no history of failure.'[18]

In any case, had the *Lady Southern Cross* gone into the sea with a dead engine, Smithy would have ditched her relatively gently, slowing her down with full flap and stalling her on to the water at less than 55mph. Yet the forensic examination of the wheel told a very different story, of a crash into the sea with such force that the aircraft, out of control, had virtually exploded on impact.

It is hard to escape the conclusion that the failure was human. Had Smithy or Pethybridge been at the controls at the time? We shall never know, but the probability is that the failure was

Smithy's rather than that of his younger and much fitter co-pilot. In poor health and low spirits when they left England, by early that Friday morning over the Andaman Sea, having had no proper sleep for more than thirty-six hours, Smithy would have been approaching the far edge of his endurance. With Bill Taylor between Hawaii and San Francisco he had nodded off with exhaustion. Had he done so again? Or had his 'aquaphobia' struck, as it had so often over the Burma seas? Because he had no shoulder harness, if he had blacked out again he would have slumped forward over the control column, held only by his lap strap. There would have been little Pethybridge could have done with his dual controls to pull the stick back against Smithy's dead weight.

Indeed, even without Smithy's weight jamming the control column forward, Pethybridge would have been hard pushed to handle the Altair safely in a dire emergency from the rear seat. In Georgia Hank Roller, the former owner of a Lockheed Orion now in the Swiss Transport Museum, was familiar with the operation of the Altair from which his Orion had been converted. A first flight in both aircraft could be likened, he wrote,

> to the breaking to harness of a 2,000-pound spooked draught horse. The rear seat man would have had the controls for maintaining straight and level cruise flight. However, if for no other reason than visibility, it is unlikely that he could have made a successful flight completion. He would have had no flaps or undercarriage controls to make a normal landing. With Smithy's limp body on the control stick Tom Pethybridge could no longer have controlled her in either pitch or roll. It would have been a bad landing – the kind that you do not walk away from.

From what height they began the fatal dive will never be known. If Melrose's flight log and diary are to be believed, the *Lady Southern Cross* had descended to below 3,000ft. What had decided Smithy to drop to that level, one can only speculate. He may have become aware of the drowsy effects of anoxia at 15,000ft without oxygen, with which, yet again, he had decided to dispense, and descended below the light broken cloud for a better view of the terrain to aid his map-reading. The 8 am weather report showed the cloud gradually thickening south of Mergui to 10/10ths cover at Victoria Point. For his flight down the long Malaya peninsula, over which the monsoon was still active, he may have elected to remain below cloud to keep the coastlines in view.

Whatever overwhelmed them, too swiftly even for the briefest radio call, will probably never be established. Nor, short of hugely expensive remote-controlled underwater camera searches, will the location of the remains of the *Lady Southern Cross* on the rocky, mud-free seabed off the southern Myanmar coast. Somewhere in those thousands of square miles of ocean, scattered across the ocean floor, a mere handful of steel components marks the site of the graves of Tommy Pethybridge and Sir Charles Kingsford Smith.

Epilogue

Catherine survived Chilla by less than two and a half years. When she died in March 1938 at the age of eighty, her ashes were flown out to sea off Sydney Heads and scattered by Eric from a Tiger Moth flown by Smithy's nephew, John. 'Kuranda', the modest house that had known in equal measure so much joy and sorrow, was sold. It has changed little with the years, and in 1997 it was the home of three elderly sisters.

Mary, the former Lady Kingsford Smith, died in Florida in the middle of 1997, as this biography was being completed. She was eighty-six. Her second marriage, to oil-industry executive Alan Tully, lasted thirty-eight years, until his death in 1975, and produced, in 1941, her second child, Belinda. In 1940 she and Tully had gone to live permanently in North America, where he went on to become head of the Ethyl Corporation's Canadian operations. The marriage wasn't always happy. 'It was haunted by Chilla's ghost,' Mary confided. 'Although I was no longer Lady Kingsford Smith, somehow in public I never ceased to be his widow. Alan grew terribly jealous of Chill. He didn't even want photographs of him in the house. Finally it led me to destroy every single one of the precious letters Chill had written me from all over the world during those five years. I must have been crazy to have done that. I still try not to think about it.' It was after Tully's death that she began to spend her winters in Florida. She bought an apartment at Holmes Beach, near Sarasota, where she met her third husband, Frank Noldin, a retired General Motors personnel manager. They were married in 1984 when she was seventy-four. Frank, who died in 1996, was almost embarrassingly proud of his wife's Kingsford Smith connection.

Charles Arthur, who is in his mid-sixties, was eight when he left Australia for America with his mother. An electronics engineer, better known to his American friends as 'Chuck', he learned to fly, but, despite acquiring over 1,700 hours, was never tempted to make it a career. However, in June 1978, on the fiftieth anniversary of the *Southern Cross*'s trans-Pacific flight, he decided to fly the ocean himself. To avoid causing his wife and mother unnecessary anxiety, he went as co-pilot on the delivery flight to Australia of a small twin-engined Cessna 340. He flew from Oakland via Hawaii, Tarawa and Fiji to Brisbane in pressurised comfort and at twice the speed of the 'old bus'. 'I wanted to feel the loneliness of that huge ocean. It helped me understand what my father had achieved,' he said. Charles and his wife, Mary, a biologist, have two sons, John, who bears a striking resemblance to his grandfather, and Stephen.

Outside the family, only a handful of Smithy's contemporaries were still alive by the end of 1997. Bill Taylor, who became Sir Gordon Taylor, had died in 1966, John Stannage in 1970 and Beau Sheil in 1978. One of the last of his pilot mates was the pugnacious and resilient Scotty Allan, who some said was Kingsford Smith's superior as a pilot, surviving more than 13,000 flying hours to handle a Boeing 707. From his nursing home near Sydney he continued, to within a few weeks of the end of his life, to answer my queries. He died there in August 1996, aged ninety-six.

Many of the women emotionally involved with Smithy in his years of towering fame I had been too late to meet. Ellen Rogers, who, unrequitedly, had loved Charles Ulm, had gone. Marge McGrath, who later became a Qantas public-relations officer, began to drink heavily and died in Sydney in 1990 in distressed circumstances and intense loneliness. I had also missed Bon Hilliard, who had ended her days at Dee-Why in her mid-eighties in 1982, and Bob Hitchcock's sister, Pretoria Bliss. On 10 April 1989, the sixtieth anniversary of the *Kookaburra*'s forced landing, eighty-eight-year-old Pretoria had been flown out to the lonely site in a helicopter. At the pink, sandy clearing in the scorched desert scrub that had witnessed the tragedy, there was now a memorial cairn and a pair of rain-fed water tanks, filled to the brim with cool, sweet water.

For the American crewmen of the 1928 Pacific flight, the moment of glory was short-lived. They had hoped, back in America, to make some money as local heroes. But, apart from $6,000 (£1,200) they each received from Hearst Newspapers and a public subscription, their rewards were few. Harry Lyon went back to his family home in Paris Hill in Maine. He became a deputy sheriff, married his second wife and, approaching sixty, saw action as the captain of an armed merchantman in the Second World War. He had been an alcoholic for much of his life and, in retirement, according to Schuyler Mott, who runs the Paris Hill library and museum in the old county jail, 'There was a porch on Harry's house facing the Baptist church across the street and he would get pretty drunk on the Fourth of July. He'd go sit on the porch with his booze and his 22 rifle and shoot at the church bell.' Harry Lyon died in May 1963 aged seventy-eight.

Except for his six marriages, Jim Warner's subsequent life had been largely unremarkable. When the Second World War came he was recalled to the US Navy as a shore-based radio instructor and afterwards resumed a precarious and itinerant existence in the radio-repair business in California. He spent his last years in Hayward, near San Francisco, often sitting on the back porch, his son Tom recalled, 'tinkering and fooling with his radio equipment, listening to short-wave Morse transmissions from around the world. From a rotten beginning he'd led a hard life. But he was a good man, with no pretences and no delusions of grandeur.' He died at the Veterans Hospital in Livermore, California, in 1970. He, too, was seventy-eight.

In 1958 Lyon and Warner returned briefly to the limelight. They had been traced by Qantas officials and flown, along with their wives, to Brisbane to attend a ceremony to dedicate a glass pavilion at the airport in which the 'old bus' was put on permanent public view. Beside the aeroplane is a print of a famous oil painting of the two Australian Pacific heroes by the artist Sir William Dargie. Romantically, they are wearing flying suits, and Charles Ulm has his arm affectionately round Smithy's shoulders.

Over all the years of my research into Smithy's death there remained a stone unturned. Was it any longer possible to verify the story of the Burmese fishermen who were said to have seen a light descend into the Andaman Sea on the night he disappeared?

In 1992 an Australian Northern Territory anthropologist and pilot, Arthur Beau Palmer, phoned me. He told me that in the late 1980s he had tried to get Mary Noldin's support for another expedition to Burma to try to find the Altair. Unlike the earlier Wixted one, which he believed had looked in the wrong place, he planned initially to conduct extensive research among the fishing communities of the south Burma coast. Palmer had already succeeded in locating a lot of aeroplanes which had gone missing in northern Australia during the Second World War. He had done so with the help of Aboriginal communities who had witnessed the crashes and absorbed the stories into their tribal folklore, sources which yielded surprisingly reliable information, he said. His trove of military planes included a Spitfire, a B25 bomber, a Mosquito, a Kittyhawk and a Japanese Zero fighter, recovered both on land and from the sea. Similar research in southern Burma, he was convinced, would help to narrow the field of search for the *Lady Southern Cross*. However, Mary Noldin had declined to support the venture – approaching eighty, she did not want the sadness of Chilla's death revived again – so Palmer had abandoned his expedition.

But could his theories have worked? Were there among Burma's south coast people similar ethnic traditions to the Aborigines? Did significant events there become enshrined in oral history? More to the point, would the military government even consider allowing a visit to what had become an unsafe corner of the country? I put the idea to Mary. As my purpose was strictly biographical, with no interest in the Altair's physical recovery, she raised no objection. Early in 1996 I approached the Myanmar government – this time with the support of the Australian Ministry of Foreign Affairs and Trade, whose Embassy in Yangon agreed to forward to the country's Foreign Office my application to visit the prohibited Andaman Sea coast. The request was automatically viewed with suspicion. The Myanmar authorities did not welcome foreign writers: they often used the stated purpose of their visits as a cover to write damaging articles about the totalitarian regime and its alarming human-rights record. My application, which sought permission to visit Aye Island, where the aircraft wheel was found, coastal villages near Tavoy (now Dawei) and the Middle Moscos Islands (now the Maungmagans), was refused 'on security grounds'.

The precise security concerns were not explained. They were, however, being copiously reported in an informative Internet daily news service devoted to the closed world of Myanmar. Parts of the long, narrow strip of the southern peninsula between the Andaman Sea and the Thailand border were apparently in the throes of civil war. One of the country's most spirited ethnic minorities, the Karen, seeking independence from Myanmar, had created a well-organised army which the government forces, the Tatmadaw, were attempting to crush. The area was not a healthy place to visit. Indeed, on the 80-mile road that ran north from Dawei to Ye, from where I had planned to get a boat to visit nearby Aye Island, travellers risked being shot.

I decided to try another tack. I offered to be accompanied by a government official who could decide exactly where, in the troubled south, I could go and what questions I could ask in the villages. The new application moved slowly. It rose through the Foreign Office's director-general to his minister, then to the defence minister, to military intelligence and finally, unbelievably, it seemed, to the Myanmar Cabinet, the country's supreme body, now benignly renamed the State Peace and Development Council. Early in 1998, when the Tatmadaw had regained control of most of the south, the Cabinet issued me, to my astonishment, with a 'special permit' to visit both Ye and Dawei.

I flew to Yangon in March. Time in this city of golden pagodas seemed to have stood still. Unlike the booming high-rise cities of the rest of the Orient, its wide streets were still dominated by ancient colonial buildings with corrugated-iron roofs. There was scarcely a neon sign to be seen. There were no freeways, no metro, no night life. The entire throb of this city of 5 million seemed to cease at around 9 pm and lapse into virtual silence. It was several days before I set eyes on another Western visitor.

At the Ministry of Hotels and Tourism I was allocated a guide, a serious, conscientious man in blue-checked *longyi* and cream silk jacket. U Ohn Kyaw was a devout Buddhist who had once been a lawyer. His normal work was escorting foreign parties round the country's tourist sites, but now his interest and his interpreting was the key to my enterprise. He listened politely as I described Charles Kingsford Smith's demise in Burma airspace, and if he thought mine was a hopeless mission, he did not betray it. We boarded a plane to travel the 250 miles south to Dawei, climbing out across the Gulf of Martaban along the very route that Smithy had flown. I peered out for a glimpse of Aye Island, but the windows of the Myanmar Airways F28 were so scarred with sparkling cracks and the heat haze so dense we might have been flying inside a grey ping-pong ball.

Soldiers in green uniforms with fixed bayonets surrounded the aircraft as we taxied in at Dawei through shimmering heat. Mosquitos whined around the bare arrivals building, and there were sparrows nesting among the stationary ceiling fans. An immigration official studied my special permits searchingly, entering the details in a large ledger. He spoke rapidly to my guide. 'We must report to the regional army headquarters,' U Ohn Kyaw said ominously. 'Without permission of the military you are not to leave Dawei.' Things had not begun well. Dawei lay inland at the head of a long estuary. The fishing villages I had come 7,000 miles to visit were on the coast, 16 miles to the west, and the Maungmagan Islands lay 25 miles offshore.

Outside we retrieved our bags from a bowl of dust beneath a collapsed iron lean-to, and hired a taxi – a small Toyota pick-up with hard, wooden seats and worn shock-absorbers. As we jolted off through the bush towards Dawei a wave of heat engulfed us. The temperature was 40 degrees centigrade. It was like travelling in a fan oven. The sound of cicadas, like batteries of electric drills, came in gusts from the trees as we entered the suburbs. When Lores Bonney passed through here on her 1937 flight to South Africa, Dawei was a small river-port headquarters of the British colonial district administration. It had grown into a city of over 100,000 people, choked with tooting cars, buses, pony carts, bicycles, ox wagons and trishaws. 'People's Desire,' huge government hoardings declared in English. 'Crush all internal and external destructive elements.'

The Tatmadaw headquarters was a camp in baking, parched bush outside town. The building's weatherboards were rotting, the window frames collapsing. Inside soldiers sat in a haze of cheroot smoke, chewing betel and typing documents with carbon papers and correction fluid. The duty officer, a young captain with rows of campaign ribbons, slowly studied my permits. The regional commands, I had been warned, functioned like autonomous fiefdoms. I was, he confirmed, restricted to the city limits. A special permit issued by the highest authority in the land was obviously not permission enough in a forward military area.

It took U Ohn Kyaw three hours to negotiate an extension. Asked to wait outside, I sheltered from the blazing sun under a tree, plagued by small, voracious flies. It was not until mid-afternoon that permission to visit the coastal villages arrived at last by radio from defence headquarters in Yangon. Authority to go out to the Maungmagan Islands was refused. The islands were uninhabited, we were told: there was no point in visiting them. Nor would I be permitted to travel either by sea or by road the 80 miles north to Ye and Aye Island. Ye was in another military district whose commander would have to authorise the visit. It couldn't be arranged from Dawei.

This was only the beginning of the formalities. 'We must report also to the regional civil authorities, as well as the city authorities – and the People's Police,' U Ohn Kyaw informed me. That took most of what was left of the day. Next we tried to find somewhere to stay. There was no hotel in Dawei – it was not a tourist town. I was probably the only foreigner there at that moment. When I walked into the central market to take photographs I was enthusiastically cheered. People crowded round just to look at me. A woman seized me, sat me down and proceeded, amid applause, to give my neck and shoulders a vigorous and soothing massage.

There turned out to be only two private guest houses. Both were full. 'We must try the government guest house,' my guide suggested. We drove to a seventy-year-old, two-storey, wooden building with a large, open, first-floor veranda, set among lawns and tall trees. It must have been an elegant mansion when the last British deputy commissioner lived there; now, with pigeons nesting in the ceilings and its paint peeling, it was a dilapidated shell of its former splendour, its accommodation reduced to two dormitories like military barracks. The caretaker offered us one each. But there was, he explained, a slight problem: there was no water. The tanks had run dry. For US$6 he arranged for the Dawei fire brigade to come and replenish them, and we moved in. By now we had

been joined by a cherubic young man with gold-rimmed spectacles and a thin wisp of beard sprouting from a mole on his chin.
He was, I was told, a Special Branch agent, assigned to follow me
for the duration of my stay. He spoke no English and wasn't permitted to reveal his name. 'Then we shall call him Number
Thirteen,' I suggested to U Ohn Kyaw.

In the centre of Dawei stood the grand stone edifice of the
former colonial administration. It was now the headquarters of the
local political commissar – the regional chairman of the State
Peace and Development Council. In the hope that records of the
search for Kingsford Smith might have survived there, I went to
meet the chairman, an intimidating, unsmiling man with a commanding presence. He sat beneath a framed motto: 'Stability of the
State: community peace and tranquillity, prevalence of law and
order.' When my mission had been outlined he summoned the
regional secretary and explained it to him. The secretary shook his
head. The local records went back only to 1966, he said. At the
port authority on the banks of the Dawei River on the muddy tidal
estuary, the story was the same. If a fisherman had reported a
crashing aircraft, the record would not have survived.

There was no newspaper or library in 1935; indeed, there was
still none. But I discovered that a writer and historian, U Than
Swe, lived in the town. I went to see him at his comfortable home
that would not have been out of place in Beverly Hills. Valuable
Burmese landscape paintings adorned the walls and, rare for
Myanmar, a television and video-recorder were conspicuous in a
corner. U Than Swe, plump and owlish, was in his late fifties and
spoke good English. He had never heard of Kingsford Smith, but
sparked a glimmer of hope when he said: 'I know where there is a
crashed aeroplane.' Alas, it was not in the Andaman Sea, but lay in
the jungle a few miles east of Dawei: the wreckage of a Second
World War plane, in which an Indian general, according to local
legend, had been fleeing to Thailand with a stash of gold.

Early the next morning we set out for the coast, jolting through
rice paddies and rubber plantations on a narrow road teeming
with pony carts, ox wagons and tooting Japanese cars. The Special
Branch man had been joined by a colleague, again nameless, who
became Number 14. They followed us on motorbikes in formation, riding through the red dust trailing in our wake as we wound

over a range of jungle-clad hills whose slopes were scarred by the ravages of cyclonic storms. Not only had they smashed the trees, as Hodder had seen at Aye Island, but in places entire hillsides had been eroded down to bare, pink rock.

In these airless weeks before the monsoon exploded back on the coast, the ocean at Maungmagan Beach lay in a hazy, flat calm. Here, lying among palms and casuarina pines, was the first of the villages. Scattered along the broad white beach and visible in silhouette at sea was the fishing fleet of primitive, open wooden boats. Apart from the addition of small petrol engines precariously mounted on their sterns, their design and motive power of sail and paddle had not changed for centuries. Had the crew of one such craft witnessed Smithy's Lockheed, landing lights on, descending out of the night for a desperate emergency ditching? In Maungmagan village I set out to ask.

Protocol demanded that the process begin with the headman. At his wooden, bamboo-thatched house, shoes and socks removed, we climbed the stairs leading up to the dimly lit family room, in which a shrine of the Buddha glowed serenely. Away from the wilting heat it was deliciously cool. U O Kyaing, small, bald and in his late sixties, greeted us with affable charm. We sat on the floor, cross-legged as custom decreed, while his wife produced cups of China tea and a multitude of grandchildren gathered wide-eyed to listen at a respectful distance. In the background the Special Branch men hovered unobtrusively. But at this point Number 13, who had been diligently writing in his notebook, came into his own: he spoke the Maungmagan coast dialect, which U Ohn Kyaw confessed he didn't entirely understand, so he agreed to put my questions to the headman.

The village chief was awed by the invasion. It was not every day that the village welcomed a foreigner with a special permit from the Cabinet, or a government official all the way from Yangon. Number 13, now familiar with the details of my quest, related at length the story of the Australian aviator's disappearance over the nearby ocean. Everyone listened attentively. The headman was only five years old at the time, and he knew nothing of the event. But, he said, there were some old people in the village who might remember. He asked a younger man, the village's deputy head, to take me to them.

Many villagers, the deputy explained as we set off, lived to ripe old ages. This was thanks to their simple diet of fish, rice and vegetables and their amazingly stress-free existence. Down on the beach, which today boasts an open-air market and holiday houses on stilts that people from Dawei rent during the hot season, we found Daw San Kyin, seventy-seven, toothless and acutely hunched. She had been fourteen when Smithy disappeared, but had never heard the story, either. Instead, with much gesticulation and pointing to the sea, she told me about a ship that, following 'a loud noise', she had watched sink near Maungmagan in the 1940s. The villagers had gone out to the rescue, she recalled, but no one had been saved. Perhaps it was the *Sir Harvey Adamson*, the ship that reported seeing an aeroplane pass over the Middle Moscos Islands the night the *Lady Southern Cross* vanished: the British India Steam Navigation Company's vessel had been blown up by a mine near here in 1947, with the loss of all on board.

Eighty-four-year-old Daw Tun May was still running a general store in the village. In 1935 she had been twenty-one, and married to a fisherman, but her husband had never mentioned such an incident. Much more dramatic, she said, had been the disappearance around that time of an entire fishing crew of six men. When they had failed to return after several months all hope had been abandoned, yet twelve years later they walked back into the village. They had been blown far out into the Bay of Bengal by a storm. An Indian fishing boat had rescued them and taken them to India, where they had been living ever since. The elderly shopkeeper had never even seen an aeroplane until recent years. The Second World War and the Japanese invasion had not touched Maungmagan. She had heard stories of soldiers somewhere descending by parachute, but the village never saw a single Japanese or Allied soldier.

Two miles up the coast to the north another village, Pantinin, lay at the end of a narrow, bare-earth track which wound through ricefields and banana groves past pagodas and monasteries. Orange-robed monks clutching black-lacquered alms bowls were obscured in the swirling dust stirred up by the pick-up as it squealed and scraped over the rocks studding the track. It was so rough that the Special Branch men had to abandon their motorbikes and climb aboard the Toyota. At Pantinin the ritual began again. When the mats had been laid and cold drinks served, the headman sent for the village's oldest inhabitant, U Tun Swe, who was nervous and bewildered by the summons to meet a foreigner asking about a pilot from a country he had never heard of. He did remember stories about an aircraft crash, but it was on land and a long time ago, and his memory had faded. He could not elaborate.

'The trouble is,' explained U Ohn Kyaw, 'the aged people here were illiterate in those days. The village had no school, no electricity, no telephones, no radio, no newspapers. Their only transport was the bullock cart. They would marry someone from the next village, two miles away. Most never even visited Dawei in their whole lives. They knew little of the outside world. Their world was this small stretch of coast. They wouldn't have heard of England or Australia. The whole concept of an aeroplane would have been foreign to most of them in 1935. They were very simple people.'

We bumped our way back to Maungmagan village. The next day, along a road cratered and fissured by the monsoon, we went south to Thabawseik, the only other Andaman Sea village from which it was likely that the story could have reached Dawei. Thabawseik nestled among tall palms in the curve of a bay beneath a hill whose jungle slopes were dotted with bright, white pagodas. This village had one of the biggest fishing fleets on the coast. The beach in front of the palm-thatched houses was crowded with boats and lined with frames hung with sun-drying fish. Out in the bay, bigger boats with flimsy thatched cabins rolled gently at anchor. Further out at sea, toward the Middle Moscos Islands, others were specks on the horizon against the setting sun. Surely, in such a big community of fishing families, a whisper of the legend would linger? But Thabawseik was a village of active young people. The headman, who sat on a chair on the sand outside his house, smoking a cheroot, told us there was no one there over forty. Had the legend existed in their folklore, he would certainly have been aware of it, but there was no such legend.

'Sadly, I think the story has died,' commiserated U Ohn Kyaw as we drove back in the dark through the paddies and rubber trees. 'You can see they are not very curious about anything beyond fishing and rice cultivation – and village gossip. The tale of the big light was probably soon forgotten – it didn't relate to anything they could immediately comprehend. Because they couldn't understand it, it became unimportant. It wasn't significant enough to join their folklore.'

On my last day in Dawei I went back to Maungmagan. Our driver knew of a very old man there whom we hadn't met earlier. U Aye Dun, ninety years old, was a small, gnome-like figure with a long, sad face. He had been twenty-eight when Smithy crashed, and an obvious candidate to have been out that night in the Moscos, since he did sometimes fish there. As my questions were translated he became suddenly animated. The sadness disappeared from his face and he began excitedly to describe something. His thin arms jabbed upwards, pointing to the sky. My heart quickened. All I needed was one witness. Had I found him?

'He is describing an aeroplane,' U Ohn Kyaw translated, with Number 13's help. 'It was a plane, he says, with two wings – a biplane. It was before the war. It flew over the village very low. They had never seen an aeroplane before and didn't know what this noisy bird was. They were so terrified that they fled and hid in the forest until it had gone.'

The old fisherman knew nothing of a night crash into the sea. Neither he nor anyone else in the village had ever seen any of the leaflets the RAF had dropped during the search for the *Lady Southern Cross*.

There were no more ocean fishing villages within reach of Dawei, and no more old people to question – or so it seemed. Three months later, back in New Zealand, a registered letter arrived for me from Dawei. It came from U Than Swe. The historian had been making inquiries about the falling light supposedly seen on the night of Smithy's disappearance. Amazingly, he had tracked down in Dawei, 'an old reporter', U Aung Nyunt, who clearly remembered the event. 'A fisherman who saw a big light descending into the sea had reported it to the township officer,' U Than Swe wrote. Alas, the municipal files for the 1930s no longer exist. But it does seem that, after all, there might be some substance to the story. Perhaps the last stone has indeed yet to be turned.

Sir Charles Kingsford Smith's
Principal Flights

Times – when he entered them – and aircraft registrations are taken from his logbooks.

1927 (28–31 January): Perth–Sydney
Failed record attempt, with two passengers, in Bristol Tourer (G-AUDK). Flight made in formation with second Tourer (G-AUDJ), flown by Keith Anderson. Journey took over 4 days and 30 flying hours; record 21½ hours.
Route: Perth–Kalgoorlie–Naretha–Cook–Wirraminna–Broken Hill–Parkes–Sydney

1927 (19–29 June): Around Australia
Record 7,500-mile flight of 10 days 5¼ hours with passenger Charles Ulm in Bristol Tourer (G-AUDJ).
Route: Sydney–Brisbane–Longreach–Darwin–Broome–Carnarvon–Perth–Naretha– Wirraminna–Adelaide–Melbourne–Sydney

1928 (17–19 January): San Francisco: World endurance flight record attempt
Fokker trimotor FVIIb-3m *Southern Cross* (US identification No. 1985). Co-pilot: Commander George Pond. Airborne time of 50 hours 5 minutes failed to break the 52-hour 22-minute record.

1928 (31 May–9 June): America–Australia
First trans-Pacific flight between the two countries (7,200 miles). Fokker *Southern Cross* (1985). Co-pilot: Charles Ulm; navigator: Harry Lyon; wireless-operator: Jim Warner. Total flying time: 83 hours 50 minutes.
Route: Oakland–Honolulu (27 hrs 25 mins); Honolulu–Kauai (55 mins); Kauai–Suva (34 hrs 30 mins); Suva–Naselai beach (1 hr); Naselai–Brisbane (20 hrs)

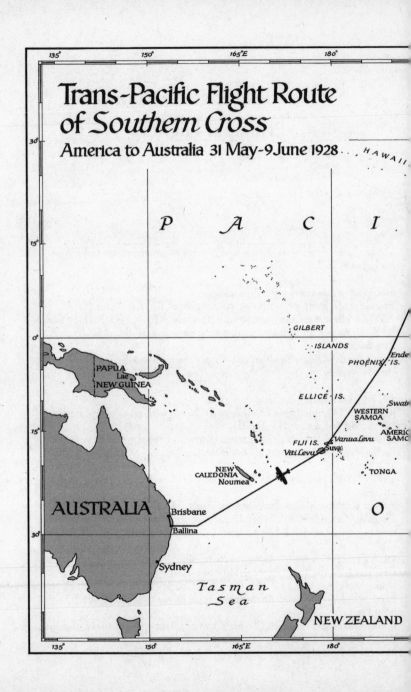

Trans-Pacific Flight Route of *Southern Cross*

America to Australia 31 May-9 June 1928

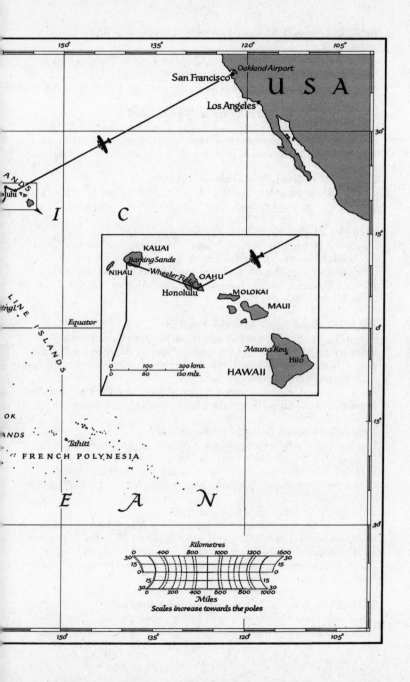

150° 135° 120° 105°

Oakland Airport

San Francisco

U S A

Los Angeles

30°

A N D S

lulu

I   C   15°

KAUAI
Barking Sands
NIHAU   Wheeler Field   OAHU
Honolulu   MOLOKAI
8°   MAUI

L I N E

Equator

ingl   Mauna Kea
                                         Hilo
0   100   200 kms.   HAWAII
0   60   120 mls.

I S L A N D S

OK   15°
ANDS   Tahiti

F R E N C H   P O L Y N E S I A

E   A   N   30°

Kilometres
0   400   800   1000   1200   1600
30   30
15   15
15   15
30   30
0   200   400   600   800   1000
Miles
Scales increase towards the poles

150° 135° 120° 105°

1928 (8–9 August): Melbourne–Perth. First non-stop flight across Australia
Fokker *Southern Cross* (G-AUSU). Co-pilot: Charles Ulm; navigator: Harold Litchfield; wireless-operator: Tom McWilliams. Distance: 2,000 miles; time: 23 hours 25 minutes.

1928 (10–11 September): Australia–New Zealand
First flight across the Tasman Sea. Fokker *Southern Cross* (G-AUSU). Co-pilot: Charles Ulm; navigator: Harold Litchfield; wireless-operator: Tom McWilliams. Sydney–Christchurch. Time: 14 hours 25 minutes.

1928 (8–9 October): New Zealand–Australia
First westbound Tasman crossing. Fokker *Southern Cross* (G-AUSU). Crew as for eastward journey. Blenheim–Sydney time: 23 hours.

1929 (30–31 March): Sydney–'Coffee Royal'
Disastrous attempt to fly from Australia to England in *Southern Cross* (G-AUSU). Co-pilot: Charles Ulm; navigator: Harold Litchfield; wireless-operator: Tom McWilliams. Lost in bad weather in North-Western Australia, Smithy force-landed on Kimberley mudflat. Time: 28 hours 30 minutes.

1929 (25 June–8 July): Australia–England
Record flight between the two countries. *Southern Cross* (G-AUSU). Resumed flight to England following Coffee Royal forced landing. Co-pilot: Charles Ulm; navigator: Harold Litchfield; wireless-operator: Tom McWilliams. Time: 12 days 18 hours.
Route: Sydney–Derby–Singapore–Singora–Rangoon–Calcutta–Allahabad–Karachi–Bandar Abbas–Basra–Baghdad–Athens–Rome–London

1930 (23–24 June): Ireland–Newfoundland
First fully successful westbound north Atlantic flight. *Southern Cross* (VH-USU). Co-pilot: Evert van Dijk; navigator: Paddy Saul; wireless-operator: John Stannage. Portmarnock Beach (near Dublin)–Harbour Grace (Newfoundland). Distance: 1,900 miles; time: 31 hours 30 minutes

1930 (9–19 October): England–Australia
Record solo flight in Avro Avian *Southern Cross Junior* (G-ABCF). Time of 9 days 22 hours (London–Darwin) broke Hinkler's 1928 15½-day record.
Route: London–Rome–Athens–Aleppo–Bushire–Karachi–Allahabad–Rangoon–Singapore–Surabaya–Atamboea (Timor)–Darwin–Cloncurry–Brisbane–Sydney

1931 (24 September–7 October): Australia–England
Failed solo record attempt in Avro Avian *Southern Cross Minor* (VH-UQG). Bad weather necessitated a forced landing in Malaya; illness

another in Turkey where he was temporarily detained. Later rested for four days in Athens. Australia–England time of 14 days failed to beat the under-9-day record of Jim Mollison.
Route: Melbourne–Adelaide–Oodnadatta–Alice Springs–Wyndham–Ceribon (Java)–Malayan beach–Victoria Point–Rangoon–Calcutta–Jhansi–Karachi–Jask–Bushire–Baghad–Aleppo–Milas (Turkey)–Athens–Rome–London

1931 (30 November–16 December): Australia–England
First all-Australian airmail flight to England. Avro 10 trimotor *Southern Star* (VH-UMG). Co-pilot: Scotty Allan; engineer: Wyndham Hewitt. Time: 17 days.
*Route:*Sydney–Brisbane–Cloncurry–Camooweal–Darwin–Kupang–Surabaya–Alor Star–Bangkok–Rangoon–Calcutta–Gaya–Allahabad–Jodhpur–Karachi–Jask–Bushire–Baghdad–Aleppo–Athens–Rome–Lyon–Le Touquet (beach)–London

1932 (7–22 January): England–Australia return mail flight
(London–Melbourne)
Avro 10 *Southern Star* (VH-UMG). Co-pilot: Scotty Allan. Time: 16 days.
Route: Hamble–Le Bourget–Marseilles–Rome–Athens–Aleppo–Bushire–Jask–Jodhpur–Calcutta–Bangkok–Alor Star–Singapore–Surabaya–Kupang–Darwin–Camooweal–Cloncurry–Longreach–Brisbane–Sydney–Melbourne

1933 (11 January): Australia–New Zealand
Southern Cross (VH-USU) to NZ for joyriding tour. Gerringong Beach, NSW–New Plymouth. Time: 14 hours. Co-pilot/navigator: P. G. (Bill) Taylor; wireless-operator: John Stannage

1933 (27 March): New Zealand–Australia
Southern Cross (VH-USU) return Tasman flight. Co-pilot/navigator: P. G. (Bill) Taylor; wireless-operator: John Stannage. Ninety Mile Beach, NZ–Sydney. Time: 13 hours 42 minutes.

1933 (4–11 October): England–Australia (Lympne–Wyndham)
Solo flight time of 7 days 4 hours 43 minutes was briefly an absolute record for the route. Percival Gull 4 *Miss Southern Cross* (G-ACJV – later VH-CKS).
Route: Lympne (Kent)–Brindisi–Baghdad–Gwadar–Karachi–Jodhpur–Akyab–Alor Star–Surabaya–Wyndham (then via Camooweal, Brisbane and Sydney to Melbourne, arriving 14 October)

1934 (13 January): Australia–New Zealand
Southern Cross (VH-USU) to NZ for second summer joyriding visit.

Co-pilot: Tommy Pethybridge; navigator: P. G. (Bill) Taylor; wireless-operator: John Stannage. Time: 15 hours 25 minutes (Sydney–New Plymouth)

1934 (29 March): New Zealand–Australia
Southern Cross (VH-USU). Return Tasman flight. Co-pilot: Tommy Pethybridge; navigator: P. G. (Bill) Taylor; wireless-operator: John Stannage. Time: 13 hours 23 minutes (Ninety Mile Beach, NZ–Sydney)

1934 (8 September): Sydney–Perth
Trans-Australia record. Lockheed Altair *Lady Southern Cross* (VH-USB). Co-pilot: P. G. (Bill) Taylor. Time: 10 hours 19 minutes (Melbourne–Perth)

1934 (20 October–3 November): Australia–America
World's first eastbound trans-Pacific flight. Lockheed Altair *Lady Southern Cross* (VH-USB). Co-pilot/navigator: P. G. (Bill) Taylor. Total flying time: 52 hours.
Route and sector times: Brisbane–Suva (12 hours); Suva–Honolulu (25 hours); Honolulu–San Francisco (15 hours)

1935 (15 May): Tasman forced return flight
Failed Australia–New Zealand special Jubilee airmail flight. *Southern Cross* (VH-USU). Co-pilot/navigator: P. G. (Bill) Taylor; wireless-operator: John Stannage. Aircraft returned to Sydney on two engines when starboard propeller was smashed in mid-Tasman. Time: 6 hours out, 9 hours back

1935 (6–8 November): England–Burma
Kingsford Smith's final flight – a failed attempt to break Scott and Black's England–Australia record of 2 days 4 hours 38 minutes to Darwin. Lockheed Altair *Lady Southern Cross* (G-ADUS). Co-pilot: Tommy Pethybridge.
Route and cumulative times according Sydney Morning Herald: Lympne (Kent)–Athens (8 hours)–Baghdad (15 hours 52 minutes)– Allahabad (29 hours 27 minutes – compared with Scott and Black's 26 hours 41 minutes)–crashed into Andaman Sea off south Burma

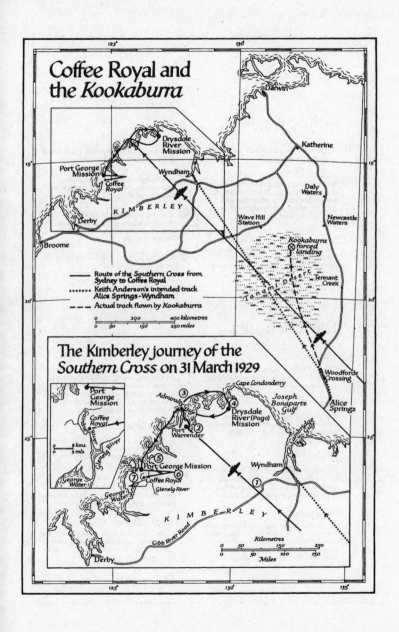

Coffee Royal and the *Kookaburra*

Darwin

Drysdale
River
Mission

Katherine

Port George
Mission

Wyndham

Daly
Waters

Coffee
Royal

KIMBERLEY

Wave Hill
Station

Newcastle
Waters

Derby

Kookaburra
forced
landing

Broome

Tennant
Creek

Tanami Desert

——— Route of the *Southern Cross* from
Sydney to Coffee Royal
········ Keith Anderson's intended track
Alice Springs–Wyndham
– – – Actual track flown by *Kookaburra*

200   400 kilometres
50   150   250 miles

Woodforde
Crossing

Alice
Springs

The Kimberley journey of the *Southern Cross* on 31 March 1929

Port
George
Mission

Cape Londonderry

Joseph
Bonaparte
Gulf

Coffee
Royal

③

Admiralty

④

Drysdale
River (Pago)
Mission

Cambridge Gulf

8 kms.
5 mls.

②

Port
Warrender

Glenelg River

⑤

Wyndham

George
Water

⑦

Port George Mission

①

⑥

Coffee Royal

Glenelg River

George
Water

KIMBERLEY

Gibb River Road

Kilometres
50   150   250
50   100   150
Miles

Derby

Coffee Royal

① Aircraft, in cloud and dark, passes south-west of Wyndham.

② Reaches coast around Port Warrender. Crew believe they are 350 miles to the east on the coast south of Darwin. Smithy mistakenly heads west to try to find Wyndham.

③ Realisation dawns at last that they have reached the Timor Sea. They now turn to follow the Kimberley coast eastward, hoping it will lead them to Wyndham.

④ Stumble upon the Drysdale mission and get wrongly directed south-west

⑤ Port George mission correctly directs them eastward to Wyndham, to which they set out to fly.

⑥ After flying about 50 miles east Smithy abandons the flight and tries unsuccessfully to relocate the Port George mission.

⑦ With fuel almost exhausted he force-lands on a mudflat.

The last hours

12·45am

Jimmy Melrose in Percival Gull Westley leaves Rangoon to resume his flight to Australia.

1·30am

Smithy and Tom Pethybridge, in Lockhead Altair Lady Southern Cross, pass over Rangoon en route to Singapore.

2·50 am

Burma government ship Sir Harvey Adamson, cruising in the vacinity of Middle Moscos (Maungmagan) Islands, reports seeing one aircraft fly past.

2·50 am (approx.)

The faster Altair (Melrose later reports) overtakes him over the Andaman Sea. Times and relative speeds of the two aircraft put most likely position at around 250 miles from Rangoon.

May 1937

Starboard wheel of Lady Southern Cross found by Burmese fishermen. In January 1938 fragments of metal from the wheel's closure panel are discovered nearby by Australian engineer Jack Hodder.

January 1938

Jack Hodder sails from Kanbauk to Aye I. and creates the myth that Lady Southern Cross crashed there.

May 1937

Australian pilot Lores Bonney hears story that fishermen saw light descend into sea early on 8 November 1935.

2·50-3·50am

Lady Southern Cross crashes into sea somewhere along the 200 or so miles between the Moscos Islands and the Kra Isthmus.

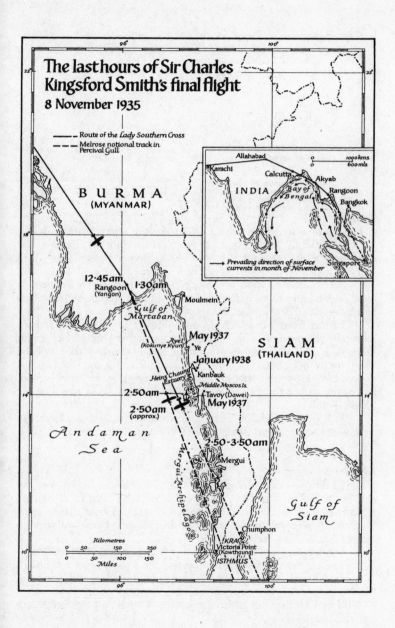

The last hours of Sir Charles Kingsford Smith's final flight

8 November 1935

——— Route of the *Lady Southern Cross*
- - - - Melrose notional track in
Percival Gull

BURMA
(MYANMAR)

12·45am
Rangoon
(Yangon)

1·30am

Moulmein

*Gulf of
Martaban*

May 1937

Ye (Kokunye Kyun)

January 1938

Heinz Chaung
Estuary

Kanbauk

Middle Moscos Is.

2·50am

Tavoy (Dawei)

2·50am
(approx.)

May 1937

*Andaman
Sea*

2·50-3·50am

Mergui

Mergui Archipelago

SIAM
(THAILAND)

*Gulf of
Siam*

Chumphon

Kilometres
0 50   150   250
0   50   100   150
Miles

IKRA

Victoria Point
(Kawthaung)

ISTHMUS

(Inset map)

Allahabad
Karachi
Calcutta
Akyab
Rangoon
Bangkok

INDIA

*Bay of
Bengal*

0   1000 kms.
0   600 mls.

Singapore

→ *Prevailing direction of surface
currents in month of November*

Notes

Preface

1. *Caesar of the Skies* (Beau Sheil), *Smithy* (John Stannage), 'Air Master Supreme' in *Flying Matilda* (Norman Ellison), *Smithy: The Kingsford Smith Story* and *The Man on the Twenty Dollar Note* (Ward McNally), *Charles Kingsford Smith* (Pedr Davis).

2. An account of Ward McNally's criminal past, his years spent in New Zealand prisons and reformed life in Australia is the substance of his autobiography *Cry of a Man Running*.

3. Letters from Ward McNally to publisher Paul Hamlyn, Sydney, November/December 1977. Recalling his encounter with McNally, Pedr Davis said: 'The introduction to his book *Smithy* thanked "the late Beau Sheil" for his help. Beau was, however, very much alive and when I interviewed him many years later he was still spitting chips. McNally, he said, had never spoken to him in his life. He had simply taken words out of Sheil's own book.'

4. In-flight notes held in Ernest Crome Collection, National Library of Australia, Canberra, and Charles Ulm Collection, State Library of NSW, Sydney.

Chapter 1

1. Corbea was never listed in the Post Office street directory of the day, but a former neighbour, Edward Cullen, who lived in Whyenbah Road from 1870 to 1950, told his granddaughter, Julia Fryar, that he knew the Smith family, who lived in what was then the next house, and remembered Charles being born there in 1897.

2. 'Reminiscences of Kingsford Smith's Childhood', by Winifred Sealby.

3. The eighteen-bedroomed house, which for some years contained a 'Kingsford Smith Restaurant' and disco, was burned to the ground in 1993.

4. 'Little Mother', an undated tribute to Catherine Kingsford Smith by Winifred Sealby.

5.   'Reminiscences of Kingsford Smith's Childhood', op. cit.

6.   Ibid.

7.   Smithy was referring to Vincent Patrick Taylor, popularly known as 'Captain Penfold'.

8.   'The New Magellan: Sailor of the Skies', by S. J. Woolf, in *New York Times* magazine, 6 July 1930. Another version of the story has Charles, around this time, building a pair of wooden wings and, along with his cousin Hal Southerden, using them to make 10ft jumps from the veranda roof of the Southerden's home in Strathfield, Sydney.

9.   Queen's School, Vancouver. Kingsford Smith's Form 2 report for the term ending 25 October 1907.

10. Much later Smithy learned that he and Rupert had made Australian surf life-saving history: they had been the first people saved using the newly introduced reel-and-line system. One of Smithy's rescuers was Warwick Wilce, to whom Catherine wrote on 4 January 1907: 'I cannot tell you how I feel towards all those heroic men who risked their lives to save a little child. I should have written yesterday, but Charlie wanted to send you a small gift.' She enclosed it, but there is no record of what it was.

Chapter 2

1.   Commemorative material supplied by St Andrew's Cathedral School gave a range of conflicting dates for Kingsford Smith's years there. Catherine's diary establishes his arrival date as 28 April 1909 and it is fairly certain that he left at the end of 1911.

2.   Sydney Technical High School Class 1C result sheet, final term, 1912.

3.   Colonial Sugar Refining Company personnel file on Kingsford Smith held in the Business and Labour Archives of the Australian National University, Canberra.

4.   'Reminiscences of Kingsford Smith's Childhood', op. cit.

5.   Ibid.

6.   Between 1915 and 1925 Smithy wrote hundreds of letters to his parents. Those that have survived are today in the Norman Ellison Collection (MS 1882) in the National Library of Australia, Canberra.

7.   Now in the Queensland Museum.

8.   *Aces High*, by Alan Clark. In the last twelve months of the war German pilots began to save their lives with static-line parachutes.

9.   In 1998 the British Public Record Office began to release First World War officers' personal records and correspondence under the seventy-five-year rule. Among them were the RFC service records of Charles Kingsford Smith. They contained no more than the bare details of his successive postings, which were already in the public domain.

Chapter 3

1.   Sir Charles Kingsford Smith, as told to Edwin C. Parsons in 'My Co-Pilot was called Death', *Liberty* magazine, 1935.

2.   James Cross died at the end of 1996 in his ninety-ninth year.

3.   Laurie Coombes (1899–1988) became a distinguished aeronautical scientist. He worked for the British Royal Aircraft Establishment before emigrating in 1938 to Australia, where he founded the country's Aeronautical Research Laboratory in Melbourne.

4.   Laurie Coombes, 'Barnstorming with Charles Kingsford Smith' in *Cross & Cockade International*, Vol. 9, No. 4.

5.   When Smithy left the RAF, with the rank of lieutenant, his commanding officer at Eastchurch, Major B. J. Moore, gave him a warm reference, describing his flying as 'excellent'. The note, dated May 1919, listed twenty types of aircraft he had flown: Maurice Farman BE2e; Martinsyde; Sopwith 1½ Strutter; Sopwith Pup, Camel, Snipe and Dolphin; Avro 504K; SPAD 7; SE5; DH6; DH4; Bristol Fighter; Armstrong Whitworth FK2; Nieuport Scout; FE2B; RE8; Bristol Monoplane – and two German aircraft: the Albatross D5 and the Fokker biplane.

6.   Laurie Coombes, 'Barnstorming with Charles Kingsford Smith', op. cit.

Chapter 4

1.   *These are Facts*, by Air Marshal Sir Richard Williams.

2.   Observation by vintage-aircraft consultant Michael Vaisey, of Little Gransden in Cambridgeshire, England.

3.   Australian Archive, ACT: A457/1, item C506/6.

Chapter 5

1.   *Australian Aviator*, by Sir Norman Brearley.

2.   For quaint commercial reasons the weekly service was not allowed to start from Perth. Because a railway ran to Geraldton, 240 miles to the north, the flights began from there to avoid taking business from the trains.

3.   Letter to author from Michael Prevost, Aldham, Suffolk, 27 December 1994.

4.   Verona subsequently married a prosperous Australian wool-buyer, Benjamin Prevost, and Smithy remained a good friend of them both. But her affluent life descended into tragedy and attempted suicide. In London in 1948 she submitted to a horrifying full prefontal leucotomy, which reduced her, according to Michael Prevost, to a 'semi-vegetable' state for ten years. She died in London in 1976 at the age of eighty.

5.   *Smithy: The Kingsford Smith Story*, by Ward McNally.

6.   *The Man on the Twenty Dollar Note*, op. cit.

7.   *A Thousand Skies*, a six-part Australian television drama, 1985.

8.   *Pilbara Bushman – The Life Experience of W. Dunn*, by Graham Wilson (Hesparian Press, Perth, 1989).

9.   John Kingsford-Smith (born 1911) has spent most of his life in the Australian film industry, having started out as a cinema newsreel

cameraman. After service as a fighter pilot in the RAAF during the Second World War, in which he became a wing commander, he created his own successful film production company, Kingcroft, in Sydney.

Chapter 6

1. *Australian Aviator*, op. cit.

2. Sources for Smithy's sacking are *Australian Aviator*, op. cit.; 'Western Australian Airways Ltd', by G. Goodall, in Aviation Historical Society of Australia journal; 'The Father of Australia's Airline Industry' by Angela Prime, in *Aircraft* magazine, December 1991/January 1992.

3. The accident report, still on file at the Australian Bureau of Air Safety Investigation (A8323), casually declared the cause as 'undetermined'. Most probably it was a control-wire or structural failure.

4. *Pilbara Bushman*, op. cit.

5. *NZ Truth*, 8 November 1928.

6. *To the Bar Bonded*, by Kathleen Mallett.

Chapter 7

1. Australian Archives: A795 Department of Air, file 21/1/61 Part 1.

2. Today, as Gascoyne Trading, the company is one of Western Australia's biggest road-transport firms.

3. Transcript of evidence in action Henry Smith Hitchcock v. Kingsford Smith and others, Supreme Court of NSW in causes before judge and jury of four, 19 March 1929. NSW State Archives.

4. Personal dossiers for 1st Australian Imperial Forces ex-service members, Australian Archives (ACT): Charles Thomas Ulm, 'Famous People', Box SVZ (214.4.4.5).

5. Their route round Australia was: Sydney–Brisbane–Longreach–Camooweal–Darwin–Broome–Minilya Station (emergency landing)–Carnarvon–Perth–Naretha–Cook–Wirraminna–Adelaide–Melbourne–Sydney.

Chapter 8

1. Supreme Court of NSW in equity: Case No. 5633 of 1928 – Keith Vincent Anderson v. Charles Edward Kingsford Smith and Charles Thomas Phillippe Ulm. Transcript of evidence in NSW State Archives, ref. K180390.

2. Ibid.

3. 'The Southern Cross Complex', by Gregory C. Kohn, in American Aviation Historical Society journal, Vol. 4, No. 3 (third quarter, 1959). A false myth developed that the trimotor offered to Smithy was still fitted with the *Alaskan*'s smaller 63ft-span wing. In fact its original 71ft 2in wing had been reattached.

Chapter 9

1. Supreme Court of NSW in equity: transcript of evidence in Case No. 5633 of 1928.

2. *A Pioneer Heritage*, by Sam T. Clover and *G. Allan Hancock*, by De Witt Meredith.

3. *A Pioneer Heritage*, op. cit.

4. Bud Morriss, who held Pilot's Licence No. 10, became the first president of America's Early Birds.

5. Pilots George Hood and John Moncrieff disappeared on 10 January 1928 while attempting to make the first flight from Australia to New Zealand in the much-acclaimed Ryan monoplane.

6. Letter from C. E. Kingsford Smith and C. T. P. Ulm in San Francisco to Keith Anderson in Sydney, 16 May 1928. Exhibit in Case No. 5633 of 1928, Supreme Court in equity.

Chapter 10

1. 'The Trans-Pacific Flight – Being the Saga of the *Southern Cross*', by James W. Warner, as told to John Robert Johnson, in *Liberty* magazine, 19 April 1930. The article was based on an unpublished manuscript of Warner's.

2. San Francisco *Examiner*, 2 June 1928.

3. Locke Harper's letter to Walter Phillips, 13 September 1957, op. cit.

4. Not all the notes got through. Some dropped off the stick's clip and fell underneath the tank. Several years later, when the *Southern Cross* was at Mascot being converted for use as an airliner, Ernest Aldis, a young apprentice, found a small pile of them which had lain there for over two years. Today many of the notes are in the Ernest Crome Collection, National Library of Australia, Canberra and the Charles Ulm Collection, Mitchell Library, Sydney.

5. Lyon's charts are held today in the Rare Map Collection (RM2811/1-6) in the National Library of Australia, Canberra.

Chapter 11

1. Lyon used eight charts to navigate the Pacific. Two of them – covering a section of the mid-Pacific between latitudes 12° and 3°S and the area immediately east of the Australian coast – have not survived. It is believed that Smithy gave these to someone as a souvenir.

2. The *Southern Cross* was in the air for one hour longer than Lindbergh's 1927 New York–Paris flight of thirty-three and a half hours for the greater non-stop distance of 3,610 miles. The grandstand in Suva's Albert Park was named the Kingsford Smith Pavilion in Smithy's honour. Also in 1927 Chamberlin and Levine had completed a forty-one and a half-hour non-stop flight of nearly 4,000 miles from New York to Eisleben in Germany in the Wright-Bellanca *Columbia*, but only around half that distance was over the ocean.

3. 'Breach Denied by Australian Flyers', *Los Angeles Times*, 6 June 1928.

4. According to the times Smithy entered in his pilot's logbook, which included the short positioning flights in Hawaii and Fiji.

Chapter 12

1.   US$50,000 was the figure quoted by Ulm as 'personal liabilities' in the contracts he had drawn up for Lyon and Warner in Suva.

2.   The guess of the Sydney Police on the day. Huge licence was subsequently taken in estimates of the Mascot crowd. Most of Smithy's biographers raised the figure, as he did in his autobiography, to 300,000. Ulm's memoirs give it as 400,000. The London *Times* settled for 500,000.

3.   *Faith in Australia: Charles Ulm and Australian Aviation*, by Ellen Rogers.

4.   Sydney *Sun*, 2 August 1938.

5.   Melbourne *Herald*, 6 August 1928.

6.   Melbourne *Herald*, 9 June 1928.

7.   Australian House of Representatives Hansard, 12 June 1928.

Chapter 13

1.   Its third and final registration was the Australian VH-USU.

2.   Report of Kingsford Smith's divorce hearing, *NZ Truth*, 8 November 1928.

3.   Letter from Elsie Pike to June Dupre, 24 September 1928, in the possession of Mrs Dupre.

4.   With characteristic carelessness Smithy entered the date as 9 October in his often unmethodically maintained logbook.

5.   In an interview later that day, Ulm corrected Smithy's figure to 30 gallons, which would have given them only another fifty minutes' flying.

Chapter 14

1.   Neither Smithy nor Ulm sank any of their own money into the airline: they were each issued with a £6,250 free parcel of shares. Their ANA had no connection with the much longer-lived company of the same name which was created in 1936.

2.   This had no connection with the trouble-plagued amphibian of the same name which was designed for the RAAF by Lawrence Wackett.

3.   Kingsford Smith's evidence at the 'Coffee Royal' inquiry.

4.   Transcript of evidence in action Henry Smith Hitchcock v. Kingsford Smith and others, Supreme Court of NSW in causes before judge and jury of four, 19 March 1929. NSW State Archives.

5.   In an attempt to improve the audibility of reception against the inflight noise, the radio system had been modified since the Pacific and Tasman flights on which the 400ft aerial had been used for medium wave, short-distance work and the 15ft one for short-wave long-range communication. The long aerial was now used for reception and the short one for transmission.

6.   The winding mechanism appears to have been defective. On takeoff from Sydney it suddenly ran out involuntarily and McWilliams had to frantically wind it back before the dangling wire was ripped off by trees.

7. Letter produced at the 'Coffee Royal' inquiry, from George Beard to N. A. Paull, 10 April 1929.

Chapter 15
1. Department of Air memorandum in Australian Archives (A705, File 21/1/84, Pt 2).
2. 'Gallantry of Keith Anderson', by William Berg, Sydney *Guardian*, 28 June 1929.
3. Article in Sydney *Sun*, 20 April 1929, cabled by Smithy from Derby.

Chapter 16
1. *Labour Daily*, Sydney, 20 April 1929.
2. Sydney *Daily Guardian*, 16 April 1929. Many years later the New Zealand journalist Eric Baume, who was news editor of the *Guardian* during the Coffee Royal affair, wrote in his autobiography, *I Lived These Years*: 'I'm afraid we headed our own matter in such a way that the meaning was ambiguous. "Ulm's Tale" was our headline and our poster. It was a very wrong one, because these two men – the one the greatest airman, the other the greatest air organiser Australia has ever known – were above faking a stunt when the whole of their careers in big commercial aviation depended upon a successful flight.'
3. Flight Lieutenant Eaton cut from the rudder fabric the text of the diary. It is today on display in the Perth Museum.

Chapter 17
1. Sydney *Daily Telegraph Pictorial*.
2. Around 1939 Bon married an army officer, Major Thomas Marshall Tate, an Ulsterman who had served in the First World War and in the Indian Army. He died eleven years later. But Bon's true love remained Keith Anderson, and she requested that her ashes be scattered from the air over his memorial. Unfortunately, by the time she died – in 1982, aged eighty-five – no one was able to arrange this.
3. *Plain Talk*, 27 April 1929.
4. Article in an American magazine (name and date not supplied), quoted by Beau Sheil in *Caesar of the Skies*, op. cit.
5. Heavily dependent on advertising from British aircraft manufacturers, *Aircraft* rarely had a good word for foreign aeroplanes, including the *Southern Cross*, whose 1928 Pacific flight it dismissed as a valueless stunt. Nonetheless, during his editorship through the 1920s, Ted Hart fought a ceaseless battle for the development of a safe, well-regulated aviation industry in Australia, waging in the process war on official apathy and aviators he saw as cowboys and stunt pilots in search of personal glory.
6. In 1958, prompted by the publication of his short biography of Smithy in *Flying Matilda*, Ellison was attacked by Harold Litchfield and

Tom McWilliams for whom, despite the passage of years, Coffee Royal was still a sensitive issue. In a joint statement they formally deplored Ellison's references to the loss of public esteem Smithy had suffered as a result of the forced landing, 'more especially', they added, 'as we both know quite definitely that Kingsford Smith and Ulm blamed him for the articles inferring [sic] that the forced landing was not genuine but a publicity stunt'. Around the same time Ellen Rogers was still conducting a lone campaign to force Ellison to admit publicly that he had written the articles she believed had permanently blackened the names of Kingsford Smith and Ulm. In June 1958 she told Locke Harper in a letter (held in the papers of Walter Phillips, Australian managing director of Atlantic Union Oil): 'I asked him if he could make a written statement that these shocking articles were the result of a newspaper war. He said he hadn't written them.' However, she added, she had subsequently learned from Eric Kingsford-Smith that Ellison had confessed to Smithy's mother 'how sorry he was, but that he had been forced into doing them at the risk of losing his job'.

7.   In fact the white wood smoke they sent up was far more conspicuous against the mudflat than black oil smoke.

8.   Comment made by Captain John Myers to Australian aviation historian Darcy Williams, who passed it on to the author in a letter dated 5 November 1995.

Chapter 18

1.   George Minton Combes papers (MS 11176), La Trobe Collection, State Library of Victoria, Melbourne.

2.   *Sydney Morning Herald*, 19 July 1929.

3.   Letter of 5 June 1978 from Mary A. Ralston, West Range Historical Society, Bonalbo, NSW to Smithy's son, Charles Kingsford-Smith.

4.   Fysh, in his autobiography *Qantas Rising*.

5.   *Death Cometh Soon or Late* by J. A. Mollison.

6.   Ibid.

7.   *Over den Oceaan* by Evert van Dijk.

8.   Stannage was born in South Africa of English parents but grew up in New Zealand and became a New Zealander. He spent the first ten years of his career at sea.

9.   Metrically, every kilo of weight saved was worth a litre and a quarter of fuel.

10.   Flown by Hermann Köhn, Baron von Hünefeld, and an Irish Army Air Corps pilot, Colonel James Fitzmaurice, the aircraft was an all-metal Junkers W33. In October 1928 the Atlantic had been flown non-stop again by a luxury German airship, the *Graf Zeppelin*, which flew successfully from Friedrichshaven to Lakehurst, New Jersey and back again.

Chapter 19

1.   The Frenchmen, Costes and Bellonte, succeeded in September

1930 in making the first non-stop flight from Paris to New York in thirty seven and a half hours in a Bréguet 19.

2.   Captain Ray Hinchcliffe, an Imperial Airways pilot, flying the Hon. Elsie Mackay, daughter of Lord Inchcape, left England in March 1928 in a single-engined Stinson. The wreckage of the aircraft was later washed up on the coast of Ireland. The previous year the French First World War fighter ace Charles Nungesser and a companion disappeared on a Paris–New York attempt and later in 1927 a single-engined Fokker, the *St Raphael*, piloted by Lt Col F. Minchin, set off from Wiltshire bound for Ottawa carrying Princess Anne Lowenstein-Wertheim. They disappeared in the Atlantic.

3.   *Over den Oceaan*, op. cit.

4.   At Gander International Airport, 100 miles north of Harbour Grace, local pilots and air-traffic controllers consulted on behalf of the author had never heard of either of the phenomena described by Kingsford Smith.

5.   Built in South Australia in the 1980s for the Southern Cross Museum Trust, this replica of the 'old bus' has three 300hp Jacobs radial engines in place of the original Wright Whirlwinds, variable-pitch propellers, brakes, a tail wheel instead of the original skid, modern flight instruments and radio. In 1990 it was flown across the Tasman to New Zealand and back via Norfolk Island.

6.   'Over the Ditch With Smithy', by Captain J. P. Saul, in *Aviation* magazine, Dublin, April 1935.

7.   *Aviatrix*, by Elinor Smith.

8.   Doolittle was a famous American aviator of the 1930s. He became a USAF general and led a spectacular daylight bomber raid on Tokyo in 1942.

9.   Elinor Smith, in a June 1992 telephone conversation with the author.

10.   *These Are Facts*, op.cit.

11.   *Playboy of the Air*, by J. A. Mollison.

Chapter 20

1.   The wreckage of the *Southern Cloud* was 4,500ft up in the Toolong Mountains of the Great Dividing Range above the Tooma River gorge near Kiandra, not far from the NSW–Victoria border. Parts of its three Lynx engines are now on permanent display in a memorial in Southern Cloud Park in the nearby town of Cooma.

2.   *Southern Cloud*, by I. R. Carter.

3.   Dr Moore has made an extensive study of the New Guard – and another less militant underground organisation, the Old Guard – and has written about them both in his book *The Secret Army and the Premier* (NSW University Press, 1989).

4.   In 1932, under pressure from the federal government, whose loans Lang had long since ceased to repay, and with advice from the British government, the state governor, Sir Philip Game, dismissed Lang from office. The fascist movement subsequently faded away.

5.   Smithy's account of his sickness-plagued 1931 flight to England is drawn from *My Flying Life*, from 'Smithy: One Sleep Too Many?', a *Sunshine Coast Daily* article by his friend Jack Manton (15 October 1985) and from the *Sydney Morning Herald* of 9 October 1931, reporting a London interview with him.

6.   Wireless message from Brinsmead to Australian defence liaison officer, London, 9 October 1931. Australian Archives: RAAF ref. 192/20/68.

7.   Wireless message from Australian defence liaison officer, London, to Brinsmead, 10 October 1931. Australian Archives: RAAF ref. 192/20/68.

8.   Letter to author, 23 March 1994, from Wing Commander K. D. Craig, FRCPsych.

9.   *Sydney Morning Herald*, 10 October 1931.

Chapter 21

1.   *Wings and the Man – The Private Papers of Charles Ulm, Aviator* by Percy Cogger. Written after Ulm's death, and largely a repetition of Ulm's memoirs *My Yesterdays, Todays and Tomorrows*, woven into an expanded narrative by Cogger. The manuscript is in the Ulm Collection in the Mitchell Library, Sydney.

2.   Brinsmead never made it to London. The KLM trimotor in which he resumed his journey crashed on take-off at Bangkok. He was too crippled to work again, and eventually died of his injuries in 1934.

3.   Smithy's logbooks end abruptly on 23 July 1932, a day when he was joyriding in Queensland, with his total hours at 5,299. It appears that he lost that week the second major logbook recording his flights since 1921 and switched to a new one that almost certainly disappeared with him on his last flight.

4.   'Personal and confidential' letter from Rudder to Woods Humphery, 6 July 1932. In Imperial Airways Collection, BA Archives, Heathrow, London.

5.   Letter from Rudder to Woods Humphery, 7 March 1933, BA Archives.

6.   *Outback Airman*, by Harry Purvis with Joan Priest.

7.   'Kingsford Smith as I Remember Him', lecture to NSW branch of the Royal Aeronautical Society, 12 November 1959, by Sir Gordon Taylor.

Chapter 22

1.   Confusingly, there are at least two versions of Kingsford Smith's 1933 England–Australia flight log. One was quoted by Geoffrey Rawson in Smithy's posthumously published *My Flying Life*; another by the Sydney *Telegraph*. Both have been used as sources.

2.   *The Times*, London, 12 October 1933.

3.   Following his England–Australia flight Ulm produced for the prime minister, in support of a petition seeking a knighthood for him, a league table in which he attempted to show that he had set more records than Smithy, crediting to himself eleven and conceding only six to

Smithy. In addition to the records broken by the *Faith in Australia* flight, among the extra five he rather desperately included such intermediate milestones as Australia to Singapore and Karachi, England–Calcutta and England–Singapore. But of course he had not captained, as pilot in charge, any of the flights concerned. It was his practice to enter into his pilot's logbook, in addition to the genuine light-aircraft hours to which he was entitled, large amounts of flying in the *Southern Cross* and in Avro 10s when, as co-pilot, he had relieved people like Smithy and Scotty Allan of some of the tedium at the controls. So of the 2,045 hours shown by his logbook at the end of 1931, only about a third had he flown as the pilot in command – and this of light aircraft.

4.   Letter from Harman to Rudder, 16 October 1933.

5.   Letter from Rudder to Woods Humphery, 12 December 1933, BA Archives.

6.   A Bomber Command wing commander at the age of twenty-four, Rollo Kingsford-Smith was one of the RAF's youngest Second World War squadron commanders. He flew more than 30 operations and was awarded the DSO and DFC during a tour in which his Australian Lancaster squadron, No. 463, lost 90 per cent of its air crew. After the war he became business manager of de Havilland in Australia, and following its merger with Hawker Aircraft was for many years managing director or chairman of Hawker de Havilland, Australia's biggest aircraft manufacturer.

7.   'Tenders   for   Overseas   and   Internal   Air   Services   – Recommendations of Air Contracts Committee'. Australian Archives (ACT): A5954, 9011/6.

8.   Dominion Airways was not Smithy's only business disaster at this time. Early in 1934 he sank money into Marks Motor Construction Ltd, which planned to manufacture an Australian car with a laminated-wood body. He became chairman of the company and allowed the strange-looking vehicle to be named Southern Cross. The car was a flop and the company failed.

9.   *The Defeat of Distance – Qantas 1919–1939*, by John Gunn.

Chapter 23

1.   Campbell Black, a former RAF pilot, had been a pioneer of flying in East Africa, where he had taught the celebrated Beryl Markham to fly and had become one of her lovers. He later married the British comedy actress Florence Desmond.

2.   Of the eleven Lockheed Altairs that were built, six were originals and five conversions of the Sirius.

3.   Acronym for Australian and New Zealand Army Corps, the force, revered in both countries, with which Smithy had landed in Gallipoli in 1915.

4.   'Kingsford Smith Puts His Cards on the Table', *Smith's Weekly*, Sydney, 13 October 1934.

5.   Letter from Shelmerdine to Wing Commander R. Marsden, RAAF liaison officer in London, 21 April 1934. Australian Archives (VIC): A.795, Department of Air, 1922–60, 21/1/86.

6.   Letter from Murray Jones to St Barbe, 25 July 1934.

7.   *Smith's Weekly*, Sydney, 4 January 1936.

Chapter 24

1.   Scott and Campbell Black's time from Mildenhall to Melbourne was seventy hours fifty-four minutes. They were followed by a KLM Douglas DC2 in a little over ninety hours and a Boeing 247D in just under ninety-three. Amy Johnson and Jim Mollison, in the Comet *Black Magic*, withdrew at Allahabad with engine trouble. After Mollison had left the cockpit an engineer found three empty whisky bottles beside his seat.

2.   Lecture by Sir Gordon Taylor, op.cit.

3.   In the seven years the author was researching this biography, no one in any country ever emerged to claim that Kingsford Smith was his or her father.

4.   'Kingsford Smith Harassed', *Southland Times*, New Zealand, 19 November 1934.

5.   Ulm had planned to fly the Pacific in easier stages than the *Southern Cross* flight of 1928. From Hawaii to Sydney he had intended going via Fanning Island, Fiji and Auckland, having arranged for a temporary runway to be built on Fanning Atoll (now Tabuaeran) in the Line Islands.

6.   'Loss of Ulm – Flying Pal Grief-Stricken', by John W. Stannage, Sydney *Sun*, 11 December 1935.

7.   Lecture by Sir Gordon Taylor, op.cit.

Chapter 25

1.   Had Ulm made it to Australia the knighthood he'd desired for so long would have been his: according to the prime minister's publicity officer, Irvine Douglas, it was to have been awarded in the New Year's honours list of 1935.

2.   *Luck and the Record Breaker*, by Jean Batten, unpublished memoirs held by the Batten family. Batten became the first woman pilot to fly the South Atlantic and for a time held both the England–Australia and Australia–England records for either sex with much faster times than Smithy ever achieved.

3.   Flying boats were then favoured because they could be more heavily loaded than landplanes, which were restricted by small and often rough airfields. The spacious Short S30 Empire flying boat could carry twenty-four passengers, some luxuriously in sleeping berths.

Chapter 26

1.   'When the great fixed undercarriage hit the water the aircraft would have immediately flipped over and broken up, injuring, if not killing them all,' said Ernest Aldis. 'Had they survived all that, they

wouldn't have sawn through all those engine-bearers with one small hack-saw – nor the wing with that modest wood saw. As for buoyancy from the fuel tanks, it wouldn't have been enough just to block off the vent as Smithy did. In the water they would have had to have found and sealed the fuel lines as well – an almost impossible task. Smithy may have been a superb pilot, but frankly, he wasn't always the most practical of people.'

2. This account was written by Taylor in *Call to the Winds*. Smithy, in his posthumous biography, left behind a rather different version which claimed that Stannage had tried to go out to the starboard engine first. This never happened, although Stannage did later try without success to take oil collected from the starboard engine to the port engine. Kingsford Smith's ghost-writer, Geoffrey Rawson, got it wrong: he confused the port and starboard engines – and gave the *Southern Cross*'s open-sided flight deck windows which it never had – and Smithy disappeared before seeing the draft.

3. Report of the *Southern Cross* Tasman accident investigation com-mittee, which sat on 22 May 1935. Australian Archives (VIC): A705 Department of Air 1922–60, 21/1/61, Pt 6.

4. Dr Banks was another Australian folk hero. He had been an outback flying doctor and in the Second World War served as a pilot and surgeon in the Fleet Air Arm, going on to become a Harley Street plastic surgeon.

5. Surprisingly, Taylor's cool heroism brought no immediate reward. It was two years before recognition came with an Empire Gallantry Medal, which became the George Cross in 1941. His flying log entry for that day made no reference to what he had done. All it said was: 'Exhaust manifold broke and smashed propeller in starboard motor. Returned on two motors: 6 hours out, 9 hours back.' What Smithy wrote in his logbook we will never know.

6. The suitcase in which Stannage collected the oil is now in the National Library in Canberra (PIC OBJ A 40004414 LOC LG1).

7. The fractured propeller has also survived and is in the Power House Museum in Sydney.

Chapter 27

1. Letter from Colonel Harold Burchall, general manager, Imperial Airways, to Lt-Col Francis Shelmerdine, director-general of civil aviation, 26 July 1935, BA Archives.

2. Letter from Rudder to Hamilton, 18 July 1935.

3. Interview with Molly Hudson, September 1992.

4. Kingsford Smith is credited with his own farewell poem in honour of the *Southern Cross*:

Old faithful friend, a long adieu!
These are poor words with which to tell
Of all my pride, my joy in you.
True to the end, you've served me well.

I pity those who cannot see
That heart and soul are housed within
This thing of steel and wood – to me
You live in every bolt and pin.

And so, staunch and steadfast steed
Your deep and mighty voice must cease.
Faithful to death.
If God will heed
My prayer, dear pal,
You'll rest in peace!

5. Letter from Freddie Kent to author, 1 May 1992.
6. *Aviators of the Charles Ulm and Kingsford Smith Era*, by Bob Boulton.
7. *Daily Express*, London, 24 October 1935.
8. Letter from Barbara Allan to author, 26 May 1996.
9. *Luck and the Record Breaker*, op.cit.
10. 'Smithy's PR Man: Beau Sheil', in *Australian Flying Reference Book: Kingsford Smith*, by Fred Morton.
11. *Daily Telegraph*, London, 7 November 1935.
12. *Daily Telegraph*, London, 9 November 1935.
13. *The Pioneer*, Lucknow, 9 November 1935.
14. *The Jimmy Melrose Story – Australia's Youngest Air Ace*, by Eric Gunton.
15. *The Statesman*, New Delhi, 8 November 1935.
16. Burma moonset time and phase data from HM Nautical Almanac Office, Royal Greenwich Observatory, Cambridge, England.
17. *The Jimmy Melrose Story*, op.cit.
18. Journey times for the last flight of the *Lady Southern Cross* from report of director of civil aviation, Burma: 'The Loss of G-ADUS, flown by the late Sir Charles Kingsford Smith', 11 May 1939. Australian Archives (VIC): A705, Department of Air 1922–60, 21/1/58, Pt 4.

Chapter 28
1. 'He Passed Me Like a Comet', *Daily Telegraph*, London, 9 November 1935.
2. *Sydney Morning Herald*, 22 November 1935.
3. The Polish pilots were Major Stanislaus Karpinski and a Mr Rogalski.
4. *Flight*, London, 21 November 1935.
5. Bill Taylor, knighted in 1954, became a distinguished long-distance aviator in his own right. In 1939 he piloted the first flight across the Indian Ocean and in 1951 the first crossing of the southern Pacific, from Australia to Chile. He died in Honolulu at the age of seventy in 1966.
6. Smithy's feats were five first-ever route flights (the Pacific and

Tasman in both directions and the Atlantic westbound) and three intercontinental records (1929 Australia–England; 1930 and 1933 England–Australia solo flights). Mollison's were six first-time route achievements – England–Cape Town via the Sahara (1932), North Atlantic westward non-stop solo (1932), South Atlantic westward non-stop solo (1933), UK–South America solo (1933), UK–USA direct, with Amy Johnson (1933), New York–London, via Harbour Grace, (1936) – plus three records.

Chapter 29

1. *Pioneer Aviator: The Remarkable Life of Lores Bonney*, by Terry Gwynn-Jones. Bonney, one of Australia's most celebrated pilots, lived to the age of ninety-six. She was not an admirer of Kingsford Smith, who believed women lacked the stamina and fortitude for long-distance flying. He once upset her when she was preparing for a gruelling round-Australia flight by saying: 'You might make it – if you've got the guts.' She was often quoted as saying that he was 'not a gentleman'.

2. 'Loss of Sir Charles Kingsford Smith's Aeroplane – Interim Report on Salvaged Wreckage', from Michael A. Doyle, assistant director of civil aviation, Burma, 11 April 1938. Australian Archives (VIC): A705, 21/1/58, Pt 4. In his positioning of Aye Island Doyle miscalculated the longitude by 1 degree, putting it nearly 70 miles off the coast.

3. Ibid.

4. 'Search for Plane – Smithy's Fate – Important Clues', letter to Sydney *Sun* from Jack Hodder, published 2 February 1938.

5. Ibid.

6. Ibid.

7. Interview with Ted Wixted by author, 5 August 1991.

8. 'Accident to Lockheed Altair G-ADUS', report for author by G. Clark and J. L. Kepert, File BM2/03/38, Aeronautical Research Laboratory, Department of Defence, Melbourne, October 1992.

9. The alloy experts at ALCOA in Pittsburg took a more optimistic view of the longevity of duralumin. Tropical waters, they said, 'are not particularly corrosive to aluminium. The parts could survive sixty years or more in Burma waters.'

10. *The Jimmy Melrose Story*, op.cit.

11. Letters to the author from Eric Gunton, February and March 1993.

12. Drift data transmitted daily from hundreds of ships around the world is held by the Meteorological Office at Bracknell in England. An atlas of the Indian Ocean information – 'Surface Currents of the Indian Ocean – Institute of Oceanographic Sciences', Report No. 187 – was produced in 1984 by two scientists, A. N. Cutler and J. C. Swallow.

13. Letter to author from Dr Bryden aboard *R/V Knorr*, Indian Ocean, 14 October 1995.

14. Letter to author from Dr Shetye, 15 June 1995.

15. Letter to author from Dr Parulekar, 14 August 1995.

16.   Report prepared for author by Dr Tin Hlaing, Extra Master Mariner UK, Msc PhD (Wales).

17.   'Some Aspects of Sir Charles Kingsford Smith's Flights', sixteenth Sir Charles Kingsford Smith Memorial Lecture to the Royal Aeronautical Society, Sydney, September 1974.

18.   Letter to author from Kenneth Bird, former chief of overhaul liaison, Pratt & Whitney Aircraft Division, 29 April 1994.

Bibliography

Allan, G. U. (with Elizabeth Shearman): *Scotty Allan: Australia's Flying Scotsman* (Clarion, Sydney, 1992)

Allen, Richard S.: *Revolution in the Sky: The Lockheeds of Aviation's Golden Age* (Orion Books, New York, 1964)

Beattie, Tasman: *A Thousand Skies* (Fontana Australia, 1985)

Boulton, Bob: *Aviators of the Charles Ulm and Kingsford Smith Era* (Echnida Publishing, Sydney, 1993)

Brearley, Sir Norman: *Australian Aviator* (Rigby Books, Sydney, 1971)

Bruce, J. M.: *The Aeroplanes of the Royal Flying Corps Military Wing* (Putnam, London, 1982)

Carter, Isobel R.: *Southern Cloud* (Angus & Robertson, London, 1964)

Clark, Alan: *Aces High* (Weidenfeld & Nicolson, London, 1973)

Clennell, W. Jack: *Eastern Odyssey* (privately published, Isle of Man, 1990)

Clover, Sam T.: *A Pioneer Heritage* (Saturday Night Publishing Company, Los Angeles, 1932)

Cluett, Douglas (with Joanna Nash and Bob Learmonth): *Croydon Airport: The Great Days 1928–1939* (London Borough of Sutton Libraries and Arts Services, 1980)

Davis, Pedr: *Charles Kingsford Smith: Smithy, the World's Greatest Aviator* (Lansdowne Press, Sydney, 1977)

Davis, Pedr (with Dick Smith): *Kookaburra* (Lansdowne Press, 1980)

Dunstan, Keith: *Knockers* (Cassell Australia, 1972)

Ellison, Norman: *Flying Matilda* (Angus & Robertson, Sydney, 1957)

Eustis, Nelson: *The Greatest Air Race: England–Australia 1919* (Rigby Books, Adelaide, 1969)

Ewing, Ross and Macpherson, Ross: *History of New Zealand Aviation* (Heinemann NZ, 1986)

Fokker, Anthony H. G. (with Bruce Gould): *Flying Dutchman* (George Routledge, London, 1931)

Forden, Lesley: *Glory Gamblers: The Story of the Dole Race* (Nottingham Press, Alameda, California, 1986)

Gero, David: *Aviation Disasters* (Patrick Stephens Ltd, Somerset, England, 1993)

Gunn, John: *The Defeat of Distance – Qantas 1919–1939* (University of Queensland Press, 1985)

Gunn, John: *Challenging Horizons – Qantas 1939–1954* (University of Queensland Press, 1987)

Gunton, Eric: *The Jimmy Melrose Story: Australia's Youngest Air Ace* (published by author, Adelaide, 1990)

Gwynn-Jones, Terry: *Pioneer Aviator: The Remarkable Life of Lores Bonney* (University of Queensland Press, 1988)

Gwynn-Jones, Terry: *Wings Across the Pacific* (Allen & Unwin, Sydney, 1992)

Hardie, Jenny: *Nor'Westers of the Pilbara Breed* (Hesperian Press, Perth, 1981)

Herman, Dr Judith Lewis: *Trauma and Recovery* (HarperCollins, New York, 1992)

Hordern, Lesley: *Children of One Family* (Retford Press, Sydney, 1985)

Kingsford Smith, C. E. and Ulm, C. T. P.: *Story of 'Southern Cross' Trans-Pacific Flight 1928* (Penlington & Somerville, Sydney, 1928)

Kingsford Smith, Sir Charles: *The Old Bus* (Herald Press, Melbourne, 1932)

Kingsford Smith, Sir Charles: *My Flying Life* (Andrew Melrose, London, 1937)

Luff, David: *Mollison – The Flying Scotsman* (Lidun Publishing, Lancashire, England 1993)

Mackersey, Ian: *Jean Batten: The Garbo of the Skies* (Macdonald, London, 1990)

Mallett, Kathleen: *To the Bar Bonded* (Hesperian Press, Perth, 1993)

McNally, Ward: *Smithy: The Kingsford Smith Story* (Robert Hale, London, 1966)

McNally, Ward: *Cry of a Man Running* (Angus & Robertson, Sydney, 1968)

McNally, Ward: *The Man on the Twenty Dollar Note* (A. H. & A. W. Reed, Sydney, 1976)

Meredith, De Witt: *G. Allan Hancock* (privately published by subject, Los Angeles, 1964)

Mitchell, Alan: *No Man Despairs – The Story of Matthew Banks, Plastic Surgeon* (Harrap, London, 1958)

Mollison, Jim: *Death Cometh Soon or Late* (Hutchinson, London, 1932)

Mollison, Jim: *Playboy of the Air* (Michael Joseph, London, 1937)

Morgan, Sally: *Wanamurraganya: The Story of Jack McPhee* (Fremantle Arts Centre Press, 1989)

Morton, Fred: *Australian Flying Reference Book: Kingsford Smith* (Page Publications, Sydney, c.1972)

Muss, Dr David: *The Trauma Trap* (Doubleday, London, 1991)

Parnell, Neville and Boughton, Trevor: *Flypast: A Record of Aviation in Australia* (Australian Government Publishing Service, Canberra, 1988)

Penrose, Harald: *Wings Across the World* (Cassell, London, 1980)

Purvis, Harry (with Joan Priest): *Outback Airman* (Rigby Books, Sydney, 1979)

Rogers, Ellen: *Faith in Australia: Charles Ulm and Australian Aviation* (Book Production Services, Sydney, 1987)

Sheil, Beau: *Caesar of the Skies* (Cassell, London, 1937)

Smith, Dick: *Solo Around the World* (Australian Geographic, Sydney, 1992)

Smith, Elinor: *Aviatrix* (Harcourt Brace Jovanovich, New York, 1981)

Stannage, John: *High Adventure* (privately published, Christchurch, NZ, 1944)

Stannage, John: *Smithy* (Oxford University Press, London, 1950)

Swinson, Arthur: *The Great Air Race* (Cassell, London, 1968)

Taylor, Sir Gordon: *Pacific Flight* (Angus & Robertson, Sydney, 1937)

Taylor, Sir Gordon: *Call to the Winds* (Angus & Robertson, 1939)

Taylor, Sir Gordon: *The Sky Beyond* (Cassell, Melbourne, 1963)

Van Dijk, Evert: *Over Den Oceaan* (Scheltens & Giltay, Amsterdam, 1930)

Williams, Air Marshal Sir Richard: *These Are Facts* (Australian War Memorial & Australian Government Printing Service, Canberra, 1977)

Wilson, Graham: *Pilbara Bushman – The Life Experience of W. Dunn* (Hesperian Press, Perth, 1989)

Wixted, Edward P: *North West Aerial Frontier* (Boolarong Publications, Brisbane, 1985)

Wixted, Edward P.: *The Life and Times of Sir Charles Kingsford Smith: an illustrated chronology* (published by author, Brisbane, 1996)

Index